上海对外经贸大学一流本科建设引领计划系列教材

祝卫 程洁 谈英 ■ 著

出口贸易
模拟操作教程
第四版

CHUKOU MAOYI
MONI CAOZUO JIAOCHENG

上海人民出版社

第 四 版 前 言

在本书第四版付梓之际，中国成为第二大经济体和货物贸易第一大国已有很多年，全球贸易格局也发生了显著变化，国际贸易中服务贸易对货物贸易的比例、货物贸易中中间品对产成品的比例都有了跨越性的改变，正在影响和产生新的世界贸易规则。

在这样的时代背景下，一方面，社会和企业对国际贸易人才的要求越来越高，各种新的业态迅速崛起又不断烟花式地陨落，强大的互联网解构了近乎所有的信息垄断，另一方面，国际贸易的跨境交换本质没有变，学习者能力养成的路径也没有变，只有尊重认知规律，才能谈教学效果，也才会有学生的竞争力、企业的接受度和社会的美誉度。

本书作者团队有着丰富的企业实践经验，也长期从事国际贸易专业一线课堂教学，多年与学生的互动使我们深刻领悟到教学训练需要的是一个载体，而不是一个模具，留下知识与技能的痕迹固然重要，但更重要的是建立起各种连接：情境与操作之间的连接，规则与实践之间的连接，前因与后果之间的连接……所以本次修订，我们在根据实际业务变化全面更新内容的同时，仍旧保持了原书"案例"—"示范"—"指南"—"练习"的框架体例，并为每一页都标注了所属章节和模块。这些设计透露着我们内心真诚的希望：期待本书的使用者们能时常借助索引将学习内容前后关联，比如第 6 章的案例是第 5 章的示范的后续发展，第 4 章的案例为第 13 章的案例埋下了伏笔等等。当本书的文字图表被这样再次还原成一个完整的出口交易，你定会在生动的案例中收获到互动的欢愉：原来"David Wang"是这样想的，原来"Tivolian"是这样做的。当你合上书时，心中涌动着对国际贸易具体而多样的理解，那就去勇敢地实践，在实践中诠释和更新自己的理解，这才是面向未来的学习。

本书编写的初衷是连接专业与行业、学院与企业、校园与社会，打通理论学习与社会实践之间厚重的围墙，激发青年学子脚踏实地的学习热情。《资治通鉴》中有"口说不如身逢，耳听不如目睹"的古训，本书及其对应的课程也是本着这样的理念，旨在为学生提供一个提前实习见习的机会。对于缺乏生活现实感的 00 后来说，"任务驱动"、"做中学"和"在情境中学"这样三位一体的课程结构能够调动他们自我发现、自我教育、自我成长的积极性，了解出口业务的全貌，熟悉各个环节的操作流程，提高处理实际问题的能力，强化英语交际的沟通技巧，为将来的实习和工作打下坚实的基础。从历年学生的学习小结中可以看出，这样的教学组织在知识传授、技能习得、习惯养成、视野拓展，乃至人格培育诸多方面皆有发力，称得上一门大学里的好课程了。

参加第四版修订的有上海高校国际商务实习中心的银辉、许良靓和姜琳。感谢华东理工大学蔡惠伟老师给予本次修订的指导与帮助，感谢上海对外经贸大学对"国际贸易模拟"课程一如既往的支持，特别感谢多年来一直使用并关心本书发展的广大读者，"唯学生与读者不可辜负"，这是我们的初心，也是坚守的理由。衷心希望更多有缘的读者和同行发现本书的价值，同时也竭诚期待大家对本书反馈宝贵的意见和建议，联系邮箱：workbook@scicib.com。书中若有不当或错误之处，尚祈鉴宥并拨冗惠告。

作　者
2019 年 8 月于上海

第 三 版 前 言

《出口贸易模拟操作教程》自 2002 年修订以来已经走过了六个年头。六年来,国际贸易实践课程、实训教学软件和教材建设都得到了迅速的发展。随着中国高等教育向大众化和普及化的转变,探索开设以培养学生实践能力、思考能力、创新能力和职业素养的仿真实践课程已经成为提高高等教育教学质量的重要手段。

六年中,以开展国际贸易仿真实践教学为己任的上海高校国际商务实习中心及其教学研发团队也在上海市教委和上海对外贸易学院的关心和支持下,在广大积极参与国际贸易模拟实习学员的关注和推动下,在锐意进取、不懈求索的道路上取得了长足的进步。基于"做中学(Learning by Doing)"的教学理念,在开展"国际贸易模拟实习(Teach Me Trade,TMT)"实践课程的同时,我们还开设了"网络贸易模拟(Internet Trade Simulation,ITS)"课程,开发了"国际贸易操作训练系统(PTOT)",并与国内外、海内外多所高校展开了多种形式的教学平台研发合作及课程共享。特别令人欣喜的是在上海市教委的积极支持下,自 2006 年起,"国际贸易模拟实习 TMT"已经作为上海市第一门免费的公共实训课程向市属高校在校学生开放共享。

《出口贸易模拟操作教程》作为"国际贸易模拟实习"课程的配套教材,以其独具特色的编排风格和内容设计,受到了广大读者的好评。本次修订,我们在继续保持原书框架体系的前提下,对全书进行了很大的改动,包括案例的重新设计、指南的修改完善以及练习的重组等。其中,对于出口合同的履行环节以及信用证的审核及单据缮制等,均根据实际业务的变化和 2007 年修订的《跟单信用证统一惯例》(UCP600)进行了全新编写。

值得一提的是,在本次修订后,我们将在上海高校国际商务实习中心的网站(www.scicib.com)上专门开辟"教材"栏目,为广大读者提供本书中涉及的合同、单据的空白样式,以方便下载练习,为"做中学"提供更多的支持和互动。

出于仿真教学训练和贴近实际业务的需要,本书中的商品图片、合同、单证等都基于真实业务文件的外观样式,但涉及的交易内容、当事人等信息均是虚拟的,其相关内容如不慎与真实生活中的人物、组织或事件发生雷同，实属巧合，凡有第三方签章的文件也都进行了水印处理，请勿移作他用，谨此声明。

感谢上海高校国际商务实习中心全体同仁对本书编写的贡献和支持，感谢周秉成先生给予本次修订的审核及指导，特别感谢广大读者对于"国际贸易模拟实习"多种方式的参与，正是你们的厚爱鞭策着我们在仿真实践教学训练的探索中不断前行。

祝 卫

2008 年 6 月

再 版 前 言

《出口贸易模拟操作教程》自 1999 年出版至今已有三年。在这短短三年中，随着中国加入世界贸易组织以及越来越多的企业进入国际市场，社会对外经贸业务人员的需求不断的发展，同时，在教育界，随着教学观念的进步和信息技术的普及，在国家教育部和全国各地教育主管部门的大力倡导下，高等院校尤其是经济管理类高校和相关专业的实验教学和实验室建设有了长足的发展。在此期间，以"做中学"为特征的"国际贸易模拟实习"项目业已在全国一百三十多所高校推广实施。继 1998 年"进出口业务模拟操作"项目获奖之后，上海对外贸易学院的"国际贸易模拟实验室建设"在 2001 年再次荣获上海市优秀教学成果一等奖。

《出口贸易模拟操作教程》作为"国际贸易模拟实习"项目的配套教材，自出版以来，以其独特的框架设计和务实的训练风格受到了广大读者的欢迎，曾多次重印，此次应读者要求作再版修订。本着方便读者自主训练的原则，再版后的《出口贸易模拟操作教程》对原书的章节结构作了一定的调整。

参加再版修订的有程洁和王艮。感谢上海市教委和上海对外贸易学院对"国际贸易模拟实习"项目的重视和支持，感谢广大读者对本书的厚爱和建议，所有这一切将始终鞭策我们不懈地努力和不倦地追求。

祝 卫

2002 年 7 月

前　　言

不同国家之间进行跨越国界的商品买卖为进出口贸易。由于进行交易的双方隶属于两个不同的国家或地区,因此从事这种商业活动比进行国内贸易更为复杂、困难、因而也更具挑战性。从事国际商务活动,尤其是国际间货物的买卖,其工作的最大特点就是要求商务人员在掌握基本知识的同时,必须具有很强的实际工作能力。而现代国际商务活动,对从业人员的知识结构、实践能力和基本素质提出了更高的要求。作者多年从事进出口贸易以及实务教学工作,深感学习进出口贸易实务如同临床医学,必须通过具体的实际业务操作,才能切实掌握运用,否则只能是纸上谈兵,无法做到学以致用。因此,1994 年开始,作者开始进行进出口贸易实务仿真模拟化教学的探索和尝试,开设了独具特色的实习项目"进出口业务模拟操作"。该项目以其独具匠心的创意、科学系统的教学内容、新颖独特的训练方式以及满意的教学训练效果荣获上海市优秀教学成果一等奖,并成为上海高校国际商务实习中心首推的仿真模拟实习项目,受到国内外同行及企业界的一致赞誉。

"进出口业务模拟操作"主要是通过精心设计、组织、控制和指导下的进出口交易模拟训练,让学员能够在一个仿真的国际商业环境中切身体会商品进出口交易的全过程,在实际业务的操作过程中使其全面、系统、规范地掌握从事进出口交易的主要操作技能。《出口贸易模拟操作教程》为"进出口业务模拟操作"项目的教材,该书以出口交易的基本过程为主线,以模拟设定的具体出口商品交易作背景,针对出口贸易中业务函电的草拟、商品价格的核算、交易条件的磋商、买卖合同的签订、出口货物的托运订舱、报验通关、信用证的审核与修改以及贸易文件制作和审核等主要业务操作技能,通过生动具体的案例、详尽的操作指南、具体的图表实例和大量的操作练习,为读者提供了一个在仿真模拟实践中了解和掌握出口交易基本程序和主要操作技能的有效途径。

《出口贸易模拟操作教程》着重培养读者的自学和动手能力、理解能力以及动态思维能力,它可以作为大中专院校相关专业开展"进出口业务模拟实习"的教材,也可以作为有志从事进出口贸易的人员自我学习训练的良师益友。

参加本书编写的有程洁和王艮等。感谢上海市教育委员会主任、上海高校国际商务实习中心张伟江理事长，上海市教委高等教育办公室许宝元、李进主任以及上海对外贸易学院王新奎、王兴孙院长对"进出口业务模拟操作"项目的关心和支持以及对本书编写及出版的指导和帮助。同时感谢英国东方国际公司姚文卿先生为本书审定。

祝 卫

1999 年 7 月

目　　录

第一章　建立业务关系

案　例

　　上海环宇贸易有限公司（Shanghai Universal Trading Co.，Ltd.）成立于 1997 年 1 月，是经国家批准的具有进出口经营权的综合性贸易公司，主要经营各类轻工业产品的进出口业务。

　　公司与多家供货厂商联系紧密，货源基础稳固，业务力量雄厚。同时，面对多变的国际市场，公司也十分重视新产品的开发。最近玩具部与工厂联手开发了一系列毛绒玩具新品，如 KB 玩具熊、KD 玩具狗、KP 玩具猪、KR 玩具兔等。这批新品均选用上等原料制成，手感柔软，造型逼真，可水洗，并可按客户要求大批量定制，受到了欧美进口商的普遍欢迎。

营业执照

统一社会信用代码　913101177653073652
证照编号　17000000201702280175

名　　　称	上海环宇贸易有限公司
类　　　型	有限责任公司（国内合资）
住　　　所	上海市东方路131号美陵广场1201室
法 定 代 表 人	马衍飞
注 册 资 本	人民币500.0000万元整
成 立 日 期	1997 年 1 月 20 日
营 业 期 限	1997 年 1 月 20 日至 2027 年 1 月 19 日
经 营 范 围	自营或代理各类商品和技术的进出口，但国家限定公司经营或禁止进出口的商品及技术除外，承办中外合资经营，合作生产，三来一补，易货贸易，对销贸易，对外经济贸易咨询，技术交流，国内贸易业务。【依法须经批准的项目，经相关部门批准后方可开展经营活动】

登记机关

2017 年 02 月 28 日

在 2018 年德国科隆国际婴幼儿及少儿用品展览会上,荷兰 Tivolian 公司的
Chila Trooborg 先生对我公司展出的毛绒玩具颇感兴趣,并留下名片:

Chila Trooborg

Purchase Manager

Heiman Dullaertolein 3,
P. O. Box 1783,
3024CA Rotterdam, Netherlands
chtrooborg@tivolian.nl
Tel: 31-10-4767418
Fax: 31-10-4767422

2018 年 9 月 23 日,环宇公司向 Tivolian 公司发出建立业务关系函。

工作任务

根据上述背景资料,以上海环宇贸易公司玩具部业务员的身份拟写电子邮件
发送给荷兰客户,表达与其建立业务关系的愿望,并随附公司部分新产品的插页。

示 范

Plush Toys - Followup on Fair Cologne

发件人：	David Wang <d.wang@universal.com.cn>
日 期：	2018年9月23日
收件人：	Chila Trooborg <chtrooborg@tivolian.nl>
附 件：	1个 (📊 latest leaflets for plush toys.xlsx)

上海环宇贸易有限公司
Shanghai Universal Trading Co., Ltd.

Dear Mr. Trooborg

It was great to meet you at the *Kind+Jugend International Baby to Teenage Fair Cologne* and thank you for your interest in our plush toys. We are glad of the opportunity to start a happy and mutual beneficial association with you.

As a leading trading company in Shanghai and backed by more than 20 years of export experience, we have good connection with reputable toy factories, and sufficient supplies and on-time delivery are thus guaranteed.

Attached are some leaflets for our latest plush toys, which may meet with your demand. You'll see they are all made of high quality materials and vividly designed. They have already enjoyed a high popularity in other European cities for their fine craftsmanship, comfortable feel and washable traits.

In addition, we can also produce according to your designated styles so long as the quantity is substantial. If you have any specific requirement, please just let us know.

As to our financial standing, you may refer to the Bank of China, Shanghai Branch (200 Mid. Yincheng Road, Pudong new District, Shanghai 200121, China Tel: +86-21-38824588 Fax: +86-21-50372847). We shall appreciate it if you could inform us of your bank reference.

We are pleased to add you to our list of clients and look forward to your enquiries.

Best wishes

David Wang
Sales Manager
Shanghai Universal Trading Co., Ltd.
Tel: +86 21 58818863
Email: d.wang@universal.com.cn

中国上海市东方路 131 号美陵广场 1201-1216 室
Rm. 1201-1216 Mayling Plaza, 131 Dongfang Rd., Shanghai, 200120, China
电话/Tel: 86-21-58818844 传真/Fax: 86-21-58818766 网址/Web: www.universal.com.cn

上海环宇贸易有限公司
Shanghai Universal Trading Co., Ltd.

TWIN BEAR

ART. NO.	KB0278	SIZE 25 / 25cm
PACKING	2 pcs / set, 4 sets / ctn	
CTN. DIMENSION	55×45×40cm	
CTN. G.W. / N.W.	8 kg / 5.5 kg	
MOQ	400 sets	

BROWN BEAR WITH RED BOW

ART. NO.	KB0677	SIZE 30 / 20 / 15cm
PACKING	3 pcs / set, 8 sets / ctn	
CTN. DIMENSION	48×64×60cm	
CTN. G.W. / N.W.	8.5 kg / 6 kg	
MOQ	400 sets	

TWIN BEAR IN BALLET COSTUME

ART. NO.	KB5411	SIZE 25 / 25cm
PACKING	2 pcs / set, 4 sets / ctn	
CTN. DIMENSION	55×45×40cm	
CTN. G.W. / N.W.	8 kg / 5.5 kg	
MOQ	400 sets	

BEAR IN PINK T-SHIRT

ART. NO.	KB7900	SIZE 30 / 20 / 15cm
PACKING	3 pcs / set, 8 sets / ctn	
CTN. DIMENSION	48×64×60cm	
CTN. G.W. / N.W.	8.5 kg / 6 kg	
MOQ	400 sets	

FEATURES

100% polyester velboa, 100% polyester fiberfill
Wash by hand in warm water
Suitable for ages 3+

上海环宇贸易有限公司
Shanghai Universal Trading Co., Ltd.

TWIN BEAR

ART. NO.	KB8752	SIZE 30 / 30cm
PACKING	2 pcs / set, 4 sets / ctn	
CTN. DIMENSION	42×36×32cm	
CTN. G.W. / N.W.	8.3 kg / 5.8 kg	
MOQ	400 sets	

DOG COUPLE

ART. NO.	KD2346	SIZE 30 / 30cm
PACKING	2 pcs / set, 4 sets / ctn	
CTN. DIMENSION	42×36×32cm	
CTN. G.W. / N.W.	8.3 kg / 5.8 kg	
MOQ	400 sets	

PEPPA'S FAMILY

ART. NO.	KP2273	SIZE 30/30/19/19cm
PACKING	4 pcs / set, 4 sets / ctn	
CTN. DIMENSION	56×42×30cm	
CTN. G.W. / N.W.	8.7 kg / 6.2 kg	
MOQ	400 sets	

RABBIT COUPLE

ART. NO.	KR2048	SIZE 50 / 50cm
PACKING	2 pcs / set, 4 sets / ctn	
CTN. DIMENSION	50×44×30cm	
CTN. G.W. / N.W.	8.3 kg / 5.8 kg	
MOQ	400 sets	

FEATURES

100% polyester bright velvet & knitted fabric, 100% polyester fiberfill
Wash by hand in warm water
Suitable for ages 3+

💬 示范评析

对于一封陌生者的来函，收信人通常会顺着"How do you know us？ →Why are you writing to us？ →Who are you？"的思路来思考，所以，作为写信人，我们一般会遵循"信息来源→致函目的→公司和产品介绍"的顺序来撰写建立业务关系函。如果以其他内容，如公司介绍，作为信的开头并非不可以，但假如用很大的篇幅、撇开具体客户、一味地泛泛而谈公司情况，这样做不但会因缺乏针对性而难有成效，而且很容易让人产生厌烦情绪。毕竟，建立业务关系函作为一种促成业务关系建立的手段，始终都应考虑到对方的感受与兴趣。

当然，在建立业务关系函中提及信息来源，主要是希望给对方留下正规可信的第一印象。所以并无必要在信中详细叙述获得信息的具体过程。试比较：

On Mar. 5，we noticed your information on the International Business Daily. We immediately further contacted the Echo Corner，a section in that newspaper. We paid the fee and obtained your name and address.

From the March 5 issue of the International Business Daily we have learned that you are in the market for plush toys.

Q：可以套用公司网站或宣传资料上的公司介绍吗？

A：建立业务关系函总是面对特定客户、针对不同人，其中的公司介绍也理应有所变化。除了应介绍一些最基本的情况，如公司的经营范围，还应选取一些对这个客户有意义的优势，而不宜简单地套用公司进行公开宣传时的简介。试比较：

Our company，Universal Trading Co.，Ltd.，was established in 1997 with registration capital of RMB5,000,000. So far, it has developed into a comprehensive firm with import and export rights approved by the government. We specialize in various light industrial products and our motto is "Clients' needs come first". We are associated with many factories through long-term cooperation agreement thus to have qualified suppliers. Many experienced sales personnel have joined our company and strengthened our business power. Meanwhile，much has been concentrated on R&D to promote the flexibility of competing in the brisk world market. Each department will launch several new products or product lines every year. We sincerely hope to explore cooperation opportunities with clients both at home and abroad on the basis of mutual benefit and common development.

As a leading trading company in Shanghai and backed by more than 20 years of export experience，we have good connection with reputable toy factories，and sufficient supplies and on-time delivery are thus guaranteed.

Q：为什么在建立业务关系时会要求客户提供银行信息？

A：在与国外客户建立业务关系时，我们有时会询问对方的往来银行以方便我们通过银行进行资信调查。同时我们一般也会主动提供有关我方往来银行的信息。

Q：建立业务关系函好像总是以"**We are looking forward to your enquiry**"结尾，是不是太程式化了？

A：建立业务关系函通常会以若干邀请对方询盘（enquiry）或回应（reply，feedback 等）的语句结尾。虽然简短，却不宜省略，否则让人感觉信函戛然而止，推进力度锐减。同时，也不能随意将其改为直接邀请对方下订单，如"We are looking forward to your order"，这样的结尾有强迫交易之嫌，会给客户留下交易流程不清、专业经验缺乏的不良印象。

Q：这封信每一段开头都没有空格缩进，称呼语、结尾套语部分也没有标点，这是一种特别的格式吗？

A：这是目前商务英语信函中使用最广泛的格式——完全平头式（fully blocked style）。采用这种格式，每一行字都靠左顶格，新段落或结尾部分都不需要空格缩进，在计算机上使用起来非常方便，而且看上去也比较现代。完全平头式的信函通常也使用开放式标点（open punctuation），即删掉所有不必要的句号和逗号，例如信内地址每一行末尾、称呼语之后、结尾套语之后的标点等。

需要说明的是，尽管完全平头式很普遍，但有些公司仍偏好采用缩进式的信函格式，只要保持一致性，都有助于树立和提升公司形象。

指 南

> ⓘ 建立业务关系函的基本结构　　第 *8* 页
> ⓘ 商务英语信函的基本组成　　　第 *10* 页

ⓘ 建立业务关系函的基本结构

　　商务英语信函,特别是电子邮件(e-mail),是当今国际间货物买卖磋商的主要载体。从书信、函电到传真、电子邮件,商务信函的形式虽在变化,但其目的都是为了有效交流商务信息,因此主体内容的组织规则还是相同的。合格的商务英语信函应该是以简洁的语言、明晰的结构来表述完整的内容,同时,还要体现出业务思维和商业风格。

　　一笔具体的出口交易往往始于出口商主动向潜在客户发函建立业务关系。因此,建立业务关系函是出口商务英语信函中较为重要的信函。

　　就标准规范而言,建立业务关系函一般应包括如下内容:

(一) 信息来源

　　作为贸易商,可以有各种途径来获取客户资料,如通过驻外使馆商务参赞处、商会、商务办事处、银行或第三方公司的介绍;或在企业名录、各种传媒广告、互联网上查得;或在交易会、展览会上结识。在建立业务关系时,发函者通常都会告知对方自己是通过何种途径得到对方信息的,例如:

◇ We learned from the Commercial Counselor's Office of our Embassy in your country that you are in the market for Chinese handicraft.

◇ Mr. Jacques, Canadian Ambassador in Beijing, has recommended you to us as a leading importer of lithium batteries for vehicles in Quebec.

◇ We have obtained your name and address from your company website.

◇ Our market survey has shown that you are the largest importer of cases and bags in Egypt.

(二) 致函目的

　　一般说来,出口商主动联系进口商,总是以扩大交易地区及对象、建立长期业务关系、拓宽产品销路为目的。例如：

◇ In order to expand the sales of our products into South America，we are writing to you to seek cooperation possibilities.

◇ We are writing to you to establish long-term trade relations with you.

◇ We wish to express our desire to enter into business relationship with you.

（三）公司介绍

我们这里所说的公司介绍，包括对公司性质、业务范围、宗旨等基本情况的概述以及对公司某些竞争优势的凸显，例如，贸易经验丰富、供货渠道稳定、有广泛的销售网等。例如：

◇ We are a leading company with many years of experience in machinery export business.

◇ We enjoy a good reputation internationally in the circle of textile.

◇ We have our principle as "Clients' needs come first".

◇ Located in Shanghai，we take the advantage to set up our solidifying production basis in coastal and inland areas.

（四）产品介绍

建立业务关系信函中的产品介绍，大致有两种形式：在较明确对方需求时，我们会选取某类特定产品，进行具体的推荐性介绍；否则，我们通常只就公司经营产品的整体情况，如质量标准、价格水平、目前销路等，作较为笼统的介绍。当然，附上目录、报价单或另寄样品供对方参考也是公司经常采取的做法。例如：

◇ Art. No.76 is our newly launched one with superb quality, fashionable design，and competitive price.

◇ We have a good variety of colors and sizes to meet your different needs.

◇ Our products are enjoying popularity in Asian markets.

◇ To give you a general idea of our products，we are enclosing our catalogue for your reference.

(五) 盼望答复

与其他商业促销信函一样,在结尾部分,我们通常都会写上一两句希望对方给予回应或希望对方尽快做出反馈的语句。例如:

◇　Your comments on our products or any information on your market demand will be really appreciated.

◇　We are looking forward to your specific enquiries.

ⓘ 商务英语信函的基本组成

商务英语书信通常由六部分组成:信头、信内地址、称呼、正文、结尾套语、签署,及其他选择性项目,包括注意、主题、附件、附言等。

(一) 信头(Heading)

信头位于信纸的上方,包括寄信人名称、地址和日期。一般公司信笺上已印有中英文名称和地址、电话、传真等,所以写信时只需打上日期即可。但如临时打印信头,一般在第一页信纸上打上寄信人的名称和地址,而其他续页可用空白信纸,表明页码、日期和收信人名称即可。

日期应打在寄信人名称和地址的下方,也可打在信内地址的下方。各国日期的写法习惯不尽相同,例如美式写法为月/日/年,英式写法为日/月/年,而日式写法为年/月/日。因此,月份最好不要用数字来代表,以免引起误解。

(二) 信内地址(Inside Address)

信内地址是指收信人姓名、公司名称和地址,通常打在信纸的左边、信头的下方。如果知道收信人的姓名,则应使用敬语,如 Mr., Ms., Mrs.等。如果不确定收信人名字,则常打上 To whom it may concern。

(三) 称呼(Salutation)

如已知收信人姓名,则男性以 Mr.称呼,女性一般以 Ms.称呼,除非对方要求以 Mrs.(已婚)或 Miss(未婚)称呼。如不知收信人姓名,则常用 Dear Sirs, Dear Sir or Madam, Gentlemen 等。注意,没有 Dear Gentleman 的说法。

(四) 正文(Body)

正文是信的主体。商务信函讲究清晰明了,正文内容通常分段呈现,而且段落宜短不宜长,每段之间空一行。同时要注意各段的前后排序,确保信息过渡自然、符合逻辑。

(五) 结尾套语(Complimentary Close)

结尾套语紧贴正文最后一行下一二行书写。常见的有 Sincerely, Yours sincerely, Sincerely Yours, Yours truly, Truly yours, Very truly yours, Yours faithfully, Faithfully yours。一般来说,只有在不清楚收信人姓名的情况下,才用 Yours faithfully/Faithfully yours 做结尾套语。

(六) 签署(Signature)

商务信函一般都是以公司的名义发出,所以签署时要注明发信人的姓名、所代表的公司,也有再加其职衔的。

商务电子邮件中,信头和信内地址部分一般不再赘述,邮件主题(Subject)的拟写倒值得仔细斟酌。一般而言,主题应该具体确切,而不要单纯使用"Update"、"Urgent"等模糊的字眼,但也不宜太长,过长的主题无法在邮件列表里完整显示。有些人从不在意修改邮件主题,总是直接回复,以至于磋商到最后邮件的主题变为"Re:Re:Re:Re:Plush Toys",这实则是个懒惰的习惯,应该予以改进。

近年来商务电子邮件更为轻松、自然、简洁,但仍然建议恰当地使用称呼和结尾套语作为基本的礼节。如果觉得书信中常用的称呼和结尾套语过于正式,我们可以用"Hi Peter"来替换"Dear Peter",用"Best wishes"来替换"Yours sincerely"。

练 习

1.

 Profile 上海正源进出口公司主营各类家用电器和消费类电子产品

Information 公司曾名列上海市出口额前五十名

Attention! 新近营销目标：开拓北欧市场

News! 经中国国际贸易促进会介绍，得知丹麦一经销商 Toneveal Products Corp.对中国的家电产品感兴趣。

根据上述情况，试以该公司销售的身份拟写一封建立业务关系函，随附全套产品插页。

2.

小王：

1）Barrison Bros Ltd.的 Mr. Cooper 今早发来传真，希望增订 6000 套 SPT007 绣花枕套，请你与新乐厂联系落实。

2）Mr. Cooper 提到伦敦的 MPE Enterprise UK Ltd.有意进口一批木制工艺品，请你直接给 MPE 发传真了解具体情况，并推荐我们公司的木制饰品。请另寄一份旧的价目表（带产品图片的）给 MPE，别忘了解释一下上面的价格与实际价格会有出入，还有些新产品没来得及汇编进去。新的价目表正在制作，完成后会立即寄出。

试根据上述要求向 MPE 公司发送建立业务关系的传真。（注：我司主营工艺品出口业务）

3.

一日，你在整理工作笔记时发现了上述尼日利亚客户的信息。试向该公司致函建立业务关系并附寄最新产品目录。

4.

上海新际贸易公司成立于 2006 年,注册资金 200 万元,专营轻工业产品的出口业务。十多年来,经营商品种类已增至上百种。现仍不断致力于与国内生产厂家建立联系,向国外客户介绍中国高品质的轻工业产品。

新际贸易公司总经理

Wit Co. Ltd.是韩国一家颇具实力的经销商,在当地有广泛的商销渠道。

中国银行

公司新近设计开发了一组台式打火机,款式新颖大方,制作精巧,选材独特,既可用于点缀桌面,又可作为馈赠佳品。该产品已在日本试销成功。

新际贸易公司
采购部经理

根据上述情景,试以新公司的名义与 Wit 公司联系,推荐上述产品,随寄公司目录,并另寄样品。

5.

Warlaka Al-Adasani Ent.是科威特一家颇有信誉的中间商,专营各类纺织品,具有广阔的销售渠道。捷信公司曾与其做过几笔交易,但由于去年一批货物出了质量问题,发生了点摩擦,至今未再有联系。为了开拓市场,试去信重新建立业务关系,介绍本公司新近的发展并了解当地的市场信息,同时向其推荐全棉桌布和餐巾,并寄最新样本。

第二章　发盘与出口报价核算

案　例

2018 年 9 月 24 日,环宇公司收到荷兰客户 Tivolian 公司的询盘函(第 16 页)。

2018 年 9 月 25 日,环宇公司完成出口报价核算并向 Tivolian 公司发送发盘函。

✍ 工作任务

1. 根据客户的询盘函,结合下列报价信息,填写《报价核算表》,分别计算 FOB、CFR 和 CIF 价格。

采购成本:
KB0278 人民币 55 元/套
KB0677 人民币 90 元/套
KB5411 人民币 70 元/套
KB7900 人民币 95 元/套
(以上价格均含 16％增值税)

出口退税:毛绒玩具的出口退税率为 15％

起订数量:各货号的最低起订量均为 400 套

出口费用:
公司定额费：　5％
贷款年利率：　6.5％(一年按 12 个月 360 天计),预计垫款时间为 45 天
银行手续费：　0.25％(按结算金额计)
国内包干费：　拼箱:每运费吨人民币 80 元,计费标准为 W/M
　　　　　　　整箱:每个 20 英尺集装箱为人民币 1200 元,每个 40 英尺集装箱为人民币 1500 元
海洋运费：　　从上海港至鹿特丹港的整箱运价为 1010/1840 美元(20'GP/40'GP);拼箱运价为每运费吨 95 美元,计费标准为 W/M
海运保险费：　CIF 价加一成投保一切险和战争险,保险费率合计为 0.65％

预期利润：利润率 12%（按出口报价计）

外汇汇率：6.85 元人民币兑换 1 美元

2. 根据客户询盘及报价核算结果，拟写发盘函，清楚列明各项主要交易条件，并同意向 Tivolian 免费寄送四个货号的样品。

付款方式：　　　即期信用证

装运期：　　　　收到信用证后 45 天内

询盘函

Inquiry on plush toys

Sender：　　Chila Trooborg <chtrooborg@tivolian.nl>
Date：　　　24-Sep-2018
Receiver：　David Wang <d.wang@universal.com.cn>

Tivolian
TRADING B.V.

Dear Mr. Wang,

We are pleased to receive your email of September 23 and the leaflets.

We are large dealers in toys and wish to expand our present range with more fashionable plush toys. We believe there is a promising market here for moderately priced products.

After studying your leaflets, we are particularly interested in the following items:

KB0278　　　Twin Bear
KB0677　　　Brown Bear with Red Bow
KB5411　　　Twin Bear in Ballet Costume
KB7900　　　Bear in Pink T-Shirt

Please quote us your best CIF Rotterdam prices on both 20'FCL and LCL basis as well as the terms of shipment, payment and insurance.

Meanwhile we would like to request some samples to test the market demand. If the feedback is good, and your prices are competitive, we'd certainly be able to place a substantial order.

For your information, our banker is F.Van Lanschot Bankiers N.V. (Westersingel 74, 3015 LB Rotterdam, Netherlands, Tel: +31 10 440 20 20　Fax: +31 10 440 20 90).

We hope to hear from you soon.

Yours truly,
Chila Trooborg

Chila Trooborg
Purchase Manager
Tivolian Trading B.V.
Heiman Dullaertolein 3, 3024 CA Rotterdam, the Netherlands
Tel: 31 - 10 - 4767418
Fax: 31 - 10 - 4767422
www.tivolian.nl

报价核算表

上海环宇贸易有限公司
Shanghai Universal Trading Co., Ltd.

报 价 核 算 表

填表日期：＿＿＿ 年 ＿＿＿ 月 ＿＿＿ 日　填表人：＿＿＿＿＿＿＿　编号：＿＿＿＿＿＿＿

为保证报价的精确性，计算过程一律保留4位小数，数值小于1时保留5位，最终报价结果保留2位。

进口商	询价数量	贸易术语	装运港	目的港

包干费 (RMB)			海洋运费(USD)		
LCL / FT	20'FCL	40'FCL	LCL / FT	20'FCL	40'FCL
增值税率	出口退税率	公司定额费率	银行手续费	银行贷款年利率	垫款时间(天)
保险加成率	保险费率	佣金率	其他费用	利润	汇率(USD1=RMB)

货号	计价单位	采购成本（RMB)	包装	包装方式	毛重 kg	净重 kg	长 cm	宽 cm	高 cm
起订数量	报价数量	件数 / 20'FCL	件数 / 40'FCL	数量 / 20'FCL	数量 / 40'FCL				

计算过程		核算单位：	计算结果
出口退税额(¥)			
包干费(¥)			
公司定额费(¥)			
垫款利息(¥)			
海洋运费(¥)			
FOB (US$)			
CFR (US$)			
CIF (US$)			

货号	计价单位	采购成本（RMB)	包装	包装方式	毛重 kg	净重 kg	长 cm	宽 cm	高 cm
起订数量	报价数量	件数 / 20'FCL	件数 / 40'FCL	数量 / 20'FCL	数量 / 40'FCL				

计算过程		核算单位：	计算结果
出口退税额(¥)			
包干费(¥)			
公司定额费(¥)			
垫款利息(¥)			
海洋运费(¥)			
FOB (US$)			
CFR (US$)			
CIF (US$)			

示　范

上海环宇贸易有限公司
Shanghai Universal Trading Co., Ltd.

报 价 核 算 表

填表日期：　**2018**　年　**9**　月　**25**　日　　填表人：　**王凯**　　　编号：　**HYBJ-E0373**

为保证报价的精确性，计算过程一律保留4位小数，数值小于1时保留5位，最终报价结果保留2位。

进口商	询价数量	贸易术语	装运港	目的港
Tivolian Trading B.V.	20'FCL & LCL	CIF	Shanghai	Rotterdam

包干费 (RMB)			海洋运费(USD)		
LCL / FT	20'FCL	40'FCL	LCL / FT	20'FCL	40'FCL
80	1200	1500	95	1010	1840
增值税率	出口退税率	公司定额费率	银行手续费	银行贷款年利率	垫款时间(天)
16%	15%	5%	0.25%	6.5%	45
保险加成率	保险费率	佣金率	其他费用	销售利润率	汇率(USD1=RMB)
10%	0.65%	/	/	12%	6.85

货号	计价单位	采购成本(RMB)	包装	包装方式	毛重 kg	净重 kg	长 cm	宽 cm	高 cm
KB0278	set	55.00		4 sets/ctn	8	5.5	55	45	40
起订数量	报价数量	件数 / 20'FCL		件数 / 40'FCL		数量 / 20'FCL		数量 / 40'FCL	
400	20'FCL (1008 sets)	252		/		1008		/	

	计算过程	核算单位：	set	计算结果
出口退税额(¥)	55 ÷ (1＋16%) × 15%			7.1121
包干费(¥)	1200 ÷ 1008			1.1905
公司定额费(¥)	55 × 5%			2.7500
垫款利息(¥)	55 × 6.5% ÷ 360 × 45			0.44688
海洋运费(¥)	1010 ÷ 1008 × 6.85			6.8636
FOB (US$)	(55−7.1121＋1.1905＋2.75＋0.44688) ÷ (1−0.25%−12%) ÷ 6.85			8.70
CFR (US$)	(55−7.1121＋1.1905＋2.75＋0.44688＋6.8636) ÷ (1−0.25%−12%) ÷ 6.85			9.84
CIF (US$)	(55−7.1121＋1.1905＋2.75＋0.44688＋6.8636) ÷ (1−0.25%−12%−110% x 0.65%) ÷ 6.85			9.92

货号	计价单位	采购成本(RMB)	包装	包装方式	毛重 kg	净重 kg	长 cm	宽 cm	高 cm
KB0278	set	55.00		4 sets/ctn	8	5.5	55	45	40
起订数量	报价数量	件数 / 20'FCL		件数 / 40'FCL		数量 / 20'FCL		数量 / 40'FCL	
400	LCL	/		/		/		/	

	计算过程	核算单位：	set	计算结果
出口退税额(¥)	55 ÷ (1＋16%) × 15%			7.1121
包干费(¥)	80 × (0.55 × 0.45 × 0.4) ÷ 4			1.9800
公司定额费(¥)	55 × 5%			2.7500
垫款利息(¥)	55 × 6.5% ÷ 360 × 45			0.44688
海洋运费(¥)	95 × (0.55 × 0.45 × 0.4) ÷ 4 × 6.85			16.1061
FOB (US$)	(55−7.1121＋1.98＋2.75＋0.44688) ÷ (1−0.25%−12%) ÷ 6.85			8.83
CFR (US$)	(55−7.1121＋1.98＋2.75＋0.44688＋16.1061) ÷ (1−0.25%−12%) ÷ 6.85			11.51
CIF (US$)	(55−7.1121＋1.98＋2.75＋0.44688＋16.1061) ÷ (1−0.25%−12%−110%×0.65%) ÷ 6.85			11.60

货号	计价单位	采购成本(RMB)	包装	包装方式	毛重 kg	净重 kg	长 cm	宽 cm	高 cm
KB0677	set	90.00		8 sets/ctn	8.5	6	48	64	60
起订数量	报价数量		件数 / 20'FCL	件数 / 40'FCL		数量 / 20'FCL		数量 / 40'FCL	
400	20'FCL (1080 sets)		135	/		1080		/	

	计算过程	核算单位:	set	计算结果
出口退税额(¥)	90 ÷ (1＋16%) × 15%			11.6379
包干费(¥)	1200 ÷ 1080			1.11111
公司定额费(¥)	90 × 5%			4.5000
垫款利息(¥)	90 × 6.5% ÷ 360 × 45			0.73125
海洋运费(¥)	1010 ÷ 1080 × 6.85			6.4060
FOB (US$)	(90－11.6379＋1.1111＋4.5＋0.73125) ÷ (1－0.25%－12%) ÷ 6.85			14.09
CFR (US$)	(90－11.6379＋1.1111＋4.5＋0.73125＋6.406) ÷ (1－0.25%－12%) ÷ 6.85			15.16
CIF (US$)	(90－11.6379＋1.1111＋4.5＋0.73125＋6.406) ÷ (1－0.25%－12%－110%×0.65%) ÷ 6.85			15.28

货号	计价单位	采购成本(RMB)	包装	包装方式	毛重 kg	净重 kg	长 cm	宽 cm	高 cm
KB0677	set	90.00		8 sets/ctn	8.5	6	48	64	60
起订数量	报价数量		件数 / 20'FCL	件数 / 40'FCL		数量 / 20'FCL		数量 / 40'FCL	
400	LCL		/	/		/		/	

	计算过程	核算单位:	set	计算结果
出口退税额(¥)	90 ÷ (1＋16%) × 15%			11.6379
包干费(¥)	90 × (0.48 × 0.64 × 0.6) ÷ 8			1.8432
公司定额费(¥)	90 × 5%			4.5000
垫款利息(¥)	90 × 6.5% ÷ 360 × 45			0.73125
海洋运费(¥)	95 × (0.48 × 0.64 × 0.6) ÷ 8 × 6.85			14.9933
FOB (US$)	(90－11.6379＋1.8432＋4.5＋0.73125) ÷ (1－0.25%－12%) ÷ 6.85			14.21
CFR (US$)	(90－11.6379＋1.8432＋4.5＋0.73125＋14.9933) ÷ (1－0.25%－12%) ÷ 6.85			16.71
CIF (US$)	(90－11.6379＋1.8432＋4.5＋0.73125＋14.9933) ÷ (1－0.25%－12%－110%×0.65%) ÷ 6.85			16.85

货号	计价单位	采购成本(RMB)	包装	包装方式	毛重 kg	净重 kg	长 cm	宽 cm	高 cm
KB5411	set	70.00		4 sets/ctn	8	5.5	55	45	40
起订数量	报价数量		件数 / 20'FCL	件数 / 40'FCL		数量 / 20'FCL		数量 / 40'FCL	
400	20'FCL (1008 sets)		252	/		1008		/	

	计算过程	核算单位:	set	计算结果
出口退税额(¥)	70 ÷ (1＋16%) × 15%			9.0517
包干费(¥)	1200 ÷ 1008			1.1905
公司定额费(¥)	70 × 5%			3.5000
垫款利息(¥)	70 × 6.5% ÷ 360 × 45			0.56875
海洋运费(¥)	1010 ÷ 1008 × 6.85			6.8636
FOB (US$)	(70－9.0517＋1.1905＋3.5＋0.56875) ÷ (1－0.25%－12%) ÷ 6.85			11.01
CFR (US$)	(70－9.0517＋1.1905＋3.5＋0.56875＋6.8636) ÷ (1－0.25%－12%) ÷ 6.85			12.16
CIF (US$)	(70－9.0517＋1.1905＋3.5＋0.56875＋6.8636) ÷ (1－0.25%－12%－110%×0.65%) ÷ 6.85			12.26

货号	计价单位	采购成本(RMB)	包装	包装方式	毛重 kg	净重 kg	长 cm	宽 cm	高 cm
KB5411	set	70.00		4 sets/ctn	8	5.5	55	45	40
起订数量	报价数量	件数 / 20'FCL		件数 / 40'FCL		数量 / 20'FCL		数量 / 40'FCL	
400	LCL	/		/		/		/	

	计算过程	核算单位:	set	计算结果
出口退税额(¥)	70 ÷ (1＋16%) × 15%			9.0517
包干费(¥)	80 × (0.55 × 0.45 × 0.4) ÷ 4			1.9800
公司定额费(¥)	70 × 5%			3.5000
垫款利息(¥)	70 × 6.5% ÷ 360 × 45			0.56875
海洋运费(¥)	95 × (0.55 × 0.45 × 0.4) ÷ 4 × 6.85			16.1061
FOB (US$)	(70－9.0517＋1.98＋3.5＋0.56875) ÷ (1－0.25%－12%) ÷ 6.85			11.15
CFR (US$)	(70－9.0517＋1.98＋3.5＋0.56875＋16.1061) ÷ (1－0.25%－12%) ÷ 6.85			13.83
CIF (US$)	(70－9.0517＋1.98＋3.5＋0.56875＋16.1061) ÷ (1－0.25%－12%－110%×0.65%) ÷ 6.85			13.94

货号	计价单位	采购成本(RMB)	包装	包装方式	毛重 kg	净重 kg	长 cm	宽 cm	高 cm
KB7900	set	95.00		8 sets/ctn	8.5	6	48	64	60
起订数量	报价数量	件数 / 20'FCL		件数 / 40'FCL		数量 / 20'FCL		数量 / 40'FCL	
400	20'FCL (1080 sets)	135		/		1080		/	

	计算过程	核算单位:	set	计算结果
出口退税额(¥)	95 ÷ (1＋16%) × 15%			12.2845
包干费(¥)	1200 ÷ 1080			1.1111
公司定额费(¥)	95 × 5%			4.7500
垫款利息(¥)	95 × 6.5% ÷ 360 × 45			0.77188
海洋运费(¥)	1010 ÷ 1080 × 6.85			6.4060
FOB (US$)	(95－12.2845＋1.1111＋4.75＋0.77188) ÷ (1－0.25%－12%) ÷ 6.85			14.86
CFR (US$)	(95－12.2845＋1.1111＋4.75＋0.77188＋6.406) ÷ (1－0.25%－12%) ÷ 6.85			15.93
CIF (US$)	(95－12.2845＋1.1111＋4.75＋0.77188＋6.406) ÷ (1－0.25%－12%－110%×0.65%) ÷ 6.85			16.06

货号	计价单位	采购成本(RMB)	包装	包装方式	毛重 kg	净重 kg	长 cm	宽 cm	高 cm
KB7900	set	95.00		8 sets/ctn	8.5	6	48	64	60
起订数量	报价数量	件数 / 20'FCL		件数 / 40'FCL		数量 / 20'FCL		数量 / 40'FCL	
400	LCL	/		/		/		/	

	计算过程	核算单位:	set	计算结果
出口退税额(¥)	95 ÷ (1＋16%) × 15%			12.2845
包干费(¥)	80 × (0.48 × 0.64 × 0.6) ÷ 8			1.8432
公司定额费(¥)	95 × 5%			4.7500
垫款利息(¥)	95 × 6.5% ÷ 360 × 45			0.77188
海洋运费(¥)	95 × (0.48 × 0.64 × 0.6) ÷ 8 × 6.85			14.9933
FOB (US$)	(95－12.2845＋1.8432＋4.75＋0.77188) ÷ (1－0.25%－12%) ÷ 6.85			14.99
CFR (US$)	(95－12.2845＋1.8432＋4.75＋0.77188＋14.9933) ÷ (1－0.25%－12%) ÷ 6.85			17.48
CIF (US$)	(95－12.2845＋1.8432＋4.75＋0.77188＋14.9933) ÷ (1－0.25%－12%－110%×0.65%) ÷ 6.85			17.62

示范评析

1. 在计算整箱货的单位海洋运费时，关键是必须计算出正确的整箱装货数量。
我们以货号 KB0278 为例说明：

KB0278 的包装纸箱尺码为 $55 \times 45 \times 40$ cm，包装毛重为 8kg，所以，

按 20'FCL 的理论有效容积计算，可装：$55 \times 45 \times 40 = 99000$ cm^3 $= 0.099$ m^3，$25 \div 0.099 = 252.5253$，舍位取整为 252 箱；

按 20'FCL 的理论载货重量计算，可装：$17500 \div 8 = 2187.5$，舍位取整为 2187 箱；

故 20'FCL 可装 252 箱；

而货号 KB0278 的包装方式为 4 套/纸箱，

因此，其 20'FCL 的装货数量为 $252 \times 4 = 1008$ 套。

2. 在计算拼箱货的单位海洋运费时，关键是按计费标准确定正确的计费基数。
我们以货号 KB0278 为例说明：

KB0278 的包装纸箱尺码为 $55 \times 45 \times 40$ cm，包装毛重为 8kg，所以，

其尺码吨（以每立方米为运费计算单位）为：$55 \times 45 \times 40 = 99000$ cm^3 $= 0.099$ m^3；

其重量吨（以每公吨为运费计算单位）为：8 kg $= 0.008$ mt；

因其拼箱运价的计费标准为 W/M，即重量吨与尺码吨比较，择高计算，
而 $0.099 > 0.008$，

故，货号 KB0278 应按其尺码吨 0.099 计收拼箱运价；

又因拼箱运价为每运费吨 95 美元，包装方式为 4 套/纸箱，汇率为 6.85，

因此，拼箱运价应为人民币每套 $95 \times 0.099 \div 4 \times 6.85 = 16.1061$ 元。

3. 示范采用了通用公式来显示其报价的核算过程，但其基本原理还是：价格 ＝成本＋费用＋利润。

我们以货号 KB0278 为例演示其 20'FCL、CIF 价格的计算过程：

价格＝成本＋费用＋利润

CIF＝（采购成本－退税收入）＋（包干费＋公司定额费＋垫款利息＋银行手
续费＋海洋运费＋海运保险费）＋利润

CIF＝$(55 - 7.1121) + (1.1905 + 2.75 + 0.44688 + \text{CIF} \times 0.25\%$
$+ 6.8636 + \text{CIF} \times 110\% \times 0.65\%) + \text{CIF} \times 12\%$

CIF$- \text{CIF} \times 0.25\% - \text{CIF} \times 110\% \times 0.65\% - \text{CIF} \times 12\%$

$= 55 - 7.1121 + 1.1905 + 2.75 + 0.44688 + 6.8636$

CIF×（1－0.25％－110％×0.65％－12％）＝55－7.1121＋1.1905＋2.75＋
　　0.44688＋6.8636

CIF＝（55－7.1121＋1.1905＋2.75＋0.44688＋6.8636）÷（1－0.25％－110％
　　×0.65％－12％）

CIF＝ 人民币 67.9484 元＝9.92 美元

指南中的通用公式可以帮助我们迅速地报价，但要正确运用通用公式的前提还是清晰地掌握核算原理。

Q："海洋运费：从上海到鹿特丹港的整箱运价为 1010/1840 美元（20'GP/40'GP）"，其中的"20'GP"和"40'GP"是什么含义？

A：20'GP 是指 20 feet container for general purpose，即 20 英尺通用集装箱，俗称 20 尺普箱，40'GP 是指 40 feet container for general purpose，即 40 英尺通用集装箱，俗称 40 尺普箱。

Q："海运保险费：CIF 价加 10％投保一切险和战争险"，既然投保了一切险，为什么还要投保战争险？

A：一切险并不涵盖一切风险，不应从名称上望文生义。一切险是中国保险条款中的一个险别，有其具体的责任范围。详细的内容可以参看**第八章　出口货运投保中关于"一切险"的解释**（第 246 页）。

Q：如果供货方能提供商品的 20 英尺整箱数量，是否还需要按示范中的方法进行估算？

A：我们应当了解，有效容积25m³ 仅是一般经验值，在不明确（不了解）实际装箱件数时可依此进行理论上的估算。由于这种方法比我们用 20 英尺集装箱的长宽高分别除以每件包装的长宽高来计算更接近实际装箱结果、更快捷，所以得到了较广的运用。同样，载货重量 17500kg 也仅是通用平均值，实际上，各国各船公司对集装箱配货重量的限制不尽相同。所以当供货方能提供准确的装箱件数时，贸易商自然就不必按理论估算了。

Q：为什么利息率出现在通用公式的分子中，而银行费用率却出现在分母中？

A：垫款利息应按垫款金额计，而出口报价核算中的垫款利息是由于出口商垫付了采购款项而产生的，因此应按采购成本计收。这样在尚未计算出对外报价时，我们就可以依据采购成本得出一个明确的费用额，按上述的演算过程，我们可以看到它一定是作为一项费用出现在分子中。

银行费用是银行收取的服务费用,而出口报价核算中的银行费用往往是指银行向出口商提供收款、结算服务时,按结算金额的一定比率收取的费用,因此应按成交价(在此阶段即为对外报价)计收。在得出最终报价之前,我们不可能得出其具体金额,按上述的演算过程,它只能以一个百分率的形式出现在分母中。当然,也有某些银行费用是按某个固定额收取的,这时它就会作为一项费用额出现在分子中了。银行费用究竟是定额还是定率,应按银行的实际规定执行。

其实,我们可以将众多的出口费用大致分为两类:出口商公司内部的费用(业务费)和出口商向其他机构支付的费用。业务费的计算由出口商自行决定,通常以定额费率的形式核算;而外部费用则根据收费机构的规定去核算,对于那些按费用率方式收取的费用,我们应特别注意其征收基数。

Q:据了解,有相当多的公司采用 CFR＝FOB＋F(海洋运费),CIF＝FOB＋F(海洋运费)＋I(海运保险费)的方式来进行 FOB、CFR 和 CIF 报价的转换。这是否与示范所采用的报价方法相悖呢?

A: 我们以货号 KB0278 的 20 英尺整箱价为例来分析。

在示范中,我们可以清晰地看到其 FOB 价 8.70 美元的构成,即:

采购成本 55－出口退税 7.1121＋包干费 1.1905＋公司定额费 2.75＋垫款利息 0.44688＋银行手续费 0.14899(＝8.7×6.85×0.25%)＋利润 7.1514(＝8.7×6.85×12%)

(＝¥59.5757＝US $8.70)

按照示范的核算方法,我们得出了 CFR 价 9.84 美元,其构成为:

采购成本 55－出口退税 7.1121＋包干费 1.1905＋公司定额费 2.75＋垫款利息 0.44688＋银行手续费 0.16851(＝9.84×6.85×0.25%)＋利润 8.0885(＝9.84×6.85×12%)＋海洋运费 6.8636

(＝¥67.3959＝US $9.84)

但若我们采用 CFR＝FOB＋F 的核算方法,则可得出 CFR＝(59.5757＋6.8636)÷6.85＝US $9.70,细分其构成实际上为:

采购成本 55－出口退税 7.1121＋包干费 1.1905＋公司定额费 2.75＋垫款利息 0.44688＋银行手续费 0.14899(＝8.7×6.85×0.25%)＋利润 7.1514(＝8.7×6.85×12%)＋海洋运费 6.8636

(＝¥66.4393＝US $9.70)

对比以上三种价格构成,我们不难发现,这两种计算 CFR 价格的方法之区别主要存在于银行手续费和利润的计算上。在采用 CFR＝FOB＋F 的方法计算时,CFR

价格中的银行手续费和利润额与 FOB 价格中的完全一致,这表明了运用 CFR＝FOB＋F 方法的默示条件是核算者认为当 FOB 转换成 CFR 术语成交时,除了多加了一项海洋运费以外,其他所有的费用和价格中包含的利润均不会发生变化。然而,就本案例的情况而言,由于银行手续费是按结算金额的一定比率来计收,公司的预期利润也是根据销售利润率(即销售价格的一定比率)来衡量,故当 FOB 报价改为 CFR 报价时,由于报价金额(即结算金额、销售价格)发生了变化,银行手续费和销售利润也理应随之发生变化。从这个意义上而言,示范所演示的核算方法,与 CFR＝FOB＋F 的简易核算方法相比,实际上能更精确地反映出价格中那些以最后报价为核算基数的要素的变化,从而不会导致出口商实际利润的减少。

接下来,让我们做一个不同的比较分析。

假设,银行手续费由按结算金额的 0.25％ 计收调整为按每单 US＄200 征收,公司的预期利润由按 12％ 的销售利润率调整为按采购成本的 12％(即成本利润率)去计算,而其他条件均不发生变化,那么:

按照示范的核算方法,

CFR ＝成本＋费用＋利润

　　＝采购成本 55－出口退税 7.1121＋包干费 1.1905＋公司定额费 2.75＋垫款利息 0.44688＋海洋运费 6.8636＋银行手续费 1.3591(＝200×6.85÷1008)＋利润 6.6(＝55×12％)

　　＝￥67.0980＝US＄9.80

按照 CFR＝FOB＋F 的核算方法,

FOB ＝成本＋费用＋利润

　　＝采购成本 55－出口退税 7.1121＋包干费 1.1905＋公司定额费 2.75＋垫款利息 0.44688＋银行手续费 1.3591(＝200×6.85÷1008)＋利润 6.6(＝55×12％)

　　＝￥60.2344

CFR＝FOB＋F＝(60.2344＋6.8636)÷6.85＝US＄9.80

由此,我们可以看到,示范所运用的核算方法与 CFR＝FOB＋F 的核算方法,在原理上其实是相通的,即"价格＝成本＋费用＋利润",只是前者更为精确,后者则粗略便捷,而在一定的条件下,二者的核算结果就会是完全相同的。

同理,我们可以参照以上的分析方法来理解 CIF＝FOB＋F＋I。

Quotation for plush toys

发件人： David Wang <d.wang@universal.com.cn>
日 期： 2018年9月25日
收件人： Chila Trooborg <chtrooborg@tivolian.nl>

上海环宇贸易有限公司
Shanghai Universal Trading Co., Ltd.

Dear Mr. Trooborg

We are pleased to receive your enquiry of Sept. 24 and the samples you asked for will be sent to you by separate post.

We think you have made an excellent choice in selecting these four items, and once you have seen the samples we feel sure you will be impressed by the quality of inner and outer fabric.

As requested, we would like to quote our favorable CIF Rotterdam prices as follows:

Art. No.	Commodity Name	Min. Order Quantity	Unit Price (LCL Basis)	20' FCL Quantity	Unit Price (20'FCL Basis)
KB0278	Twin Bear	400 sets	USD11.60 / set	1008 sets	USD 9.92 / set
KB0677	Brown Bear with Red Bow	400 sets	USD16.85 / set	1080 sets	USD15.28 / set
KB5411	Twin Bear in Ballet Costume	400 sets	USD13.94 / set	1008 sets	USD12.26 / set
KB7900	Bear in Pink T-Shirt	400 sets	USD17.62 / set	1080 sets	USD16.06 / set

Packing: KB0278 & KB5411: 2 pcs / set, 4 sets / ctn
KB0677 & KB7900: 3 pcs / set, 8 sets / ctn
Payment: By sight L/C
Shipment: To be effected within 45 days from receipt of the relevant L/C
Insurance: For 110% invoice value against All Risks and War Risks

Because of fluctuating exchange rates, we can only hold these prices for three weeks.

We believe you will find a ready sale for our products in Netherlands as have other retailers throughout Europe and America, and we do hope we can reach an agreement on the terms quoted.

Thank you for your interest and look forward to working with you.

Best wishes

David Wang
Sales Manager
Shanghai Universal Trading Co., Ltd.
Tel: +86 21 58818863
Email: d.wang@universal.com.cn

中国上海市东方路 131 号美陵广场 1201-1216 室
Rm. 1201-1216 Mayling Plaza, 131 Dongfang Rd., Shanghai, 200120, China
电话/Tel: 86-21-58818844 传真/Fax: 86-21-58818766 网址/Web: www.universal.com.cn

💬 示范评析

鉴于发盘函的特殊业务功能及法律含义，我们格外强调信函内容的完整性，即必须一一列明六项主要交易条件，即货物的品质、数量、包装、价格、交货和支付条件，而保险作为交货条件的从属内容通常也需列明。有时，客户在询盘函中会指定某项交易条件，如"We would like to point out that we usually settle our accounts on a documents against acceptance basis payable by a draft at 30 days after sight"，"We request the December delivery..."等，出口商无论同意与否，都应在发盘函作明确的表述，而不宜采取"不提及即表示默认接受"的方式。

Q：除了完整地提出各项交易条件外，发盘函中还应有哪些内容呢？

A：发盘函作为对询盘函的回复，仅是简单地回答客户可以供货及供货的条件是远远不够的。我们必须意识到，除了应在建立业务关系函中对产品进行推荐介绍，更应在发盘函中对该客户感兴趣产品的"卖点"（selling point）予以突出强调，这样才能更好地吸引、说服客户。

而对于客户在询盘函中提出的特殊要求或询问，在发盘函中也必须及时予以回应，即使有些问题一时无法答复，也应告知客户会稍后明确，切忌对客户的提问视而不见，留下缺乏服务意识和交流能力的印象。

Q：发盘时为什么要明确商品的数量呢？不是应该由客户来决定吗？

A：在进行报价核算时，我们已经注意到价格与数量是密不可分的，数量的改变会直接影响到国内费用的分摊，海洋运费的拼箱费率和包箱费率也会相去甚远，所以如果进口商在询价时没有确定数量，出口商在报价时则必须说明每一个价格所对应的数量：在对外报 LCL 价格时，应注意告知客户由供货厂商提出的最低起订量，即购买某商品的最小数量；而若报 FCL 价格，则应向客户明确整箱对应的商品数量，以便其决策。所谓发盘时应明确商品数量，并非是替客户决定订购数量，而是要告知所报价格的对应数量。当然，如果客户在询价时已提出了采购数量，则无论报价核算还是发盘均应据此进行。

指 南

价格的表示方法

进出口商品的价格可以用单价（UNIT PRICE）和总值（TOTAL VALUE）来表示，总值是单价和数量的乘积，而单价则由计价的货币、金额、数量单位和价格术语四个部分组成。例如：

US $75.00 PER PIECE FOB SHANGHAI（每件 75 美元上海港船上交货）

由于进出口交易的双方分别处于两个不同的国家或地区，商品单价中的计价货币、计量单位和贸易术语会发生许多变化。

进出口交易中常用的计价货币有：

美元	USD	United States Dollar
欧元	EUR	Euro，European Dollar
英镑	GBP	Great Britain Pound
瑞士法郎	CHF	Swiss Franc
日元	JPY	Japanese Yen

进出口交易中常用的计量单位通常包括六个大类，它们是：

◇ 重量

gram，g.（克）	kilogram，kg（千克）	ounce，oz.（盎司）
pound，lb.（磅）	metric ton，M/T（公吨）	

◇ 个数

piece，pc.（个/只）	pair，pr.（对/副）	dozen，doz.（打）
gross，gr.（罗）	set（台/套）	carton，ctn.（纸箱）
case，c/s（箱）	package，pkg.（件）	

◇　长度

　　metre，m.（米/公尺）　　　　foot，ft.（英尺）　　　yard，yd.（码）

◇　面积

　　square metre，sq.m.（平方米）　　square foot，sq.ft.（平方英尺）

◇　体积

　　cubic metre，cbm（立方米）　　cubic foot，cb.ft.（立方英尺）

◇　容积

　　litre，l.（升）　　　　　　gallon，gal.（加仑）　　bushel，bu.（蒲式耳）

国际货物买卖中最为常见的价格术语有以下三种：

FOB	Free on board	装运港船上交货
CFR	Cost and freight	成本加运费
CIF	Cost，insurance and freight	成本加保险费、运费

　　价格术语的重要作用是表明了价格的组成部分，例如：成本加保险费及运费（CIF）就清楚地表明该价格中除了包含货物本身的价值外，还包括了货物由装运港至目的港的运输费用和保险费用。

　　掌握主要价格术语的基本要素构成、熟悉不同计量单位以及计价货币之间的换算是进行出口价格核算的前提。

ⓘ 价格的构成

　　出口商品的价格包括成本、费用和利润三大要素。

（一）成本（COST）

　　出口商品的成本有生产成本、加工成本和采购成本三种类型。生产成本是制造商生产某一产品所需的投入；加工成本是加工厂商对成品或半成品进行加工所需的成本；而采购成本则是贸易商向供应厂商采购商品的价格，亦称进货成本。在出口价格中，成本所占的比重最大，因而成为价格中的重要组成部分。

（二）费用（EXPENSES/CHARGES）

　　由于进出口交易通常为跨越国界的买卖，其间所要发生的费用远比一般国内交易复杂。在出口商品价格中,费用所占的比重虽然不大,但因其内容繁多,且计算方法又不尽相同,因而成为价格核算中较为复杂的一个方面。出口业务中通常会发生的费用有:

◇　包装费(packing charges)

包装费用通常包含在采购成本之中,但如果客户对货物的包装有特殊的要求,由此产生的费用就会作为包装费另加。

◇　仓储费(warehousing charges)

出口商需要提前采购或另外存仓的货物往往会发生仓储费用。

◇　国内运输费(inland transport charges)

出口货物在装运前所发生的内陆运输费用,通常有卡车运输费、内河运输费、路桥费、过境费及装卸费等。

◇　港区港杂费(port charges)

出口货物装运前在港区码头所需支付的各种费用。

◇　认证费(certification charges)

出口商办理出口许可、配额、原产地证明以及其他证明所支付的费用。

◇　商检费(inspection charges)

出口商根据国家的有关规定或进口商的要求向商品检验机构申请对货物实施检验所支付的费用。

◇　国内包干费(domestic service charges)

在出口业务中,出口商往往委托货物运输代理来办理货物的托运、订舱、报关、装箱及长、短途驳运等涉及货物的运输、通关的事项。各货运代理公司提供的服务项目不尽相同,其收费涵盖也就各有不同,通常包括国内运输费、港区港杂费、商检费、报关费、单证费等,这些费用统称为国内包干费。

◇　捐税(duties and taxes)

国家对出口商品征收、代收的有关税费,如出口关税。

◇　垫款利息(interest)

出口商自国内采购至收到国外进口商付款期间因垫付资金所产生的利息。

◇　银行费用(banking charges)

出口商委托银行向国外客户收取货款、办理结算等所支付的费用。

◇　业务费用(operating charges)

出口商在经营中发生的有关费用,如通信费、交通费、交际费等。业务费用又被称为经营管理费或出口定额费。

◇　出口运费(freight charges)

货物出口时支付的海运、陆运或空运费用。

◇　保险费（insurance premium）
　　出口商向保险公司购买货运保险或信用保险所支付的费用。

◇　佣金（commission）
　　出口商向中间商支付的报酬。

（三）利润（EXPECTED PROFIT）

在出口商品价格中，对于出口商而言，利润无疑是最重要的部分。

了解出口价格的构成，掌握成本、利润和出口交易中各种费用的含义和计算方法，对于准确地核算出口价格是十分重要的。

ⓘ 成本核算

对于从事贸易的出口商而言，成本即为采购成本，也就是贸易商向供货厂商购买货物的支出。供货厂商报出的价格一般会包含增值税，所以供货厂商的报价也常被称为"含税价"、"含税（采购）成本"。然而，由于增值税是以商品进入流通环节所发生的增值税额为课税对象的一种流转税，而出口商品是进入国外流通领域的，所以许多国家为了降低出口商品的成本，增强其产品在国际市场上的竞争力，往往对于出口商品采取退还增值税款的全额或一定比例的做法，称之为"出口退税"。所以在实施出口退税制度的情况下，出口商在进行成本核算时，为了增加其产品在售价上的竞争力，往往会将含税的采购成本中的出口退税部分予以扣除，也就是说出口商实际的成本支出为采购成本减去退税收入。

值得注意的是，增值税的征收和退还都是以不含税的价格，即货物本身的价格（货价）为基数的，即：

$$增值税额＝货价×增值税率$$

$$出口退税额＝货价×出口退税率$$

而我们知道贸易商支付给供货厂商的采购款项是含税的，即

$$采购成本＝含税价＝货价＋增值税额$$

因此，

$$采购成本＝货价＋增值税额＝货价＋货价×增值税率＝货价×（1＋增值税率）$$

即：

$$货价＝采购成本÷(1＋增值税率)$$

$$出口退税额＝货价×出口退税率＝采购成本÷(1＋增值税率)×出口退税率$$

例如：某仪器的采购成本为每台 1160 元人民币(含 16％增值税)，则其货价和增值税额分别为：

$$货价＝采购成本÷(1＋增值税率)＝1160÷(1＋16％)＝1000 元/台$$
$$增值税额＝货价×增值税率＝1000×16％＝160 元/台$$

若其出口可享有 13％的退税，那么退税收入为：

$$退税收入＝采购成本÷(1＋增值税率)×出口退税率$$
$$＝1160÷(1＋16％)×13％＝130 元/台$$

故若出口该仪器，实际的成本支出为：

$$采购成本－退税收入＝1160－130＝1030 元/台$$

(i) 费用核算

(一) 海运运费核算

进出口货物的运输通常采用的是海洋运输方式，而在海运方式中，根据承运货物船舶的不同营运方法又可以分为班轮运输和租船运输两种。进出口交易中除了大宗初级产品的交易外，多数采用班轮运输的方式。在班轮运输中，根据托运货物是否装入集装箱运输又可以将进出口货物分为件杂货物与集装箱货物两类。出口交易中，在以 CFR(CPT)、CIF(CIP)术语成交的情况下，出口方需要进行海运运费的核算。

◇　件杂货物(散货)运费核算

1. 运费构成

件杂货物海运运费主要由基本运费和附加运费两部分，基本运费一般不常发生变动，但由于构成海运运费的各种因素会经常发生变化，各船公司就采取征收各种附加费的办法以维护其营运成本，附加运费主要有：

① 燃油附加费(Bunker Adjustment Factor，简称 B.A.F.)

因燃油价格上涨，船公司营运成本增加而加收的费用。燃油附加费有的航线按基本运费率的百分比加收,有的航线则按运费吨加收一定金额。

② 货币附加费(Currency Adjustment Factor,简称 C.A.F.)

由于用以收取运费的货币贬值使船公司收入减少而加收的费用。

③ 港口拥挤费(Port Congestion Surcharge)

由于装卸港口堵塞拥挤,造成船舶停靠时间拉长,增加船期成本,船公司将视港口情况好坏,在不同时期根据基本费率收取的不同百分比的费用。

④ 转船附加费(Transshipment Surcharge)

因运往非基本港口的货物需在途中经转运至目的港而加收的费用。

⑤ 港口附加费(Port Surcharge)

由于卸货港港口费用太高或港口卸货效率太低影响船期而向货主加收的费用。

2. 运费计算标准

件杂货海运运费的计算标准共有以下七种:

① 重量法

按货物毛重来计算,以每公吨即 1000 千克为运费计算单位,又称重量吨(weight ton),吨以下取小数三位。费率表上以"W"表示。

② 体积法

按货物的体积来计算,以每立方米为运费计算单位,又称尺码吨(measurement ton),立方米以下取小数三位。费率表上以"M"表示。

注意,以重量吨或尺码吨计算运费的,统称为运费吨(freight ton,FT)。

③ 从价法

按货物价值作为运费计算标准,费率表上以"AD VAL"表示。

④ 选择法

有以下四种选择方法:

W/M	最为常见的选择方法,即在重量法与体积法之间选择;
W or AD VAL	在重量法与从价法之间选择;
M or AD VAL	在体积法与从价法之间选择;
W/M or AD VAL	在重量法、体积法和从价法之间由承运人根据不同的货物,决定具体的选择方法,择高收取运费。

⑤ 综合法

按重量吨或尺码吨计收运费外,再加收从价运费,即 W & AD VAL;M & AD VAL。

⑥ 按件法

按每件为一单位计收。

⑦ 议价法(OPEN RATE)

由船货双方临时协商议定运价的计费方法。

3. 运费计算

件杂货物(散货)海运运费计算的一般步骤为:

① 根据货物名称,在运价本中的货物分级表上查到货物的等级(CLASS)和运费计算标准(BASIS);

② 根据货物的装运港、目的港,找到相应的航线,按货物的等级查到基本运价;

③ 查出该航线和港口所要收取的附加费项目和数额(或百分比)及货币种类;

④ 根据基本运价和附加费算出实际运价(单位运价);

⑤ 根据货物的托运数量算出应付的运费总额。

◇　集装箱货物运费核算

1. 集装箱运输介绍

集装箱是一种容器,能够作为运输辅助设备反复使用。集装箱的外形像一个箱子,由于人们可以将货物集中装入箱内,故称集装箱,又称"货柜"或"货箱"。

国际标准化组织(ISO)为了统一集装箱的规格,推荐了十三种规格的集装箱,而在国际货物运输中经常使用的是 20 英尺和 40 英尺集装箱,其型号和具体规格如下:

1C 型　　$20' \times 8' \times 8'6''$

【内径】$5898 \times 2352 \times 2390$mm

1A 型　$40' \times 8' \times 8'6''$
【内径】12024×2352×2390mm

由于集装箱型号规格不尽相同,为使集装箱箱数计算统一化,便把 20 英尺集装箱作为一个计量单位 TEU(Twenty Equivalent Unit),也称国际标准箱单位,40 英尺集装箱折算成 2 个 TEU。TEU 通常被用来表示船舶装载集装箱的能力,也是集装箱和港口吞吐量的重要统计、换算单位。

随着集装箱运输的发展,为适应装载不同种类货物的需要,出现了不同种类的集装箱,除了通用的干货集装箱(Dry Cargo Container)外,还有罐式集装箱、冷藏集装箱、框架集装箱、平台集装箱、通风集装箱、牲畜集装箱、散装集装箱、挂式集装箱等。

根据托运货物是否装满一个集装箱,可分为整箱货(Full Container Load,简称 FCL)与拼箱货(Less than Container Load,简称 LCL)两类。整箱货由货方在工厂和仓库进行装箱,货物装箱后直接交运集装箱堆场(Container Yard,简称 CY)等待装运,货到目的地(港)后,收货人可直接从目的地(港)集装箱堆场提取货物。拼箱货是指货量不足一整箱,需由承运人在集装箱货运站(Container Freight Station,简称 CFS)负责将不同发货人的少量货物拼装在一个集装箱内,货到目的地(港)后,再由承运人拆箱后分拨给各收货人。

2. 集装箱运费构成
海运集装箱货物运输通常会发生以下费用:
① 内陆运输费(Inland Transportation Charge)
② 堆场服务费(Terminal Handling Charge)
③ 拼箱服务费(LCL Service Charge)
④ 设备使用费(Fee for Use Container and Other Equipments)
⑤ 海运运费(Ocean Freight)
根据不同的集装箱交接方式,计收不同的费用项目。

3. 集装箱海运出口费率表
海运集装箱费率表有不同的形式,实际业务中最为常见的集装箱货物海运出口费率表为 FAK(Freight for All Kinds)费率表,即不分货物级别统一收取运费,示例如下:

单位:美元

装运港 PORT OF LOADING	货物种类 COMMODITIES	拼箱(重量/尺码) LCL(W/M)	20英尺整箱 20′FCL	40英尺整箱 40′FCL
黄浦 HUANGPU	普通货物 GENERAL CARGO	63.00	800.00	1450.00
	半危险品 SEMI-HAZARDOUS	86.00	1250.00	2300.00
	全危险品 HAZARDOUS		1550.00	2850.00
	冷藏货物 REEFER		2200.00	4050.00
上海 SHANGHAI	普通货物 GENERAL CARGO	78.00	1100.00	2050.00
	半危险品 SEMI-HAZARDOUS	97.00	1450.00	2700.00
	全危险品 HAZARDOUS		1850.00	3400.00
	冷藏货物 REEFER		2700.00	5000.00

此外,还有以下两种费率表:

FCS(Freight for Class)费率表,即按不同的货物等级收取不同的运费,示例如下:

单位:美元

等 级 CLASS	LCL W/M	CY/CY	
		20′	40′
1—7	55.00	770.00	1460.00
8—10	58.00	820.00	1560.00
11—15	61.00	870.00	1650300
16—20	64.00	920.00	1750.00
CHEMICALS, N.H.	61.00	870.00	1650.00
SEMI-HAZARDOUS	68.00	1200.00	2280.00
HAZARDOUS		1650.00	3100.00
REEFER		2530.00	4800.00

FCB(Freight for Class & Basis)费率表,即按不同的货物等级以及计算标准收取不同的运费,示例如下:

单位:美元

等　　级	计算标准	拼　箱	CY/CY 整箱	
CLASS	BASIS	CFS/CFS	20' /	40'
1—7	M	90.00	1750.00	3500.00
8—10	M	94.00	1900.00	3800.00
11—15	M	101.00	2050.00	4100.00
16—20	M	107.00	2200.00	4400.00
1—7	W	118.00	1750.00	3500.00
8—10	W	127.00	1900.00	3800.00
11—15	W	136.00	2050.00	4100.00
16—20	W	145.00	2200.00	4400.00
CHEMICAL	W/M	128.00	2050.00	4100.00
SEMI-HAZARDOUS CARGO	W/M	166.00	2550.00	5100.00
HAZARDOUS CARGO	W/M	224.00	3550.00	7100.00
REFRIGERATED CARGO	W/M	246.00	3900.00	7850.00

4. 集装箱货物海运运费的计算方法

集装箱货物海运费根据货量的大小,即拼箱货(LCL)和整箱货(FCL),分为以下两种不同的计算方法:

① 拼箱货

拼箱货的运费一般以运费吨为计费单位,按照传统的件杂货等级费率收取基本运费外,再加收一定的附加费。

拼箱货的运费计算的一般步骤为:

● 根据货物名称,在运价本中的货物分级表上查到货物的等级(CLASS)和运费计算标准(BASIS);

● 根据货物的装运港、目的港,找到相应的航线,按货物的等级查到基本运费(LCL 栏或 CFS 栏)和附加费,确定拼箱费率;

● 根据运费计算标准,确定实际计费数量;

● 根据拼箱费率、计费数量算出实际运价。

例如：某商品用纸箱包装，2 打装 1 个纸箱，每个纸箱的尺码是 40×40×50 厘米，毛重是 20 千克，净重是 18 千克，共出口 200 打即 100 个纸箱。经查，拼箱费率为每运费吨 90 美元，运费计算标准是 W/M，则该批货物的海运总运费和单位商品的海运运费分别为：

尺码吨（M）：0.4×0.4×0.5×100＝8 立方米

重量吨（W）：20×100＝2000 千克＝2 吨

因为尺码吨（M）大于体积吨（W），所以应按尺码吨（M）计算运费，

总海运运费为 90×8＝720 美元

单位商品的海运运费为 720÷200＝3.6 美元/打

② 整箱货

整箱货以每个集装箱为计费单位，收取包箱费率（Box Rate）。

整箱货的运费计算的一般步骤为：

● 确定一个集装箱所容纳的货物数量（装箱数量）；

● 根据货物的装运港、目的港，找到相应航线的包箱费率（及附加费）；

● 包箱费率除以商品装箱总数量，即可得出单位商品的运费。

我们可以看到，在整箱货的情况下，总运费是很容易确定的，因为我们只需用包箱费率乘以集装箱个数即可。而如何将这笔总运费平摊到单位商品上，就成为了计算运费的关键。

要计算单位商品的运费，就必须先确定商品的装箱（集装箱）数量。在进出口交易中，集装箱货物的装箱方法对于贸易商减少运费开支起着很大的作用。运费开支减少了，就意味着贸易商可以报出更低的价格但能保证同等的利润，提高了其价格竞争力。所以贸易商非常重视货物外包装箱的尺码、重量设计，讲究货物在集装箱内的配装、排放以及堆叠，以达到充分利用集装箱空间的目的。当然，这需要在实践中不断摸索，而且也和货物的种类、特性以及客户的要求有关。

如不清楚实际装货数量，我们可以用一个理论限额来测算 20 英尺和 40 英尺集装箱的装箱数量，即：

20 英尺集装箱的有效容积为 $25m^3$，最大载货重量为 17500 千克

40 英尺集装箱的有效容积为 $55m^3$，最大载货重量为 24500 千克

显然，货物的装箱数量既应在有效容积范围内，又不能超过最大载货重量。

例 1：某货物的包装方式为 8 台装 1 个纸箱，纸箱的尺码为 54×44×40cm，毛

重为 42 千克,试计算该类货物集装箱运输出口时的装箱数量。

20 英尺整箱装箱数量

按体积计算:25÷(0.54×0.44×0.40)=263.0471,取整为 263 箱

按重量计算:17500÷42=416.6667,取整为 416 箱

取较小值,故 20 英尺整箱可装 263 箱,装箱数量为 263×8=2104 台

40 英尺整箱装箱数量

按体积计算:55÷(0.54×0.44×0.40)=578.7037,取整为 578 箱

按重量计算:24500÷42=583.3333,取整为 583 箱

取较小值,故 40 英尺整箱可装 578 箱,装箱数量为 578×8=4624 台

例 2:某货物的包装方式为 8 台装 1 个纸箱,纸箱的尺码为 54×44×40cm,毛重为 68 千克,试计算该类货物集装箱运输出口时的装箱数量。

20 英尺整箱装箱数量

按体积计算:25÷(0.54×0.44×0.40)=263.0471,取整为 263 箱

按重量计算:17500÷68=257.3529,取整为 257 箱

取较小值,故 20 英尺整箱可装 257 箱,装箱数量为 257×8=2056 台

40 英尺整箱装箱数量

按体积计算:55÷(0.54×0.44×0.40)=578.7037,取整为 578 箱

按重量计算:24500÷68=360.2941,取整为 360 箱

取较小值,故 40 英尺整箱可装 360 箱,装箱数量为 360×8=2880 台

注意,这里的箱数取整,应该是"舍位取整",而不是"四舍五入";按体积计算的箱数与按重量计算的箱数比较后,应取较小值。

明确了装箱数量之后,我们将包箱费率平均分摊到每单位商品,就可以迅速得出单位海运运费了。

例如:出口一个 40 英尺集装箱的装饰灯串,每 20 套装 1 个纸箱,纸箱的尺码为 38×38×28 厘米,毛重为每箱 12 千克,净重为 10 千克,40 英尺集装箱的海运包箱费为 2100 美元,人民币对美元的汇率为 1 美元兑换 6.4 元人民币,试计算每套灯串的出口运费为多少元人民币。

按体积计算:55÷(0.38×0.38×0.28)=1360.3760,取整为 1360 箱

按重量计算:24500÷12=2041.6667,取整为 2041 箱

因此,一个 40 英尺整箱可装 1360 箱,货物数量为 1360×20=27200 套

故,每套灯串的海运运费为 2100×6.4÷27200=人民币 0.49 元

（二）保险费核算

出口交易中，在以 CIF（或 CIP）术语成交的情况下，出口方就需要进行保险费的核算。

保险费是投保人向保险公司交纳的费用，按照货物的保险金额（即投保人对保险标的的投保金额，也是保险公司承担赔偿的最高限额）乘以一定的百分比（即保险费率）来计算。各国的保险法一般都规定进出口货物运输保险的保险金额可在货物 CIF 价值基础上适当加成。

$$保险费＝保险金额×保险费率$$

$$保险金额＝CIF 价×（1＋投保加成率）$$

根据有关的国际贸易惯例，投保加成率通常为 10%。当然，这并不是一成不变的。进出口双方可以根据不同的货物、不同地区进口价格与当地市价之间的不同差价幅度、不同的经营费用和预期利润水平，约定不同的加成率。

例如：某货物的 CIF 汉堡价格为每台 65 美元，投保加成率为 10%，保险费率为 0.15%，汇率为 1 美元兑换 6.4 元人民币，则应支付的保险费为：

$$65×（1＋10\%）×0.15\%×6.4＝人民币 0.69 元$$

需要注意的是，保险金额的计算是以 CIF（或 CIP）货价为基础的，因此如果在 CFR（或 CPT）合同项下买方要求卖方代为投保时，应先将 CFR 价格换算为 CIF 价格后再求出相应的保险金额和保险费，如：

$$CIF＝CFR＋保险费 I$$

$$CIF＝CFR＋CIF×（1＋投保加成率）×保险费率$$

$$CIF－CIF×（1＋投保加成率）×保险费率＝CFR$$

$$CIF×[1－（1＋投保加成率）×保险费率]＝CFR$$

$$CIF＝\frac{CFR}{1－（1＋投保加成率）×保险费率}$$

所以，

保险费 I ＝CIF×（1＋投保加成率）×保险费率

$$＝\frac{CFR}{1－（1＋投保加成率）×保险费率}×（1＋投保加成率）×保险费率$$

（三）国内包干费核算

包干费的计费标准与出口海运运费相仿，大都按照货物的类别及装箱方式来制定，分为散货、拼箱、20英尺普通箱、40英尺普通箱、特种集装箱、一般危险品和冷冻箱等，但一般均以人民币计费。计算方法也与海运运费类似。

（四）捐税核算

对出口货物，海关将根据《中华人民共和国关税条例》的规定和《中华人民共和国海关进出口税则》规定的税率，征收出口关税，目前较多采用从价计税的方法。

从价计收出口关税的计算方法为：

$$应纳关税＝出口货物完税价格×出口货物关税税率$$

税法同时规定，出口货物以海关审定的成交价格为基础的售予境外的离岸价格，扣除出口关税后作为完税价格。所以，

当以FOB价格成交时，

$$应纳关税＝\frac{FOB}{1+出口关税率}×出口货物关税税率$$

当以CFR价格成交时，

$$应纳关税＝\frac{CFR-运费}{1+出口关税率}×出口货物关税税率$$

当以CIF价格成交时，

$$应纳关税＝\frac{CIF-运费-保险费}{1+出口关税率}×出口货物关税税率$$

在我国，绝大多数货物出口免征关税。

（五）垫款利息核算

垫款利息是指出口商由向国内供货商购进货物至从国外买方收到货款期间由于资金的占用而造成的利息损失，所以垫款利息通常按采购成本计。

例如,某商品的采购成本为人民币 100 元,银行贷款年利率为 9%,预计垫款周期为 2 个月,那么,单位商品的垫款利息则为 $100 \times 9\% \times 2 \div 12 =$ 人民币 1.5 元。

(六) 银行费用核算

银行费用是指出口商委托银行向进口商收取货款时所需交纳的费用。其计费方式一般有两种:一是按交易笔数收取一定金额,例如每笔交易的银行手续费为 100 美元,二是按委托收款金额的一定百分比收取。在前一种情况下,银行费用应平均分摊到单位商品上,在后一种情况下,银行费用应按照报价来计算。

(七) 出口定额费核算

所谓定额费用率是指公司对业务操作中,诸如邮电通信费用、交通费用、差旅费、招待费及其他业务费用,按公司年度实际支出状况规定的一个百分比,一般为公司购货成本的 5% 左右,也可根据不同的商品类别有所区别。定额费用率的计费基础通常是含税的采购成本。出口定额费也被称为经营管理费。

(八) 佣金核算

佣金是买方或卖方付给中间商的报酬,按成交价格的一定百分比来计算。包含佣金的价格即为含佣价,价格中不包括佣金则称为净价(Net Price)。CIFC5 价即指包含 5% 佣金的含佣价。

净价与含佣价之间的换算关系是:

因为　　　　　　　　佣金＝含佣价×佣金率

所以　　　　　　　含佣价＝净价＋佣金

含佣价＝净价＋含佣价×佣金率

含佣价－含佣价×佣金率＝净价

含佣价×(1－佣金率)＝净价

$$含佣价 = \frac{净价}{1 - 佣金率}$$

ⓘ 利润核算

利润是出口价格的三要素之一,贸易商计算利润的方法不尽相同,有的规定某一固定的数额作为利润,有的则用一定的百分比来核算利润(利润率)。在用利润率来核算利润额时,应当注意计算的基数,以采购成本为基数的利润率称为成本利润率,以销售价格为基数的利润率称为销售利润率。

ⓘ 综合报价核算

报价核算的基本原理:价格＝成本＋费用＋利润

其中,成本核算时应注意扣除退税收入,即核算实际支出的成本;费用核算时,必须首先明确应核算哪些费用项目,例如在计算 FOB 报价时,海运运费和保险费均不应计入费用,然后梳理各费用项目的计费方法,特别是那些按费用率计费的项目其计算基数是如何规定的;利润核算时,应注意区分究竟是采用销售利润率还是成本利润率。

下面我们可以通过一次具体的报价过程来理解报价核算的原理。

例如:某公司收到丹麦客户求购离心泵的询价,要求分别按照拼箱(LCL)和 20 英尺整箱(20′FCL)报出包含 3‰佣金的 FOB 上海和 CFR、CIF 哥本哈根的价格。

该产品的采购成本为每台人民币 1160 元,增值税率为 16％,出口退税率为 5％;2 台装一个木箱,木箱尺码为 50×40×40 厘米,净重为 78 千克,毛重为 83 千克。最低起订量为 100 台。

出口的各项费用有:

海洋运费:	拼箱(LCL):USD100/FT,计费标准为 W/M
	整箱(FCL):USD1000/20′FCL,USD1850/40′FCL
海运保险费:	按 CIF 价值的 120％投保,保险费率为 0.4％
国内包干费:	拼箱(LCL):每运费吨人民币 70 元,计费标准为 W/M
	整箱(FCL):每个 20 英尺箱人民币 800 元,
	每个 40 英尺箱人民币 1200 元
垫款利息:	银行贷款年利率为 9％,预计垫款时间为 120 天(一年按 360 天计)
银行费用:	每笔交易 200 美元
公司定额费率:	4％

公司的预期利润为采购成本的 10％。

汇率按 1 美元兑换 6.4 元人民币折算。

成本核算

采购成本＝1160 元/台

退税收入＝货价×出口退税率＝采购成本÷(1＋增值税率)×出口退税率

$\qquad$ ＝1160÷(1＋16％)×5％＝50 元/台

费用核算

海洋运费 LCL　　　W：83 千克＝0.083 吨

M：50×40×40＝80000 立方厘米＝0.08 立方米

因为 W＞M，所以按重量吨计算运费

100×0.083×6.4÷2＝26.56 元/台

海洋运费 20′FCL　　按尺码计算装箱件数：25÷(0.5×0.4×0.4)＝312.5，取整为 312 箱

按重量计算装箱件数：17.5÷0.083＝210.8434，取整为 210 箱

故 20 英尺整箱可容纳的包装件数为 210 箱，即 210×2＝420 台

均摊的海运运费为：1000×6.4÷420＝15.2381 元/台

海运保险费　　　　CIF 价×(1＋投保加成率)×保险费率

＝CIFC3×120％×0.4％

包干费 LCL　　　　因重量吨 0.083＞尺码吨 0.08，所以按重量吨计算包干费

70×0.083÷2＝2.905 元/台

包干费 20′FCL　　　因 20 英尺整箱可容纳的商品数量为 420 台

均摊的包干费为：800÷420＝1.9048 元/台

垫款利息　　　　　采购成本×贷款年利率×垫款天数÷360

＝1160×9％×120÷360＝34.8 元/台

银行费用　　　　　拼箱按最低起订量均摊：200×6.4÷100＝12.8 元/台

整箱按装箱数量均摊：200×6.4÷420＝3.0476 元/台

公司定额费　　　　采购成本×定额费率＝1160×4％＝46.4 元/台

客户佣金　　　　　含佣价×佣金率

＝FOBC3×3％或 CFRC3×3％或 CIFC3×3％

利润核算

预期利润　　　　　　　＝采购成本×成本利润率＝1160×10％＝116元/台

LCL 报价

FOBC3　　　　　　　　＝成本＋费用＋利润

FOBC3　　　　　　　　＝采购成本－退税收入＋包干费＋垫款利息＋银行费用＋
　　　　　　　　　　　公司定额费＋客户佣金＋利润

FOBC3　　　　　　　　＝1160－50＋2.905＋34.8＋12.8＋46.4＋FOBC3×3％＋
　　　　　　　　　　　116

FOBC3－FOBC3×3％＝1160－50＋2.905＋34.8＋12.8＋46.4＋116

FOBC3×97％　　　　　＝1322.905

FOBC3　　　　　　　　＝1363.8196元/台

FOBC3　　　　　　　　＝213.10美元/台

CFRC3　　　　　　　　＝成本＋费用＋利润

CFRC3　　　　　　　　＝采购成本－退税收入＋**海洋运费**＋包干费＋垫款利息＋
　　　　　　　　　　　银行费用＋公司定额费＋客户佣金＋利润

CFRC3　　　　　　　　＝1160－50＋**26.56**＋2.905＋34.8＋12.8＋46.4＋CFRC3×
　　　　　　　　　　　3％＋116

CFRC3－CFRC3×3％＝1160－50＋26.56＋2.905＋34.8＋12.8＋46.4＋116

CFRC3×97％　　　　　＝1349.465

CFRC3　　　　　　　　＝1391.201元/台

CFRC3　　　　　　　　＝217.38美元/台

CIFC3　　　　　　　　＝成本＋费用＋利润

CIFC3　　　　　　　　＝采购成本－退税收入＋**海洋运费**＋**保险费**＋包干费＋垫
　　　　　　　　　　　款利息＋银行费用＋公司定额费＋客户佣金＋利润

CIFC3　　　　　　　　＝1160－50＋**26.56＋CIFC3×120％×0.4％**＋2.905＋34.8
　　　　　　　　　　　＋12.8＋46.4＋CIFC3×3％＋116

CIFC3－CIFC3×120％×0.4％－CIFC3×3％＝1160－50＋26.56＋2.905＋
　　　　　　　　　　　34.8＋12.8＋46.4＋116

CIFC3×96.52％＝1349.465

CIFC3　　　　　　　　＝1398.1196元/台

CIFC3　　　　　　　　＝218.46美元/台

20′FCL 报价

FOBC3	＝成本＋费用＋利润
FOBC3	＝采购成本－退税收入＋**包干费**＋垫款利息＋**银行费用**＋公司定额费＋客户佣金＋利润
FOBC3	＝1160－50＋**1.9048**＋34.8＋**3.0476**＋46.4＋FOBC3×3％＋116
FOBC3－FOBC3×3％	＝1160－50＋1.9048＋34.8＋3.0476＋46.4＋116
FOBC3×97％	＝1312.1524
FOBC3	＝1352.7344 元/台
FOBC3	＝211.36 美元/台

CFRC3	＝成本＋费用＋利润
CFRC3	＝采购成本－退税收入＋**海洋运费**＋**包干费**＋垫款利息＋**银行费用**＋公司定额费＋客户佣金＋利润
CFRC3	＝1160－50＋**15.2381**＋**1.9048**＋34.8＋**3.0476**＋46.4＋CFRC3×3％＋116
CFRC3－CFRC3×3％	＝1160－50＋15.2381＋1.9048＋34.8＋3.0476＋46.4＋116
CFRC3×97％	＝1327.3905
CFRC3	＝1368.4438 元/台
CFRC3	＝213.82 美元/台

CIFC3	＝成本＋费用＋利润
CIFC3	＝采购成本－退税收入＋**海洋运费**＋**保险费**＋**包干费**＋垫款利息＋**银行费用**＋公司定额费＋客户佣金＋利润
CIFC3	＝1160－50＋**15.2381**＋**CIFC3×120％×0.4％**＋**1.9048**＋34.8＋**3.0476**＋46.4＋CIFC3×3％＋116
CIFC3－CIFC3×120％×0.4％－CIFC3×3％	＝1160－50＋15.2381＋1.9048＋34.8＋3.0476＋46.4＋116
CIFC3×96.52％	＝1327.3905
CIFC3	＝1375.2492 元/台
CIFC3	＝214.88 美元/台

由以上出口报价的实例不难看出,报价核算并不深奥,其关键是掌握各项内

容的计算依据并细心地加以汇总，也要特别注意计费单位和货币单位。我们也可以由此归纳出一个出口报价的通用公式：

$$出口报价 = \frac{采购成本 - 退税收入 + 费用额 + 利润额}{1 - 以出口报价为基数的费用率 - 销售利润率} \div 人民币汇率$$

其中，

"采购成本－退税收入"等于出口商实际支出的成本，即"实际成本"；

"费用额"是指那些可以直接计算得出的费用，如包干费、海洋运费等，包括那些与采购成本相关的费用，如公司定额费、银行贷款利息、银行费用额等。这些费用的数额是在尚未得出出口报价的最后结果时就已明确了的；

"利润额"是指当公司采用固定的数额或是成本利润率来控制利润水平时，在尚未得出出口报价的最后结果时，利润额就已经明确；

"以出口报价为基数的费用率"是指那些与出口报价成一定比例的费用率，如银行费用率、客户佣金率、保险费率（还应考虑到投保加成）等。

"销售利润率"是指当公司采用销售利润率来决定利润水平时，在尚未得出出口报价的最后结果时，不能明确具体数额，只能以率的形式来表现。

上述报价公式体现了一种基于成本精确定价的思路。在实际交易中，贸易商往往会采用一些粗略、简化的计算方法或自动化的计算工具以使报价核算过程更为简便、快捷。

ⓘ 发盘函的基本结构

发盘函（offer）也称报价函（quotation），通常是出口商（卖方）应进口商（买方）询价的要求发出的。

从标准规范的角度而言，发盘函一般应包括如下内容：

（一）确认收到询盘

◇　Thank you for your enquiry about our porcelain ware.

◇　Many thanks for your letter of 15 March. We are pleased to learn you are impressed with our selection of silk shirts.

◇　Thanks for your email and interest in our bicycles. I am pleased to tell you that we are able to supply you with the high quality products.

（二）强调产品的优势特色

　　在发盘函中仅简单地回复客户可以供货、列明交易条件是远远不够的，因为客户极有可能同时发出了多个询盘。在发盘函中，我们应就客户询盘商品作具体的推荐，突出其一两个卖点，这对于鼓励客户订货是很有帮助的。

◇　We think you have made an excellent choice in selecting this line, and once you have seen the samples we are sure you will agree that this is unique both in texture and colour.

◇　Once you have seen the machine in operation we know you will be impressed by its trouble-free performance.

◇　We can assure you that the Ultra 2019 is one of the most outstanding machines on the market today, and our confidence in it is supported by our three-year guarantee.

（三）按客户要求发盘，列明主要交易条件

　　主要交易条件是指品名规格、数量、包装、价格、交货和支付条件，当然，如果有 CIF 报价，一般还会加上保险条件。这些交易条件是成立买卖合同所不可缺少的交易条件，因此也是买卖双方交易磋商的主要内容。

◇　For the Fancy Brand AGT-4 garment sewing machine, the best price is USD78.00 per set FOB Shanghai.

◇　We confirm our price for the Automatic Dishwasher at US $211.00 per set CFR Nagoya.

◇　In reply to your enquiry of May 28, we have the pleasure of quoting on 100 dozen nylon stockings at US $18 a dozen CIF Singapore.

◇　The minimum quantity is one 20'FCL and with the purchase of two or more containers, the price is reduced by 2%.

◇　All these blankets are packed in plastic bags with zip of 1 piece each, 20 pieces to a carton.

◇　The wheat is to be packed in new gunny bags of 100kgs., and each bag weighs about 1.5kgs.

◇ The trip scissors are packed in boxes of one dozen each，100 boxes to the carton.

◇ Delivery is to be made within 45 days upon receipt of order.

◇ Our delivery terms are shipment within three months from receipt of L/C.

◇ The earliest shipment possible is December. We hope this will be acceptable to your customers.

◇ Our usual terms of payment are by irrevocable L/C available by draft at sight.

◇ We may accept L/C at 30 days' sight to help your financing.

◇ The insurance shall be effected by the seller for the invoice value plus 10% against Institute Cargo Clauses(A).

◇ We usually cover shipment against WPA and War Risks. If you wish to add any extra risks，please let us know in advance.

◇ We generally insure our export shipments with the People's Insurance Company of China.

◇ We will insure the goods against All Risks and War Risks for invoice value plus 10%.

如果报价是有期限的,或是还需卖方最后确认,也应明确表示。

◇ This offer is valid for ten days.

◇ The quotation is for acceptance within two weeks.

◇ This quotation is effective while stocks last.

◇ This offer is subject to our final confirmation.

(四) 回复客户提出的其他问题和要求

◇ The samples you asked for will follow by separate post.

◇ The requested samples of our silk handkerchiefs have been sent to you.

◇　Enclosed please find the copy you requested for the inspection report.

（五）鼓励客户订货

发盘的目标是为了获得订单，所以我们通常会以一些鼓励、刺激对方下订单的语句来结尾。例如：

◇　We believe our offer will give you full satisfaction and hope to receive a favorable reply from you soon.

◇　We look forward to an initial order，which will convince you of the high quality of our goods.

◇　As we have been receiving a rush of orders now，we would advise you to place your order as soon as possible.

◇　This favorable offer will not be repeated for some time，and we accordingly look forward to an early order from you.

出口报价核算

一、单项核算

1. 根据以下增值税发票回答问题：

1）该发票的总金额为多少元？

其中，货款为多少元？

税款为多少元？

2）如果上述产品的退税率为 11％，则出口该产品的出口退税收入为多少元？

3）扣除退税收入后，出口商采购该商品的实际成本为多少元？

2. 根据以下运价表回答问题：

（保留 4 位小数，小于 1 的数值保留 5 位小数）

港　　口	计费标准	LCL 费率	20′FCL 费率	40′FCL 费率
SINGAPORE		US $25.00	US $570.00	US $890.00
SOUTHHAMPTON	W/M	US $54.00	US $1100.00	US $2100.00
HAMBURG		US $72.00	US $1100.00	US $2050.00
BRISBANE		US $82.00	US $1300.00	US $2150.00

某货物包装方式为 30 套装 1 纸箱,纸箱尺码为 68×35.5×86 厘米,毛重为每箱 25 千克,净重为每箱 23.5 千克,如果出口一个 40 英尺集装箱该货物,则:

1）按重量推算,其理论装箱数量为多少套?

2）按体积推算,其理论装箱数量为多少套?

3）出口至新加坡,总运费为多少美元? 每套的运费为多少美元?

某货物包装方式为 2 台装 1 纸箱,纸箱尺码为 30×44×44 厘米,毛重为每箱 61.5 千克,净重为每箱 59.5 千克,则:

4）每箱的重量经换算为多少吨?

5）每箱的体积经换算为多少立方米?

如果出口 300 台至汉堡,那么:

6）总运费为多少美元? 每台的运费为多少美元?

如果出口一个 20 英尺整箱该货物,那么:

7）按重量推算,其理论装箱数量为多少台?

8）按体积推算,其理论装箱数量为多少台?

9）出口至布里斯班,总运费为多少美元? 每台的运费为多少美元?

某货物包装方式为 16 打装 1 纸箱,纸箱尺码为 62×48×38.5 厘米,毛重为每箱 28 千克,净重为每箱 26 千克,如果出口一个 20 英尺集装箱该货物,则:

10）按重量推算,其理论装箱数量为多少打?

11）按体积推算,其理论装箱数量为多少打?

12）出口至南安普顿,总运费为多少美元? 每打的运费为多少美元?

3. 某商品的采购成本为每件 55 元人民币,其中包括 17% 的增值税,该商品的出口退税率为 11%,如果出口该商品的国内各类费用总额为每件 2.24 元,国外客户要求的佣金率为 3%,美元对人民币汇率为 1:6.7,试进行以下核算:

（计算过程中和计算结果均保留 3 位小数）

1）实际成本为每件多少元人民币？

2）若出口商预期利润为每件 2.75 元人民币，则包含 3% 佣金的 FOB 价格应为每件多少美元？

3）若出口商预期成本利润率为 8%，则包含 3% 佣金的 FOB 价格应为每件多少美元？出口该商品的利润额为每件多少元人民币？

4）若出口商预期销售利润率为 8%，则包含 3% 佣金的 FOB 价格应为每件多少美元？出口该商品的利润额为每件多少元人民币？

二、综合报价核算

4.

商品名称：12 套陶瓷餐具

包装方式：4 套装一个纸箱

纸箱尺码：66×48×52cm（长×宽×高）

纸箱重量：21/18kg（毛重/净重）

国内采购成本：每套 240 元（含增值税 16%）

出口退税率：13%

各项出口费用如下：

出口商的定额费用率为 3%；

国内包干费为每运费吨 55 元，每个 20 英尺集装箱 800 元，每个 40 英尺集装箱 1300 元；

海洋运费件杂货物或拼箱货物为每运费吨 62 美元（运费的计算标准为"W/M"），每个 20 英尺集装箱的海运包箱费率为 1000 美元；40 英尺集装箱的包箱费率为 1600 美元；

该笔交易预计垫款周期为 1 个月，银行贷款的年利率为 6%；

海运出口的保险费率为 0.3%，投保加成率为 10%；

银行手续费率为 0.25%（按结算金额计）；

国外客户要求在报价中包含 3% 的佣金；

出口商的预期利润为出口报价的 10%；

汇率按 1 美元兑换 7 元人民币计。

根据上述报价核算资料，试分别计算出口 300 套、1 个 20 英尺整箱和 1 个 40 英尺整箱时的 FOB、CFR 和 CIF 美元出口单价。（计算过程中保留 4 位小数，小于 1 的数值保留 5 位小数，最终美元报价保留 2 位小数。）

5.

商品信息

品名：	Lelpro 牌自行车
货号：	T118
计量单位：	辆
包装：	纸箱
包装方式：	1 辆/纸箱
每个纸箱尺码：	48×40×80cm
每个纸箱毛/净重：	15/13kg
报价数量/起订量：	100 辆

核算信息

采购成本：	185 元人民币/辆(含增值税)	
出口费用：	单位商品出口的包干费约为：(每辆)	￥5.50
	20 英尺集装箱的包干费率为：	￥800.00
	40 英尺集装箱的包干费率为：	￥1400.00
	件杂货/拼箱海运费率为：(每运费吨)	US $60.00
	20 英尺集装箱的海运包箱费率为：	US $1200.00
	40 英尺集装箱的海运包箱费率为：	US $2100.00
	出口定额费率为：	4.00%
	银行贷款年利率为：(1 年按 360 天计)	6.00%
	垫款时间为：	30 天
	银行手续费额为：(按每笔交易计)	US $80.00
	海运货物保险费率为：	0.80%
	投保加成率为：	10.00%
	增值税率为：	16.00%
	出口退税率为：	9.00%
	国外客户的佣金率为：	3.00%
	汇率为：(1 美元兑换人民币元)	￥6.60
预期利润：	成本利润率为：	10.00%

核算要求：

1) 填写下列核算表,用数字列出计算过程并将结果填入规定的栏目内,如:

计算过程

计算过程	计算结果
（100＋45）＊20/（1－10％）	3222.2222

2）计算过程和计算结果均保留 4 位小数。

拼箱报价核算：

	计算过程	计算结果	
退税收入			人民币/辆
实际成本			人民币/辆
定额费			人民币/辆
贷款利息			人民币/辆
海洋运费			人民币/辆
海运保险费			人民币/辆
FOBC 报价			美元/辆
CFRC 报价			美元/辆
CIFC 报价			美元/辆

20 英尺整箱报价核算：

	计算过程	计算结果	
装箱数量			辆
包干费			人民币/辆
海洋运费			人民币/辆
海运保险费			人民币/辆
FOBC 报价			美元/辆
CFRC 报价			美元/辆
CIFC 报价			美元/辆

40 英尺整箱报价核算：

	计算过程	计算结果	
装箱数量			辆
包干费			人民币/辆
海洋运费			人民币/辆
海运保险费			人民币/辆
FOBC 报价			美元/辆
CFRC 报价			美元/辆
CIFC 报价			美元/辆

6.

出 口 报 价 核 算 表

| TY-12/JH012 | TY-12/JH015 | SP-16/MY005 | CL-16/MY007 |

报价商品及费用明细					
货号	计量单位	品名		采购成本(¥)	包装方式	包装种类
TY-12/JH012	set	12pc Dinnerware Set		320.00	4sets/ctn.	carton
毛重(kg)	净重(kg)	长(cm)	宽(cm)	高(cm)	LCL数量	
21	18	62	48	52	200	

货号	计量单位	品名		采购成本(¥)	包装方式	包装种类
TY-12/JH015	set	12pc Dinnerware Set		290.00	4sets/ctn.	carton
毛重(kg)	净重(kg)	长(cm)	宽(cm)	高(cm)	LCL数量	
21	18	60	48	50	200	

货号	计量单位	品名		采购成本(¥)	包装方式	包装种类
SP-16/MY005	set	16pc Dinnerware Set		310.00	2sets/ctn.	carton
毛重(kg)	净重(kg)	长(cm)	宽(cm)	高(cm)	LCL数量	
18	16	55	46	44.5	200	

货号	计量单位	品名		采购成本(¥)	包装方式	包装种类
CL-16/MY007	set	16pc Dinnerware Set		280.00	2sets/ctn.	carton
毛重(kg)	净重(kg)	长(cm)	宽(cm)	高(cm)	LCL数量	
18	16	52	48	42	200	

包干费(¥)			海洋运费(USD)		
LCL / Unit	20′FCL / CTNR	40′FCL / CTNR	LCL / FT	20′FCL	40′FCL
5.2	920	1550	76	1230	2130
增值税率	出口退税率	销售利润率	公司定额费率	银行手续费率	银行贷款年利率
16%	13%	15%	3%	0.3%	5.22%
垫款时间(天)	汇率(USD1=RMB¥)	佣金率	保险加成率	保险费率	其他费用(¥)
45	6.5	/	10%	0.65%	/

（注：计算过程及结果均保留4位小数）

拼箱（LCL）报价核算

TY-12/JH012　　　　计算过程　　　　　　　　　　　　　　　　核算单位：　**set**　　计算结果

实际成本(¥)		
公司定额费(¥)		
垫款利息(¥)		
海洋运费(¥)		
FOB (US$)		
CFR (US$)		
CIF (US$)		

TY-12/JH015　　　　计算过程　　　　　　　　　　　　　　　　核算单位：　**set**　　计算结果

实际成本(¥)		
公司定额费(¥)		
垫款利息(¥)		
海洋运费(¥)		
FOB (US$)		
CFR (US$)		
CIF (US$)		

SP-16/MY005　　　　计算过程　　　　　　　　　　　　　　　　核算单位：　**set**　　计算结果

实际成本(¥)		
公司定额费(¥)		
垫款利息(¥)		
海洋运费(¥)		
FOB (US$)		
CFR (US$)		
CIF (US$)		

CL-16/MY007　　　　计算过程　　　　　　　　　　　　　　　　核算单位：　**set**　　计算结果

实际成本(¥)		
公司定额费(¥)		
垫款利息(¥)		
海洋运费(¥)		
FOB (US$)		
CFR (US$)		
CIF (US$)		

20英尺整箱（20′FCL）报价核算			
TY-12/JH012	计算过程	核算单位： **set**	计算结果
出口退税额(¥)			
海洋运费(¥)			
包干费(¥)			
FOB (US$)			
CFR (US$)			
CIF (US$)			

TY-12/JH015	计算过程	核算单位： **set**	计算结果
出口退税额(¥)			
海洋运费(¥)			
包干费(¥)			
FOB (US$)			
CFR (US$)			
CIF (US$)			

SP-16/MY005	计算过程	核算单位： **set**	计算结果
出口退税额(¥)			
海洋运费(¥)			
包干费(¥)			
FOB (US$)			
CFR (US$)			
CIF (US$)			

CL-16/MY007	计算过程	核算单位： **set**	计算结果
出口退税额(¥)			
海洋运费(¥)			
包干费(¥)			
FOB (US$)			
CFR (US$)			
CIF (US$)			

40英尺整箱（40′FCL）报价核算

TY-12/JH012　　计算过程　　　　　　　　　　　　　　　核算单位：　**set**　　计算结果

项目	计算过程	计算结果
海洋运费(¥)		
包干费(¥)		
FOB (US$)		
CFR (US$)		
CIF (US$)		

TY-12/JH015　　计算过程　　　　　　　　　　　　　　　核算单位：　**set**　　计算结果

项目	计算过程	计算结果
海洋运费(¥)		
包干费(¥)		
FOB (US$)		
CFR (US$)		
CIF (US$)		

SP-16/MY005　　计算过程　　　　　　　　　　　　　　　核算单位：　**set**　　计算结果

项目	计算过程	计算结果
海洋运费(¥)		
包干费(¥)		
FOB (US$)		
CFR (US$)		
CIF (US$)		

CL-16/MY007　　计算过程　　　　　　　　　　　　　　　核算单位：　**set**　　计算结果

项目	计算过程	计算结果
海洋运费(¥)		
包干费(¥)		
FOB (US$)		
CFR (US$)		
CIF (US$)		

出口报价核算汇总

货号	TY-12/JH012	TY-12/JH015	SP-16/MY005	CL-16/MY007
品名	12pc Dinnerware Set	12pc Dinnerware Set	16pc Dinnerware Set	16pc Dinnerware Set
拼箱（LCL）报价				
FOB				
CFR				
CIF				
20英尺整箱（20′FCL）报价				
FOB				
CFR				
CIF				
40英尺整箱（40′FCL）报价				
FOB				
CFR				
CIF				

发 盘 函 草 拟

7.

昨日收到国外来函如下：

 G WOOD & SONS TRADING COMPANY

36 Castle Street, Bristol,
BS1 ABO, U.K.

5 Sep, 2018

Shanghai Tianyuan Trading Company
No. 451 Zunyi Road,
Shanghai, China

Dear Sir or Madam,

Armstrong & Smith of Sheffield inform us that you are suppliers of polyester cotton bed-sheets and pillowcases. We'd like you to send us details of your various ranges and some samples. Please state terms of payment and discounts you would allow on purchases of no less than five thousand of individual items.

We believe there is a promising market in our area for moderately priced goods.

Looking forward to your favorable reply.

Yours sincerely,
Christine Marji
G Wood & Sons Trading Company

请以出口部业务员的身份拟写回信，告知：1)产品的详细资料，诸如规格、价格和包装等，可参见随附的目录和价目表；2)样品另寄；3)通常采用即期信用证付款；4)所提数量可给予 3‰ 的优惠；5)订货若早于本月底，可保证在到证日后 30 天内交货。

8.

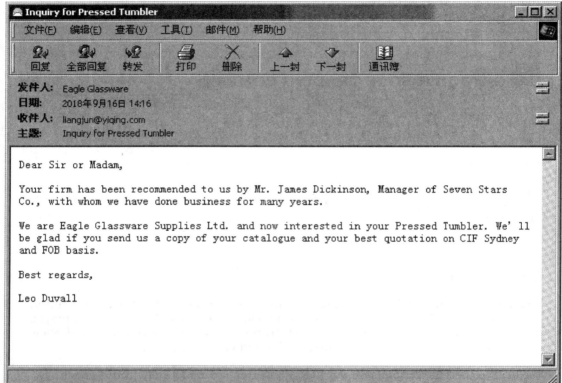

> 按 10%的销售利润率计算，AF101 的 20 英尺整箱价为：CIF 每罗 15 美元，FOB 每罗 12.60 美元，4 罗一纸箱，800 罗装一个 20 英尺整箱；AF102 的 20 英尺整箱价为：CIF 价每罗 14.20 美元，FOB 每罗 12.30 美元，5 罗一纸箱，1000 罗装一个 20 英尺整箱。初次交易，即期信用证方式付款，证到后 30 天出运，保险按常规保一切险。发盘有效期 15 天。同时随邮件附上产品目录。

请以上海益清进出口公司业务员的身份，回复该电子邮件。

9.

Margaret Trading Company

TO: Shanghai Union Trading Co. Ltd. (Fax No. 86-21-6456 8932)
FM: Margaret Trading Company (Fax No. 1-604-507 2944)
DT: October 10, 2018

Dear Miss Li,

Thanks for your information that you are supplying these kinds of gloves and mittens.

Today we have sent you by courier 4 pairs of ski gloves and mittens for which we need your quotation on CFR Vancouver.

Moreover we need to offer more different styles to our clients. Please kindly select from your makers some 5 or 6 styles and send to us with prices as soon as possible. This is very urgent if we want to catch up their purchasing plan this year. Please do not wait until our samples reach you, because we are losing too much time.

All the styles have to be lined, outside nylon. The styles should be fancy, some with structured nylon material, with zippers and adjustable straps for width, some with print and/or embroidery or plastic labels.

Thanks and best regards.

Yours truly,
Clarence M. Woods (Ms.)
Margaret Trading Company

1）把佳伦厂前天送来的五对样品寄给客户，CFR Vancouver 报价如下：
ST001 USD3.80/副，ST002 USD4.50/副，ST003 USD5.10/副，YE101 USD4.70/副，YE115 USD5.30/副。
60 天远期信用证付款，若月底开到，则 12 月上旬能交货。
ST 系列 8 打装一纸箱，YE 系列 5 打装一纸箱，起订量都是 4800 副。
发盘 2 周有效。

2）等客户样品寄到，立即与海源厂联系打样、核算成本。

试根据客户要求及 **TO DO LIST** 的提示，回复传真。

10.

　　2018 年 9 月 25 日，阿里巴巴网站上有一条求购信息如下：

　　试向新加坡客户发送电子邮件，简单介绍公司情况（专营轻工业产品，货源稳定充足，产品远销中东、欧美等），并表达建立长期业务联系的愿望。按起订量报出 CIF 新加坡的美元价格（保留 1 位小数），付款方式为远期信用证，提单日后 30 天付款。能保证在年底出运，但信用证需于 10 月底前开到。

　　公司的不锈钢快餐餐具共有 3 个型号，其价格核算数据如下表：

商　　品	Stainless Steel Server Sets		
货　　号	S9420	S9320	S9411
采购价（元/套）	105.00	128.00	155.00
包装方式（套/纸箱）	5	4	3
退税收入（元/套）	9.96	12.14	14.70
起订量（套）	1000	800	600
国内费用（元/套）	3.15	3.85	4.65
出口运费（元/套）	12.40	15.50	20.67
保险加成率	10%		
保险费率	0.6%		
汇率（1 美元兑换人民币）	6.5		
预期销售利润率	8%	9%	10%

第三章 还盘与出口还价核算

案 例

2018 年 9 月 26 日,环宇公司收到 Tivolian 公司的还盘函(第 64 页)。

2018 年 9 月 27 日,环宇公司完成出口还价核算,向 Tivolian 公司发送还盘函。

工作任务

1. 根据客户的还盘函,结合下列核算要求,填写《还价核算表》:

1) 若接受客户的还价,四个货号商品的利润额分别为多少元人民币? 销售利润率又分别为多少?

2) 若接受客户的还价,同时维持公司原定的 12% 的销售利润率,那么,四个货号的国内采购价格应分别控制在每套多少元人民币?

2. 根据以下信息,拟写还盘函:

1) 出口价格:无法接受客户的还价,但为促成首笔交易,同意将货号 KB0278 降至每套 9.6 美元,货号 KB0677 降至每套 14.5 美元,货号 KB5411 降至每套 11.5 美元,货号 KB7900 降至每套 15.4 美元。

2) 付款方式:坚持以即期信用证付款。

 还盘函

Re: Quotation for plush toys

Sender ： Chila Trooborg <chtrooborg@tivolian.nl>

Date ： 26-Sep-2018

Receiver ： David Wang <d.wang@universal.com.cn>

Tivolian
TRADING B.V.

Dear Mr. Wang,

We are glad to receive your email of September 25 and the plush toy samples.

We really appreciate the good workmanship and lovely designs of your products, but we feel your prices are not competitive enough. Information here indicates plush toys from other suppliers are sold about 7%~8% lower than yours. As you know, the price level counts much, especially in the initial sales stage.

To set up the trade, may we suggest you reduce the prices as follows:

KB0278　USD　9.20 / set　　　KB0677　USD 14.20 / set
KB5411　USD 11.40 / set　　　KB7900　USD 14.90 / set
CIF Rotterdam on 20'FCL basis

Meanwhile, we usually deal with our clients on D/P terms, which is easier and cost-saving than L/C. We hope this method of payment will be acceptable to you also.

Competitive prices and flexible payment terms for a trial order can often lead to a big market share with great profit in the future. We hope you will take this factor into account and wait for your early reply.

Yours truly,
Chila Trooborg

Chila Trooborg
Purchase Manager
Tivolian Trading B.V.
Heiman Dullaertolein 3, 3024 CA Rotterdam, the Netherlands
Tel: 31 - 10 - 4767418
Fax: 31 - 10 - 4767422
www.tivolian.nl

出口还价核算表

上海环宇贸易有限公司
Shanghai Universal Trading Co., Ltd.

还价核算表

填表日期: ＿＿＿ 年 ＿＿＿ 月 ＿＿＿ 日　　填表人: ＿＿＿＿＿＿＿＿　　编号: ＿＿＿＿＿＿＿＿

利润总额 核算时，成本、费用及利润项目一律保留2位小数。
单位成本 核算时，计算过程一律保留4位小数，数值小于1时保留5位，最终结果保留2位。

进口商	装运港	目的港	报价核算表编号

包干费 (RMB)			海洋运费(USD)		
LCL / FT	20'FCL	40'FCL	LCL / FT	20'FCL	40'FCL
增值税率	出口退税率	公司定额费	银行手续费	银行贷款年利率	垫款时间(天)
保险加成率	保险费率	佣金率	其他费用	汇率(USD1=RMB)	

还价利润核算

	货号	计价单位	采购成本 RMB	客户还价 USD	贸易术语	还价数量
包装	包装方式	毛重 kg	净重 kg	长 cm	宽 cm	高 cm

计算过程	核算单位:	计算结果
销售收入总额(¥)		
退税收入总额(¥)		
采购成本总额(¥)		
包干费总额(¥)		
公司定额费总额(¥)		
银行手续费总额(¥)		
垫款利息总额(¥)		
海洋运费总额(¥)		
保险费总额(¥)		
其他费用总额(¥)		
利润总额(¥)		
销售利润率(%)		

还价成本核算

	货号	计价单位	客户还价 USD	贸易术语	还价数量	利润
包装	包装方式	毛重 kg	净重 kg	长 cm	宽 cm	高 cm

计算过程	核算单位:	计算结果
销售收入(¥)		
包干费(¥)		
银行手续费(¥)		
海洋运费(¥)		
保险费(¥)		
利润(¥)		
采购成本(¥)		

示 范

上海环宇贸易有限公司
Shanghai Universal Trading Co., Ltd.

还价核算表

填表日期： **2018** 年 **9** 月 **27** 日　　填表人： **王凯**　　　　编号： **HYHJ-E0373**

*利润总额*核算时，成本、费用及利润项目一律保留2位小数。
*单位成本*核算时，计算过程一律保留4位小数，数值小于1时保留5位，最终结果保留2位。

进口商	装运港	目的港	报价核算表编号
Tivolian Trading B.V.	Shanghai	Rotterdam	HYBJ-E0373

包干费 (RMB)			海洋运费(USD)		
LCL / FT	20'FCL	40'FCL	LCL / FT	20'FCL	40'FCL
80	1200	1500	95	1010	1840
增值税率	出口退税率	公司定额费	银行手续费	银行贷款年利率	垫款时间(天)
16%	15%	5%	0.25%	6.5%	45
保险加成率	保险费率	佣金率	其他费用	汇率(USD1=RMB)	
10%	0.65%	/	/	6.85	

还价利润核算

货号	计价单位	采购成本 RMB	客户还价 USD	贸易术语	还价数量	
KB0278	set	55.00	9.20	CIF	1008 sets	1 × 20'FCL

包装	包装方式	毛重 kg	净重 kg	长 cm	宽 cm	高 cm
	4 sets/ctn	8	5.5	55	45	40

	计算过程	核算单位： 1 × 20'FCL　　计算结果
销售收入总额(¥)	9.2×1008×6.85	63524.16
退税收入总额(¥)	55×1008÷(1+16%)×15%	7168.97
采购成本总额(¥)	55×1008	55440.00
包干费总额(¥)	1200	1200.00
公司定额费总额(¥)	55×1008×5%	2772.00
银行手续费总额(¥)	9.2×1008×0.25%×6.85	158.81
垫款利息总额(¥)	55×1008×6.5%÷360×45	450.45
海洋运费总额(¥)	1010×6.85	6918.50
保险费总额(¥)	9.2×1008×110%×0.65%×6.85	454.20
其他费用总额(¥)	/	/
利润总额(¥)	63524.16+7168.97−55440−1200−2772−158.81−450.45−6918.5−454.2	3299.17
销售利润率(%)	3299.17 ÷ 63524.16	5.19%

货号	计价单位	采购成本 RMB	客户还价 USD	贸易术语	还价数量	
KB0677	set	90.00	14.20	CIF	1080 sets	1 × 20'FCL
包装	包装方式	毛重 kg	净重 kg	长 cm	宽 cm	高 cm
	8 sets/ctn	8.5	6	48	64	60

	计算过程	核算单位: 1 × 20'FCL	计算结果
销售收入总额(¥)	14.2×1080×6.85		105051.60
退税收入总额(¥)	90×1080÷(1+16%)×15%		12568.97
采购成本总额(¥)	90×1080		97200.00
包干费总额(¥)	1200		1200.00
公司定额费总额(¥)	90×1080×5%		4860.00
银行手续费总额(¥)	14.2×1080×0.25%×6.85		262.63
垫款利息总额(¥)	90×1080×6.5%÷360×45		789.75
海洋运费总额(¥)	1010×6.85		6918.50
保险费总额(¥)	14.2×1080×110%×0.65%×6.85		751.12
其他费用总额(¥)	/		/
利润总额(¥)	105051.6+12568.97－97200－1200－4860－262.63－789.75－6918.5－751.12		5638.57
销售利润率(%)	5638.57÷105051.6		5.37%

货号	计价单位	采购成本 RMB	客户还价 USD	贸易术语	还价数量	
KB5411	set	70.00	11.40	CIF	1008 sets	1 × 20'FCL
包装	包装方式	毛重 kg	净重 kg	长 cm	宽 cm	高 cm
	4 sets/ctn	8	5.5	55	45	40

	计算过程	核算单位: 1 × 20'FCL	计算结果
销售收入总额(¥)	11.4×1008×6.85		78714.72
退税收入总额(¥)	70×1008÷(1+16%)×15%		9124.14
采购成本总额(¥)	70×1008		70560.00
包干费总额(¥)	1200		1200.00
公司定额费总额(¥)	70×1008×5%		3528.00
银行手续费总额(¥)	11.4×1008×0.25%×6.85		196.79
垫款利息总额(¥)	70×1008×6.5%÷360×45		573.30
海洋运费总额(¥)	1010*6.85		6918.50
保险费总额(¥)	11.4×1008×110%×0.65%×6.85		562.81
其他费用总额(¥)	/		/
利润总额(¥)	78714.72+9124.14－70560－1200－3528－196.79－573.3－6918.5－562.81		4299.46
销售利润率(%)	4299.46÷78714.72		5.46%

货号	计价单位	采购成本 RMB	客户还价 USD	贸易术语	还价数量	
KB7900	set	95.00	14.90	CIF	1080 sets	1 × 20'FCL
包装	包装方式	毛重 kg	净重 kg	长 cm	宽 cm	高 cm
	8 sets/ctn	8.5	6	48	64	60

	计算过程	核算单位: 1 × 20'FCL	计算结果
销售收入总额(¥)	14.9×1080×6.85		110230.20
退税收入总额(¥)	95×1080÷(1+16%)×15%		13267.24
采购成本总额(¥)	95×1080		102600.00
包干费总额(¥)	1200		1200.00
公司定额费总额(¥)	95×1080×5%		5130.00
银行手续费总额(¥)	14.9×1080×0.25%×6.85		275.58
垫款利息总额(¥)	95×1080×6.5%÷360×45		833.63
海洋运费总额(¥)	1010×6.85		6918.50
保险费总额(¥)	14.9×1080×110%×0.65%×6.85		788.15
其他费用总额(¥)	/		/
利润总额(¥)	110230.2+13267.24－102600－1200－5130－275.58－833.63－6918.5－788.15		5751.58
销售利润率(%)	5751.58÷110230.2		5.22%

还价成本核算					

货号	计价单位	客户还价 USD	贸易术语	还价数量		利润
KB0278	set	9.20	CIF	1008 sets	1 × 20'FCL	12%

包装	包装方式	毛重 kg	净重 kg	长 cm	宽 cm	高 cm
	4 sets/ctn	8	5.5	55	45	40

	计算过程	核算单位: set	计算结果
销售收入(¥)	9.2×6.85		63.0200
包干费(¥)	1200÷1008		1.1905
银行手续费(¥)	9.2×0.25%×6.85		0.15755
海洋运费(¥)	1010÷1008×6.85		6.8636
保险费(¥)	9.2×110%×0.65%×6.85		0.45059
利润(¥)	9.2×12%×6.85		7.5624
采购成本(¥)	(63.02−1.1905−0.15755−6.8636−0.45059−7.5624)÷[1−15%÷(1+16%)+5%+6.5%÷360×45]		50.38

货号	计价单位	客户还价 USD	贸易术语	还价数量		利润
KB0677	set	14.20	CIF	1080 sets	1 × 20'FCL	12%

包装	包装方式	毛重 kg	净重 kg	长 cm	宽 cm	高 cm
	8 sets/ctn	8.5	6	48	64	60

	计算过程	核算单位: set	计算结果
销售收入(¥)	14.2×6.85		97.2700
包干费(¥)	1200÷1080		1.1111
银行手续费(¥)	14.2×0.25%×6.85		0.24318
海洋运费(¥)	1010÷1080×6.85		6.4060
保险费(¥)	14.2×110%×0.65%×6.85		0.69548
利润(¥)	14.2×12%×6.85		11.6724
采购成本(¥)	(97.27−1.1111−0.24318−6.406−0.69548−11.6724)÷[1−15%÷(1+16%)+5%+6.5%÷360×45]		83.05

货号	计价单位	客户还价 USD	贸易术语	还价数量		利润
KB5411	set	11.40	CIF	1008 sets	1 × 20'FCL	12%

包装	包装方式	毛重 kg	净重 kg	长 cm	宽 cm	高 cm
	4 sets/ctn	8	5.5	55	45	40

	计算过程	核算单位: set	计算结果
销售收入(¥)	11.4×6.85		78.0900
包干费(¥)	1200÷1008		1.1905
银行手续费(¥)	11.4×0.25%×6.85		0.19523
海洋运费(¥)	1010÷1008×6.85		6.8636
保险费(¥)	11.4×110%×0.65%×6.85		0.55834
利润(¥)	11.4×12%×6.85		9.3708
采购成本(¥)	(78.09−1.1905−0.19523−6.8636−0.55834−9.3708)÷[1−15%÷(1+16%)+5%+6.5%÷360×45]		64.50

货号	计价单位	客户还价 USD	贸易术语	还价数量		利润
KB7900	set	14.90	CIF	1080 sets	1 × 20'FCL	12%

包装	包装方式	毛重 kg	净重 kg	长 cm	宽 cm	高 cm
	8 sets/ctn	8.5	6	48	64	60

	计算过程	核算单位: set	计算结果
销售收入(¥)	14.9×6.85		102.0650
包干费(¥)	1200÷1080		1.1111
银行手续费(¥)	14.9×0.25%×6.85		0.25516
海洋运费(¥)	1010÷1080×6.85		6.4060
保险费(¥)	14.9×110%×0.65%×6.85		0.72976
利润(¥)	14.9×12%×6.85		12.2478
采购成本(¥)	(102.065−1.1111−0.25516−6.406−0.72976−12.2478)÷[1−15%÷(1+16%)+5%+6.5%÷360×45]		87.55

💬 示范评析

1. 还价核算是贸易公司判断能否接受客户还价的主要决策依据。其核算的目的主要有二：一是计算出还价利润，从而了解如果接受客户还价，自身的利润会发生怎样的变化，二是计算如果接受客户还价，公司又该以何种价格水平与供应厂商谈判、以保证自己的利润。

2. 还价利润核算的原理为"收入－支出＝利润"，特别注意，收入应由"销售收入"和"退税收入"两部分来组成。核算时要特别注意价格构成要素，即成本、各项费用的变化。

3. 计算每个货号的还价利润时，我们既可以先核算单位商品的利润、再乘以商品数量，也可以先直接计算每笔收入和支出的总额、再进行加总扣除。前者我们常称为"分算法"，后者称为"总算法"。由于在交易实际履行过程中，各项收支多以总额的形式发生，所以在计算某货号的还价总利润时，采用"总算法"更为合理、准确和直观。

4. 在进行还价成本核算时，我们必须注意到两点：一是这里所谓的成本指的是从工厂采购商品的含税成本，所以计算时应考虑到出口退税的因素；二是在出口价格中，有一些费用是以采购成本（即含税成本）为基数的，如公司定额费、银行垫款利息，在还价核算时，不能再沿用报价核算时获取的数值。试以货号 KB0278 为例，分步演示计算其还价后采购成本的过程：

利润	＝收入－支出
利润	＝销售收入＋退税收入
	－采购成本－包干费－公司定额费－银行垫款利息
	－银行手续费－海洋运费－保险费
$9.2×12\%×6.85$	＝$9.2×6.85＋$采购成本$÷(1＋16\%)×15\%$
	－采购成本－$1200÷1008－$采购成本$×5\%$
	－采购成本$×6.5\%÷360×45$
	－$9.2×0.25\%×6.85－1010÷1008×6.85$
	－$9.2×110\%×0.65\%×6.85$
7.5624	＝$63.02＋$采购成本$×15\%÷(1＋16\%)－$采购成本
	－$1.1905－$采购成本$×5\%$

$$-采购成本×6.5\%÷360×45-0.15755$$
$$-6.8636-0.45059$$

采购成本＋采购成本×5％＋采购成本×6.5％÷360×45－采购成本×15％
$$÷(1＋16\%)$$
$$=63.02-1.1905-0.15755-6.8636-0.45059-7.5624$$

采购成本×(1＋5％＋6.5％÷360×45－15％÷(1＋16％))
$$=63.02-1.1905-0.15755-6.8636-0.45059-7.5624$$

$$采购成本 = \frac{63.02-1.1905-0.15755-6.8636-0.45059-7.5624}{1＋5\%＋6.5\%÷360×45－15\%÷(1＋16\%)}$$

采购成本　　　　　＝¥50.38

Q：还盘函中哪里提到了还价数量？

A：客户在还盘函中明确指出所还价格为"CIF Rotterdam on 20'FCL basis"，故还价数量应按 20 英尺整箱来计算。

Q：如果公司要保持 12％的成本利润率，又该如何核算？

A：如果公司是采用成本利润率的来计算预期利润，那么在进行还价成本核算时，情况就会发生相应的变化。

我们仍以货号 KB0278 为例。假设公司决定要保持 12％的成本利润率，在其他各项条件均未发生变化的情况下，由还价后推算出采购成本的计算过程如下：

利润　　　　　　＝收入－支出

利润　　　　　　＝销售收入＋退税收入
　　　　　　　　－采购成本－包干费－公司定额费－银行垫款利息
　　　　　　　　－银行手续费－海洋运费－保险费

采购成本×12％　＝9.2×6.85＋采购成本÷(1＋16％)×15％－采购成本－1200
　　　　　　　　÷1008
　　　　　　　　－采购成本×5％－采购成本×6.5％÷360×45
　　　　　　　　－9.2×0.25％×6.85－1010÷1008×6.85－9.2×110％×
　　　　　　　　0.65％×6.85

采购成本×12％　＝63.02＋采购成本×15％÷(1＋16％)－采购成本－1.1905
　　　　　　　　－采购成本×5％－采购成本×6.5％÷360×45－0.15755－
　　　　　　　　6.8636－0.45059

采购成本×12％－采购成本×15％÷(1＋16％)＋采购成本＋采购成本×5％＋
　　　　　　　　采购成本×6.5％÷360×45

$$=63.02-1.1905-0.15755-6.8636-0.45059$$

采购成本×（12％－15％÷（1＋16％）＋1＋5％＋6.5％÷360×45）

$$=63.02-1.1905-0.15755-6.8636-0.45059$$

采购成本 $= \dfrac{63.02-1.1905-0.15755-6.8636-0.45059}{12\%-15\%\div(1+16\%)+1+5\%+6.5\%\div360\times45}$

采购成本 ＝¥51.83

New offer for plush toys

发件人： David Wang <d.wang@universal.com.cn>
日　期： 2018年9月27日
收件人： Chila Trooborg <chtrooborg@tivolian.nl>

上 海 环 宇 贸 易 有 限 公 司
Shanghai Universal Trading Co., Ltd.

Dear Mr. Trooborg

Thank you for your email of Sept. 26, and we are glad you like the quality of our products.

But we find it impossible to comply with your requested prices. Your offer is too low and cannot serve as a basis for further negotiation with our manufacturers. As you might be aware, materials and wages have risen considerably these days. The prices we quoted on Sept. 25 were very favorable, if you take the quality and craftsmanship into consideration. It is really hard for us to make further concession.

However, in order to develop our market in your area, we have decided to give you an exceptional offer as follows:

CIF Rotterdam on 20'FCL basis
Article No. KB0278　　　USD　 9.60 / set　　　Article No. KB0677　　USD　14.50 / set
Article No. KB5411　　　USD　11.50 / set　　　Article No. KB7900　　USD　15.40 / set

Other conditions remained unchanged.

We have also noted your request for D/P terms. Unfortunately our company never offers documentary collection terms to customers until they have traded with us for over a year. We are sorry that we can't be more helpful at present.

In view of the heavy demand for this line, we advise you to place an order at your earliest convenience if prompt shipment is required.

We look forward to receiving your first order soon.

Best wishes

David Wang
Sales Manager
Shanghai Universal Trading Co., Ltd.
Tel: +86 21 58818863
Email: d.wang@universal.com.cn

中国上海市东方路 **131** 号美陵广场 **1201-1216** 室
Rm. 1201-1216 Mayling Plaza, 131 Dongfang Rd., Shanghai, 200120, China
电话/Tel: 86-21-58818844　传真/Fax: 86-21-58818766　网址/Web: www.universal.com.cn

📣 示范评析

　　本案例中交易双方除就价格进行了磋商，同时还就支付方式进行了磋商。

　　我们应当知道，在国际货物买卖中，支付方式主要有三种：汇付、跟单托收和信用证。

　　汇付（remittance）又称汇款，是指进口方通过银行直接将货款汇给出口方。根据汇款形式的不同，可分为电汇（telegraphic transfer，T/T）、信汇（mail transfer，M/T）和票汇（remittance by banker's demand draft，D/D）。其中，电汇最为迅速。而根据汇款时间的不同，汇付又可分为交货前先付款（预付）和货到后付款（后付）。显然，如能采取预付，出口方风险最小，而若采取后付，则有利于进口方控制货物的质量和资金的周转。

　　跟单托收（documentary collection）是指出口方委托银行凭货运单据向进口方收款，跟单托收可以是即期，也可以是远期。根据交单条件的不同，具体分为两种：付款交单（documents against payment，D/P）和承兑交单（documents against acceptance，D/A）。前者要求进口方必须付清货款后才能获得货运单据、提取相应的货物，而后者只要求进口方承兑远期汇票，即可向银行取得货运单据提货，在汇票到期时支付货款。可见，对于出口方来说，承兑交单（D/A）的风险较付款交单（D/P）要大得多。

　　信用证（letter of credit，L/C）则是指进口地银行应进口商的请求、向出口商做出的付款保证，承诺在出口商向其提交付款信用证规定的单据后履行付款责任。这是一种加入了银行信用的付款方式。通常来说，银行的资信要高于普通公司企业及个人，所以采取信用证交易，出口方的收款是比较有保障的。因此在与并不十分了解的新客户交易时，出口方常要求采用信用证付款方式。然而，开立信用证的手续比较繁琐，费用比较多，银行可能还需要申请人交纳较高比例的保证金等，这些都是进口方不太希望以信用证方式付款的原因。

　　这就形成了本案中双方关于付款方式的磋商。在拟写这一类信函时必须注意，应用委婉的语气拒绝对方的要求，切忌强硬拒绝或直接质疑对方的诚信。通常情况下，我们可以说这是公司的惯例，也可以提出在建立了比较稳固的业务往来后、在相互信任的基础上再考虑采用信用证以外的付款方式等。

　　有关汇付、跟单托收和信用证这三种支付方式的详细介绍可参看**第五章　信用证审核与修改**的指南（第 151 页）。

指 南

　　进出口业务中,作为一个出口商,在对外报出价格后自然十分愿意收到肯定的回复。然而,交易中很少碰上不还价的对手,在激烈的市场竞争环境中,讨价还价常常是交易磋商中的主旋律。

　　出口商将如何对待客户的还价呢? 我们首先应该依据还价进行必要的核算,以便了解如果接受客户还价将对自己的预期利润产生多少影响,同时还可以分析在构成价格的各要素中,哪些要素和成分有可能作一些变化和调整以保证自己的利益。

　　核算结果出来之后,出口商就可以做出理性的判断,采取不同的对策:

◇　努力说服客户接受原报价,不作让步。出口商采取这种策略的最大风险是可能会失去成交的机会甚至会失去客户;

◇　减少公司的利润以满足客户的降价要求。这虽然是最直接和最简便的方法,但它牺牲的是出口商自身的经济利益,因而往往是出口商最不愿意采取的对策;

◇　缩小费用开支以达到降价的目的。当然,如果出口商希望缩小的是公司业务费用以外的费用,例如运费、港口码头费等,则必须和有关方面进行磋商和协调,显然,选择在价格中占有一定比例并且有调整余地的费用去协商才是最有意义的;

◇　降低采购成本。出口商经常通过压低供货价格的办法来调整报价,但要达到降低成本的目的通常需要经过与供货商艰苦的谈判,有时甚至会有得不偿失的结果。

　　总而言之,无论采取何种方式,正确的还价核算都是决策的前提。

ⓘ 还价利润核算

　　根据进口商对于商品价格的各项要求,包括购货数量、交易价格术语等,出口商将核算此笔交易是否还有利润,总利润额与利润率分别是多少,以确定究竟是接受客户的还价,还是进一步磋商。

　　还价利润核算的基本原理是:利润＝收入－支出

　　其中,收入应包括销售收入(即如接受客户还价可得的销售收入)和退税收入两部分,而支出主要是采购成本的支出以及各项出口费用的支出。

下面我们可以通过一次具体的还价过程来理解还价利润核算的原理。

例如:某公司向丹麦客户按 20 英尺整箱出口离心泵,报价为每只 214.90 美元 CIFC3 Copenhagen,后接客户还价 US $201.00 per set CIFC3 Copenhagen。

该产品的采购成本为每只 1160 元,增值税率为 16%,出口退税率为 5%,20 英尺整箱的装箱数量为 420 只。

出口的各项费用有:

海洋运费: USD1000/20'FCL

海运保险费: 按 CIF 价值的 120% 投保,保险费率为 0.4%

国内包干费: 每个 20 英尺箱为人民币 800 元

垫款利息: 银行贷款年利率为 9%,预计垫款时间为 120 天

银行费用: 每笔交易 200 美元

公司定额费率: 4%

请据此计算还价利润,汇率按 1 美元兑换 6.4 元人民币折算。

收入核算

销售收入 $=201 \times 420 \times 6.4 = 540288$ 元

退税收入 $=1160 \times 420 \div (1+16\%) \times 5\% = 21000$ 元

支出核算

采购成本 $=1160 \times 420 = 487200$ 元

海洋运费 $=1000 \times 6.4 = 6400$ 元

保险费 $=201 \times 420 \times 120\% \times 0.4\% \times 6.4 = 2593.3824$ 元

包干费 $=800$ 元

垫款利息 $=1160 \times 420 \times 9\% \div 360 \times 120 = 14616$ 元

银行费用 $=200 \times 6.4 = 1280$ 元

定额费 $=1160 \times 420 \times 4\% = 19488$ 元

客户佣金 $=201 \times 420 \times 3\% \times 6.4 = 16208.64$ 元

利润核算

利润 =销售收入+退税收入-采购成本-海洋运费-保险费
-包干费-垫款利息-银行费用-定额费-客户佣金

利润 $=540288+21000-487200-6400-2593.3824-800-14616$
$-1280-19488-16208.64$

利润　　　　＝12701.9776 元

销售利润率　＝利润÷销售收入＝12701.9776÷540288×100％＝2.35％

成本利润率　＝利润÷采购成本＝12701.9776÷487200×100％＝2.61％

由此我们可以看到,还价利润核算的原理"利润＝收入－支出"实际上是对报价核算的原理"价格＝成本＋费用＋利润"的逆向演绎。

在进行还价利润核算时,我们要注意三点:一、对于客户的还价,不仅要关注单价数额的变化,而且要注意交易数量、价格术语的变化。二、在列明收入与支出项目时,必须全面准确,既不能遗漏项目,例如在收入中不要遗漏退税收入,在支出中不要遗漏采购成本、客户佣金等,也不能虚列实际不发生的项目,特别要注意与价格术语的对应,例如 FOB 还价计算利润时,支出项目中就不应计入海洋运费、保险费等。三、一些费用项目会随着价格的改变而变化,例如客户佣金、按结算金额计的银行费用等,注意不要贪图方便而照搬报价核算时的数据。当然,由于报价到还价有一个过程,在此期间,如果一些关键数据发生了变化,如出口退税率调整了、海洋运费有大幅度涨跌了,都应及时反映在还价利润核算中,以便出口商对自己能够获取的利润有一个正确的预估。

ⓘ 还价成本核算

在接到客户还价后,为了达成出口交易,出口商往往会选择与供货商进一步洽谈购货价格,而降低成本的幅度则需要借助还价成本核算来明确。可以说,还价成本核算是出口商在与供货商谈判前的先期工作。

还价成本核算的基本原理是:成本＝售价－费用－利润

其中,售价即为客户还价,即假设出口商满足进口商的降价要求,利润是出口商试图保证的销售利润。同时,这里的成本还必须考虑到退税的因素,也就是说,成本是指扣除退税收入后的成本。

下面我们可以通过一次具体的还价过程来理解还价成本核算的原理。

例如:某公司向丹麦客户报出每台 214.90 美元的 CIFC3 价格后,客户还价 US＄201.00 per set CIFC3 Copenhagen。

已知离心泵的增值税率为 16％,出口退税率为 5％,20 英尺整箱的装箱数量为 420 只。

出口的各项费用有:

海洋运费:　　　　　　USD1000/20'FCL

海运保险费：　　按 CIF 价值的 120％投保，保险费率为 0.4％

国内包干费：　　每个 20 英尺箱为人民币 800 元

垫款利息：　　　银行贷款年利率为 9％，预计垫款时间为 120 天

银行费用：　　　每笔交易 200 美元

公司定额费率：　4％

　　如果出口商希望保证其 10％的成本利润率，试根据客户提出的还价计算出口商能够接受的国内供货价格为每只多少元人民币，汇率按 1 美元兑换 6.4 元人民币折算。

价格

$201 \times 6.4 = 1286.4$ 元/只

费用

海洋运费　　＝$1000 \times 6.4 \div 420 = 15.2381$ 元/只

保险费　　　＝$201 \times 120\% \times 0.4\% \times 6.4 = 6.1747$ 元/只

包干费　　　＝$800 \div 420 = 1.9048$ 元/只

垫款利息　　＝采购成本$\times 9\% \div 360 \times 120$

银行费用　　＝$200 \times 6.4 \div 420 = 3.0476$ 元/只

定额费　　　＝采购成本$\times 4\%$

客户佣金　　＝$201 \times 3\% \times 6.4 = 38.592$ 元/只

利润

利润　　　　＝采购成本$\times 10\%$

成本

$$成本 \quad = 还价 - 费用 - 利润$$

$$采购成本 - 退税收入 \quad = 还价 - 费用 - 利润$$

$$采购成本 - \frac{采购成本}{1 + 增值税率} \times 退税率 = 还价 - 费用 - 利润$$

$$采购成本 - 采购成本 \div 116\% \times 5\% = 1286.4 - 15.2381 - 6.1747 - 1.9048$$
$$- 采购成本 \times 9\% \div 360 \times 120 - 3.0476$$
$$- 采购成本 \times 4\% - 38.592 - 采购成本 \times 10\%$$

$$采购成本 - 采购成本 \div 116\% \times 5\% + 采购成本 \times 9\% \div 360 \times 120 + 采购成本$$

$$×4\%＋采购成本×10\%$$
$$＝1286.4－15.2381－6.1747－1.9048－$$
$$3.0476－38.592$$

$$采购成本×(1－5\%÷116\%＋9\%÷360×120＋4\%＋10\%)＝1221.4428$$

$$采购成本＝\frac{1221.4428}{1－5\%÷116\%＋9\%÷360×120＋4\%＋10\%}＝1083.90 元/只$$

由此我们可以看到,当根据客户还价推算采购成本时,计算过程显得比较复杂,这主要是因为采购成本的变化影响着退税收入,而且费用项目中一部分费用,例如公司定额费、垫款利息等,由于是以采购成本为计算基数的,因此在尚未得出最终的采购成本时,这部分费用也无法确定具体的数额。

我们也可以归纳出一个还价成本核算的通用公式:

$$采购成本＝\frac{售价－利润额－费用额}{1－\dfrac{退税率}{1＋增值税率}＋以采购成本为基数的费用率＋成本利润率}$$

其中,

"利润额"是指当公司采用固定的数额或是销售利润率来决定利润水平时,在尚未得出采购成本的最后结果时,利润额就已明确;

"费用额"是指那些可以直接算出的费用,如包干费、海洋运费等,包括那些与售价相关的费用,如客户佣金、保险费率、银行费用。在尚未得出采购成本的最后结果时,这些费用的数额也已明确;

"$1－\dfrac{退税收入}{1＋增值税率}$"体现了采购成本扣除了退税收入的含义。

"以采购成本为基数的费用率"是指那些与采购成本成一定比例的费用率,如垫款利息(还应考虑到垫款周期)、公司定额费用率。

"成本利润率"是指当公司采用成本利润率来控制利润水平时,在尚未得出采购成本的最后结果时,不能明确具体数额,只能以率的形式来表现。

我们应该认识到,还价成本核算完全遵循了报价核算的基本原理,因此透彻掌握报价核算是完成还价成本核算的前提。

(i) 还盘函的基本结构

国际货物买卖中,由于进出口双方的立场不同,对于一方的发盘,另一方往往不会立即接受,而是会进行还盘(counter offer)。而对于还盘,也可能发生再还盘,这样还盘函的往来就构成了交易磋商的主要过程。交易磋商的主题纷繁复杂,可以是任何一项交易条件,如货物的规格、包装、数量、价格、交货、支付,也可以是关于货物的检验方法、纠纷的仲裁等任何双方未达成一致意见的贸易条件。因此,还盘函的主体内容会随着磋商内容的变化而有很大不同。

就标准规范而言,还盘函一般应包括如下内容:

(一) 确认收到对方来函

还盘函总是一封回信,因此在信的开头,我们会礼节性地感谢对方的来函,而且也可以先简洁地表明我方对来函的总体态度。

◇ We are glad to receive your letter of March 22 but sorry to learn that your customers find our prices too high.

◇ Thank you for your email of Sept. 19. We regret to say that we can't accept your counter offer.

(二) 针对对方提出变更的交易条件,作进一步的解释和说明

我们应寻找适当的理由来解释不能接受对方的交易条件的原因,如认为原报价符合市价、强调产品品质超群、或言明利润已降至极限,或指出面临成本压力、汇率压力等。可以说还盘函中的核心是理由的陈述,耐心、诚恳和有说服力的还盘理由是写好还盘函的关键。

◇ As business has been done extensively in your market at this price, we regret to say we cannot make further concession.

◇ We believe our prices are quite realistic; it is impossible that any other suppliers can under-quote us if their products are as good as ours in quality.

◇ The price we quoted is accurately calculated. We have cut the profit to the minimum in order to expand the market.

◇ We feel that your counter offer is not proper because the price for such material is on the increase at present.

（三）提出我方新的交易条件（价格、数量、交货期、付款方式等）

这部分的关键是要具有吸引力和说服力，通常带有促销的性质，如以数量折扣吸引对方大批订购、为建立合作关系而给予特别优惠等。

◇　However, in order to develop our market in your place, we have decided to accept your counter offer as an exceptional case.

◇　In order to assist you to compete with other dealers in the market, we have decided to reduce 2% of the previous price, if your order reaches 5000 sets at one time.

◇　We can give you 3% allowance if you agree to pay 10% of the order value by T/T in advance.

◇　If we receive your order within the next ten days, we will give priority to it for May shipment.

（四）期待对方回复

◇　We hope you will agree to our suggestions and look forward to receiving a trial order from you.

◇　We will appreciate it if you will consider our new offer favorably and place your order without delay.

总之，拟写还盘函的关键在于以适当的理由，从适当的角度提出各种新条件，以促进早日成交。毫无说明地接受或拒绝都是不可取的。

练 习

出口还价核算

1.

商品名称:台灯
包装方式:4 盏装一纸箱
纸箱尺码:50×62×64cm(长×宽×高)
纸箱重量:16/13.2kg(毛重/净重)
国内采购成本:每盏 81 元(含增值税 16％)
出口退税率:13％

出口费用包括:出口商的定额费用率为 3.5％;国内包干费为每个 20 英尺集装箱 750 元,每个 40 英尺集装箱 1250 元;海洋运费为每运费吨 75 美元,每个 20 英尺集装箱的海运包箱费为 1200 美元,40 英尺集装箱的海运包箱费为 2100 美元;该笔交易预计垫款周期为 1 个月,银行贷款的年利率为 5.8％;海运出口的保险费率为 0.35％,投保加成率为 10％;银行手续费率为 0.25％(按结算金额计)。

试根据上述资料进行以下出口还价核算,汇率按 1 美元兑换 6.8 元人民币计。
(计算过程中保留 4 位小数,小于 1 的数值保留小数至第 5 位,计算结果保留 2 位小数)

1) 如果客户提出的 CFR 还价为每盏 14.5 美元,试计算出口一个 20 英尺集装箱的货物出口商可以获得的利润共计多少元人民币? 其销售利润率和成本利润率又分别为多少?

2) 如果客户提出订购一个 40 英尺整箱的货物,而其能够接受的 CIF 价格为每盏 14.3 美元,在此条件下计算出口商的利润总额和利润率分别为多少?

3) 如果出口商接受客户的 CFR 还价,即每盏 14.5 美元,同时又要保持其 10％的销售利润率,那么在成本和其他费用不变的情况下,其可以接受的 20 英尺整箱海运包箱费率应降至多少美元?

4) 如果出口商接受客户的 CIF 还价,即每盏 14.3 美元,同时又必须保证其

12％的销售利润率，试计算在其他费用及海洋运费不变（每个40英尺集装箱2100美元）的情况下，出口商能够接受的国内采购成本为每盏多少元人民币？

2.

出 口 还 价 核 算 表

还价核算明细

进口商	货物总称	贸易术语	装运港	目的港
Teri International GmbH	Porcelain Dinnerware	CIF	Shanghai	Hamburg

包干费(RMB)			海洋运费(USD)		
LCL / Unit	20'FCL / CTNR	40'FCL / CTNR	LCL / FT	20'FCL / CTNR	40'FCL / CTNR
5	900	1400	85	1230	2130
增值税率	出口退税率	公司定额费率	银行手续费率	银行贷款年利率	垫款时间
16%	11%	4%	0.5%	8%	1个月
汇率(USD1=RMB)	佣金率	保险加成率	保险费率	其他费用1	其他费用2
6.2	/	10%	0.5%	/	/

还价利润总额核算（每个货号各装一个20英尺整箱）

货号	品名	计量单位	采购成本(RMB)	客户还价(USD)	还价数量
TY-12/JH012	12pc Dinnerware Set	set	320	53.8	644套
包装种类	包装方式	毛重(kg)	净重(kg)	长(cm)	宽(cm)	高(cm)
carton	4套/箱	21	18	62	48	52

货号	品名	计量单位	采购成本(RMB)	客户还价(USD)	还价数量
TY-12/JH015	12pc Dinnerware Set	set	290	48.1	692套
包装种类	包装方式	毛重(kg)	净重(kg)	长(cm)	宽(cm)	高(cm)
carton	4套/箱	21	18	60	48	50

货号	品名	计量单位	采购成本(RMB)	客户还价(USD)	还价数量
SP-16/MY005	16pc Dinnerware Set	set	310	52.5	444套
包装种类	包装方式	毛重(kg)	净重(kg)	长(cm)	宽(cm)	高(cm)
carton	2套/箱	18	16	55	46	44.5

货号	品名	计量单位	采购成本(RMB)	客户还价(USD)	还价数量
CL-16/MY007	16pc Dinnerware Set	set	280	47.0	476套
包装种类	包装方式	毛重(kg)	净重(kg)	长(cm)	宽(cm)	高(cm)
carton	2套/箱	18	16	52	48	42

（注：计算过程及结果均保留4位小数。）

	计算过程	核算单位：4*20'FCL	计算结果
销售收入总额(¥)			
退税收入总额(¥)			
采购成本总额(¥)			
海洋运费总额(¥)			
保险费(¥)			
包干费总额(¥)			
公司定额费总额(¥)			
垫款利息总额(¥)			
银行手续费总额(¥)			
利润总额(¥)			
销售利润率(%)			

还价后的采购成本核算（保持8%的销售利润率）				

TY-12/JH012 计算过程 核算单位： **set** 计算结果

销售收入(¥)		
海洋运费(¥)		
包干费(¥)		
保险费(¥)		
银行手续费(¥)		
利润(¥)		
采购成本(¥)		

TY-12/JH015 计算过程 核算单位： **set** 计算结果

销售收入(¥)		
海洋运费(¥)		
包干费(¥)		
保险费(¥)		
银行手续费(¥)		
利润(¥)		
采购成本(¥)		

SP-16/MY005 计算过程 核算单位： **set** 计算结果

销售收入(¥)		
海洋运费(¥)		
包干费(¥)		
保险费(¥)		
银行手续费(¥)		
利润(¥)		
采购成本(¥)		

CL-16/MY007 计算过程 核算单位： **set** 计算结果

销售收入(¥)		
海洋运费(¥)		
包干费(¥)		
保险费(¥)		
银行手续费(¥)		
利润(¥)		
采购成本(¥)		

还价采购成本汇总				

货号	TY-12/JH012	TY-12/JH015	SP-16/MY005	CL-16/MY007
品名	12pc Dinnerware Set	12pc Dinnerware Set	16pc Dinnerware Set	16pc Dinnerware Set
原采购成本(¥)	320元/套	290元/套	310元/套	280元/套
还价后采购成本(¥)				
降价幅度(%)				

还盘函草拟

3.

F & A

Telephone Supplies Co., Ltd.

128 taiyoun road, Kuala Lumpur, Malaysia

Tel: 0060 3 25678821　Fax: 0060 3 25679900　e-mail: naw@fatele.com.my

June 20, 2018

Shanghai Jinyuan Import & Export Co., Ltd.
224 East Jinling Road
Shanghai, China

Dear Mr. Zhao,

We are interested to receive your current catalogue and price list for your telephones.

After careful examining and comparison with other brands of similar products, such as CLEAR, SNOIRE, and YOSHOYA, we found that your prices are higher than the average in the market. In order to allow us a better competing position, we hope you will reduce your prices by 5%.

We are looking forward to your early reply.

Yours sincerely,
Noor Azman Bin Wahid
F & A Telephone Supplies Co., Ltd.

若对方订单超过 50000 美元，同意给予 1.5%的折让。

强调本公司电话机的特点，例如采用 DECT6.0 技术，频率无干扰，通话质量好，可以为不同的来电者设置个性化铃声，外壳坚固，防水级别达 JIS7，适合各种严苛环境等。

试根据上述来函及信后要求，拟写还盘函。

4.

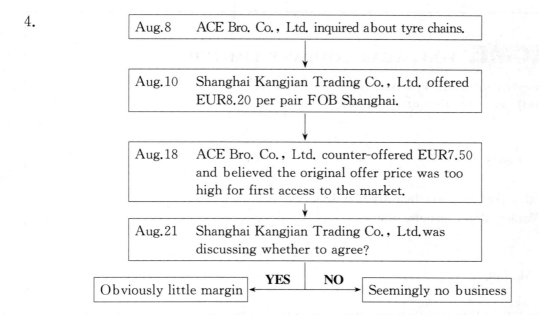

公司决定不接受客户的还价。试代为拟函，说服客户接受原报价。

5. 今收到客户来函如下。公司决定坚持原价。试拟函强调公司产品的品质，继续与对方磋商价格。

ACME FOOTWEAR COMPANY LIMITED

64 Spray St, Elwood, Melbourne, Australia
Tel : (61) 3 9531 1403 Fax : (61) 3 9531 2688

Sept. 10, 2018

Shanghai Tengyue Shoes Industrial Co., Ltd.
719 Wuning Road, Shanghai, China

Dear Mr. Lin,

Thank you for your quotation and the sample pairs of shoes which we have just received.

While appreciating the fine quality of your shoes, we regret the prices you have quoted are not competitive enough. A large number of shoes of similar designs from Malaysia, India and other areas are now commanding ready sales here, and these sell at prices from 5% to 10% below yours. We're afraid it is hard for us to penetrate the market with your shoes at their present level. We trust you will be able to make us a further concession, as we wish to place substantial orders with you.

In view of what we have said above, we would be most grateful if you would allow us a discount of 5% on an order worth approximately US$80,000.

We hope we can enter into the lasting business relationship with you and look forward to receiving your reply.

Yours sincerely,
John Smith
Acme Footwear Company Limited

6.

SOFTEE Textile S.R.L.

Figueroa Alcorta 2156, Buenos Aires, Argentina

Hello Yiwen

Thank you for your email of Oct 22 offering us six designs of Ornamental Cloth.

Unfortunately, the minimum 10,000 yards per design is too big for this period. If you can reduce it to 7,000 yards per design, there is a possibility of placing orders with you.

In addition, we are sorry that you still require payment by L/C at sight. After several years of satisfactory trading with you, we feel that we are entitled to easier terms. Most of our suppliers are allowing us 30 days' sight D/P and we shall be grateful if you can grant us the same terms.

I look forward to a prompt reply.

Many thanks

Marcelo

Marcelo Lacona
Purchasing Manager
SOFTEE Textile S.R.L.
Tel: + 54-11-48562900 Fax:+54-11-48562933

1. 订量若降至 7000 码，须提价 1%

2. 接受信用证见票后 30 天付款

试根据上述来函及信后要求，拟写还盘函。

7.

$\mathbb{S}$ AMEIM INTERNATIONAL SARL

Quai François-Mauriac 639851 Paris Cedex 13 France
Phone +33 1 52 34 32 56　Fax + 33 1 52 34 32 57

Shanghai Huixiang International Trade Co., Ltd.
344 Hubei Road, Shanghai
China

Nov. 2, 2018

Dear Ms. Xue,

Thank you for your letter of Oct. 31 sending us your quotation for Fountain Pen Art. 330.

The quality of your pen is quite good, but the price appears to be on the high side as compared with other suppliers in Asia. It is understood that to accept the price you quoted would leave us little or no margin of profit. As you know, this kind of fountain pen is mainly for students' use, so the price is an important factor. We would like to suggest that you make some allowance, say 10% on your original price. If, however, you cannot do so, then we will have no alternative but to leave the business as it is.

As to the terms of payment, we usually do business on the D/A basis. We hope it will be acceptable to you.

We are waiting for your reply with much interest.

Yours truly,
Pierre Daladier
Purchase Manager
SAMEIM International SARL

1）首次交易只接受信用证付款方式；

2）若订购 2000 打以上，给予 2%折扣；

3）保证及时装运。

试根据上述来函及信后要求,拟写还盘函。

第四章　接受与出口合同签订

案　例

2018 年 9 月 28 日,环宇公司收到 Tivolian 公司的订单(第 90 页)。

2018 年 9 月 29 日,环宇公司审核订单后,发现货号 KB0677 和 KB7900 的订购数量与货物包装方式不符。为符合客户等量拼装的要求,环宇公司决定将这两个货号的数量均调整至 536 套,并据此完成合同核算,同时接受客户的其他交易条件,向 Tivolian 公司寄送售货确认书。

工作任务

1. 填写《合同核算表》,核算此笔交易的预期总利润额及利润率。汇率按 1 美元兑换 6.85 元人民币计。

2. 制作《售货确认书》。

3. 向客户寄送《售货确认书》,并附函请求会签。

客户来函

Order No. TIV-PO-CSH0873 for plush toys

Sender：	Chila Trooborg <chtrooborg@tivolian.nl>
Date：	28-Sep-2018
Receiver：	David Wang <d.wang@universal.com.cn>
Attached:	✉ Tivolian order No.TIV-PO-CSH0873.xlsx

Tivolian
TRADING B.V.

Dear Mr. Wang,

　　Your email of Sept. 27 has convinced us to place a trial order for your plush toys. Our order number TIV-PO-CSH0873 is attached.

　　We have decided to accept your prices and terms of payment viz. sight L/C, but would like these terms to be reviewed in the near future.

　　We would like to emphasize that 4 items of toys ordered should be equally assorted as per our instructions, with each piece to be individually attached with the designated label. And we expect delivery within November.

　　We look forward to receiving hard copies of your Sales Confirmation.

Yours truly,
Chila Trooborg

Chila Trooborg
Purchase Manager
Tivolian Trading B.V.
Heiman Dullaertolein 3, 3024 CA Rotterdam, the Netherlands
Tel: 31 - 10 - 4767418
Fax: 31 - 10 - 4767422
www.tivolian.nl

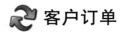 客户订单

Heiman Dullaertolein 3, 3024 CA Rotterdam, the Netherlands
Tel: 31 - 10 - 4767418
Fax: 31 - 10 - 4767422
www.tivolian.nl

PURCHASE ORDER

No. : TIV-PO-CSH0873

Date : Sept. 28, 2018

To: Shanghai Universal Trading Co., Ltd.

Rm. 1201-1216 Mayling Plaza, 131 Dongfang Rd.,

Shanghai, 200120, China

Item Description	Quantity	Price
		CIF Rotterdam
Twin bear KB0278	504 sets	US$9.60 each
Twin bear in ballet costume KB5411	504 sets	US$11.50 each
Brown bear with red bow KB0677	540 sets	US$14.50 each
Bear in pink T-shirt KB7900	540 sets	US$15.40 each

Details as per the samples dispatched by the seller on Sept. 25, 2018

Total Amount:	US$26,780.40
Trade Terms:	CIF Rotterdam Incoterms 2010
Packing:	KB0278 & KB5411: the label "CE/IMP. 087" to be attached to each piece
	KB0677 & KB7900: the label " F-TOYS 228" to be attached to each piece
	KB0278 & KB5411 assorted in one 20 feet container
	KB0677 & KB7900 assorted in one 20 feet container
Delivery Time:	During November 2018 without partial shipments
Insurance:	Covering for 110% CIF value against all risks and war risks
Payment Terms :	L/C at sight

For and on behalf of
Tivolian Trading B.V.

Henther Merton

General Manager

出口合同核算表

上海环宇贸易有限公司
Shanghai Universal Trading Co., Ltd.

universal

合同核算表

填表日期：＿＿＿年＿＿＿月＿＿＿日　填表人：＿＿＿＿＿＿　编号：＿＿＿＿＿＿

核算时，成本、费用及利润项目一律保留2位小数。

进口商	成交术语	装运港	目的港	报价核算表编号

包干费 (RMB)			海洋运费(USD)		
LCL / FT	20'FCL	40'FCL	LCL / FT	20'FCL	40'FCL
增值税率	出口退税率	公司定额费	银行手续费	银行贷款年利率	垫款时间(天)
保险加成率	保险费率	佣金率	其他费用	汇率(USD1=RMB)	

分货号成交信息

货号		计价单位	采购成本 RMB	成交价格 USD	成交数量	
包装	包装方式	毛重 kg	净重 kg	长 cm	宽 cm	高 cm

货号		计价单位	采购成本 RMB	成交价格 USD	成交数量	
包装	包装方式	毛重 kg	净重 kg	长 cm	宽 cm	高 cm

货号		计价单位	采购成本 RMB	成交价格 USD	成交数量	
包装	包装方式	毛重 kg	净重 kg	长 cm	宽 cm	高 cm

货号		计价单位	采购成本 RMB	成交价格 USD	成交数量	
包装	包装方式	毛重 kg	净重 kg	长 cm	宽 cm	高 cm

成交利润核算

	计算过程	计算结果
收入：		
销售收入总额(¥)		
退税收入总额(¥)		
支出：		
采购成本总额(¥)		
包干费总额(¥)		
公司定额费总额(¥)		
银行手续费总额(¥)		
垫款利息总额(¥)		
海洋运费总额(¥)		
保险费总额(¥)		
其他费用总额(¥)		
利润：		
利润总额(¥)		
销售利润率(%)		

售货确认书

Shanghai Universal Trading Co., Ltd.

Rm. 1201-1216 Mayling Plaza,
131 Dongfang Rd.,
Shanghai, 200120, China
Tel: 86-21-58818844
Fax: 86-21-58818766

SALES CONFIRMATION

S/C No.: _____

S/C Date: _____

To:

_____

_____

_____

We hereby confirm having sold to you the following goods on terms and conditions as specified below:

Item No.	Name of Commodity & Specifications	Quantity	Unit Price	Amount

Total Amount in Words:

Packing:

Shipment:

Insurance:

Payment:

Confirmed by:

<u>THE SELLER</u>   <u>THE BUYER</u>

(signature)   (signature)

REMARKS:

1 The Buyer shall have the covering letter of credit reach the Seller 45 days before shipment, failing which the Seller reserves the right to rescind without further notice, or to regard as still valid whole or any part of this contract not fulfilled by the Buyer, or to lodge a claim for losses thus sustained, if any.

2 In case of any discrepancy in quality, claim should be filed by the Buyer within 30 days after the arrival of the goods at port of destination; while for quantity discrepancy, claim should be filed by the Buyer within 15 days after the arrival of the goods at port of destination.

3 For transactions concluded on C.I.F. basis, it is understood that the insurance amount will be for 110% of the invoice value against the risks specified in this contract. If additional insurance amount or coverage required, the Buyer must have the consent of the Seller before shipment, and the additional premium is to be borne by the Buyer.

4 The Seller shall not hold liable for non-delivery or delay in delivery of the entire lot or a portion of the goods hereabove by reason of natural disasters, war or other causes of Force Majeure. However, the Seller shall notify the Buyer as soon as possible and furnish the Buyer within 15 days by registered airmail with a certificate issued by the China Council for the Promotion of International Trade attesting such event(s).

5 All disputes arising out of the performance of, or relating to this contract, shall be settled through negotiation. In case no settlement can be reached through negotiation, the case shall then be submitted to the China International Economic and Trade Arbitration Commission for arbitration in accordance with its arbitral rules. The arbitration shall take place in Shanghai. The arbitral award is final and binding upon both parties.

6 The Buyer is requested to sign and return one copy of this contract immediately after receipt of the same. Objection, if any, should be raised by the Buyer within 3 working days, otherwise it is understood that the Buyer has accepted the terms and conditions of this contract.

7 Special conditions: (These shall prevail over all printed terms in case of any conflict.)

示 范

上海环宇贸易有限公司
Shanghai Universal Trading Co., Ltd.

合同核算表

填表日期： **2018** 年 **9** 月 **29** 日　　填表人： **王凯**　　　编号： **HYHT-E0373**

核算时，成本、费用及利润项目一律保留2位小数。

进口商	成交术语	装运港	目的港	报价核算表编号
Tivolian Trading B.V.	CIF	Shanghai	Rotterdam	HYBJ-E0373

包干费 (RMB)			海洋运费(USD)		
LCL / FT	20'FCL	40'FCL	LCL / FT	20'FCL	40'FCL
80	1200	1500	95	1010	1840

增值税率	出口退税率	公司定额费	银行手续费	银行贷款年利率	垫款时间(天)
16%	15%	5%	结算金额的0.25%	6.5%	45

保险加成率	保险费率	佣金率	其他费用	汇率(USD1=RMB)	
10%	0.65%	/	/	6.85	

分货号成交信息

货号	计价单位	采购成本 RMB	成交价格 USD	成交数量	
KB0278	set	55.00	9.60	504 sets	与KB5411拼装1个20'FCL
包装	包装方式	毛重 kg	净重 kg	长 cm	宽 cm	高 cm

| 包装 | 4 sets/ctn | 8 | 5.5 | 55 | 45 | 40 |

货号	计价单位	采购成本 RMB	成交价格 USD	成交数量	
KB5411	set	70.00	11.50	504 sets	与KB0278拼装1个20'FCL

| 包装 | 4 sets/ctn | 8 | 5.5 | 55 | 45 | 40 |

货号	计价单位	采购成本 RMB	成交价格 USD	成交数量	
KB0677	set	90.00	14.50	536 sets	与KB7900拼装1个20'FCL

| 包装 | 8 sets/ctn | 8.5 | 6 | 48 | 64 | 60 |

货号	计价单位	采购成本 RMB	成交价格 USD	成交数量	
KB7900	set	95.00	15.40	536 sets	与KB0677拼装1个20'FCL

| 包装 | 8 sets/ctn | 8.5 | 6 | 48 | 64 | 60 |

成交利润核算

		计算过程	计算结果
收入：	销售收入总额(¥)	(9.6×504＋11.5×504＋14.5×536＋15.4×536)×6.85	182626.48
	退税收入总额(¥)	(55×504＋70×504＋90×536＋95×536)÷(1＋16%)×15%	20968.97
支出：	采购成本总额(¥)	55×504＋70×504＋90×536＋95×536	162160.00
	包干费总额(¥)	1200×2	2400.00
	公司定额费总额(¥)	(55×504＋70×504＋90×536＋95×536)×5%	8108.00
	银行手续费总额(¥)	(9.6×504＋11.5×504＋14.5×536＋15.4×536)×0.25%×6.85	456.57
	垫款利息总额(¥)	(55×504＋70×504＋90×536＋95×536)×6.5%÷360×45	1317.55
	海洋运费总额(¥)	1010×2×6.85	13837.00
	保险费总额(¥)	(9.6×504＋11.5×504＋14.5×536＋15.4×536)×110%×0.65%×6.85	1305.78
	其他费用总额(¥)	/	/
利润：	利润总额(¥)	182626.48＋20968.97－162160－2400－8108－456.57－1317.55－13837－1305.78	14010.55
	销售利润率(%)	14010.55÷182626.48	7.67%

Acknowledging Order No. TIV-PO-CSH0873

发件人：	David Wang <d.wang@universal.com.cn>
日 期：	2018年9月29日
收件人：	Chila Trooborg <chtrooborg@tivolian.nl>

上 海 环 宇 贸 易 有 限 公 司
Shanghai Universal Trading Co., Ltd.

Dear Mr. Trooborg

We are pleased to receive your order No. TIV-PO-CSH0873 for plush toys.

We have carefully noted your assorting requirement. However, the ordered quantity, 540 sets, for Article No. KB0677 and KB7900, cannot satisfy the packing mode, which is 8 sets/ctn. So we suggest adjusting the quantity to 536 sets respectively.

Expecting you will agree, we have sent out our Sales Confirmation No. HY-TIV0373 by DHL. Please countersign it and return one copy for our file. But if there is anything you want to discuss, please just let us know.

In order to help us to meet the date of delivery, please open the relevant letter of credit accordingly and courier your labels without delay. You may rest assured that we will take special care to your packing and shipping instructions.

Once again, thank you very much for your order, and please keep us updated on your end as we will keep you updated on ours.

Best wishes

David Wang
Sales Manager
Shanghai Universal Trading Co., Ltd.
Tel: +86 21 58818863
Email: d.wang@universal.com.cn

中国上海市东方路 **131** 号美陵广场 **1201-1216** 室
Rm. 1201-1216 Mayling Plaza, 131 Dongfang Rd., Shanghai, 200120, China
电话/Tel: 86-21-58818844   传真/Fax: 86-21-58818766   网址/Web: www.universal.com.cn

Shanghai Universal Trading Co., Ltd.

Rm. 1201-1216 Mayling Plaza,
131 Dongfang Rd.,
Shanghai, 200120, China
Tel: 86-21-58818844
Fax: 86-21-58818766

SALES CONFIRMATION

S/C No.: HY-TIV0373

S/C Date: Sept. 29, 2018

To: Tivolian Trading B.V.

P.O. Box 1783m Heiman Dullaertolein 3,

3024CA Rotterdam, the Netherlands

We hereby confirm having sold to you the following goods on terms and conditions as specified below:

Item No.	Name of Commodity & Specifications		Quantity	Unit Price	Amount
	Plush Toys			CIF Rotterdam Incoterms 2010	
	details as per the samples dispatched by the seller on Sept. 25, 2018				
1	KB0278	Twin Bear	504 sets	US$9.60	US$4,838.40
2	KB5411	Twin Bear in Ballet Costume	504 sets	US$11.50	US$5,796.00
3	KB0677	Brown Bear with Red Bow	536 sets	US$14.50	US$7,772.00
4	KB7900	Bear in Pink T-shirt	536 sets	US$15.40	US$8,254.40
		Total:	2080 sets		US$26,660.80

Total Amount in Words: Say U.S. Dollars Twenty Six Thousand Six Hundred and Sixty and Cents Eighty Only

Packing: KB0278 & KB5411: the label " CE/IMP. 087" to be attached to each piece,
KB0677 & KB7900: the label " F-TOYS 228" to be attached to each piece,
KB0278 & KB5411 to be packed in cartons of 4 sets each, equally assorted in one 20'FCL,
KB0677 & KB7900 to be packed in cartons of 8 sets each, equally assorted in one 20'FCL,
Total 386 cartons in two 20'FCL.

Shipment: To be effected during November 2018 from Shanghai, China to Rotterdam, the Netherlands
with partial shipments prohibited and transshipment permitted.

Insurance: To be covered by the seller for 110% of invoice value against All Risks and War Risks as per
the Ocean Marine Cargo Clauses of P.I.C.C dated Jan.1, 1981.

Payment: The buyer should open through a bank acceptable to the seller an irrevocable letter of credit
payable at sight for 100% of the contract value to reach the seller by the middle of October 2018
and valid for negotiation in China until the 15th day after the date of shipment.

Confirmed by:

THE SELLER

Shanghai Universal Trading Co., Ltd.

THE BUYER

(signature)

REMARKS:

1   The Buyer shall have the covering letter of credit reach the Seller 45 days before shipment, failing which the Seller reserves the right to rescind without further notice, or to regard as still valid whole or any part of this contract not fulfilled by the Buyer, or to lodge a claim for losses thus sustained, if any.

2   In case of any discrepancy in quality, claim should be filed by the Buyer within 30 days after the arrival of the goods at port of destination; while for quantity discrepancy, claim should be filed by the Buyer within 15 days after the arrival of the goods at port of destination.

3   For transactions concluded on C.I.F. basis, it is understood that the insurance amount will be for 110% of the invoice value against the risks specified in this contract. If additional insurance amount or coverage required, the Buyer must have the consent of the Seller before shipment, and the additional premium is to be borne by the Buyer.

4   The Seller shall not hold liable for non-delivery or delay in delivery of the entire lot or a portion of the goods hereabove by reason of natural disasters, war or other causes of Force Majeure. However, the Seller shall notify the Buyer as soon as possible and furnish the Buyer within 15 days by registered airmail with a certificate issued by the China Council for the Promotion of International Trade attesting such event(s).

5   All disputes arising out of the performance of, or relating to this contract, shall be settled through negotiation. In case no settlement can be reached through negotiation, the case shall then be submitted to the China International Economic and Trade Arbitration Commission for arbitration in accordance with its arbitral rules. The arbitration shall take place in Shanghai. The arbitral award is final and binding upon both parties.

6   The Buyer is requested to sign and return one copy of this contract immediately after receipt of the same. Objection, if any, should be raised by the Buyer within 3 working days, otherwise it is understood that the Buyer has accepted the terms and conditions of this contract.

7   Special conditions: (These shall prevail over all printed terms in case of any conflict.)

💬 示范评析

1. 交易磋商过程往往是漫长的,在这个期间,一些费用项目可能会发生变化,如海洋运费上涨或是下跌了,货币升值或是贬值了,又或者出口退税率、工厂采购成本调整了,等等。所以在进行合同核算时,不应盲目援引报价核算时的各项费率,而应根据实际情况作出调整,否则将导致合同的核算利润与实际利润产生不必要的偏差。

2. 在交易磋商中,买卖双方虽就六项主要交易条件(品质、数量、包装、价格、交货和支付)达成了基本一致,但其中仍有一些细节问题尚未明确。因此,作为有经验的卖方在拟写售货确认书时通常会在条款的完整性和规范性上下功夫,以防止和减少履约中争议的发生。

例如本案例,在磋商环节双方并未就转船问题进行磋商,在拟写装运条款时,卖方就从有利于自身利益的角度,在条款中加入了"transshipment permitted"的信息。在这样的规定下,卖方既可以采用直航的方式运输货物,也可以采用转船,这就为卖方履行交货义务争取了灵活的空间。当然,买方可以将其视作卖方提出的新的、额外的交易条件,或同意,或拒绝,双方也可能因此重回谈判桌旁继续磋商。但试想如果双方此时不在合同中予以明确,而是留待实际装运时遇到问题后再作商议,则可能会影响到合同的履行,甚至造成经济损失。

同理,在支付条款中,除了"letter of credit payable at sight"信息之外,卖方还加入了有关信用证的申请人(The buyer should open through...)、开证银行(a bank acceptable to the seller)、信用证性质(irrevocable)、信用证金额(for 100% contract value)、到证时间(to reach the seller by the middle of September 2018)、到期地点(valid in China)、信用证兑付方式(for negotiation)、到期日及交单期限(until the 15th day after the date of shipment)等一系列信息,也是出于把银行的付款保证落到实处的考虑。

由此可见,合同条款的规范与完整对于提高合同质量、减少争议的作用是不容忽视的。

3. 我们注意到,在示范售货确认书的背面印制了大量的条款,主要涉及信用证开立的时间、索赔、保险金额、险别及费用承担、不可抗力、仲裁、会签等。这就是所谓的"一般交易条件"(general terms and conditions),是出口商为出售货物而拟订的对每笔交易都适用的一套共性的交易条件,也称之为"格式条款"。一般交易条件虽然适用于所有合同,但交易双方完全可以根据具体交易的实际情况,对一般交易条件作出修正,通过在合同正面另行书写条款的方式来改变或否定背面的印刷条款的。例如,本售货确认书的第一条规定"The Buyer shall have the covering letter of credit reach the Seller 45 days before shipment",而正面的支付条款规定"The buyer should open… letter of credit… to reach the seller by the middle of October 2018",则应按支付条款的规定执行。再如,本售货确认书的第三条对CIF 术语成交时卖方的投保责任作了规定,而售货确认书的正面也有"Insurance"条款,对比后我们发现,二者并无冲突,背面的格式条款可视为对正面书写条款的进一步补充。

因此,我们除了要特别注意合同正面的主要交易条件,即品质、数量、包装、价格、交货和支付条款,同时也应仔细阅读合同的背面条款。

4. 在本案例中,Tivolian 发来的订单实际上是一项"发盘(offer)",需要环宇公司"接受(accept)"之后才能达成交易。但由于其将货号 KB0677 和 KB7900 的订量分别从 1080 套调整到了 540 套,而这两个货号的包装方式均为 8 套/箱,这样就产生了每个货号订购 67.5 箱的问题。为了使订购数量与货物包装方式匹配,同时又满足等量拼装的条件,环宇公司建议将 KB0677 和 KB7900 的订量均调整到 536套。由于改动较小,环宇公司就直接制作了售货确认书。然而,从法律意义上讲,环宇公司的售货确认书并不是一项接受,而是一项新发盘,仍需要 Tivolian 接受之后才能达成交易。因此,只有待 Tivolian 会签售货确认书后,双方的合同关系才正式确立。

Q:客户来函中的"viz."是什么意思?

A:viz.是拉丁语 videlicet 的缩写,通常读作 namely,意思是"即,那就是"。

Q:客户来函中提到拼装(assorted),是否意味着是拼箱货?

A:客户最终的订单数量为 KB0278 和 KB5411 等量拼装一个 20 英尺整箱,KB0677 和 KB7900 等量拼装一个 20 英尺整箱。尽管出现了"拼装"字眼,但无论对货主(环宇公司)还是对收货人(Tivolian 公司)而言,实际上均是两个整箱,所以在计算海洋运费或是包干费时,均应按整箱费率来计算。我们必须了解,所谓拼箱货是指货量不足一整箱,需由承运人在集装箱货运站将不同发货人的少量货物拼装在一个集装箱内,货到目的地后,由承运人拆箱分拨给各收货人。所以,货主自行在一个集装箱内进行搭配拼装,只要是发送给同一个收货人,承运人仍将其视为整箱货。当然,这也就是环宇公司同意按 20 尺整箱的价格接受此份订单的前提。

指　南

ⓘ 合同核算

合同核算从内容和过程上都与还价核算中的总利润额及利润率核算基本相同,只是在性质上有所不同而已。还价核算时,计算利润额和利润率的目的是分析客户的还价、根据核算的结果采取相应的对策,例如调整公司的预期利润、设法降低有关的费用支出或是争取得到更加具有竞争力的供货价格,而合同核算则是在双方达成交易之后,对价格磋商及整笔交易盈利状况的总结。

合同核算采用总价法计算一笔交易可以获得的人民币利润总额,在此基础上得出预期利润率。

我们可以用一个非常简单的公式来归纳合同核算:

合同利润额＝出口收入总额(销售收入＋退税收入)

－出口支出总额(采购成本＋各项费用)

合同利润率:

销售利润率＝利润总额÷出口销售收入总额×100％

成本利润率＝利润总额÷国内采购成本总额×100％

ⓘ 合同的形式与内容

在交易磋商的过程中,当一方发盘经另一方有效接受以后,交易即告达成,买卖双方就构成了合同关系。按照国际上的通常做法,买卖双方还将拟定和签署一份固定格式的书面出口交易合同,以便把各自的权利和义务用规范的合同条款的形式加以明确,作为合同成立的书面证据和合同履行的依据。

从事国际贸易的企业通常都有其固定的合同格式。出口交易达成以后,业务人员根据函电往来或口头磋商的结果,将各项内容填入合同文本中。合同通常做成一式三份,经出口商签署后,面交或航空邮寄两份给对方要求会签,进口商收到合同经审核无误签署后保留一份,并将另一份退还出口商归档。

国际上对于出口交易合同的形式并无特别的限制。在我国的出口交易中,使用最为广泛的是售货合同(Sales Contract)和售货确认书(Sales Confirmation)两种形式。二者虽在格式、项目及措辞等方面有所不同,但就其主要部分,即体现双方经磋商达成一致的各项合同条款,均是明确、完整和肯定的。因此两种形式在法律上对合同双方当事人具有同等的约束力。而其内容都不外乎以下三个方面:

(一) 约首

约首通常包括:合同名称、合同编号、缔约依据、日期和地点、当事人的名称和地址。有的合同在约首还以序言的形式说明订约意图。

(二) 本文

本文是合同的主要部分,一般以合同条款的形式具体列明交易的各项条件,规定双方当事人的权利和义务。它包括的内容主要有:出口货物的名称、规格和达成交易的数量;商品的包装和双方谈妥的价格;交付货物的时间、装运地及目的地;货物的运输保险由哪一方负责办理、保险险别与所适用的保险条款;货款支付的时间和方式等等。

此外,出口合同或售货确认书中还包括一些预防与处理争议的条款,通常作为合同的一般交易条件列明在合同的备注栏(Remarks)中或合同的背面。

(三) 约尾

约尾是合同的结束部分,通常包括:合同所使用的文字及其效力、合同的份数、缔约人签字、合同生效时间和条件以及合同所适用的法律等内容。

ⓘ 合同的主要条款

(一) 品名及规格(Commodity Name and Specifications)

品名及规格条款也称品质条款,它是构成商品说明的重要组成部分,也是交易双方在交接货物时对货物品质界定的主要依据。在出口交易中,约定商品品质的方法一般有以下两种：

◇　用实物来表示出口商品的品质。具体表现为：

1. 看货成交。即由卖方在货物存放地点向买方展示拟出售的货物，经买方现场检验满意后达成交易。看货成交一般只适合于一些古董、工艺品及首饰等贵重物品交易。

2. 凭样成交。即以样品来说明商品品质并约定以样品作为交接货物的品质依据。凭样成交又可分为"凭卖方样品成交"和"凭买方样品成交"两大类。凭样成交通常适用于那些品质难以用文字描述商品的买卖，如服装、玩具及某些轻工产品和矿产品，等等。

◇　用文字说明表示商品的品质。具体表现为：

1. 凭规格、等级或标准。根据货物的规格、等级或标准进行买卖是出口贸易中经常采用的表示品质的方法。规格是一些用以反映商品品质的主要指标；等级则是将同一种商品按其规格上的差异，分为品质上优劣不同的若干级别；而标准指的是统一化了的规格和等级及其检验方法。

2. 凭牌名或产地名称。凭牌名或产地名称进行买卖主要适用于那些买主已十分熟悉其品质的轻纺产品或农副土特产品的交易。

3. 凭说明书。对于某些结构复杂、材料、设计要求严格的技术密集型产品，一般需要凭借样本、说明书并附以图样、照片和分析图表来说明其具体的性能及构造特点。按这种方式进行的交易就是凭说明书买卖。

在出口交易中，卖方交付的货物必须与合同规定相符，这是卖方所作出的品质保证的一个基本内容。为了防止品质纠纷，合同中的品质条款应尽量订得明确具体，避免笼统含糊。在用文字说明表示商品的品质时，应针对具体的交易情况品质条款中明确规定名称、规格、等级、标准、商标等内容。在规定质量指标时不宜采用诸如"大约"，"左右"，"合理误差"等用语，所涉及的数据应力求明确，而且要切合实际，避免订得过高，过低，过繁或过细。

例如：

圣诞熊，货号 S312，16 厘米，戴帽子和围巾，详情根据 2018 年 8 月 20 日卖方寄送的样品。

S312 16cm Christmas bear with cap and scarf, details as per the samples dispatched by the seller on 20 August 2018.

威尔逊牌足球，货号 WS18，5 号球，真皮手工缝制，国际足联批准比赛用球。
Wilson Brand Football, Article Number WS18, Size 5, Genuine Leather,

Hand Sewn，FIFA Approved.

　　然而,在实际业务中,有时由于商品特性、生产和加工条件的限制以及气候等因素的影响,某些商品的品质在一定范围内会有所波动或变化。对该类商品的质量指标如果规定得过死或绝对化,卖方将那已做到货物与合同规定完全相符。为了避免交货品质与合同稍有不符而构成违约,在出口合同中,对于商品质量指标可加列品质机动幅度条款,即允许卖方交付货物的品质以在一定范围内得以机动,从而有利于生产加工和合同履行。
　　例如:
　　绿豆,水分最高 15%,杂质最高 1%。
　　Green Bean，Moisture 15% max，Admixture 1% max.

　　灰鸭毛,含绒量 18%,允许上下 1%。
　　Grey Duck Feather，Down content 18%，allowing 1% more or less.

(二) 数量(Quantity)

　　出口合同的数量条款包括计量单位、商品数量或者再加上关于数量机动幅度的规定。
　　例如:
　　800 公吨,卖方可溢装或短装 5%
　　800 metric tons，5% more or less at seller's option

　　在实际业务中,根据商品的不同性质,通常使用的计量单位有重量(如 kg、metric ton、pound 等)、容积(如 litre、gallon、bushel 等)、个数(如 piece、pair、set 等)、长度(如 metre、foot、yard 等)、面积(如 square metre、square foot、square yard 等)和体积(cubic metre、cubic foot、cubic yard 等)六种。其中,按重量计数时多使用净重,但有些单位价值不高的商品也常常采用毛重计数,称作"以毛作净"(gross for net)。数量的计量单位必须与单价的计价数量单位相一致。
　　在签订合同时,一般应明确规定买卖货物的具体数量,以作为双方当事人交接货物的数量依据。但是,在实际业务中,某些商品由于其本身的特性或是受到生产、包装、装卸和运输条件的限制,卖方要做到交货的数量与合同中的规定完全一致有一定的困难。因此,为了避免因实际交货不足或超过合同规定而导致的违约,方便合同的履行,对于一些难以严格计量的商品,如大宗的农副产品、矿产品以及集装箱运输时装箱数量不能准确把握的商品,通常在合同中规定一个允许卖方交货数量在一定范围内增减的条款,这就是合同中的溢短装条款(more or less clause)。

(三) 包装(Packing)

进出口货物根据是否加以包装可以分为三大类:散装货物(bulk cargo)、裸装货物(nude cargo)和包装货物(packed cargo),而其中以包装货物最为常见。包装又有内外包装之分:内包装又称销售包装,其作用除了保护商品外,更强调美化宣传商品、便于消费者识别、选购、携带和使用的功能;外包装也称运输包装,这种包装的主要作用在于保护商品,便于运输、储存、计数和分拨等。

通常出口合同的包装条款包含的要素有:包装方式、外包装的种类及总件数,涉及集装箱数量时一般也会明确指出。

包装种类是指采用的包装材料,如木箱(WOODEN CASE),纸箱(CARTON),捆包(BUNDLE, BALE),袋(BAG),桶(DRUM)等。包装方式是指每个包装单位内所装的商品数量。总件数是指合同项下整批货物总的包装件数。

例如:

每20只装一个纸盒,10盒装一个纸箱,共计500个纸箱装一个20英尺集装箱。

20 pieces to a box, 10 boxes to an export carton. Total 500 cartons in one 20 feet container.

每只包纸,并套塑料袋,每一打装一坚固新木箱,适合长途海运,防湿,防潮,防震,防锈,耐粗暴搬运,共计500木箱装一个40英尺整箱。

EACH TO BE WRAPPED WITH PAPER THEN TO A POLYBAG, EVERY DOZEN TO A NEW STRONG WOODEN CASE, SUITABLE FOR LONG VOYAGE AND WELL PROTECTED AGAINST DAMPNESS, MOISTURE, SHOCK, RUST AND ROUGH HANDLING. TOTAL 500 WOODEN CASES IN ONE 40'FCL.

出口合同中包装条款除了上述内容外,必要时还会列明货物的包装标志。包装标志包括运输标志、磅码产地标志以及指示性、警告性标志。

运输标志(shipping mark),又称作"唛"或"唛头",通常由三部分组成:主标志、目的地、件号。主标志通常由收/发货人名称(有时包括简单的几何图形)和参考号码(如买卖合同号码、信用证号码或发票号等)组成。目的地表明货物最终要运抵的地点,通常为港口。在货物需通过转运的情况下,有时则标明转运地点。

例如 NEW YORK VIA PANAMA,这里 NEW YORK(纽约)是卸货港,而 PAN-AMA(巴拿马)则是转运港。运输标志中的件号主要用来说明一批货物的总包装件数、本件货物的号码或是整批货物与本件货物的关系。例如某批货物共计 60件,有三种规格,每个规格 20 件,那么运输标志上的件号可以表现为三组,即NOS.1-20, NOS.21-40 和 NOS.41-60,而在各类贸易单证上填写件号时则应统一为 NOS.1-60。当然,如果该批货物只有一种规格时,那么运输标志的件号也统一为 NOS.1-60。但如果该批货物每一箱的包装方式和品种规格均不相同,则应采用顺序件号的方法,即在货物包装上用 C/NO.1, C/NO.2, C/NO.3...C/NO.60或 C/NO.1/60, C/NO.2/60, C/NO.3/60, ...C/NO.60/60 的表示方法,后一种方法说明了整批货物的总件数与本件号数的关系,如 C/NO.2/60 中的 C 表示 Car-ton 即纸箱,2/60 中的 60 表明该批货物共有 60 件,2 则表示本件是 60 件中的第二件。当然,在实际业务中,我们也常在客户的订单或来往邮件中见到这样的写法"C/NO.1-UP",这通常表明包装件数待定,在货物装运时按实际情况确定。

运输标志的样式举例如下:

ELOF HANSSEN
EFH2075641
NAVY BLUE/WHITE

6	7	$7^{1/2}$	8	$8^{1/2}$	9
1	3	3	2	2	1

STOCKHOLM
C/NOS.25-48

左边的运输标志中表明了供货人(含简单的几何图形)、合同号码、目的港和件号,右边的运输标志则较为复杂,除了有收货人的名称及订单号码外,在目的港和件号之上还加列了颜色和尺码数量的搭配,这种运输标志的表示方法在进行服装、鞋帽和手套等货物的交易时常有出现。

出口货物的外包装上,一般还刷上每件包装的毛重、净重和包装容器的尺码(长×宽×高)以及货物的产地,例如:

GROSS WEIGHT(G.W.)　　　　56KGS.
NET WEIGHT(N.W.)　　　　　52KGS.
MEASUREMENT(MEAS.)　　　42cm×28cm×20cm
MADE IN THE PEOPLE'S REPUBLIC OF CHINA

除了上述标志外,有的出口货物往往还根据商品的性质刷上一些指示性和警告性标志以促使搬运人员及开箱拆包人员注意,保障货物和操作人员的安全。指示性和警告性标志有时使用文字或是用一些简单、醒目、易懂的图标，例如：

USE NO HOOKS　　　KEEP DRY　　　SLING HERE　　　CORROSIVE
　禁用手钩　　　　　保持干燥　　　　此处起吊　　　　腐蚀品

（四）价格（Price）

通常出口合同的价格条款包含的要素有：各货号单价（Unit Price）、总值（Total Amount/Total Value）及合同总金额的大、小写等栏目。

单价由计价的货币、金额、数量单位和贸易术语四个部分组成，四部分都必须明确表述。

总值是单价和数量的乘积。总值所使用的货币应与单价所使用的货币一致，合同中数量条款的单位应与单价的数量单位相吻合、才能得出正确的合同总值。也有合同在总值栏同时列明贸易术语的。

许多出口合同还将合同总金额的大写列为专门的栏目。合同总金额的大写（Total amount in words）应与小写（Total amount in figures）保持一致。大写金额前一般应冠以"SAY"并加上货币名称的复数形式，句末以"ONLY"结尾。

例如：USD 14860.00

大写金额：SAY U.S. DOLLARS FOURTEEN THOUSAND EIGHT HUNDRED AND SIXTY ONLY.

若金额元以下有尾数，例如：USD 14860.70

大写金额有两种写法：

SAY U. S. DOLLARS FOURTEEN THOUSAND EIGHT HUNDRED AND SIXTY AND CENTS SEVENTY ONLY.

或 SAY U. S. DOLLARS FOURTEEN THOUSAND EIGHT HUNDRED AND SIXTY AND 70/100 ONLY.

如果在合同的价格中包含了支付给中间商因介绍买卖而取得的报酬，也就是佣金（commission），这样的价格就称为含佣价。含佣价可以在所使用的贸易术语中间加列佣金的英文字母缩写(C)及所付佣金的百分率来表示。例如：

US＄125 PER PC. CIFC3％ NEW YORK 或 US＄125 PER PC. CIFC3 NEW YORK

每件125美元成本加保险费、运费至纽约港含百分之三佣金

价格中不包括佣金的称为净价(net price)。有时为了说明成交价格是净价，可以在贸易术语中间插入"净价"字样。例如：

US＄125 PER PC. CIF NET NEW YORK

每件125美元成本加保险费、运费至纽约港净价

此外，在出口贸易中，有时卖方会按照原价给买方一定的减让，称为折扣(discount)，通常用文字说明，例如：

US＄125 PER PC. CIF NEW YORK LESS 2％ DISCOUNT

每件125美元成本加保险费、运费至纽约港减2％折扣

折扣一般可在合同中列项扣除，例如：

UNIT PRICE	QUANTITY	AMOUNT
US＄125 PER PC. CIF NEW YORK	1000 PC.	US＄125000.00
	LESS 2％ DISCOUNT	US＄2500.00
	TOTAL	US＄122500.00

（五）装运/交货(Shipment/Delivery)

在国际贸易中，货物的"装运"和"交货"从严格意义上讲是两个不同的概念，"装运"是指出口商将货物装上指定的运输工具或交由承运人监管，而"交货"则是指出口商将货物实际交给买方或置于买方的控制之下。然而，出口交易中因较多地使用 FOB/FCA、CFR/CPT 和 CIF/CIP 六种贸易术语，交易双方采用的是推定交货的概念，卖方在装运港或装运地将经出口清关的货物装到船上或交付给承运人，就算完成了交货义务。因此，在采用上述六种贸易术语交易时，"装运"可视作等同于"交货"，而出口合同中通常也只规定装运条款。

通常出口合同的装运条款包含的要素有：装运时间、装运港/地、目的港/地、装运的附加条件等方面的内容：

例如：Shipment during July/August 2018 from Shanghai, China to Port of Valencia, Spain in two equal lots with transshipment allowed.

2018年7/8月份分两批等量装运，从中国上海至西班牙瓦伦西亚港，允许转运。

◇ 装运时间

装运时间的规定是合同装运条款的核心,其规定方法有:

1. 规定最迟装运期限。例如:

不得迟于 2018 年 10 月 25 日装运

Shipment on or before October 25,2018

Shipment not later than October 25,2018

Shipment latest on October 25,2018

不迟于 2018 年 10 月底装运

Shipment at or before the end of October 2018

Shipment by the end of October 2018

2. 规定一段期限内装运。例如:

2018 年 3 月装运

Shipment during March 2018

2018 年 3/4 月间装运

Shipment during Mar./Apr. 2018

收到信用证后 30 天内装运

Shipment within 30 days from receipt of L/C

◇ 装运港/地和目的港/地

装运港/地通常由出口商根据便利货物出口的原则提出、经进口商同意后确定。一般装运港/地只规定一个,但在成交数量大而货源又分散几处、或在达成合同时出口商还无法确定在何处发运货物的情况下,也可以规定几个港口和地点,必要时还可以作笼统规定,装运时由出口商决定后通知进口商。目的港/地通常由进口商根据便利货物使用或转售的原则提出、经出口商同意后确定。目的港/地通常也只规定一个,必要时也可以规定两个或两个以上,在合同规定的装运期前若干天由买方确定并通知卖方或由买方在其申请开立的信用证中作出明确规定。例如:

由上海装运至费利克斯托

Shipment from Shanghai to Felixstowe

装运港：上海
Port of Loading：Shanghai

装运港：上海或宁波
Port of Loading：Shanghai/Ningbo

装运港：中国港口
Port of Loading：China Ports

目的港：汉堡
Port of Destination：Hamburg

目的港：汉堡或安特卫普
Port of Destination：Hamburg/Antwerp

目的港：欧洲主要（基本）港
Port of Destination：European Main Ports

◇ 装运的附加条件

1. 分批装运

货物是否分批装运,对交易双方都有影响,因此需要在合同中加以明确规定。例如:

2018 年 12 月间由上海装运至热那亚,允许分批。

Shipment from Shanghai to Genoa during December 2018 with partial shipments allowed.

2018 年 4/5/6 月份分三批每月平均装运。

Shipment during April/May/June 2018 in three equal monthly lots.

2. 转运

有的情况下,如从装运港至目的港没有直达船或无固定船期,或是为了防止赶不上直达船而造成迟延装运,卖方会在合同中作出允许转运的规定。例如:

允许转运。

Transshipment permitted.

货物自上海经香港转运并由马士基航运公司将货物运往洛杉矶。

Shipment from Shanghai to Los Angeles with transshipment at Hongkong by Maersk Shipping Company.

如果货物以陆运、空运方式运输,通常在装运条款中还应规定运输方式,例如:

货物由上海空运至旧金山。

Shipment from Shanghai to San Francisco by air transportation.

如果双方在合同中未明确规定采用何种运输方式,一般则理解为使用海运方式。

在出口贸易中,有时卖方为了防止因某些特殊情况延误装运而产生的违约行为,会在合同中对装运期限提出一些附加条件以保障其利益。例如:

2018 年 8 月间装运,但以获得舱位为准。

Shipment during August 2018 subject to shipping space available.

不迟于 2018 年 5 月底装运,但以卖方取得出口许可证为准。

Shipment by the end of May 2018 subject to export license available by the seller.

(六) 保险(Insurance)

◇　在以 FOB、CFR 或 FCA、CPT 术语达成交易时,应由买方自行办理保险,故保险条款可表示为:

保险:由买方负责办理。

INSURANCE：To be covered by the Buyer.

如在 FOB 术语达成的交易中,买方委托卖方代办保险,则应在合同中明确规定保险金额、投保险别以及保险费应由买方负担。

◇　以 CIF、CIP 等作为成交贸易术语的合同中,保险条款是合同的主要条款之一,必须订得明确合理。通常保险条款包含的要素有:何方办理保险,保险金额(确定方法),保险险别,按什么保险条款保险并要注明保险条款的生效日期。例如:

保险:由卖方按发票金额的110%投保一切险和战争险,按照中国人民保险公司1981年1月1日的海洋运输货物保险条款办理。

INSURANCE:To be covered by the Seller for 110% of total invoice value against All Risks and War Risks as per and subject to the relevant ocean marine cargo clauses of the People's Insurance Company of China dated 1/1/1981.

海运货物保险常见的保险条款有两种:

1. 海洋运输货物保险条款(Ocean Marine Cargo Clauses)。

该保险条款由中国人民保险公司(the People's Insurance Company of China,PICC)于1981年1月1日修订,规定了3种基本险别:平安险(free from particular average,FPA),水渍险(with average,WA或称with particular average,WPA)和一切险(all risks),以及若干项附加险,如:战争险(war risks)、罢工险(strike risks)等。

由于该保险条款与PICC制订的陆上运输货物保险条款(Overland Transportation Cargo Insurance Clauses)、航空运输货物保险条款(Air Transportation Cargo Insurance Clauses)和邮包保险条款(Parcel Post Insurance Clauses)一起被统称为"中国保险条款"(China Insurance Clauses,C.I.C.),所以也可以表述为as per and subject to C.I.C. dated 1/1/1981.

2. 协会货物条款(Institute Cargo Clauses,I.C.C.)

该保险条款由英国伦敦保险业协会于2009年1月1日修订,其中适用于海运货物保险的险别有6种:协会货物A险条款(Institute Cargo Clauses A,ICC(A)),协会货物B险条款(Institute Cargo Clauses B,ICC(B)),协会货物C险条款(Institute Cargo Clauses C,ICC(C)),协会战争险条款(Institute War Clauses(Cargo)),协会货物罢工险条款(Institute Strikes Clauses(Cargo))和恶意损害险条款(Malicious Damage Clauses)。

因此,若按协会货物条款保险则可表述为:

保险:由卖方按发票金额的110%投保协会货物险中的A险和战争险条款,根据2009年1月1日的协会货物保险条款办理。

INSURANCE:To be covered by the Seller for CIF value plus 10% against Institute Cargo Clauses A and Institute War Clauses(Cargo) dated 1/1/2009.

以上两种保险条款的详细情况可参看**第八章　出口货运投保**的**指南**(第246页)。

（七）支付（Payment）

出口合同中支付条款,也称付款条款,根据不同的结算方式而内容各异:

◇ 汇付（Remittance）

使用汇付方式结算货款时,在合同的支付条款中应明确规定汇付的时间、具体的汇付方法以及汇付的金额等。例如:

买方应在本合同签字之日起 30 天内将 100％的合同金额用电汇方式预付给卖方。

The buyer shall pay 100％ of the contract value to the seller in advance by T/T within 30 days after signing the contract.

买方应于收到卖方寄交的正本提单后立即将合同全款用电汇支付给卖方。

The buyer shall pay the total contract value by T/T upon receipt of the original Bills of Lading sent by the seller.

有关汇付的具体业务流程可参看**第五章 信用证审核与修改**的**指南**（第 152 页）。

◇ 跟单托收（Documentary Collection）

使用跟单托收结算货款时,在合同的支付条款中应明确规定付款/承兑责任、付款期限和银行交单条件等。例如:

买方应凭卖方开具的即期跟单汇票于见票时立即付款。买方付款后方可取得装运单据。

Upon first presentation the buyer shall pay against documentary draft at sight drawn by the seller. The shipping documents are to be delivered against payment only.

买方对于卖方开具的见票后 30 天付款的跟单汇票,于提示时应立即承兑,并应于汇票到期日付款。买方付款后方可取得运输单据。

Upon first presentation the buyer shall duly accept the documentary draft at 30 days after sight drawn by the sellers and make the payment on its maturity. The shipping documents are to be delivered against payment only.

买方对于卖方开具的见票后 30 天付款的跟单汇票，于提示时应立即承兑，并应于汇票到期日付款。买方承兑后可取得运输单据。

Upon first presentation the buyer shall duly accept the documentary draft at 30 days' sight drawn by the seller and make payment on its maturity. The shipping documents are to be delivered against acceptance.

有关跟单托收的具体业务流程可参看**第五章　信用证审核与修改**的**指南**（第 155 页）。

◇　跟单信用证（Documentary Letter of Credit）

使用跟单信用证结算货款时，在合同的支付条款中应明确规定开证申请人、开证银行、开证时间、信用证种类、信用证金额、信用证到期地点和到期日等。例如：

买方应通过一家为卖方所接受的银行于装运月份前 30 天按合同全额开立并送达卖方不可撤销、见票后 45 天付款的信用证，且该证于装运日后第 15 天在中国议付到期。

The buyer shall open through a bank acceptable to the seller an irrevocable letter of credit payable at 45 days' sight for 100% of the contract value to reach the seller 30 days before the month of shipment and valid for negotiation in China until the 15th day after the date of shipment.

以上条款可按其内容要点归纳如下：

开证申请人：　the buyer

开证银行：　a bank acceptable to the seller

开证时间：　to reach the seller 30 days before the month of shipment

信用证种类：　an irrevocable letter of credit payable at 45 days' sight ...for negotiation

信用证金额：　for 100% of the contract value

信用证到期日和到期地点以及交单期限：valid ...in China until the 15th day after the date of shipment

有关跟单信用证的具体业务流程可参看**第五章　信用证审核与修改**的**指南**（第 170 页）。

(i) 合同中预防与处理争议的条款

　　除了以上谈到的主要合同条款(品质、数量、包装、价格、交货、支付和保险条款)以外,为在合同履行中尽量减少争议,或者在发生争议时能妥善解决,在国际货物买卖合同中通常还需要订立一些有关预防与处理争议的条款,主要包括检验条款、索赔条款、不可抗力条款和仲裁条款。这些条款大都印就在售货合同的背面或正面的备注(Remarks)部分,是对合同主要条款的补充说明。通常只要买方不提出异议,就据以执行。

◇　检验条款实例

　　双方同意以装运港中国海关签发的品质和数量检验证书作为信用证项下议付单据的一部分。买方有权对货物的品质和数量进行复验,复验费由买方负担。如发现品质或数量与合同不符,买方有权向卖方索赔,但须提供由卖方认可的独立公证检验机构出具的检验报告。

　　It is mutually agreed that the Inspection Certificate of Quality and Quantity issued by the China Customs at the port of shipment shall be part of the documents to be presented for negotiation under the relevant L/C. The Buyers shall have the right to re-inspect the Quality and Quantity of the cargo. The re-inspection fee shall be borne by the Buyers. Should the Quality and/or Quantity be found not in conformity with that of the contract, the Buyers are entitled to lodge with the Sellers a claim which should be supported by survey reports issued by an independent public surveyor approved by the Sellers.

◇　索赔条款实例

　　质量/数量索赔:如交货质量不符,买方须于货物到达目的港后 30 天内提出索赔;如交货数量不符,则须于货物到达目的港后 15 天内提出索赔。对于应由保险公司、船公司和其他运输机构或邮政部门负责的货物不符,卖方不承担责任。

　　Quality/Quantity Discrepancy:In case of quality discrepancy, claims should be filed by the Buyers within 30 days after the arrival of the goods at port of destination; while for quantity discrepancy, claims should be filed by the Buyers within 15 days after the arrival of the goods at port of destination. It is understood that the Sellers shall not be liable for any discrepancy of the goods shipped due to causes for which the insurance company, shipping company, other transportation organizations and/or the post office are liable.

◇ **不可抗力条款实例**

如因战争或其他不可抗力的原因导致合同不能履行,若此种原因在合同到期后三个月内仍持续,则本合同的不能装运部分即视为无效,买卖双方对此均不承担责任。

If the fulfillment of the contract is prevented by reason of war or other causes of force majeure, which exists for three months after the expiring the contract, the non-shipment of this contract is considered to be void, for which neither the Seller nor the Buyer shall be liable.

◇ **仲裁条款实例**

凡与本合同有关的或因执行本合同所发生的一切争议,应由双方通过友好协商解决。如果协商不能解决,则应由中国国际经济贸易仲裁委员会根据其仲裁规则进行仲裁。仲裁在上海进行,仲裁裁决是终局的,对双方都有约束力。仲裁费用由败诉一方负担。仲裁也可在双方同意的第三国进行。

Arbitration: All disputes in connection with this contract or the execution thereof shall be settled friendly through negotiations. In case no settlement can be reached, the case may then be submitted for arbitration to China International Economic and Trade Arbitration Commission in accordance with the provisional Rules of Procedures promulgated by the said Arbitration Commission. The arbitration shall take place in Shanghai and the decision of the Arbitration Commission shall be final and binding upon both parties. Arbitration fee shall be borne by the losing party. Or arbitration may be settled in the third country mutually agreed upon by both parties.

(i) 签约函的基本结构

当出口方向进口方寄送售货确认书(S/C)时,往往会附上一封短信,我们可称之为"签约函"。签约函是一种典型的通知类信函,主要目的是告知(Informative)而非说服(persuasive),因此关键是掌握内容的完整性。

签约函的主要内容是要告知客户销售合同已寄出、希望其签退,例如:

◇ We are sending you our Sales Confirmation No. WR9023 in duplicate. Please sign it and return one copy for our filing.

通常,我们会对该笔交易成交表示高兴,并希冀合同顺利履行。例如:

◇　We are glad that through our mutual efforts we have reached the agreement.

◇　We believe the first transaction will turn out to be satisfactory to both of us.

◇　You may rest assured that we shall effect shipment strictly as contracted.

另外,在信用证交易中,信用证能否及时开到直接关系到出口方能否按时交货,所以在拟写此类签约函时,特别是在距规定到证日较近的情况下,我们一般会加上一些催促对方尽早开立信用证的语句。例如:

◇　It is understood that a letter of credit in our favor covering the above-mentioned goods will be established promptly.

◇　Please instruct your banker to issue the letter of credit as early as possible so that we can process with the preparation of the goods immediately.

练 习

出口成交核算

1. 根据以下成交明细进行出口成交核算：

成交明细				
进口商	货物总称	贸易术语	装运港	目的港
Parandar International Inc.	Porcelain Dinnerware	CIF	Shanghai	Toronto

包干费(RMB)			海洋运费(USD)		
LCL / SET	20'FCL / CTNR	40'FCL / CTNR	LCL / FT	20'FCL / CTNR	40'FCL / CTNR
5	1200	1700	180	2760	3580
增值税率	出口退税率	公司定额费率	银行手续费率	银行贷款年利率	垫款时间(天)
16%	13%	3%	0.3%	6%	90
汇率(USD1=RMB)	佣金率	保险加成率	保险费率	其他费用1	其他费用2
6.5	/	10%	0.65%	/	/

货号	品名	计量单位	采购成本(RMB)	成交价格(USD)	成交数量(套)
SHD12-P213	12pc Dinnerware Set	set	300.00	52.20	644
包装种类	包装方式	毛重(kg)	净重(kg)	长(cm)	宽(cm)	高(cm)
carton	4 sets/ctn.	21	18	62	48	52

货号	品名	计量单位	采购成本(RMB)	成交价格(USD)	成交数量(套)
SHD12-P214	12pc Dinnerware Set	set	275.00	48.00	692
包装种类	包装方式	毛重(kg)	净重(kg)	长(cm)	宽(cm)	高(cm)
carton	4 sets/ctn.	21	18	60	48	50

货号	品名	计量单位	采购成本(RMB)	成交价格(USD)	成交数量(套)
SHD16-P541	16pc Dinnerware Set	set	315.00	56.50	222
包装种类	包装方式	毛重(kg)	净重(kg)	长(cm)	宽(cm)	高(cm)
carton	2 sets/ctn.	18	16	55	46	44.5

货号	品名	计量单位	采购成本(RMB)	成交价格(USD)	成交数量(套)
SHD16-P545	16pc Dinnerware Set	set	285.00	51.70	238
包装种类	包装方式	毛重(kg)	净重(kg)	长(cm)	宽(cm)	高(cm)
carton	2 sets/ctn.	18	16	52	48	42

备注：货号 SHD12-P213 和 SHD12-P214 各装一个 20 英尺整箱，货号 SHD16-P541 和 SHD16-P545 拼装一个 20 英尺整箱。

2. 根据出口成交明细填制出口成交核算表：

出 口 成 交 核 算 表

成交明细				
进口商	货物总称	贸易术语	装运港	目的港
Alabra Home Appl. Trading Co., LLC.	Lamp	CFR	Shanghai	Duabi

包干费 (RMB)			海洋运费 (USD)		
LCL / PIECE	20'FCL / CTNR	40'FCL / CTNR	LCL / FT	20'FCL / CTNR	40'FCL / CTNR
4.5	1000	1500	90	1420	1850
增值税率	出口退税率	公司定额费率	银行手续费率	银行贷款年利率	垫款时间(天)
16%	9%	4.5%	0.25%	4.9%	60
汇率(USD1=RMB)	佣金率	保险加成率	保险费率	其他费用1	其他费用2
6.6	3%	/	/	/	/

货号	品名	计量单位	采购成本(RMB)	成交价格(USD)	成交数量（盏）
2103S	Desk Lamp	piece	160.00	32.20	1x20'FCL　320盏
包装种类	包装方式	毛重(kg)	净重(kg)	长(cm)	宽(cm)	高(cm)
carton	4 pcs/ctn	20	17.5	60	80	65

货号	品名	计量单位	采购成本(RMB)	成交价格(USD)	成交数量（盏）
2203S	Desk Lamp	piece	140.00	25.50	1x20'FCL　604盏
包装种类	包装方式	毛重(kg)	净重(kg)	长(cm)	宽(cm)	高(cm)
carton	4 pcs/ctn	22	19.5	48	52	66

货号	品名	计量单位	采购成本(RMB)	成交价格(USD)	成交数量（盏）
AMZ049	Desk Lamp	piece	125.00	22.80	1x20'FCL　712盏
包装种类	包装方式	毛重(kg)	净重(kg)	长(cm)	宽(cm)	高(cm)
carton	4 pcs/ctn	17	15	60	45	52

货号	品名	计量单位	采购成本(RMB)	成交价格(USD)	成交数量（盏）
ARG108	Desk Lamp	piece	76.00	15.10	1x20'FCL　504盏
包装种类	包装方式	毛重(kg)	净重(kg)	长(cm)	宽(cm)	高(cm)
carton	4 pcs/ctn	16	13.2	50	62	64

成交核算		

收入：	计算过程	核算单位: 4*20'FCL	计算结果
销售收入总额(¥)			
退税收入总额(¥)			
支出：			
采购成本总额(¥)			
海洋运费总额(¥)			
包干费总额(¥)			
公司定额费总额(¥)			
垫款利息总额(¥)			
银行手续费总额(¥)			
客广佣金总额(¥)			
利润：			
利润总额(¥)			
销售利润率(%)			

出口合同签订

3. 试将下列合同中的品质条款译成中文：

1) C708 Chinese Grey Duck Down
   With 90% down content，1% more or less allowed

2) Butterfly Brand Sewing Machine
   Model JA-1 Direct-drive Computerized Lockstitch Machine

3) S836 White Rabbit Plush Toy
   Quality as per samples submitted by seller by the end of July 2018

4) Quality and technical data to be in conformity with the attached technical agreement which forms an integral part of this contract.

5) 81000R Printed Shirting，Resin Finish
   30s×36s   72×69   89/91cm×38.4m

6) Buyer's designs are to reach the seller 60 days before the month of shipment and subject to the acceptance and minor modification/adjustments by the manufacturers and with reasonable tolerance in color shade allowed.

7) For the goods produced with the designs，trademarks，brand，labels and/ or stamping provided by the buyers should there be any dispute arising from infringement upon the third party's industrial property right，it is the buyers to be held responsible for it.

4. 试将下列合同中的包装条款译成中文,并推测进行交易的大致是什么货物：

1) In iron drums of 185—190kgs. net each

2) In cartons each containing 4 boxes about 9 lbs. each piece waxed and wrapped with paper

3) In new single gunny bags of about 100kgs. each

4) In cartons of 50 dozens each and size assorted.

5) Goods are in neutral packing and buyer's labels must reach the seller 45 days before the month of shipment.

6) To be packed in new strong wooden case(s)/carton(s) suitable for long distance ocean/air transportation and well protected against dampness, moisture, shock, rust and rough handling. The sellers shall be liable for any damage to the goods on account of improper packing and in such cases any and all losses and/or expenses incurred in consequence thereof shall be borne by the sellers.

5. 试为下列出口货物设计运输标志上的件号：

COMMODITY：100％ COTTON MEN'S SHIRT
PACKING：　　　EACH PIECE IN A POLYBAG, 60 PCS. TO A CARTON.

DESIGN NO. 款式	QUANTITY 数量	CARTON NO. 件号/箱号	NOS OF PKGS. 件数
93-13	1260 PCS.	（1）	（5）
93-14	1260 PCS.	（2）	（6）
93-15	1200 PCS.	（3）	（7）
93-16	1680 PCS.	（4）	（8）

以上出口商品的总数量是：　　　　　PCS
包装总件数为：　　　　箱

6. 某公司出口 350 件服装至美国纽约,成交价格为每件 125 美元 CIF 纽约。
　　1）若此成交价中包括 5％的佣金,则合同中的数量、单价和总值分别应如何表示?
　　2）若此成交价之上可再给予 5％的折扣,则合同中的数量、单价和总值分别应如何表示?

QUANTITY 数量	UNIT PRICE 单价	AMOUNT 总值
TOTAL VALUE(IN WORDS)总金额(大写)：		

7. 试将下列合同中的装运条款译成中文：

　　1）Shipment to be effected during July 2018 from Shanghai to Hamburg by ocean transportation with partial shipments and transshipment allowed.

　　2）Shipment from Shanghai to San Francisco during July/August 2018 in two lots and allowing transshipment.

　　3）Shipment from Shanghai to San Francisco during July/August 2018 in two equal lots and allowing transshipment.

　　4）Shipment to be made during July/August 2018 in monthly lots from Shanghai to San Francisco with transshipment permitted.

　　5）Shipment from Shanghai to San Francisco during July/August 2018 in two equal monthly lots and allowing transshipment.

　　6）Shipment within 30 days from receipt of L/C which must reach the seller not later than the end of June 2018 failing which the seller reserves the right to cancel this contract without further notice，or to lodge claims for direct losses sustained from.

8. 试将下列合同中有关的保险条款译成中文：

　　1）To be covered by the seller for 110％ of total invoice value against With Particular Average and War Risk as per and subject to the relevant ocean marine cargo clauses of the People's Insurance Company of China(PICC) dated 1/1/1981.

2）For transactions concluded on CIF basis, it is understood that the insurance amount will be 110% of the invoice value against the risks specified in the S/C. If additional insurance amount or coverage is required, the additional premium is to be borne by the buyer.

3）To be covered by the Buyers from shipment, for this purpose the Sellers shall advise the Buyers by cable/fax/telex of the particulars called for in Clause(11) of this Contract. In the event of the Buyers being unable to arrange for insurance in consequence of the Sellers' failure to send the above advice the Sellers shall be held responsible for all the losses thus sustained by the Buyers.（Clause 11：The Sellers shall, upon completion of loading, advise immediately the Buyers by cable/fax/telex of the contract number, name of commodity, number of packages, gross and net weights, invoice value, name of vessel and loading date.）

9. 将下列条款译成英文：

付款条件：

1）本合同项下各种款项将用美元以信用证或电汇方式支付。

2）25000美元的技术服务费将凭最终用户签发的证明技术服务已顺利完成的证明书用电汇支付。

3）除技术服务费以外，全部货款的90%将以不可撤销即期信用证支付，该信用证将于交货前一个月开出。

4）其余10%的货款将凭最终用户签署的表明安装调试和技术协助等工作已完成的证明，用中国银行签发的银行汇票支付。

10. 试将下列有关信用证支付的条款译成中文：

Unless otherwise agreed to by the sellers, payment is to be made against sight draft drawn under an irrevocable Letter of Credit for the full amount, established through a first class bank acceptable to the sellers.

The Letter of Credit in due form must reach the seller at least 30 days before the month of shipment stipulated in this S/C, failing which the seller shall not be responsible for delayed shipment; in case the buyer's credit still fails to reach the sellers after the expiry of the shipping period, the sellers shall have the right to cancel this S/C and claim for damage against the buyers.

The buyers are requested to refrain from specifying any particular shipping line, name of steamer, or insurance company in the Letter of Credit.

To facilitate negotiation of the credit by the sellers, the validity of the Letter of Credit shall be so stipulated as to remain valid for at least 10 days(expiring in China) after the last day of shipment and the amount of the credit shall allow plus or minus 5%.

To ensure timely shipment, the buyers are requested to open their Letter of Credit by full cable and stipulate that transshipment and partial shipment are allowed as well as the number of the Sales Confirmation.

11. 试将下列条款译成中文并说明该条款如此订立的目的:

THE BUYERS SHALL OPEN THROUGH A BANK ACCEPTABLE TO THE SELLERS AN IRREVOCABLE LETTER OF CREDIT AT 45 DAYS SIGHT TO REACH THE SELLERS 30 DAYS BEFORE THE MONTH OF SHIPMENT, STIPULATING THAT 50% OF THE INVOICE VALUE AVAILABLE AGAINST CLEAN DRAFT AT 45 DAYS SIGHT WHILE THE REMAINING 50% ON DOCUMENTS AGAINST PAYMENT AT 45 DAYS SIGHT ON COLLECTION BASIS. THE FULL SET OF THE SHIPPING DOCUMENTS OF 100% INVOICE VALUE SHALL ACCOMPANY THE COLLECTION ITEM AND SHALL ONLY BE RELEASED AFTER FULL PAYMENT OF THE INVOICE VALUE. IF THE BUYER FAILS TO PAY FULL INVOICE VALUE, THE SHIPPING DOCUMENTS SHALL BE HELD BY THE ISSUING BANK AT THE SELLER'S DISPOSAL. THE ABOVE TERMS SHOULD BE EXPLICITLY INCLUDED IN THE ESTABLISHED LETTER OF CREDIT.

12. 根据往来函电订立销货合约(合约号码为 YD-YYSC0827)

买方: Hong Sheng(Hongkong) Co., Ltd.
　　Address: 17/F, One Kowloon, 1 Wang Yuen Street, Kowloon Bay, Hong Kong
　　Tel: 852-2893-1521   Fax: 852-2893-1525

备注：保险通常按 CIF 金额加一成投保一切险。

收发函电：

05-08-2018（I）

　　RE：CHINESE RICE F.A.Q.

SPECIFICATION：BROKEN GRAINS（MAX.）20％ ADMIXTURE（MAX.）0.2％ MOISTURE（MAX.）10％

50KG PER NEW GUNNY BAG 5％ MORE OR LESS IN TOTAL QUANTITY IN JUL 2018 SAMPLE OF CHINESE RICE RECEIVED QUALITY TESTED OK 1000TONS NEEDED PLS INFORM CIF SINGAPORE PAYMENT BY D/P AT 30 DAYS SIGHT.

10-08-2018（O）

RE YTLX DD5/8 CHINESE RICE OFFER FIRM VALID 17TH HERE 1000TONS CIF SINGAPORE USD380/TON PAYMENT BY IRREVOCABLE SIGHT L/C SHIPMENT WITHIN 30 DAYS AFTER RECEIPT RELEVANT L/C B.RGDS

15-08-2018（I）

TKS FOR YTLX 10/8 YOUR PRICE UNACCEPTABLE 1000TONS DECEMBER 500TONS JANUARY RESPECTIVELY AT USD350/TON L/C AT 30DAYS SIGHT

20-08-2018（O）

YTLX DD 15/8 NOTED N TKS V R IN A POSITION TO ACCEPT PRC AT USD370/TON CIF SINGAPORE L/C AT SIGHT

23-08-2018（I）

PLS LOWER YOUR PRC TO USD360/TON L/C AFTER 30 DAYS 2000TONS EQUAL LOTS DEC/JAN

25-08-2018（O）

YTLX DD 23/8 NOTED YOUR PRICE ACCEPTED L/C AT SIGHT

26-08-2018(I)

YTLX DD 25/8 NOTED V CFM CHINESE RICE SAME AS SAMPLE AT USD360/TON CIF SINGAPORE 2000TONS EQUAL LOTS DEC/JAN PLS RUSH S/C FOR OPEN L/C

27-08-2018(O)

YTLX DD 26/8 NOTED TO ESTABLISH BIZ WZ U V CFM CHINA RICE SAME AS SAMPLE CIF SINGAPORE USD360/TON 2000TONS EQUAL LOTS DEC/JAN IRREVOCABLE SIGHT L/C REACH US NOT LATER THAN 15TH OCTOBER S/C DHL U AND OUR BANK COMMUNICATION BANK SHANGHAI ADD. 200 JIANG XI ZHONG RD PLS RUSH LC ASAP

上 海 远 大 进 出 口 公 司　正本
SHANGHAI YUANDA IMPORT & EXPORT COMPANY ORIGINAL
上海市溧阳路 1088 号龙邸大厦 16 楼
16th Floor, Dragon Mansion, 1088 Liyang Road, Shanghai 200081 China
电话(Tel):0086-21-56666624　传真(Fax):0086-21-56666698

销 货 合 约
SALES CONTRACT

编号 No.: _____
日期 Date: _____

买方
Buyers:_____

地址
Address:_____

电话　　　　　　　　　　　　　　　　　传真
Tel: _____　　Fax: _____

兹经买卖双方同意成交下列商品订立条款如下：
The Undersigned Sellers and Buyers have agreed to close the following transaction according to the terms and conditions stipulated below.

货物名称及规格 Name of commodity and Specifications	数 量 Quantity	单 价 Unit Price	金 额 Amount
	总 值 Total Amount		

包装
Packing

装运
Shipment

保险
Insurance

付款
Payment

卖方 SELLERS _____　　　买方 BUYERS _____

13. 根据以下成交信息填制销售合同，注意条款的正确与完整：

买方： STEPS GENERAL TRADING EST.，
P.O. BOX. 1240
DUBAI
U.A.E.

卖方： SHANGHAI LIHUA TRADING COMPANY
856 HUTAI ROAD
SHANGHAI
CHINA

成交日期：2018 年 3 月 9 日
合同编号：STEP-08BS02
成交商品：

货　号	品　　名	包装方式	
SIT4958	Baby Stroller	每辆装 1 个纸箱	
成交数量	成交价格	成交条件	
200 辆	80.5 美元/辆	CFR	

货　号	品　　名	包装方式	
SIT3455	Baby Stroller	每 2 辆装 1 个纸箱	
成交数量	成交价格	成交条件	
720 辆	46.6 美元/辆	CFR	

货　号	品　　名	包装方式	
LIE1476	Baby Stroller	每辆装 1 个纸箱	
成交数量	成交价格	成交条件	
170 辆	105 美元/辆	CFR	

每个货号装一个 20 英尺整箱，共计装 3 个 20 英尺集装箱。

2018 年 5 月底前装运，由上海港海运至阿联酋迪拜港，不允许转运。

付款方式为按合同总额开立的见票后 30 天付款的不可撤销信用证；该信用证必须在 2018 年 3 月底前开抵卖方，并明确规定至货物装船后的第十五天在中国议付有效。

SALES CONTRACT

NO. _____

DATE _____

SELLER _____ BUYER _____

_____ _____

_____ _____

ART. NO.	NAME OF COMMODITY & SPECIFICATIONS	QUANTITY	UNIT PRICE	AMOUNT
TOTAL AMOUNT IN WORDS				

PACKING: _____

_____

_____

_____

SHIPMENT: _____

_____

_____

_____

INSURANCE: _____

_____

_____

_____

PAYMENT: _____

_____

_____

_____

14.

2018 年 3 月 21 日收到温哥华客户
Kiddie Korner, Inc.订单 No. C008

与仓库联系，有现货。

缮制合同 No. CA02，达成一笔信用证交易，约定 4 月底出运。

3 月 23 日给国外客户去函，另寄合同，要求会签。

请根据上述情景，完成最后一步操作。

15.

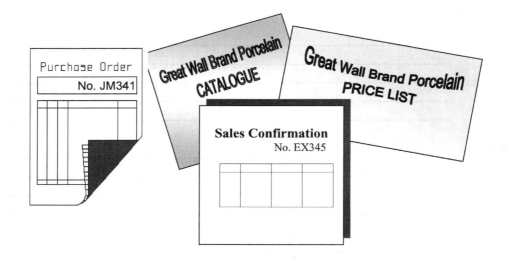

长时间磋商后，终于收到订购我方瓷器的订单。请给该客户去函，并附寄销售合同、新产品目录及价目表。

（注：该笔交易为信用证交易）

第五章　信用证审核与修改

案　例

2018 年 10 月 2 日,环宇公司收到 Tivolian 公司的会签函(第 132 页)。

2018 年 10 月 5 日,环宇公司收到 Tivolian 公司寄来的会签合同(第 133—134 页)和两种产品标签。

2018 年 10 月 8 日,环宇公司收到中国银行上海分行的信用证通知书(第 135 页)和 F. Van Lanschot Bankiers N. V. 银行开立的信用证(第 136—137 页),填写《信用证分析单》,并根据合同对信用证进行审核。

2018 年 10 月 9 日,针对审核信用证时发现的问题,环宇公司拟函联系客户。考虑到鹿特丹属于欧洲基本港,直达运输的船期完全能满足信用证的要求,故不再对信用证中禁止转运的规定提出修改。

工作任务

1. 分析审核国外来证,填写《信用证分析单》。

2. 拟写改证函,要求客户联系开证行进行相应修改。

会签函

Countersigning contract HY-TIV0373

Sender ：　Chila Trooborg <chtrooborg@tivolian.nl>
Date ：　2-Oct-2018
Receiver ：　David Wang <d.wang@universal.com.cn>

Dear Mr. Wang,

　　Your S/C No. HY-TIV0373 has been received with thanks.

　　We confirmed your adjustment in the quantity and have counter signed the contract. One hard copy has been returned by DHL as you required.

　　The relative labels for the goods have also been included in the parcel. And we will apply for the letter of credit soon. Please arrange shipment in time.

　　Thank you.

　　　　　　　　　　　　　　　　　　　　Yours truly,
　　　　　　　　　　　　　　　　　　　　Chila Trooborg

Chila Trooborg
Purchase Manager
Tivolian Trading B.V.
Heiman Dullaertolein 3, 3024 CA Rotterdam, the Netherlands
Tel: 31 - 10 - 4767418
Fax: 31 - 10 - 4767422
www.tivolian.nl

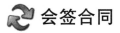 会签合同

Shanghai Universal Trading Co., Ltd.

Rm. 1201-1216 Mayling Plaza,
131 Dongfang Rd.,
Shanghai, 200120, China
Tel: 86-21-58818844
Fax: 86-21-58818766

SALES CONFIRMATION

S/C No.: HY-TIV0373
S/C Date: Sept. 29, 2018

To: Tivolian Trading B.V.

P.O. Box 1783m Heiman Dullaertolein 3,

3024CA Rotterdam, the Netherlands

We hereby confirm having sold to you the following goods on terms and conditions as specified below:

Item No.	Name of Commodity & Specifications		Quantity	Unit Price	Amount
	Plush Toys			CIF Rotterdam Incoterms 2010	
	details as per the samples dispatched by the seller on Sept. 25, 2018				
1	KB0278	Twin Bear	504 sets	US$9.60	US$4,838.40
2	KB5411	Twin Bear in Ballet Costume	504 sets	US$11.50	US$5,796.00
3	KB0677	Brown Bear with Red Bow	536 sets	US$14.50	US$7,772.00
4	KB7900	Bear in Pink T-shirt	536 sets	US$15.40	US$8,254.40
		Total:	2080 sets		US$26,660.80

Total Amount in Words: Say U.S. Dollars Twenty Six Thousand Six Hundred and Sixty and Cents Eighty Only

Packing: KB0278 & KB5411: the label " CE/IMP. 087" to be attached to each piece,
KB0677 & KB7900: the label " F-TOYS 228" to be attached to each piece,
KB0278 & KB5411 to be packed in cartons of 4 sets each, equally assorted in one 20'FCL,
KB0677 & KB7900 to be packed in cartons of 8 sets each, equally assorted in one 20'FCL,
Total 386 cartons in two 20'FCL.

Shipment: To be effected during November 2018 from Shanghai, China to Rotterdam, the Netherlands
with partial shipments prohibited and transshipment permitted.

Insurance: To be covered by the seller for 110% of invoice value against All Risks and War Risks as per
the Ocean Marine Cargo Clauses of P.I.C.C dated Jan.1, 1981.

Payment: The buyer should open through a bank acceptable to the seller an irrevocable letter of credit
payable at sight for 100% of the contract value to reach the seller by the middle of October 2018
and valid for negotiation in China until the 15th day after the date of shipment.

Confirmed by:

THE SELLER
Shanghai Universal Trading Co., Ltd.

李邓

THE BUYER
Tivolian Trading B.V.

Henther Merton

(signature)

REMARKS:

1　The Buyer shall have the covering letter of credit reach the Seller 45 days before shipment, failing which the Seller reserves the right to rescind without further notice, or to regard as still valid whole or any part of this contract not fulfilled by the Buyer, or to lodge a claim for losses thus sustained, if any.

2　In case of any discrepancy in quality, claim should be filed by the Buyer within 30 days after the arrival of the goods at port of destination; while for quantity discrepancy, claim should be filed by the Buyer within 15 days after the arrival of the goods at port of destination.

3　For transactions concluded on C.I.F. basis, it is understood that the insurance amount will be for 110% of the invoice value against the risks specified in this contract. If additional insurance amount or coverage required, the Buyer must have the consent of the Seller before shipment, and the additional premium is to be borne by the Buyer.

4　The Seller shall not hold liable for non-delivery or delay in delivery of the entire lot or a portion of the goods hereabove by reason of natural disasters, war or other causes of Force Majeure. However, the Seller shall notify the Buyer as soon as possible and furnish the Buyer within 15 days by registered airmail with a certificate issued by the China Council for the Promotion of International Trade attesting such event(s).

5　All disputes arising out of the performance of, or relating to this contract, shall be settled through negotiation. In case no settlement can be reached through negotiation, the case shall then be submitted to the China International Economic and Trade Arbitration Commission for arbitration in accordance with its arbitral rules. The arbitration shall take place in Shanghai. The arbitral award is final and binding upon both parties.

6　The Buyer is requested to sign and return one copy of this contract immediately after receipt of the same. Objection, if any, should be raised by the Buyer within 3 working days, otherwise it is understood that the Buyer has accepted the terms and conditions of this contract.

7　Special conditions: (These shall prevail over all printed terms in case of any conflict.)

信用证通知书

中国银行
BANK OF CHINA   **SHANGHAI BRANCH**

ADDRESS: 200 YIN CHENG RD(M)
TELEX: 33062 BOCSH CN
SWIFT: BKCHCNBJ300

信 用 证 通 知 书
Notification of Documentary Credit

To: 致:	WHEN CORRESPONDING PLEASE QUOTE OUR REF.NO	YEAR-MONTH-DAY
SHANGHAI UNIVERSAL TRADING CO., LTD. MAYING PLAZA, 131 DONGFANG ROAD, SHANGHAI 200120, CHINA		BP70221563 2018-10-8

Issuing Bank 开证行	Transmitted to us through 转递行/转让行
F. VAN LANSCHOT BANKIERS N.V. ROTTERDAM, NETHERLANDS	

L/C No. 信用证号 AM/VA07721SLC	Dated 开证日期 2018-10-8	Amount 金额 US$26,660.80

Dear Sirs, 迳启者

We advise you that we have received from the a/m bank a(n) letter of credit, contents of which are as per attached sheet(s).
兹通知贵司，我行收自上述银行信用证 份，现随附通知。
This advice and the attached sheet(s) must accompany the relative documents when presented for negotiation.
贵司交单时，请将本通知书及信用证一并提示。
This advice does not convey any engagement or obligation on our part unless we have added our confirmation.
本通知书不构成我行对此信用证的任何责任和义务，但我行对本证如具保兑的除外。
If you find any terms and conditions in the L/C which you are unable to comply with and/or any error(s), it is suggested that you contact applicant directly for necessary amendment(s) so as to avoid any difficulties which may arise when documents are presented.
如本信用证中有无法办到的条款及/或错误，请径与开证申请人联系，进行必要的修改，以排除交单时可能发生的问题。
THIS L/C IS ADVISED SUBJECT TO ICC UCP PUBLICATION NO.600
本信用证之通知系遵循国际商会跟单信用证统一惯例第600号出版物办理。

This L/C consists of   three   sheet(s), including the covering letter and attachment(s).
本信用证连同面函及附件共   3   页。

Remarks: 备注：

感谢您选择中行，我们将竭诚服务
我行电话总机：38824588 传真：50372594
信用证通知查询电话：22111，22108分机
信用证转让咨询：22106分机
国外银行资信调查及保兑：21126，21129分机
敬请垂询我行卜列贸易融资服务：
福费廷（包买票据）和保理业务：22046，22047分机
出口押汇业务：22028，22030，22057分机
也可就近向我们各个支行的国际结算科查询

Yours faithfully,
For **BANK OF CHINA**

信用证

```
2018OCT08        07:29:18                                 LOGICAL TERMINAL
MT  S700                  ISSUE OF A DOCUMENTARY CREDIT         PAGE
                                                               FUNC
                                                               UMR
MSGACK DWS765I AUTH OK, KEY B6852DT5E5896841, BKCHCNBJ BKCHSGSG RECORD
BASIC HEADER            F 01      BKCHCN3JA300        2576    87612
APPLICATION HEADER      O   700   7992  181008  FVLBNL2RXXX 6385 938271    181008   379  N
                                  F.VAN LANSCHOT BANKIERS N.V.
                                  *ROTTERDAM
                                  *NETHERLANDS
USER HEADER  SERVICE CODE          103:
             BANK. PRIORITY        113:
             MSG USER REF.         108:
             INFO. FROM CI         115:
SEQUENCE OF TOTAL       * 27    : 1/1
FORM OF DOC. CREDIT     * 40A   : IRREVOCABLE
APPLICABLE RULES        40E     : UCP600
DOC. CREDIT NUMBER      * 20    : AM/VA07721SLC
DATE OF ISSUE           31C     : 181008
DATE AND PLACE OF EXPIRY * 31D  : DATE 181130  PLACE  NETHERLANDS
APPLICANT               * 50    : TIVOLIAN TRADING B.V.
                                  P.O.BOX 1783, HEIMAN DULLAERTOLEIN 3, 3024CA
                                  ROTTERDAM, NETHERLANDS
BENEFICIARY             * 59    : SHANGHAI UNIVERSAL TRADING CO., LTD.
                                  MAYING PLAZA, 131 DONGFANG ROAD,
                                  SHANGHAI 200120, CHINA
CURRENCY CODE, AMOUNT   * 32B   : CURRENCY U    SD    AMOUNT      26660.80
AVAILABLE WITH/BY       * 41D   : ANY BANK BY NEGOTIATION
DRAFT AT ...            42C     : AT 30 DAYS  AFTER SIGHT FOR FULL INVOICE VALUE
DRAWEE                  42A     : F.VAN LANSCHOT BANKIERS N.V.
                                  ROTTERDAM, NETHERLANDS
PARTIAL SHIPMENTS       43P     : ALLOWED
TRANSSHIPMENT           43T     : PROHIBITED
LOADING ON BOARD / DISPATCH / TAKING IN CHARGE AT /FROM    44A:     SHANGHAI
FOR TRANSPORT TO...     44B     : ROTTERDAM
LATEST DATE OF SHIP.    44C     : 181115
DESCRIPT. OF GOODS AND/OR SERVICES              45A        :
        4 ITEMS OF TOTAL 2088 SETS OF PLUSH TOYS AS PER APPLICANT'S ORDER
        NUMBER TIV-PO-CSH0873 AND BENEFICIARY'S CONTRACT NUMBER HY-TIV0373
        LABEL: CE/IMP.087 FOR ARTICLES KB0278, KB5411
        LABEL: F-TOYS 228 FOR ARTICLES KB0677, KB7900
        TERMS OF DELIVERY: CIF ROTTERDAM (INCOTERMS 2010)
        PACKING IN NEUTRAL SEAWORTHY EXPORT CARTONS SUITABLE FOR LONG
        DISTANCE OCEAN TRANSPORTATION
        SHIPPING MARKS:            CE/IMP.087
                                   TIV-PO-CSH0873
                                   ROTTERDAM
                                   CARTON NO. 1 AND UP
                                   FOLLOWED BY: ARTICLE NUMBER   AND
```

F-TOYS 228
TIV-PO-CSH0873
ROTTERDAM
CARTON NO. 1 AND UP
FOLLOWED BY: ARTICLE NUMBER
ALL OF THE ABOVE MUST BE STATED ON THE INVOICE AND PACKING LIST.

DOCUMENTS REQUIRED　　　　46A :
+ SIGNED COMMERCIAL INVOICE IN QUINTUPLICATE MADE OUT IN THE NAME OF
APPLICANT INDICATING FOB VALUE AND THE ORIGIN OF THE GOODS SHIPPED.
+ PACKING LIST/WEIGHT MEMO IN TRIPLICATE MENTIONING TOTAL NUMBER OF CARTONS
AND GROSS WEIGHT AND MEASUREMENTS PER EXPORT CARTON.
+ 2/3 OF ORIGINAL CLEAN ON-BOARD MARINE BILLS OF LADING, PLUS 3 N.N.-COPIES MADE
OUT "TO ORDER" AND BLANK ENDORSED MARKED "FREIGHT PREPAID" SHOWING AS
NOTIFY THE APPLICANT (GIVING FULL NAME, ADDRESS AND PHONE NUMBERS) AND
INDICATING THE NAME AND ADDRESS OF THE CARRIER'S AGENT AT THE PORT OF
DISCHARGE.
+ FULL SET 3/3 OF MARINE INSURANCE POLICY OR CERTIFICATE, ENDORSED IN BLANK FOR
120 PERCENT OF FULL CIF VALUE, COVERING INSTITUTE CARGO CLAUSES (A) AND
INSTITUTE WAR CLAUSES - CARGO.
+ COPY OF G.S.P. CERTIFICATE OF ORIGIN FORM A IN DUPLICATE STATING THAT THE
GOODS ARE OF CHINESE ORIGIN.
+ BENEFICIARY'S CERTIFICATE STATING THAT ONE SET OF NON-NEGOTIABLE SHIPPING
DOCUMENTS TOGETHER WITH THE 1/3 ORIGINAL B/L AND ORIGINAL GSP FORM A
HAVE BEEN SENT TO THE APPLICANT BY DHL WITHIN 72 HOURS AFTER SHIPMENT.
+ ORIGINAL AND COPY OF QUALITY INSPECTION CERTIFICATE ISSUED AND SIGNED BY
THE APPLICANT.
+ COPY OF BENEFICIARY'S FAX SENT TO APPLICANT (FAX-NO. +(31)10 4767422) WITHIN
2 WORKING DAYS AFTER SHIPMENT INDICATING DATE OF DEPARTURE, SHIPPING MARKS,
NUMBERS OF LC, B/L, CONTRACT AND ORDER AS WELL AS NUMBER OF CARTONS SHIPPED
TOGETHER WITH THE TOTAL GROSS WEIGHT AND GOODS VALUE.

CHARGES　　　　　　　　71B　: ALL BANKING CHARGES INCLUDING OPENING FEE ARE FOR
BENEFICIARY'S ACCOUNT.

PERIOD OF PRESENTATION　　48　: DOCUMENTS TO BE PRESENTED WITHIN 15 DAYS AFTER
THE DATE OF ISSUANCE OF TRANSPORT DOCUMENT(S)
BUT WITHIN THE VALIDITY OF THIS CREDIT.

CONFIRMATION INSTRUCTIONS　*49　: WITHOUT

ADDITIONAL CONDITIONS　　47A　:
+ ALL DOCUMENTS MUST INDICATE THIS CREDIT NUMBER.
+ THE CARRYING VESSEL SHOULD BELONG TO CONFERENCE LINE AND NOT MORE THAN
20 YEARS OLD. A CERTIFICATE TO THIS EFFECT ISSUED BY THE SHIPPING COMPANY
TO BE PRESENTED WITH THE L/C DOCUMENTS UPON NEGOTIATION.
+ ALL DOCUMENTS TO BE SENT TO F.VAN LANSCHOT BANKIERS N.V. WESTERSINGEL
74 3015 L B ROTTERDAM TEL: +31 (0) 10 440 20 20 FAX +31 (0) 10 440 20 90
IN ONE LOT BY INTERNATIONAL COURIER SERVICE.

INSTRUCTION TO THE PAYING /ACCEPTING/NEGOTIATING BANK　　　　78 :
+ T.T. REIMBURSEMENT IS NOT ACCEPTABLE.
+ A DISCREPANCY FEE OF USD80 WILL BE DEDUCTED FROM THE PROCEEDS IF DOCUMENTS
ARE PRESENTED WITH DISCREPANCY(IES) AND ACCEPTANCE OF SUCH DISCREPANT
DOCUMENTS WILL NOT IN ANY WAY ALTER THE TERMS AND CONDITIONS OF THIS
CREDIT.
+ UPON RECEIPT OF CORRECT DOCUMENTS BY US, WE SHALL COVER THE NEGOTIATING
BANK AS PER THEIR INSTRUCTIONS, IN THE CURRENCY OF THIS CREDIT ONLY.

SENDER TO RECEIVER INFORMATION　　72　:　　　　PLS ACKNOWLEDGE RECEIPT

信用证分析单

上海环宇贸易有限公司
Shanghai Universal Trading Co., Ltd.

信 用 证 分 析 单

1 信用证文本格式　　☐　信开　　☐　屯开　　☐　SWIFT

2 信用证号码

3 开证日　　　　　　　　　　年　　　　　月　　　　　日

4 到期日　　　　　　　　　　年　　　　　月　　　　　日

5 到期地点

6 兑付方式　　　　　☐　付款　　☐　承兑　　☐　议付

7 兑付银行

8 信用证金额

9 金额允许增减幅度

10 交单期

11 开证申请人

12 受益人

13 开证银行

14 通知银行

15 货物名称

16 价格/交货/贸易术语

17 最迟装运日　　　　　　　　　年　　　　　月　　　　　日

18 装运港

19 目的港

20 分批装运　　　　　☐　允许　　☐　不允许

21 转运　　　　　　　☐　允许　　☐　不允许

22 运输标志

23 运输方式　　　　　☐　海运　　☐　空运　　☐　陆运

24 应向银行提交的单据及具体份数

名称	汇票	发票	装箱单	重量单	尺码单	海运提单	空运提单	货物承运收据	原产地证明	保险单
份数										

名称	检验证书	装船通知	寄单证明	受益人证明（其他内容）	承运人/船公司证明	其他单据
份数						

25 单据要求

　　1）汇票

　　　　金额

　　　　付款期限

　　　　付款人（受票人）

2）　**发票**

种类 ＿＿＿＿＿＿＿＿＿＿＿＿＿＿＿＿＿＿＿＿＿＿＿＿＿＿

出具人 ＿＿＿＿＿＿＿＿＿＿＿＿＿＿＿＿＿＿＿＿＿＿＿＿

特殊要求 ＿＿＿＿＿＿＿＿＿＿＿＿＿＿＿＿＿＿＿＿＿＿

3）　**包装单据　（装箱单/重量单/尺码单）**

种类 ＿＿＿＿＿＿＿＿＿＿＿＿＿＿＿＿＿＿＿＿＿＿＿＿＿＿

出具人 ＿＿＿＿＿＿＿＿＿＿＿＿＿＿＿＿＿＿＿＿＿＿＿＿

特殊要求 ＿＿＿＿＿＿＿＿＿＿＿＿＿＿＿＿＿＿＿＿＿＿

4）　**提单**

种类 ＿＿＿＿＿＿＿＿＿＿＿＿＿＿＿＿＿＿＿＿＿＿＿＿＿＿

出具人 ＿＿＿＿＿＿＿＿＿＿＿＿＿＿＿＿＿＿＿＿＿＿＿＿

特殊要求 ＿＿＿＿＿＿＿＿＿＿＿＿＿＿＿＿＿＿＿＿＿＿

5）　**原产地证明**

种类 ＿＿＿＿＿＿＿＿＿＿＿＿＿＿＿＿＿＿＿＿＿＿＿＿＿＿

出具人 ＿＿＿＿＿＿＿＿＿＿＿＿＿＿＿＿＿＿＿＿＿＿＿＿

特殊要求 ＿＿＿＿＿＿＿＿＿＿＿＿＿＿＿＿＿＿＿＿＿＿

6）　**保险单**

种类 ＿＿＿＿＿＿＿＿＿＿＿＿＿＿＿＿＿＿＿＿＿＿＿＿＿＿

出具人 ＿＿＿＿＿＿＿＿＿＿＿＿＿＿＿＿＿＿＿＿＿＿＿＿

特殊要求 ＿＿＿＿＿＿＿＿＿＿＿＿＿＿＿＿＿＿＿＿＿＿

7）　**检验证书**

种类 ＿＿＿＿＿＿＿＿＿＿＿＿＿＿＿＿＿＿＿＿＿＿＿＿＿＿

出具人 ＿＿＿＿＿＿＿＿＿＿＿＿＿＿＿＿＿＿＿＿＿＿＿＿

特殊要求 ＿＿＿＿＿＿＿＿＿＿＿＿＿＿＿＿＿＿＿＿＿＿

8）　**装船通知**

种类 ＿＿＿＿＿＿＿＿＿＿＿＿＿＿＿＿＿＿＿＿＿＿＿＿＿＿

出具人 ＿＿＿＿＿＿＿＿＿＿＿＿＿＿＿＿＿＿＿＿＿＿＿＿

特殊要求 ＿＿＿＿＿＿＿＿＿＿＿＿＿＿＿＿＿＿＿＿＿＿

9）　**寄单证明**

种类 ＿＿＿＿＿＿＿＿＿＿＿＿＿＿＿＿＿＿＿＿＿＿＿＿＿＿

出具人 ＿＿＿＿＿＿＿＿＿＿＿＿＿＿＿＿＿＿＿＿＿＿＿＿

特殊要求 ＿＿＿＿＿＿＿＿＿＿＿＿＿＿＿＿＿＿＿＿＿＿

10）　**受益人证明（其他内容）**

种类 ＿＿＿＿＿＿＿＿＿＿＿＿＿＿＿＿＿＿＿＿＿＿＿＿＿＿

出具人 ＿＿＿＿＿＿＿＿＿＿＿＿＿＿＿＿＿＿＿＿＿＿＿＿

特殊要求 ＿＿＿＿＿＿＿＿＿＿＿＿＿＿＿＿＿＿＿＿＿＿

11）　**承运人/船公司证明**

种类 ＿＿＿＿＿＿＿＿＿＿＿＿＿＿＿＿＿＿＿＿＿＿＿＿＿＿

出具人 ＿＿＿＿＿＿＿＿＿＿＿＿＿＿＿＿＿＿＿＿＿＿＿＿

特殊要求 ＿＿＿＿＿＿＿＿＿＿＿＿＿＿＿＿＿＿＿＿＿＿

12）　**其他单据**

种类 ＿＿＿＿＿＿＿＿＿＿＿＿＿＿＿＿＿＿＿＿＿＿＿＿＿＿

出具人 ＿＿＿＿＿＿＿＿＿＿＿＿＿＿＿＿＿＿＿＿＿＿＿＿

特殊要求 ＿＿＿＿＿＿＿＿＿＿＿＿＿＿＿＿＿＿＿＿＿＿

26 特别条款

       ① _____

       ② _____

       ③ _____

27 银行费用

       ① _____

       ② _____

       ③ _____

28 信用证审核意见

    1) 信用证条款：_____

       存在问题：_____

       修改意见：_____

    2) 信用证条款：_____

       存在问题：_____

       修改意见：_____

    3) 信用证条款：_____

       存在问题：_____

       修改意见：_____

    4) 信用证条款：_____

       存在问题：_____

       修改意见：_____

    5) 信用证条款：_____

       存在问题：_____

       修改意见：_____

    6) 信用证条款：_____

       存在问题：_____

       修改意见：_____

    7) 信用证条款：_____

       存在问题：_____

       修改意见：_____

    8) 信用证条款：_____

       存在问题：_____

       修改意见：_____

    9) 信用证条款：_____

       存在问题：_____

       修改意见：_____

   10) 信用证条款：_____

       存在问题：_____

       修改意见：_____

示 范

上海环宇贸易有限公司
Shanghai Universal Trading Co., Ltd.

信 用 证 分 析 单

1 信用证文本格式	☐ 信开	☐ 电开	☑ SWIFT	
2 信用证号码	AM/VA07721SLC			
3 开证日	2018 年 10 月 8 日			
4 到期日	2018 年 11 月 30 日			
5 到期地点	荷兰			
6 兑付方式	☐ 付款	☐ 承兑	☑ 议付	
7 兑付银行	任何银行			
8 信用证金额	USD26660.80			
9 金额允许增减幅度	/			
10 交单期	运输单据签发日后15天内，且在信用证的有效期内			
11 开证申请人	TIVOLIAN TRADING B.V.			
12 受益人	SHANGHAI UNIVERSAL TRADING CO., LTD.			
13 开证银行	F. VAN LANSCHOT BANKIERS N.V., ROTTERDAM, NETHERLANDS			
14 通知银行	BANK OF CHINA, SHANGHAI BRANCH			
15 货物名称	4 ITEMS OF TOTAL 2088 SETS OF PLUSH TOYS			
16 价格/交货/贸易术语	CIF ROTTERDAM (INCOTERMS 2010)			
17 最迟装运日	2018 年 11 月 15 日			
18 装运港	SHANGHAI			
19 目的港	ROTTERDAM			
20 分批装运	☑ 允许	☐ 不允许		
21 转运	☐ 允许	☑ 不允许		
22 运输标志	CE/IMP. 087 / TIV-PO-CSH0873 / ROTTERDAM / CARTON NO.1 AND UP / KB0278			
	CE/IMP. 087 / TIV-PO-CSH0873 / ROTTERDAM / CARTON NO.1 AND UP / KB5411			
	F-TOYS 228 / TIV-PO-CSH0873 / ROTTERDAM / CARTON NO.1 AND UP / KB0677			
	F-TOYS 228 / TIV-PO-CSH0873 / ROTTERDAM / CARTON NO.1 AND UP / KB7900			
23 运输方式	☑ 海运	☐ 空运	☐ 陆运	

24 应向银行提交的单据及具体份数

名称	汇票	发票	装箱单	重量单	尺码单	海运提单	空运提单	货物承运收据	原产地证明	保险单
份数	1式2联	5份	3份	/	/	2/3正本+3份副本	/	/	2份副本	全套3份

名称	检验证书	装船通知	寄单证明	受益人证明（其他内容）	承运人/船公司证明	其他单据
份数	1份正本+1份副本	1份	1份	/	1份	/

25 单据要求

　　1）汇票

　　　　金额　　　　　发票全额

　　　　付款期限　　　见票后30天

　　　　付款人(受票人) F.VAN LANSCHOT BANKIERS N.V., ROTTERDAM, NETHERLANDS

　　2）发票

　　　　种类　　　　　商业发票

　　　　出具人　　　　/

　　　　特殊要求　　　经签署，以开证申请人为抬头，注明FOB金额及其原产地，注明信用证中的货物描述

　　3）包装单据　（装箱单/重量单/尺码单）

　　　　种类　　　　　装箱/重量单

　　　　出具人　　　　/

　　　　特殊要求　　　显示总箱数、每箱的毛重和尺码，注明信用证中的货物描述

　　4）提单

　　　　种类　　　　　清洁、已装船、海运提单

　　　　出具人　　　　/

　　　　特殊要求　　　凭指示抬头，空白背书，标明"运费已付"，被通知方为开证申请人（指明其全称、地址和电话号码），注明承运人在卸货港的代理的名称和地址

　　5）原产地证明

　　　　种类　　　　　普惠制原产地证格式A

　　　　出具人　　　　/

　　　　特殊要求　　　说明货物原产自中国

　　6）保险单

　　　　种类　　　　　海运保险单或保险凭证

　　　　出具人　　　　/

　　　　特殊要求　　　空白背书，按CIF总金额的120%投保协会货物（A）险和协会战争险

　　7）检验证书

　　　　种类　　　　　品质检验证书

　　　　出具人　　　　开证申请人

　　　　特殊要求　　　经签署

　　8）装船通知

　　　　种类　　　　　传真副本

　　　　出具人　　　　受益人

　　　　特殊要求　　　装船后2个工作日内受益人向开证申请人发出传真，告知离港日期、运输标志、信用证号码、提单号码、合同号码、订单号码、装运箱数、总毛重和货物价值

　　9）寄单证明

　　　　种类　　　　　/

　　　　出具人　　　　受益人

　　　　特殊要求　　　证明一套不可议付的装运单据连同3份正本海运提单中的1份及正本普惠制原产地证明格式A已在装运后72小时内通过DHL寄给了开证申请人

10）受益人证明（其他内容）

种类　　　　/

出具人　　　/

特殊要求　　/

11）承运人/船公司证明

种类　　　　/

出具人　　　船公司

特殊要求　　证明承运船只隶属于班轮公会，船龄不超过20年

12）其他单据

种类　　　　/

出具人　　　/

特殊要求　　/

26 特别条款

① 所有单据须注明信用证号码

② 所有单据须通过国际快递一次性寄往开证行

③

27 银行费用

① 所有银行费用包括开证费用均由受益人承担。

② 不符单据处理费为每次80美元。

③

28 信用证审核意见

1）信用证条款：　**31D　EXPIRY PLACE NETHERLANDS**

存在问题：　与合同规定 valid in China 不符

修改意见：　改为在中国到期

2）信用证条款：　**59　MAYING PLAZA**

存在问题：　与合同规定 Mayling Plaza 不符

修改意见：　改为 MAYLING PLAZA

3）信用证条款：　**42C　AT 30 DAYS AFTER SIGHT**

存在问题：　与合同规定 payable at sight 不符

修改意见：　改为即期

4）信用证条款：　**43P　ALLOWED**

存在问题：　与合同规定 partial shipments prohibited 不符

修改意见：　宽于合同规定，不必提出修改

5）信用证条款：　**43T　PROHIBITED**

存在问题：　与合同规定 transshipment permitted 不符

修改意见：　改为允许转运

6）信用证条款：　**44C　181115**

存在问题：　与合同规定 shipment during November 2018 不符

修改意见：　改为 181130

7) 信用证条款： **31D   181130**

存在问题： 最迟装运日推迟后，信用证到期日应作相应的顺延

修改意见： 改为 **181215**

8) 信用证条款： **45A   TOTAL 2088 SETS OF PLUSH TOYS**

存在问题： 与合同规定 **2080 SETS** 不符

修改意见： 改为 **2080 SETS**

9) 信用证条款： **46A   +   2/3 OF ORIGINAL CLEAN ON-BOARD MARINE BILLS OF**
LADING ...

+   BENEFICIARY'S CERTIFICATE STATING THAT ... 1/3
ORIGINAL B/L ... HAVE BEEN SENT TO THE APPLICANT
BY DHL WITHIN 72 HOURS AFTER SHIPMENT.

存在问题： 装运后72小时内将1/3正本提单直接寄给客户，无法保证出口商在收款之前
掌握货权

修改意见： 将3/3正本提单提交给银行，删除寄单证明中有关寄送1/3正本提单的内容

10) 信用证条款： **46A   ... INSURANCE POLICY ... FOR 120 PERCENT OF FULL CIF VALUE**
COVERING INSTITUTE CARGO CLAUSES (A) AND INSTITUTE WAR CLAUSES -
CARGO.

存在问题： 与合同规定 **for 110% of invoice value against All Risks and War Risks** 不符

修改意见： 改为按**110%**的CIF金额投保，险别可不要求修改

11) 信用证条款： **46A   ORIGINAL AND COPY OF QUALITY INSPECTION CERTIFICATE ISSUED**
AND SIGNED BY THE APPLICANT.

存在问题： 品质检验证书的签发权掌握在开证申请人手中，无法保证受益人及时正确交单

修改意见： 改为官方机构签发的品质检验证书

12) 信用证条款： **71B   ALL BANKING CHARGES INCLUDING OPENING FEE ARE FOR**
BENEFICIARY'S ACCOUNT.

存在问题： 按贸易惯例，开证费用不应由受益人承担

修改意见： 改为受益人承担发生在开证国以外的银行费用

Amending L/C under S/C HY-TIV0373

发件人：　David Wang <d.wang@universal.com.cn>
日　期：　2018年10月9日
收件人：　Chila Trooborg <chtrooborg@tivolian.nl>

上 海 环 宇 贸 易 有 限 公 司
Shanghai Universal Trading Co., Ltd.

Dear Mr. Trooborg

Thank you for your L/C No. AM/VA07721SLC issued by F.Van Lanschot Bankiers N.V. dated Oct. 8, 2018. However, we have found the following discrepancies after checking with our S/C No. HY-TIV0373.

1. Latest date of ship. 44C

Latest date of shipment should be 181130 as contracted, instead of 181115.

2. Date and place of expiry 31D

Expiry date should be extended to 181215 as contracted, i.e. 15 days after shipment.
Expiry place should be China as contracted, instead of Netherlands.

3. Beneficiary 59

Our address is Mayling Plaza, not Maying Plaza.

4. Draft at 42C

Draft should be payable at sight as contracted, instead of at 30 days after sight.

5. Descript. of goods and/or services 45A

Total quantity should be 2080 sets instead of 2088 sets, as you have confirmed to adjust so.

6. Documents required 46A

+ Please amend "2/3 of original" bills of lading to "Full set (3/3) original", and consequently delete the wording "the 1/3 original B/L" in the clause "Beneficiary's certificate stating that … sent to the applicant by DHL within 72 hours after shipment".

+ Please amend quality inspection certificate "issued and signed by the applicant" to "issued by competent authority at port of loading".

+ We notice you have increased the insurance amount to 120% of full CIF value instead of 110%. This will incur the additional premium, which is contracted to be borne by you. Please confirm.

7. Charges 71B

L/C opening fee is to be borne by the applicant according to the usual practice. So please amend to "All banking charges outside Netherlands are for beneficiary's account".

Please let us have the L/C Amendment soon so that we can effect shipment within the contracted time.

Best wishes

David Wang
Sales Manager
Shanghai Universal Trading Co., Ltd.
Tel: +86 21 58818863
Email: d.wang@universal.com.cn

中国上海市东方路 **131** 号美陵广场 **1201-1216** 室
Rm. 1201-1216 Mayling Plaza, 131 Dongfang Rd., Shanghai, 200120, China
电话/Tel: 86-21-58818844　传真/Fax: 86-21-58818766　网址/Web: www.universal.com.cn

🗨 示范评析

1. 在审核信用证之前,必须对信用证的信息进行分析、归纳。因此,填写《信用证分析单》是多数公司采用的一种有效方法。在分析信用证时,单据条款往往是其中的难点却又是重点,因为它直接关系到受益人日后是否能顺利交单结汇。无论单据条款如何复杂,都可以从单据种类、单据份数、出具人和特殊要求这四个方面进行分析。

2. 审核信用证的依据是买卖双方签订的合同,但并不意味着要将信用证修改成与合同完全一致。出具信用证审核意见时,应遵循以下审核原则:若信用证的要求比合同的要求更为严格,或使卖方权利受损,卖方(即受益人)可依据合同提出修改;若信用证的要求比合同的要求更为宽松,或对卖方履约不会造成实质性影响,卖方一般不提出修改。

例如本案例,合同规定以即期信用证结算,而信用证规定见票后 30 天付款,卖方原本即期收款的权利受到了损害,所以应当修改。相反,如果合同规定见票后 30 天付款,而信用证是即期的,卖方就不会提出修改。又如,合同规定按 110% CIF 金额投保中国保险条款的一切险和战争险,而信用证规定按 120% CIF 金额投保协会货物 A 险和战争险,我们不难发现,提高投保加成率会造成卖方保费支出增加,但由一切险改投协会货物 A 险,由于这两种险别的承保范围相近,保险公司计征的保险费率无二,对卖方并无实质性影响,所以应就投保加成率进行修改,而对险别的变化则可同意接受。

第二条审核原则是:若信用证中出现了双方未曾商议的条款,卖方应从是否限制了受益人权利,是否增加了受益人负担,是否会影响受益人交单,是否增加了受益人收汇风险的角度进行审核,如出现不能接受的条件,则要求修改。

例如本案例,寄单证明中要求将 1/3 正本提单直接用特快专递寄给客户,这就对出口商在收款之前掌握货物的控制权产生了不利影响。因为正本提单作为货物所有权的凭证,其中的任何一份都可以凭以提货,在开证行因单证不符拒付时,出口商很可能将面临货款两空的局面,因为进口商完全可以凭借已收到的 1/3 正本提单将货物提走。又如,信用证要求商检证书必须由开证申请人出具签署,这使得出口商处于不定的危险之中,因为开证申请人可能履行检验义务,也可能不履行,检验后可能签发商检证书,也可能不签发,受益人是否能交单就完全处在了开证申请人的控制之中。诸如此类影响出口商向银行提交符合信用证要求的单据或是影响出口商安全收款的信用证条款就一定要提出修改。

可见,信用证中那些与合同不相符合的条款,或是买卖双方未曾协商的条款,均可看作是买方提出的新条件,卖方应根据自身的利益来严谨判断,既不能草率牺牲磋商中争取到的利益,也不宜提出无谓的修改,更不能盲目接受附带高风险的交单条件。

3. 对信用证提出的修改意见必须完整,否则将无法达到修改的目的,甚至造成信用证条款之间的互相矛盾。例如,在提出删除寄单证明中自寄 1/3 正本提单的要求时,也需要相应地将向银行提交 2/3 正本提单的要求修改为向银行提交 3/3 正本提单。又如,在提出推迟最迟装运日的同时,还必须考虑到信用证的到期日需做相应变更。再如,若提出修改货物单价、数量,就必须关注信用证总金额的变化。

4. 我们必须明确,买方与开证行之间存在委托代理的关系,买方可以凭开证申请人的身份要求开证行修改信用证,而作为信用证受益人的卖方也只有通过买方向开证行提出改证的请求。所以改证函的收信人依然是买方,即开证申请人。

在根据审核意见提出改证要求时,应灵活处理、寻求更好的修改方式。例如本案例中,卖方在对待投保加成变更时,并没有简单地强调必须按合同规定修改,而是仔细地询问了买方的需求。这就使得若变更是由于买方笔误造成的,那卖方就尽到了善意提醒的职责,若变更是由于买方实际需要导致的,那卖方也给出了可行的解决方案。我们再举个例子,信用证中货物的数量有时会发生偏差,如果是少了,毫无疑问,我们应该要求进口方按照合同进行修改,如果是多了,我们除了简单地要求修改货物数量,也可以在货源充足的情况下,询问对方是否真的需要增订,如:When we checked the L/C, we have found the quantity specified is 600 sets instead of 500 sets as contracted. For your information, we are able to supply as much as you require in case you really wish to do so.

Q:客户来函中提到"… labels … sent … by DHL",请问 DHL 是指什么?

A:DHL,又称"敦豪国际",是知名的全球速递公司,DHL 这个名称来自其三位创始人姓氏首字母的缩写。国际上比较著名的速递公司还有 Fedex(联邦快递)、TNT(天地快运)、UPS(联合包裹)等。

Q:如何理解提单条款"2/3 OF ORIGINAL CLEAN ON-BOARD MARINE BILLS OF LADING, PLUS 3 N.N.-COPIES"? 2/3 是什么含义? N.N.-COPIES 又是指什么?

A:2/3 of original bills of lading 是指承运人一共出具 3 份正本提单、其中的

2 份正本提单，1/3 即指其中的 1 份正本。N.N.-COPIES 是指 non-negotiable cop-ies，意思是不可议付的副本。因此该提单条款对提单份数的要求是 2 份正本（共 3 份正本）加 3 份副本。值得注意的是，这里说的份数是指提交给银行的份数，并非船公司签发的份数。

Q：单据条款第 6 款提到的"shipping documents"是指提单吗？

A： Shipping documents 是指"装运单据"，通常指信用证项下除汇票以外的所有单据，包括商业发票、装箱单、运输单据、保险单据以及各类证明证书等。Transport documents（运输单据）在海运方式下才是指提单。

Q：信用证分析单中"包装单据（装箱单/重量单/尺码单）"是什么含义？是指包装单据有三种类型吗？"寄单证明"与"受益人证明（其他内容）"又是什么关系？

A： 包装单据泛指所有显示货物包装细节的单据，装箱单、重量单、尺码单只是最常见的三种类型，还有诸如规格单、搭配单等多种类型。受益人证明泛指所有由受益人签发的证明（certificate），寄单证明特指内容是证明其已按信用证要求寄发相关单据的受益人证明，也就是说，寄单证明仅是受益人证明的一种，还有很多其他内容的受益人证明。有关结汇单据的种类具体可参见**第十二章　出口交单结汇**的**指南**（第 332 页）。

附：本案例信用证的全文翻译

应用报头（开证行信息）：		F. VAN LANSCHOT BANKIERS N.V.
		＊　鹿特丹
		＊　荷兰

基本报头

报文页次	＊ 27	：	第 1 页，共 1 页
跟单信用证形式	＊ 40A	：	不可撤销跟单信用证
适用规则	40E	：	UCP600
跟单信用证号码	＊ 20	：	AM/VA07721SLC
开证日期	31C	：	2018 年 10 月 8 日
到期日及到期地点	＊ 31D	：	日期：2018 年 11 月 30 日，地点：荷兰
开证申请人	＊ 50	：	TIVOLIAN TRADING B.V.
			P.O. BOX 1783，HEIMAN DULLAERTOLEIN
			3，3024CA

ROTTERDAM，NETHERLANDS

受益人	* 59	:	上海环宇贸易有限公司
			中国上海市东方路 131 号美陵广场，邮编 200120
跟单信用证的货币及金额	* 32B	:	币种：美元，金额：26660.80
兑付银行及兑付方式	* 41D	:	在任何银行议付
汇票付款期限	42C	:	见票后 30 天、按发票全额付款
汇票付款人	42A	:	F. VAN LANSCHOT BANKIERS N.V.
			ROTTERDAM，NETHERLANDS
分批装运条款	43P	:	允许
转运条款	43T	:	不允许
装船、发运和接受监管的地点	44A	:	上海
货物发送最终目的地	44B	:	鹿特丹
最迟装运日期	44C	:	2018 年 11 月 15 日
货物/服务描述	45A	:	

4 个货号共计 2088 套毛绒玩具，与开证申请人的第 TIV-PO-CSH0873 号订单和受益人的第 HY-TIV0373 号合同一致；

标签：货号 KB0278 和 KB5411 为 CE/IMP.087

标签：货号 KB0677 和 KB7900 为 F-TOYS 228

交货条件：成本加保险费、运费至鹿特丹港（2010 年国际贸易术语解释通则）

采用中性包装、适合于长途海洋运输的出口纸箱

运输标志：CE/IMP.087

TIV-PO-CSH0873

ROTTERDAM

CARTON NO.1 AND UP

紧跟：货号

和

F-TOYS 228

TIV-PO-CSH0873

ROTTERDAM

CARTON NO.1 AND UP

紧跟：货号

上述内容均须在发票和装箱单上说明。

应提交单据	46A	:

- 经签署的商业发票一式五份,以开证申请人为抬头,注明货物的离岸价值及其原产地。
- 装箱/重量单一式三份,显示总箱数和每个出口纸箱的毛重和尺码。
- 三份正本清洁已装船海运提单中的二份加上三份不可议付的副本,作成凭指示抬头,空白背书,标明运费已付,显示被通知方为开证申请人(指明其全称、地址和电话号码),注明承运人在卸货港的代理的名称和地址。
- 全套(一式三份)海运保险单或保险凭证,空白背书,按到岸价值的120%投保协会货物条款中的协会货物 A 险和战争险。
- 普惠制原产地证明格式 A 副本一式二份,说明货物系中国原产。
- 受益人证明,证明一套不可议付的装运单据连同三份正本海运提单中的一份及正本普惠制原产地证明格式 A 已在装运后 72 小时内通过 DHL 寄给开证申请人。
- 由开证申请人出具并签署的品质检验证书的正本和副本。
- 受益人传真副本,该传真于装船后 2 个工作日内由受益人向开证申请人发出,通知离港日期、运输标志、信用证号码、提单号码、合同号码、订单号码、装运箱数、总毛重和货物价值。

费用负担	71B	：	所有银行费用包括开证费用均由受益人承担。
交单期限	48	：	单据须在运输单据签发日后 15 天内且在信用证的有效期内提交。
保兑指示	＊49	：	无保兑
附加条款	47A	：	

- 所有单据须注明本信用证号码。
- 由船公司签发的表明承运船只隶属于班轮公会、且船龄不超过 20 年的证明,该证明须随附其他信用证项下单据一并提交议付。
- 所有单据须通过国际快递的方式一次性寄往：F. VAN LANSCHOT BANKIERS N. V. ， WESTERSINGEL 74 3015 LB, ROTTERDAM，TEL：＋31(0) 10 4402020， FAX ＋31(0) 10 4402090

给付款行、承兑行或议付行的指示　　　　　78　：

- 不接受电汇索偿。
- 如提交单据含有不符点,我行将从款项收入中扣除 80 美元作为不符单据费用。接受存在不符点的单据无论如何都不会改变本信用证的条款。
- 我行收到正确的单据后,将按议付行的指示、仅以本信用证的货币对其进行偿付。

附言　　　　72　　：　　　请确认收到。

指　南

国际贸易货款结算的方式

　　货物买卖的基本特征表现为交易的一方交付货物,另一方给付货款。在日常生活中,购物付款是一件十分简单的事,交易双方一手交钱,一手交货,银货两讫,当场结算,十分方便。然而,当买卖较大数量的货物,且交易的双方分别处于两个不同地点时,货款的结算就会变得复杂起来。进出口交易是不同国家的商人之间进行的货物买卖,进出口货款的收付和国内贸易货款的结算相比,不仅使用的货币不同,结算方式及其操作方法也有很大差异。不仅如此,国际货物买卖的货款结算还会涉及各国有关的法律、国际结算惯例以及各国银行的业务处理习惯等。

　　那么,进出口贸易中买卖双方是如何结算货款的呢? 简单地说,不外乎三种方法:易货、付现和通过银行结算。以货换货是进出口商人结算货款最古老的方法,即一国的商人将本国的货物运往他国以换回本国所需的货物,这种结算方法不仅麻烦,而且成交的机会也十分有限。现金结算是在易货贸易基础上的一大进步,交易的双方用现金来结算货款,这种方法虽然十分简单,但是交易货币的运送对于商人来讲存在着很大的风险。而通过银行结算则为不同国家商人之间进行货款的结算提供了一种更为简便、快速和安全的方法。

　　在当今的国际贸易中,绝大多数交易的货款都是通过银行来结算的,银行进行贸易结算的具体方式通常有三种:汇付、跟单托收和信用证。根据结算操作中资金的流向还可将这些方式分为顺汇和逆汇两种:债务人主动支付款项给债权人的为顺汇;而债权人向债务人索取款项的则为逆汇。贸易结算中,以汇付方式收付货款属于顺汇,而以跟单托收和信用证方式收付货款则属于逆汇。

在进出口贸易中,交易的双方分处两个不同的国家或地区,尤其是在首次洽谈时,彼此之间不可能完全信任。因此,如何实现货物和货款的对流,对于买卖双方都是一个难题。采用汇付方式,尽管手续十分简便,费用也不高,但是它依托买卖双方中的一方对另一方商业信誉的信赖,提供信用和资金融通的一方将承受很大的资金负担和风险。采用跟单托收方式,进口商的资金压力较小,但出口商在货物出运后却面临着较大的收款风险,尽管出口商可以通过采用相对谨慎的交单条件来控制货物,但一旦进口商拒绝付款仍会使出口商遭受损失。相比而言,信用证支付方式下,银行向进口商提供了交单保证、进而在一定程度上约束了出口商的货物交付,还可以提供一定的资金融通的便利,同时银行也为出口商提供了信用保障:只要出口商在信用证规定的期限内向银行提交符合信用证规定的单据,银行将对出口商履行付款责任。因此,信用证结算方式较易得到买卖双方的同意而成为进出口贸易中使用较为广泛的结算方式。

(i) 汇付

进出口交易中,进口商主动将货款通过银行交付给出口商即为汇付(remittance,也称汇款)。

(一) 汇付的形式和流程

汇付可以分为信汇、电汇和票汇三种形式。

◇ 信汇和电汇

信汇,mail transfer,简称 M/T,是指进口商将货款交给当地的一家银行(汇出行),要求该行用信件的方式委托出口商所在地的一家银行(汇入行)付款给出口商。

电汇,telegraphic transfer,简称 T/T,是指进口商请求汇出行用电讯手段委托汇入行付款给出口商。

信汇/电汇业务的基本流程如下:

~ **信汇/电汇业务流程图** ~

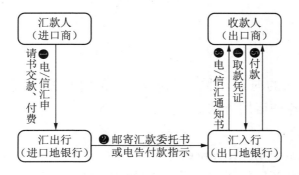

◇　票汇

票汇是债务人使用某种票据来支付款项的付款形式。它通常是由进口商向其所在地的一家银行（出票银行）购入一张由该行签发的银行汇票或银行本票,或者是由进口商自己签发一张支票寄交出口商,由出口商向票据上指定的付款人收取票款。由于在票汇业务中,使用银行汇票较为普遍,因此票汇常被简称为 D/D,即 remittance by banker's demand draft。

以银行汇票为例,票汇业务的基本流程如下:

~ **票汇业务流程图** ~

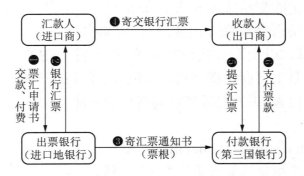

由于票据本身仅仅是一个付款的命令或承诺,所以对于出口商来讲,只有在兑现了票据后方为收妥货款。在进出口贸易中,通常出口商收到的票据上的付款人是进口地银行或第三国银行,因此,出口商往往还须将票据交到其所在地的银行,委托该银行通过其在付款地的分行或代理行代收票款。这也就是银行的票据托收（光票托收）业务。

从付款速度而言,电汇最快,信汇次之。票汇由于其付款行多为非收款人所在国,所以速度最慢。

(二) 汇付的应用

根据进口商付款的时间不同,汇付又有"预付货款"、"货到付款"、"凭单付现"、"凭单付汇"等各种运用方法。

◇ 预付货款(Payment in Advance)

预付货款顾名思义是指进口商先将货款用电汇、信汇或是票汇的形式汇交出口商。

这种方式对出口商最为有利,他甚至可以在收到货款以后再去采购发货,无需占用自有资金。不仅如此,由于是先收款后发货,出口商掌握充分的主动权,基本上不承担贸易风险。但对于进口商来说,预付货款不仅占用大量的资金而且是否能够安全收取货物完全取决于出口商的信用,因此有很大的风险。

◇ 货到付款(Payment after Arrival of the Goods)

在采用货到付款方式时,出口商先发货,而进口商在收到货物时或收货后再过一段时间以电汇、信汇或票汇的形式支付货款。这种方式对进口商最为有利,而对出口商则意味着大量的资金占用和极高的贸易风险。

货到付款又有记账交易(Open Account,O/A)和寄售(Consignment)两种形式。记账交易通常是指交易双方达成协议,由卖方先行向买方发运货物,货款一季、半年或一年结算。以记账方式结算货款时,通常货物的价格以及付款时间均是确定的。寄售则是出口商先将货物运至国外,委托国外商人在当地市场按照事先规定的条件代为出售,买方要等到货物售出后才将货款汇给卖方。

◇ 凭单付现(Cash against Documents,CAD)

凭单付现方式是指交易双方采取"一手交钱、一手交货(单)"的结算方法。通常的做法是出口商在发货之后将代表货物所有权的凭证——货运单据寄交进口商或其代理人,进口商在收到货运单据后即用电汇或其他形式将货款汇给出口商。这种方式在业务实践中通常被称为后 T/T。

这种单到付款的方式对于出口商来讲,减少了货到付款时的资金负担,收款时间也大大加快,但出口商是要承担寄交单据后进口商不付的风险。

因此,在实践中,又逐步发展起另一种做法:出口商在发货之后将代表物权的货运单据传真给进口商,在收到正本货运单据的传真后,进口商立即以电汇方式将货款支付给出口商,出口商在收到电汇款项后,再将货运单据正本寄交进口商。实际业务中通常将这种付款安排称为前 T/T。这种款到交单的做法可以大大降低出口商的收款风险,但进口商需承担付款后无法获得正本货运单据的风险。

◇　凭单付汇(Remittance Against Documents)

凭单付汇是指进口商先将货款通过信汇或电汇的方式由汇出行汇交汇入行,并指示其凭指定的单据或装运凭证付款给出口商。

对于进口商而言,采用凭单付汇可以防止出口商收到货款后不交货(单)或不按期交货(单);对于出口商而言,只要及时按合同规定交货并向汇入行提交指定的货运单据,便可立即得到货款。所以凭单付汇与预付货款和货到付款相比,通常更易为进出口双方所接受。

但是,由于汇款在尚未被收款人支取以前是可以撤销的,进口商有权在出口商向汇出行交单取款前通知银行将汇款退回,所以,出口商在收到汇入行的汇款通知后应尽快发运货物,并及时向汇入行交付单据支取货款。

在进出口贸易中,汇付方式虽然手续简便、费用少,但由于提供信用保障的一方所承担的风险很大而且资金负担也极不平衡,所以在实际业务中,除了对少数有长期业务往来和有良好资信客户使用外,汇付方式主要用于支付交易定金、货款尾数、佣金或其他贸易从属费用。当然,在采用分期付款或延期付款的交易中,也比较多地采用汇付方式。

ⓘ 跟单托收

托收,collection,即委托银行收取货(票)款的意思。在进出口贸易中,出口商将票据或其他付款凭证、货运单据交给其所在地的一家银行,委托该银行通过进口商所在地的银行向进口商收取款项即为托收方式。

托收可分为光票托收和跟单托收两大类:委托银行收取不随附货运单据的票据款项称为光票托收(clean bill for collection);将随附货运单据的汇票委托银行收款的则称为跟单托收(documentary bill for collection)。在进出口贸易中,货款结算主要采用的是跟单托收。

(一) 跟单托收的种类和货款收付流程

跟单托收根据交单条件的不同,可以分为付款交单和承兑交单二种,简述如下:

◇　付款交单（Documents against Payment，D/P）

付款交单是指进口商在向其所在地银行（代收银行）支付货款之后才能取得货运单据的托收安排。

付款交单又可分为即期和远期两种：

即期付款交单（D/P at sight）是由出口商开立即期汇票、通过代收银行向进口商提示，进口商见到票据以后立即付款，付清票款后方能取得货运单据。

远期付款交单（D/P after sight）是由出口商开立远期汇票、通过代收行向进口商提示，进口商见票后作承兑，即保证承担到期付款的责任。在汇票到期以前，经过承兑的汇票和货运单据通常保留在代收银行。汇票到期后，进口商在支付票款后方可获取货运单据。

即期付款交单和远期付款交单的货款收付流程如下所示：

～ 即期付款交单流程图 ～

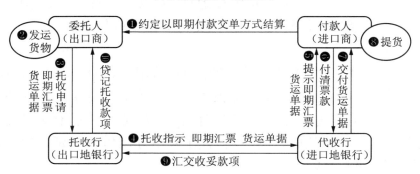

～ 远期付款交单流程图 ～

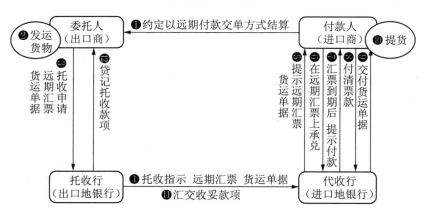

◇　承兑交单（Documents against Acceptance，D/A）

承兑交单是指进口商只要在出口商提交的汇票上作承兑即可取得货运单据的托收安排。

～ 承兑交单流程图 ～

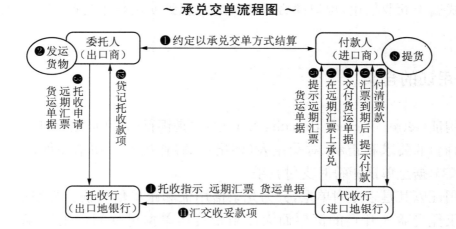

（二）跟单托收的特点及风险

跟单托收方式的特点在于它是一种建立在商业信用基础上的结算方式。虽然在跟单托收业务中,有托收银行和代收银行的加入,但在整个收付过程中,银行所提供的仅仅是服务而不承担任何付款保证。按照有关的国际惯例,银行在办理跟单托收业务时,只是以委托人的代理人身份行事,它既没有检查货运单据是否齐全或正确的义务,也不承担保证进口商必须付款的责任。如果进口商拒绝付款赎单或拒绝承兑,除非事先约定,银行无须承担代委托人提货、存仓和保管的义务,因此采用跟单托收方式对出口商来讲,能否安全收取货款完全取决于进口商的商业信誉。

在付款交单条件下,进口商在未付清货款前,通常无法取得货运单据、提取货物,出口商始终通过掌握代表货物所有权的货运单据控制着物权,如进口商拒不付款赎单,出口商除了可依据合同向进口商交涉外,还可以将货物另找买主或回运,但出口商必须承担额外费用损失以及其他的风险。而在承兑交单条件下,进口商只要办理了对远期跟单汇票的承兑手续即可得到货运单据提取货物,一旦作为承兑人的进口商到期不履行付款责任,出口商即便可凭经进口人承兑的汇票向法院起诉,但如遇进口商破产倒闭、无力支付,出口商仍将面临货款两空的境地。

除了需要承担较大收款风险以外,跟单托收方式下,出口商需先发货,再将单据委托银行向进口人收取货款,即使采用即期付款交单,从出口商发货到由托收行得到货款,往往需要一段时间,而在远期付款交单和承兑交单的情况下,出口商的资金占用时间就更长了。

综上所述,跟单托收实际上是出口商通过向进口商授信和提供资金融通便利来达到吸引客户、争取成交和提高其产品在市场上的竞争力的目的。但由于这种收付方式属于商业信用,出口商必须清醒地意识到使用跟单托收方式时其承担的风险。

(i) 信用证的含义

信用证(letter of credit, credit, L/C)通常是银行(即开证银行)应开证申请人(即进口商)的要求和指示,对受益人(即出口商)作出的一项书面保证,承诺在受益人提交单据且单证相符时支付款项。

信用证以其是否随附单据,分为光票信用证和跟单信用证。光票信用证是指开证行仅凭受益人开具的汇票而无需附带货运单据付款的信用证,跟单信用证(documentary credit)是开证行凭跟单汇票或仅凭单据付款的信用证。在国际货物买卖货款结算中主要使用的是跟单信用证。

2007年修订的国际商会第 600 号出版物《跟单信用证统一惯例》,简称UCP600,对信用证作出了如下定义:

Credit means any arrangement, however named or described, that is irrevocable and thereby constitutes a definite undertaking of the issuing bank to honour a complying presentation.

信用证意指一项安排,无论其如何命名或描述,该约定不可撤销并因此构成开证行对于相符交单予以承付的确定承诺。

据此我们可以了解到:信用证方式下银行作出了有条件的付款承诺,而在汇付和跟单托收方式下,银行均无此承诺。所谓的条件是指受益人在规定的期限内向指定银行提交符合信用证要求的单据。

信用证的基本功能就是给予建立在商业信用基础上的交易添加了银行的信用保障,这可以解决买卖双方在交货和付款方面的矛盾,增加进出口交易的确定性,并可在一定情况下提供资金融通的便利,从而减轻双方的资金负担。因此,信用证结算方式在国际货物买卖中始终占据着非常重要的地位,特别是在初次交易以及中小商人间的交易中得到了较为广泛的运用。

(i) 信用证结算方式的特点

在信用证业务中,各有关当事人所依据的国际惯例是国际商会(International Chamber of Commerce, ICC)制定的《跟单信用证统一惯例》(Uniform Customs and Practice for Documentary Credits)。现行的统一惯例是于 2007 年 7 月 1 日生

效的国际商会第 600 号出版物。

根据 UCP600 的规定,信用证结算主要有以下三大特点:

◇ 开证银行承担第一性付款责任。

信用证是开证银行开立的有条件的承诺付款的书面文件。在信用证业务中,只要出口商(受益人)在信用证规定的期限内向信用证指定的银行提交相符的单据,开证银行就必须保证付款。在信用证业务中,开证银行对受益人作出的付款承诺是一种独立的责任。相比而言,在汇付和跟单托收业务中,银行仅提供服务,而不作付款承诺。

◇ 信用证是一项独立的文件。

在进出口贸易中,信用证的开立虽然是以买卖双方订立的贸易合同为基础,其内容也理应符合买卖合同的规定,但信用证一经开立就成为独立于贸易合同以外的文件。买卖合同是进出口商之间的契约,而信用证则是开证行与受益人之间的契约。开证行和其他参与信用证业务的银行只根据信用证规定办事,不受买卖合同的约束。

◇ 信用证业务是纯单据业务。

在信用证业务中,各有关方面处理的是单据,而不是与单据有关的货物或服务。银行在审核单据时仅以单据为基础决定单据表面是否与信用证规定相符,只需遵循相关惯例及实务标准,而无需去探究单据背后的实际情况。银行将以受益人向其提交的单据是否符合信用证的规定、作为其付款或拒绝付款的唯一依据。

ⓘ 信用证的开立形式

信用证的开立形式可分为信开本和电开本两种形式。

信开本信用证是指以信函格式开立、并用航空挂号等方式寄给通知行的信用证。

电开本信用证是指采用电文格式开立并以电讯方式传递的信用证。电开本有电报(cable)、电传(telex)和 SWIFT(Society for Worldwide Interbank Financial Telecommunication,环球同业银行金融电讯协会)三种格式。

其中,SWIFT 信用证由于方便、迅速、安全、格式统一、条款明确,目前已成为信用证开立时最普遍的格式。

～ 信开本信用证 ～

QNB قطر الوطني

Foreign Trade Department, P.O.Box 1002, Doha, Qatar

Phone: 0974-4407407
Telex: 4357 QATBK DH
Fax: 0974-4414345
SWIFT: QNBAQAQA

Issuance of Irrevocable Documentary Credit Number: **ILC/2018/00739** **Issued on : 06 Nov 2018**	Date of Expiry 15 Jan 2019	Place of Expiry CHINA

Applicant	**Beneficiary**
Tamim Al Marri PO Box 23334 Doha, Qatar	SHANGHAI HUIYUAN TRADE CO., LTD. 1660 DA DU HE ROAD, 200333 SHANGHAI CHINA

Advising Bank	**Amount in Figures and Words**
Bank Of China Shanghai	USD 45,850.00 (Forty Five Thousand Eight Hundred Fifty US DOLLARS) **Tolerance Percentage** Plus 10 and/or Minus 10

Partial Shipment Not Allowed	**Transshipment** Allowed	**Credit Available With** Advising bank CHINA By Negotiation against presentation of stipulated documents and Beneficiary's drafts payable at Sight drawn on Issuing Bank and marked "Drawn under Qatar National Bank Documentary Credit No. ILC/2018/00739 dated 06 Nov 2018"
Shipment		
From : CHINA To : DOHA By : Sea Not Later Than : 31 Dec 2018		

Description of Goods:
ALARM LCD CLOCK WITH CALENDAR
CFR DOHA

Documents Required:
- Signed Commercial invoice(s) authenticated as to the value and origin of goods in one original plus 4 copies. Original only to be certified by the China Council for the promotion of Intl. Trade.
- Invoice must certify the following:
- Goods shipped are strictly as per order TAM 3478 dated 26/10/2018 of M/s. Mamoon Import & Export Co., Doha, and beneficiary's S/C No. GYMJ05Q021-18 dated 28/10/2018.
- Each PC. is inserted in polybag and panda brand to be marked on each PC.
- Packing. 100 PCS per strong sea worthy carton.

- Full set (3/3) of clean On Board Bills of Lading issued to the order of Qatar National Bank, marked Freight Prepaid and notifying buyers.

- Certificate of Origin certified by the China Council for the promotion of International Trade.

- Packing List.

- A Certificate from the Supplier or Steamship Company showing the name, flag and nationality of the carrying vessel also confirming that the vessel will not pass by any Israeli Port through its present voyage and that it is permitted to enter Arab Ports. This Certificate is not required when the shipment is effected on Vessels owned by United Arab Shipping Company.

LC Number: ILC/2018/00739   nal Bank   Page 1 of 2

ISS001/HF 83

QNB القطري

Foreign Trade Department, P.O.Box 1002, Doha, Qatar

Phone: 0974-4407407
Telex: 4357 QATBK DH
Fax: 0974-4414345
SWIFT: QNBAQAQA

Additional Conditions:

- Shipment by Conference Line Vessles only. Certificate to this effect from the Shipping Company or their Agents should accompany the documents.

- Upon negotiation 3 percent of the invoice value is to be deducted being commission and made payable to M/s. Mamoon Import & Export, A/c No. 8930 278492 173 with Commercial Bank of Qatar, Souq Branch, Doha, Qatar.

- All bank charges outside Qatar including reimbursement charges are for the account of beneficiary.

- Trade Marks or Brand Names must be clearly mentioned on the invoices or Certificate of origin.

- USD 100/- or equivalent in the L/C currency and related charges should be deducted from the reimbursement claim for each presentation of discrepant documents under this Credit, not withstanding any instruction to the contrary, this charge shall be for the account beneficiary.

- Legalisation of documents will be done locally by openers.

- Payment under reserve against guarantee and or indemnity is not allowed.

- Insurance covered locally by Openers.

- Payment under this Credit will be made 3 business days after the date of negotiating of documents. The negotiating bank should telex/swift advise us details of negotiation indicating value date applied.

- Tolerance of 10 percent plus or minus in quantity and amount allowed.

We request you to notify the credit to the beneficiary **without adding your** confirmation.
Documents to be presented within **21 days** from the date of shipment but within the validity of the credit.

This credit is subject to the **Uniform Customs and Practice** for Documentary Credits (2007 Revision, International Chamber of Commerce, Paris, France, Publication No.600).
All presentations under this credit must be marked on the reverse thereof.
Kindly forward the original/first set of documents direct to us by **Registered air mail** and duplicates by subsequent airmail.
In reimbursement of negotiations under the terms and condition of this Credit, the negotiating Bank is authorized to claim on our account with the reimbursing bank mentioned below certifying that all terms and conditions under this credit have been complied with.

Reimbursing Bank:	**For Qatar National Bank**
Jp Morgan Trade Services Bank To Bank Reimb Tampa, Usa	

LC Number: ILC/2018/00739 　　　　　　For Qatar National Bank 　　　　　　Page 2 of 2

～ TELEX 信用证 ～

TELEX   INCOMING REPORT
FILE NUMBER 0484   FILE NAME   13174674
INCOMING TELEX REFERENCE NUMBER :   SIEN/2260

03.14   14:23
333062 BOCATNSH D CN

DD: 03/14/2018
TO: BANK OF COMMUNICATIONS, SHANGHAI BRANCH
FM: BANK CENTRAL ASIA/JAKARTA

WE OPEN IRREVOCABLE SIGHT DOCUMENTARY CREDIT NO. RICK-PTB064

FAVOR: MAOTIAN IMPORT & EXPORT CORPORATION 102 HONGQIAO ROAD,
                SHANGHAI 200335, CHINA

FOR A/C OF: PIXBAC PERKASA, JALAN DAAN MOGOT NO. 84 E,
                JAKARTA 11510, INDONESIA

FOR US DOLLARS 115,672.50
(SAY US DOLLAR ONE HUNDRED AND FIFTEEN THOUSAND SIX HUNDRED AND
 SEVENTY TWO AND CENTS FIFTY ONLY)

SHIPPING TERMS: CIF JAKARTA
EXPIRY DATE : 05/15/2018   IN BENEFICIARY'S COUNTRY

AVAILABLE BY ADVISING BANK'S NEGOTIATION AGAINST BENEFICIARY'S DRAFT
30 DAYS AFTER B/L DATE DRAWN ON APPLICANT FOR 97% OF INVOICE VALUE.

ACCOMPANIED BY THE FOLLOWING DOCUMENTS:
- SIGNED COMMERCIAL INVOICE IN TWO COPIES.

- FULL SET CLEAN ON BOARD OCEAN BILL OF LADING CONSIGNED TO OUR ORDER,
MARKED FREIGHT PREPAID, AND NOTIFYING APPLICANT WITH TEL NUMBER.

- INSURANCE POLICY IN DUPLICATE TRANSFERABLE FOR 110 PCT OF INVOICE
VALUE COVERING ICC (A) AS PER INSTITUTE CARGO CLAUSE DATED OF 1/1/2009
INDICATING THAT CLAIMS, IF ANY, ARE PAYABLE IN JAKARTA.

- PACKING LIST IN DUPLICATE.

- CERTIFICATE OF ORIGIN LEGALISED BY C.C.P.I.T. AND INDICATING THAT
ORIGIN OF THE GOODS HAS BEEN LABELLED/PRINTED ON THE SURFACE OF EACH
CARTON / CASE /PACKAGE.

COVERING SHIPMENT OF:
MAINGO BRAND PAINTING BRUSHES 619 SERIES IN STANDARD EXPORT PACKING
SUBJECT TO S/C NO. TIXE0301 OF MARCH 5, 2018

SHIPMENT FROM : ANY PORT IN CHINA   TO: JAKARTA IN INDONESIA
PARTIAL SHIPMENT : PROHIBITED   TRANSSHIPMENT : PROHIBITED
LATEST SHIPMENT DATE: 04/30/2018

SHIPPING MARKS: PIXBAC/PI NO.4854/JAKARTA/C/NO. 1-UP

SPECIAL CONDITIONS:
- ALL BANKING CHARGES OUTSIDE INDONESIA ARE FOR ACCOUNT OF BENEFICIARY.

- A FEE OF USD 80.00 (OR ITS EQUIVALENT) WILL BE DEDUCTED FROM THE
PROCEEDS OF EACH PRESENTATION OF DISCREPANT DOCUMENTS.

- ALL DRAFTS AND DOCUMENTS SHALL BE PRESENTED TO THE NEGOTIATION BANK
 WITHIN 10 DAYS AFTER THE SHIPMENT DATE.

INSTRUCTIONS TO THE NEGOTIATING BANK:
1.THE AMOUNT OF EACH DRAWING MUST BE ENDORSED ON THE REVERSE HEREOF.

2. ALL DOCUMENTS TO BE DISPATCHED IN ONE LOT BY COURIER SERVICE
TO BCA JL. ASEMKA 27-30 JAKARTA 11110 ATTN IMPORT DEPT.

WE HEREBY ENGAGE WITH DRAWERS AND/OR BONAFIDE HOLDERS THAT DRAFTS
DRAWN AND NEGOTIATED IN CONFORMITY WITH THE TERMS OF THIS CREDIT
WILL BE DULY HONOURED ON PRESENTATION.

THIS CREDIT IS SUBJECT TO THE UNIFORM CUSTOMS AND PRACTICE FOR
DOCUMENTARY CREDITS (2007 REVISION) ICC (PUBLICATION NO.600).
THIS TELEX IS AND OPERATIVE CREDIT INSTRUMENT AND NO MAIL CONFIRMATION
FOLLOWS.

333062 BOCATNSH D CN

TELEX RECEIVED   ON 14-MARCH-2018 AT 14:35 FROM LINE

～ SWIFT 信用证 ～

```
****   RECEIVED MESSAGE   ****        18/12/5   14:55 PAGE NO.    1412
STATUS:   MESSAGE DELIVERED
STATION:   1  BEGINNING OF MESSAGE

27    SEQUENCE OF TOTAL                1/1
40A   FORM OF DOCUMENTARY CREDIT       IRREVOCABLE
20    DOCUMENTARY CREDIT NO.           614-3000806
31C   DATE OF ISSUE                    181205
40E   APPLICABLE RULES                 UCPURR LATEST VERSION
31D   DATE AND PLACE OF EXPIRY         190123
                                       IN THE COUNTRY OF BENEFICIARY


50    APPLICANT:                       SHILU CO.,LTD.
                                       29-3,5-CHOME, KURAMAE, TAITO-KU,
                                       TOKYO 155 JAPAN

59    BENEFICIARY:                     SHANGHAI SHENGHUA TRADING CO., LTD.
                                       NO 45 NANCHANG RD
                                       SHANGHAI CHINA

32B   CURRENCY CODE AMOUNT             USD20000,00

39A   PERCENTAGE CREDIT AMOUNT TOLERANCE 10/10

41D   AVAILABLE WITH/BY                ANY BANK BY NEGOTIATION

42C   DRAFTS AT                        SHIPPER'S USANCE 30 DAYS
                                       AFTER B/L DATE

42D   DRAWEE                           SAKURA BANK LTD.(FORMERLY
                                       MITSUI TAIYO KOBE) TOKYO

43P   PARTIAL SHIPMENTS                PROHIBITED

43T   TRANSSHIPMENT                    ALLOWED

44A   PORT OF LOADING                  SHANGHAI

44B   PORT OF DISCHARGE                YOKOHAMA

44C   LATEST DATE OF SHIPMENT          190113

45A   DESCRIPTION OF GOODS AND/OR SERVICES
      SMS NONWOVENS 60G/M2
      WHITE     24,000M
      YELLOW    20,000M
      QUANTITY AND AMOUNT 10 PCT MORE OR LESS ALLOWED
```

```
46B   DOCUMENTS REQUIRED
      +SIGNED COMMERCIAL INVOICE IN 3 COPIES

      +3/3 SET OF CLEAN ON BOARD OCEAN BILLS OF LADING MADE OUT TO
      ORDER OF SHIPPER AND BLANK ENDORSED MARKED 'FREIGHT PREPAID'
      NOTIFY: APPLICANT

      +INSURANCE IS TO BE EFFECTED BY BUYER

      +PACKING LIST IN 3 COPIES

      +BENEFICIARY'S CERTIFICATE STATING THAT ONE SET OF SHIPPING
      DOCUMENTS INCLUDING ONE ORIGINAL B/L AND G.S.P. CERTIFICATE OF
      ORIGIN FORM A  HAS BEEN SENT DIRECTLY TO APPLICANT BY EMS AS
      SOON AS SHIPMENT.

47A   ADDITIONAL CONDITIONS

      1)GOODS TO BE PACKED IN EXPORT STANDARD PACKING

      2)T.T. REIMBURSEMENT IS NOT ACCEPTABLE

71B   DETAILS OF CHARGES:            ALL BANKING CHARGES OUTSIDE JAPAN
                                     ARE FOR ACCOUNT OF BENEFICIARY

48    PERIOD FOR PRESENTATION        DOCUMENTS MUST BE PRESENTED WITHIN
                                     15 DAYS AFTER DATE OF SHIPMENT

49    CONFIRMATION INSTRUCTIONS:     WITHOUT

53A   REIMBURSING BANK               CORESTATES BANK N.A.
                                     PHILADELPHIA.PA

78    INSTRUCTIONS TO PAY/ACC/NEG BK IN REIMBURSEMENT NEGOTIATING BANK
                                     SHOULD SEND THE ORIGINAL LETTER TO
                                     REIMBURSING BANK,CORESTATES BANK
                                     N.A. PHILADELPHIA. PA  U.S.A.
                                     NEGOTIATING BANK SHOULD FORWARD THE
                                     DOCUMENTS DIRECT TO THE SAKURA BANK
                                     LTD. TOKYO INT'L OPERATIONS CENTER
                                     P.O.BOX 766 TOKYO, JAPAN BY
                                     REGISTERED AIRMAIL IN ONE LOT
                                     REIMBURSEMENT IS SUBJECT TO ICC
                                     URR725.


MAC: Authentication Code 7495D4CD
CHK: CheckSum          25E1436A24ET
SAC: SWIFT Authentication Correct
```

(i) 信用证的内容

信用证是银行开立给受益人(出口商)的有条件付款保证文件,虽然有不同的形式、格式,各银行使用的文字语句也有很多差别,但根据《跟单信用证统一惯例》(UCP600),其基本内容主要包括以下几个方面:

(一) 信用证本身的说明

◇ 跟单信用证的类型
例如:irrevocable 不可撤销
transferable 可转让
confirmed 保兑

可转让信用证是指可按受益人的请求,使该信用证的全部或部分供另一受益人兑付的信用证。保兑信用证是指开证行请求另一家银行对该信用证加以保证兑付的信用证,即由开证行和保兑行两家银行共同保证兑付并独立向受益人负责。在 SWIFT 格式信用证中,信用证是否可转让应关注 40A Form of documentary credit,信用证是否加具了保兑,可关注 49 Confirmation instructions 栏目。

◇ 信用证号码 documentary credit number
◇ 开证日期 date of issue
◇ 兑付 availability

信用证必须明确地规定兑付方式和兑付银行(available with ... by ...)。具体规定兑付银行的形式通常有两类:

特指某家银行: available with the advising bank only
不明确规定: available with any bank in China

而兑付的方式又有以下四种:

by sight payment 即期付款,即指定银行见单即付
by deferred payment 延期付款,即指定银行承担延期付款责任和到期付款
by acceptance 承兑付款,即指定银行承兑由受益人出具的汇票并到期付款
by negotiation 议付,即指定银行买入汇票和/或单据,向受益人预付资金

◇　到期日 date of expiry

信用证必须规定一个到期日,即交单到期日,也就是说受益人(或其代表)的交单行为必须在到期日或之前完成,同时,在要求提交正本运输单据的信用证项下,还不得迟于装运日后 21 天内提交。当然,开证行还可在信用证中另行约定交单期限,如在 presentation period of documents 中明示 within 15 days after the date of shipment。

(二) 信用证的当事人

◇　开证申请人 applicant

即向银行提起开证申请的人,一般为进口商,又称开证人 opener,出账人 accountee。

◇　受益人 beneficiary

即信用证指定的有权使用该信用证的人,一般为出口商。

◇　开证银行 issuing bank,opening bank

即开立信用证的银行,一般为进口地银行。

◇　通知银行 advising bank,notifying bank

即按开证行请求、通知信用证的银行,一般为出口地银行。

◇　议付行 negotiating bank

即根据开证行授权、买入受益人提交的汇票和/或单据、向受益人预付资金的银行。议付行对受益人的付款有追索权。

◇　付款行 paying bank,drawee bank

即作出付款行为的银行,通常是汇票的受票人,故亦称受票行(drawee bank)。开证行一般兼为付款行,也可以是受开证行委托、代为付款的另一家银行。付款行对受益人一经付款,即无追索权。

◇　偿付行 reimbursing bank,clearing bank

即受开证行的委托或授权,对有关代付行或议付行的索偿(reimbursement)予以照付的银行。

◇　保兑行 confirming bank

即应开证行请求或授权对信用证加具保兑的银行,具有与开证行相同的责任和地位。保兑行在已经付款后,不论开证行倒闭或无理拒付,都不能向受益人追索。

（三）信用证的金额

◇　货币种类 currency
◇　金额 amount

（四）信用证的汇票条款 draft

一般会涉及以下内容：
◇　汇票金额 amount
◇　付款期限 tenor
◇　出票人 drawer
◇　受票人 drawee

（五）信用证的货物条款

可能会涉及以下内容：
◇　货物名称、规格 commodity name and specifications
◇　数量 quantity
◇　包装 packing
◇　单价 unit price
◇　参考号码，如合同号码（Contract No.或 S/C No.）、订单号码（Order No.）、形式发票号码（Proforma Invoice No.）等
◇　交货条件 terms of delivery

（六）信用证的运输条款

◇　运输方式 mode of transportation
◇　装运港 port of loading
◇　卸货港或目的地 port of discharge or destination
◇　最迟装运日 latest date of shipment
◇　分批装运规定 partial shipments
◇　转运规定 transshipment

（七）信用证的单据条款

特别需要注意的是，关于信用证要求的单据一般会统一列在 documents required 项下，但有时也会在信用证的其他地方出现，例如 additional conditions 或 special conditions 中体现。

信用证的单据条款一般会涉及提交单据的种类、份数、内容要求等。常见的单据有：

◇　商业发票 commercial invoice
◇　装箱单/重量单/尺码单 packing list/weight list/measurement list
　　这三种单据均属包装单据，名称不同，缮制内容相近但略有侧重。
◇　提单 bill of lading
◇　保险单或保险证明 insurance policy or certificate
◇　检验证书 inspection certificate
◇　原产地证明 certificate of origin
◇　受益人证明 beneficiary's certificate，beneficiary's declaration
　　其中，内容为证明受益人已按信用证要求自行寄出了某些单据的受益人证明，又常被称为"寄单证明"。
◇　装船通知副本 copy of shipping advice
◇　第三方临时性证明
　　如，承运人/船公司出具的船舶证明、航线证明等。

（八）信用证的其他规定

◇　附加条款或特别条款 additional conditions or special conditions
◇　银行费用 banking charges
◇　开证行对议付行的指示 instructions to negotiating bank
　　一般包含背批议付金额条款（endorsement clause）、索汇方法（method of reimbursement）、寄单方法（method of dispatching documents）等内容。

（九）信用证的责任文句

◇　开证行付款保证 engagement/undertaking clause

◇　惯例适用条款 subject to UCP clause

在 SWIFT 格式的信用证中,可关注 40E Applicable Rules 栏目。

(十) 授权签字人的签名或密押

◇　信开本中的开证行签字(Signature)
◇　电开本中的密押(Test key)

对信用证内容作全面准确的理解,是审核与修改信用证的前提,更是正确缮制信用证项下单据的前提。虽然传统的信开本由于其排版、语言的多样性显得较为复杂,在实际中的运用也越来越少,但熟悉和掌握信开本信用证对于我们理解内容按栏位分列的 SWIFT 格式信用证是非常有帮助的。

(i) 跟单议付信用证的结算程序

使用跟单议付信用证方式来收付货款大致需要经过以下步骤:
◇　进出口双方签订买卖合同,约定以议付信用证作为结算方式。
◇　进口商向当地银行(开证行)申请开立信用证。
◇　开证银行开立信用证,并传递到通知行(一般为出口地银行)。
◇　通知行向受益人(即出口商)通知信用证。
◇　出口商(即受益人)审核信用证无误后装运货物,制作单据。
◇　出口商(即受益人)向指定的议付行(一般也为出口地银行,有时由通知行兼为议付行)交单议付。
◇　议付行审单无误后向出口商(即受益人)预付货款。
◇　议付行向开证行寄单索偿。
◇　开证行审单无误后作承付:如为即期,则立即向议付行偿付;如为远期,则立即承兑。
◇　开证行向开证申请人(即进口商)提示单据。
◇　如为即期,进口商(即开证申请人)付款赎单;如为远期,进口商(即开证申请人)承兑取单。
◇　开证申请人凭单提货。
◇　如为远期,则开证行于到期后向议付行偿付,进口商(即开证申请人)向开证行付款。

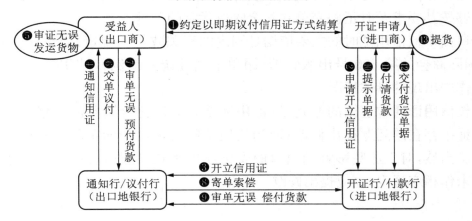

~ 即期议付信用证流程图 ~

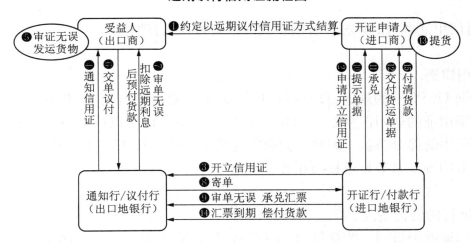

~ 远期议付信用证流程图 ~

在上述结算程序中,我们应注意到:(1)无论是即期信用证还是远期信用证,议付行都是在审单无误之后就把款项预付给了受益人(即出口商);(2)开证行的付款时间在即期信用证和远期信用证项下是不同的。(3)即便是远期信用证,开证申请人(即进口商)也是在开证行向其提示单据时就可以取得单据并凭以提货。

议付行为受益人(即出口商)提供了资金融通的便利,而在远期议付信用证项下,开证行更为开证申请人(进口商)提供了资金融通的便利。

信用证的审核

信用证结算方式对于出口商来讲,其最大的优越性在于,只要出口商按时提交的单据完全符合信用证的规定,就可以获得开证行的付款。而通知行只负责核对信用证的真实性,对其传递的完整性负责,而不审核信用证的具体内容。因此,在执行出口合同的过程中,认真细致地对国外来证进行审核就成为关系到出口商是否能够按其要求及时正确交单并安全收取货款的关键。

　　出口商审核信用证时的主要依据是国内的有关政策和规定、交易双方成交的合同、国际商会的第 600 号出版物即《跟单信用证统一惯例》(UCP600)以及实际业务操作中出现的具体情况。

　　审核信用证通常遵循的原则是:信用证条款规定比合同条款严格时,应当作为信用证中存在的问题提出修改;而当信用证的规定比合同条款宽松时,可不要求修改。当然,对于那些影响到出口商安全收汇和顺利履行合同义务的条款,即便合同未作相应规定,也应提出修改。

　　信用证审核的基本要点为:

(一) 对信用证本身的审核,关注其可靠性、有效性、合理性

◇　适用惯例。

　　根据 UCP600 的规定,只有当信用证文本中明确指出受 UCP600 约束,才意味着该信用证的适用惯例是 UCP600,信用证当事人也可以按照自己的意愿修改和排除其中的部分条款。因此我们必须先确认该证是按 UCP600 开立的,然后才能基于 UCP600 来分析审核信用证。

◇　开证行的资信情况。

　　信用证能否得到有效兑付,开证行的资信是重要因素之一。如对开证行资信不清楚,可委托相关银行仔细查清其信用等级;对于资信欠佳的银行或局势紧张动荡的国家开来的信用证,应尽量避免接受,或要求其他银行对其进行保兑。

◇　信用证的付款保证。

　　虽然 UCP600 规定信用证是不可撤销的,但并不排除信用证中会出现各种限制信用证生效的条款,例如:

　　This credit is non-operative unless the name of carrying vessel has been approved by the applicant.

　　运输工具经开证申请人确认后,本信用证方才生效。

　　This credit is not operative only after your receipt of our telex confirming that the import license has been obtained.

待开证申请人获得进口许可证并由我方电传向你方确认后，本信用证方才生效。

This credit will become effective provided that you receive authorization from our bank in the form of LC amendment

待你方收到我行以信用证修改书的形式发出的授权后，本信用证方才生效。

如果发现开证行在其相符交单即保证付款的承诺上，又加上了其他付款条件，也应要求删除，例如"开证行在货到目的港后通过进口商品检验后才付款"、"在货物清关后开证行才支付货款"等。

如果合同规定应开具保兑信用证，要注意核查信用证是否加具了保兑。

◇　费用问题。
银行费用如事先未商定，应由双方共同承担，一般情况下，发生在开证行的所有费用应由进口商负担，而开证行所在国以外的费用通常会规定由出口商负担。

◇　兑付方式、到期日、到期地点、交单期限。
合同中规范的信用证支付条款会约定信用证的兑付方式、到期日和到期地点的，例如：

... and valid for negotiation in China until 15th day after date of shipment
　　　　　兑付方式　到期地点　　　　　　　　　到期时间/交单期限

审核信用证时可据此进行。
即便双方事前未在合同中约定，对于信用证规定在国外到期或是到期时间过早、交单期限过短，例如装运日后 5 天交单，也应在审核意见中作修改表述，以保证出口商及时顺利交单收款。

(二) 专项审核，要关注其与合同的一致性，以及是否给受益人带来了额外的风险或费用支出：

◇　申请人和受益人是否与合同相符。

◇　信用证金额、币种、付款期限规定是否与合同的支付条款一致，例如：

... a letter of credit payable <u>at 30 days after B/L date</u> <u>for 100％ contract value</u>
　　　　　　　　　　　　　付款期限　　　　　　　　　　金额

　　如果信用证的付款期限迟于合同规定,例如合同规定付款期限为提单日后 30 天,而信用证规定付款期限为 at 30 days' sight(见票后 30 天),由于见票日是晚于提单日的,如接受就意味着受益人将比合同约定的更晚取得货款,所以在审核时应就此提出修改。反过来,如果受益人将比合同约定的更早取得货款,在审核时就不必提出修改。

◇　商品品名、货号、规格、数量、包装规定,特别是贸易术语,是否与合同一致。如合同有溢短装条款,则在信用证的数量和金额上均应有相应体现。

◇　信用证中装运期限、装运港、卸货港、分批装运、转运规定是否与合同的装运条款一致。

　　例如:

Shipment <u>by the end of May 2018</u> from <u>China port</u> to <u>Liverpool</u>,U.K.
　　　　　　装运期限　　　　　　　　装运港　　　　　　卸货港
<u>allowing partial shipments and transshipment</u>
　　　　分批装运　　　　　　转运

◇　单据条款是否合理,是否给受益人带来了额外的风险或费用支出。
　　第一,应注意审核提交的单据是否与交易的实际情况相冲突。例如 CFR 交易中,信用证要求提交保险单;FOB 交易中,信用证要求提单显示运费已付;在采用海洋运输的情况下,信用证要求提交空运单。
　　第二,应注意是否存在限制出口商装运、交单的条件。例如"Shipment can only be effected upon receipt of applicant's shipping instructions by means of L/C amendment through opening bank nominating the name of carrying vessel. Such amendment must accompany the documents for negotiation(货物只能待收到申请人指定船名的装运通知后装运,而装运通知将由开证行以信用证修改书的方式发出。该修改书应随单据一起提交议付)",又如"The beneficiary cannot present the documents until the shipping samples have been approved by the applicant(船样经开证申请人确认后受益人方可交单)"。
　　第三,应注意是否有将单据的出具权掌握在申请人或其代理人手中的情况。例如"Inspection certificate signed by applicant or its agent(由开证申请人或其代表签署的检验证书)"。

第四,应注意是否额外增加了受益人的费用支出。例如信用证中规定单据须由指定机构或使领馆签署或认证;再如信用证的投保加成率比合同有所提高等等。当然,如果信用证中规定的保险险别虽与合同不同,只要其没有增加出口商额外的保险费支出,就无需修改。例如合同规定投保 ICC(B)险而信用证规定投保 WPA,合同规定投保 FPA 而信用证规定投保 ICC(C),这些一般都不作为审证不符点。

第五,应特别关注货物的控制权问题。例如:信用证规定提单以进口商作为记名收货人(Bill of lading ... consigned to applicant ...)、或收货人凭进口商指示(Bill of lading ... made out to applicant's order ...);信用证要求提交空运单、并以进口商为收货人;信用证规定在货物装运后将正本提单直接寄给进口商。

ⓘ 改证函的基本结构

出口商在审核信用证后,如发现有不符合买卖合同或不利于出口方安全收汇的条款,应及时联系进口商通过开证银行对信用证进行修改。修改信用证的要求应尽可能一次性具体明确地提出,以避免或减少往返改证,延误时间。

从标准规范的角度而言,改证函一般应包括如下内容:

(一) 确认收到信用证

一般来说,应明确指出所收到信用证的号码、开证行及开证日期。例如:

◇　Thank you for your L/C No. SG07WE34 issued by West Country Bank, Los Angeles Branch dated February 5, 2018.

◇　We are very pleased to receive your L/C No. YUC9022 established by the National Bank of Bangladesh dated March 1, 2018 against S/C No. 13DXB15.

(二) 列明经审核后发现的不符点,并说明需要如何修改。例如:

◇　However, we are sorry to find it containing the following discrepancies.

◇　But the following points are in discrepancy with the stipulations of our S/C No. ERT12.

◇　As to the description of the goods, please insert the word "red" before "sun".

◇ Please delete the clause "The invoice evidences that the goods are packed in wooden cases." and insert the wording "The invoice evidences that the goods are packed in seaworthy cartons."

◇ Please amend the amount in figure to USD78,450.00.

◇ The expiry date should be February 15, 2018 instead of February 5, 2018.

◇ Please extend the shipment date and the validity of the L/C to March 15, 2018 and March 30, 2018 respectively.

(三) 要求对方尽快修改信用证,以保证按期交货。例如:

◇ Please see to it that the L/C amendment reach us within next week, otherwise we cannot effect punctual shipment.

练 习

信用证审核与修改

1. 试将下列短文译成中文：

ADVANTAGE AND DISADVANTAGE OF COLLECTION

The most unsatisfactory feature of the D/P form of transaction is the possibility of the buyer or his banker refusing to honor the draft and take up the shipping documents, especially at a time when the market is falling. In such a case, the seller may not receive his payment, although he is still the owner of the goods.

Under D/P method, before making payment, the buyer cannot get documents of title to the goods and take delivery of the goods. The ownership of the goods still remains in the hands of the seller. If the buyer dishonors the draft, the seller can sell the goods to others.

In the case of payment by D/A, the further difficulty arises that, on the buyer accepting the draft, the documents of title will be surrendered to him. Hence, if the buyer goes bankrupt or becomes insolvent before the payment of the draft, the loss will fall on the seller.

Therefore, seldom does a seller accept payment by D/P or D/A, unless the buyer is of unquestionable integrity or if there is a special relation between the seller and the buyer. It is far better for the exporter to use L/C rather than D/P or D/A. However, under certain circumstances or for certain purposes, payment by D/P or D/A is still deemed necessary, for instance:

1) For implementation of foreign trade policy, especially for the promotion of trade with developing countries.
2) For promotion of exports, especially to push the sale of our new products and difficult-sell commodities.
3) For promotion of trade with the small enterprises by granting credits to them.

4）For simplifying procedures of payment while doing business with affiliated corporations.

2. 试用图示简要说明即期付款交单(D/P at sight)的结算流程：

委托人
（出口商）

付款人
（进口商）

托收行
（出口地银行）

代收行
（进口地银行）

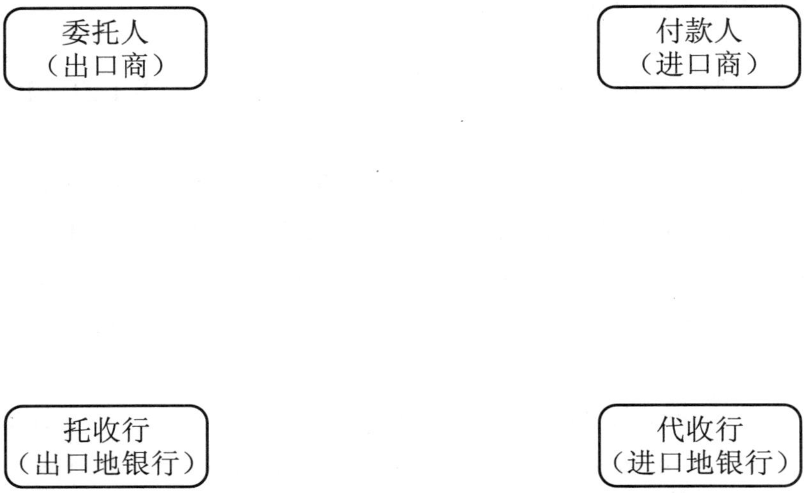

3. 试用图示简要说明远期付款交单(D/P at ××× days after sight)的结算流程：

委托人
（出口商）

付款人
（进口商）

托收行
（出口地银行）

代收行
（进口地银行）

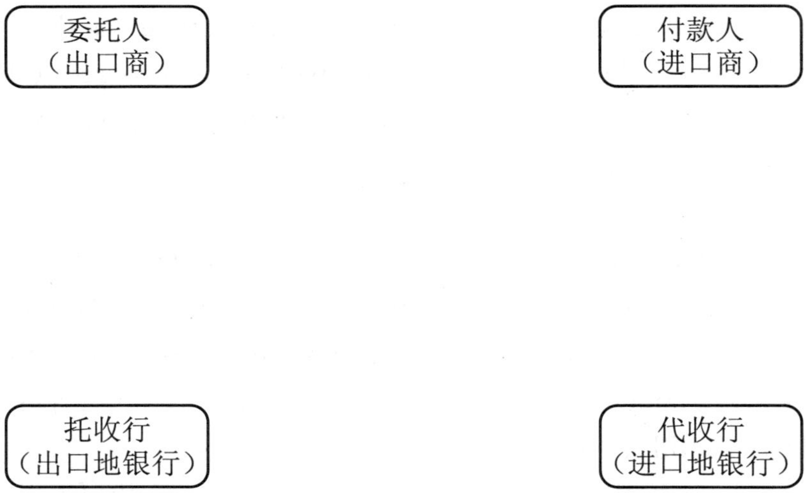

4. 试用图示简要说明承兑交单(D/A at ××× days after sight)的结算流程：

委托人
（出口商）

付款人
（进口商）

托收行
（出口地银行）

代收行
（进口地银行）

5. 根据下列表格中的内容,按照不同的跟单托收条件分别填写承兑日,付款日和交单日。

交易合同中规定的托收条件	代收银行向进口商提示汇票和单据的日期	进口商在汇票上作出承兑的日期	进口商向代收银行支付票款的日期	代收银行向进口商提交货运单据的日期
即期付款交单（D/P at sight）	8月8日			
远期付款交单见票后 30 天付款（D/P at 30 days after sight）	8月8日			
承兑交单见票后 30 天付款（D/A at 30 days after sight）	8月8日			

6. 将下列电开本信用证译成中文:

TO: THE INDUSTRIAL AND COMMERCIAL BANK OF CHINA SHANGHAI

FM: TOKAI BANK TOKYO

JUN 15 2018 OUR SRL 91388

ISSUE OF A DOCUMENTARY CREDIT

PLS ADVISE

THAT WE ISSUED IRREVOCABLE CREDIT LC635-38564

ON JUN 15, 2018

EXPIRY JUL 30, 2018 CHINA

APPLICANT   DAITO TSUSHO Co., LTD. 504, 18-18 2-CHOME, TATSUNUMA,
               ADACHI-KU, TOKYO, 121, JAPAN

BENEFICIARY   SHANGHAI MORNING STAR CORPORATION, 375 DONG DA MING ROAD,
               SHANGHAI CHINA

AMOUNT   USD186,400.00

CREDIT AVAILABLE WITH ANY BANK BY NEGOTIATION OF BENEFICIARY'S DRAFTS
AT SIGHT FOR FULL INVOICE VALUE DRAWN ON THE TOKAI BANK, LTD., NEW YORK

PARTIAL SHIPMENTS ALLOWED

TRANSHIPMENT PROHIBITED

SHIPMENT FROM SHANGHAI CHINA

NOT LATER THAN JUL 15, 2018

FOR TRANSPORTATION TO NAGOYA, JAPAN

SHIPMENT OF 8,000 SETS OF GARMENTS AS PER ORDER NO.DAITO3746 DATED APR
6,2018. CIF NAGOYA

DOCUMENTS REQUIRED:

+ COMMERCIAL INVOICE IN 3 COPIES DULY SIGNED, INDICATING THE
  CREDIT NUMBER.

+ FULL SET OF CLEAN ON BOARD MARINE BILLS OF LADING MADE OUT TO
  ORDER OF SHIPPER BLANK ENDORSED MARKED FREIGHT PREPAID NOTIFY
  APPLICANT.

+ PACKING LIST IN 3 COPIES.

+ MARINE INSURANCE POLICY OR CERTIFICATE IN DUPLICATE ENDORSED IN BLANK
    FOR 110 PCT OF THE INVOICE VALUE INCLUDING: OCEAN MARINE CARGO WAR
    RISKS CLAUSES, OCEAN MARINE CARGO CLAUSES (ALL RISKS), SUBJECT TO C.I.C.
    OF PICC CLAIMS TO BE PAYABLE IN JAPAN IN CURRENCY OF DRAFTS.
+ G.S.P. CERTIFICATE OF ORIGIN FORM 'A' IN ONE COPY.
+ CERTIFICATE OF QUALITY AND QUANTITY IN ONE COPY.

DOCUMENTS TO BE PRESENTED WITHIN 15 DAYS AFTER DATE OF ISSUANCE OF
TRANSPORT DOCUMENTS BUT WITHIN VALIDITY OF CREDIT.

OTHER CONDITIONS:
+ ONE SET COPY OF ABOVE SHIPPING DOCUMENTS AND ORIGINAL OF CERTIFICATE
    OF ORIGIN (FORM A) MUST BE AIRMAILED TO APPLICANT BY EXPRESS WITHIN
    48 HOURS AFTER SHIPMENT.
+ INSURANCE IS TO BE EFFECTED BY SHIPPER.
+ T.T. REIMBURSEMENT PROHIBITED.
+ ALL BANKING CHARGES OUTSIDE JAPAN ARE FOR BENEFICIARY'S ACCOUNT.
+ DRAFTS DRAWN HEREUNDER MUST BEAR THIS CREDIT NO.AND DATE.
+ NEGOTIATING BANK MUST FORWARD DRAFTS TO DRAWEE BANK AND ALL DOCUMENTS
    TO US IN TWO REGISTERED AIRMAILS.

WE AGREE THAT DRAFTS DRAWN IN COMPLIANCE WITH THE TERMS OF THIS
CREDIT SHALL BE DULY HONORED ON DUE PRESENTATION SUBJECT TO U.C.P.
2007 REVISION, ICC PUBLICATION NO.600.

7. 信用证条款翻译：

1）Available by beneficiary's drafts at sight together with the following documents bearing our credit number.

2）All drafts drawn under this credit must contain the clause "Drawn under Bank of ... credit No ... dated ...".

3）Signed commercial invoice in quintuplicate indicating applicant's Import License No ... as well as this credit number.

4）Full set of clean on board ocean bills of lading made out to shipper's order，endorsed to the order of Bank of China Singapore Branch marked "Freight prepaid" and notify the above applicant.

5）Marine insurance policies or certificates in negotiable form for 110% of

CIF invoice value covering All Risks and War Risks as per ocean marine cargo clause of the People's Insurance Company of China dated 1/1/1981 with extended cover up to Kuala Lumpur with claims payable at destination in the currency of draft.

6）Packing list in triplicate detailing the complete inner packing specification and contents of each package.

7）Evidencing shipment of 1500 cartons of sporting balls from China ports to Kuwait by steamer not later than July 20th, 2018 with partial shipments and transshipment not allowed.

8）Draft(s) drawn under this credit must be presented for negotiation in China on or before 30th August 2018.

9）All documents must be presented to the negotiating bank within 15 days after the issuance of the transportation document but within the credit validity.

10）We hereby engage with the drawers, endorsers and bona-fide holders of drafts drawn under and in compliance with the terms of the credit that such drafts, if drawn and negotiated within the validity of this credit, shall be duly honored on due presentation and delivery of documents as specified.

11）This documentary credit is subject to the Uniform Customs and Practice for Documentary credit(2007 Revision, International Chamber of Commerce, Paris, France, Publication No.600) and engages us in accordance with the terms thereof and especially in accordance with the terms of article 7 & 8 thereof. The number and the date of the credit and the name of our bank must be quoted on all drafts required. The amount and date of each negotiation must be endorsed on the reverse of this credit by the negotiating bank.

8. 信用证审核：

试根据出口合同审核国外来证，指出信用证存在的问题并说明应如何修改。

1）大米交易

2）缝纫机交易

3）纺织品交易

上 海 远 大 进 出 口 公 司
SHANGHAI YUANDA IMPORT & EXPORT COMPANY
上海市溧阳路 1088 号龙邸大厦 16 楼
16th Floor, Dragon Mansion, 1088 Liyang Road, Shanghai 200081 China
电话(Tel):0086-21-56666624　　传真(Fax):0086-21-56666698

销 货 合 约
SALES CONTRACT

编号 No.:　YD-MDSC1211
日期 Date:　Nov. 8, 2018

买方
Buyers:　MAURICIO DEPORTS INTERNATIONAL S.A.

地址
Address:　AVENIDA CUBA No. 45B, PANAMA CITY, REPUBLIC OF PANAMA

电话　　　　　　　　　　　　　传真
Tel:　　507-25192334　　　　　Fax:　　507-25192333

兹经买卖双方同意成交下列商品订立条款如下：

The Undersigned Sellers and Buyers have agreed to close the following transaction according to the terms and conditions stipulated below.

货物名称及规格 Name of commodity and Specification	数　量 Quantity	单　价 Unit Price	金　额 Amount
Chinese Rice　F.A.Q. Broken Grains (max.) 20% Admixture (max.) 0.2% Moisture (max.) 10% 5% more or less both in Amount and Quantity allowed at Sellers' option	200 tons	CIFC3 US$ 360.00	Colon US$72,000.00
	总　值 Total Amount Say US Dollars Seventy Two Thousand Only		

包装
PACKING: 50KG to one gunny bag. Total 4000 bags.

装运
SHIPMENT: To be effected during December 2018 from Shanghai, China to Colon, R.P. allowing partial shipments and transshipment.

保险
INSURANCE: To cover 110% of invoice value against All Risks as per C.I.C. dated 1/1/1981.

付款
PAYMENT: The buyer shall open through a first-class bank acceptable to the seller an irrevocable L/C at 30 days after B/L date to reach the seller before November 25, 2018 and valid for negotiation in China until the 15th day after the date of shipment.

卖方 SELLERS
Shanghai Yuanda Import & Export Company
赵国斌

买方 BUYERS
Mauricio Deports International S.A.
D.H. STEVE

CITIBANK N.A.　　　　　　　　ORIGINAL

P.O.Box 555 Panama, R.P.

CABLE ADDRESS:"CITIBANK"	PLACE & DATE OF ISSUE PANAMA NOVEMBER 23, 2018	
DOCUMENTARY CREDIT IRREVOCABLE	**CREDIT NUMBER** **OF ISSUING BANK** **OF ADVSING BANK** 180-43672	
ADVISING BANK CITI BANK OF SHANGHAI SHANGHAI, CHINA	**APPLICANT** MAURLCIO DEPORTS INTERNATIONAL S.A. AVENIDA CUBA NO. 45V, PANAMA CITY, REPUBLIC OF PANAMA	
BENEFICIARY SHANGHAI YUANDA EXPORT & IMPORT COMPANY 16 FLOOR, DRAGON MANSION, 1088 LIYANG ROAD, SHANGHAI 200081 CHINA	**AMOUNT** US$73,332.00 (SAY US DOLLARS SEVENTY THREE THOUSAND THREE HUNDRED AND THIRTY TWO ONLY)	
	EXPIRY DATE:　　　JANUARY 15, 2019 AT THE COUNTER O CITIBANK N.A. PANAMA	

Dear sir(s),

We hereby issue in your favor this documentary credit which is available by your at 30 days' sight draft(s) drawn on CITIBANK N.A. PANAMA BRANCH, PANAMA for 100 % invoice cost accompanied by the following documents:

1) 2/3 set of original clean on board ocean bill of lading dated no later than December 15, 2018 issued to our order notify APPLICANT marked freigh to be collected.

2) Commercial invoice in triplicate duly signed and original certified by CCPIT.

3) Packing list in triplicate showing gross weight of package and certified that the goods are packed in new gunny bags.

4) Beneficiary's certificate stated that 1/3 set of original bill of lading has been airmailed directly to applicant within 48 hours after shipment.

5) Insurance policy or certificate in duplicate in the currency of the credit and in assignable form for the full invoice value plus 110 pct, covering Institute Cargo Clauses Clause A of 1/1/2009.

Covering:　　　4000 bags of Chinese Rice as per Sales Contract No. YD-MDSC1211 dated November 18, 2018
　　　　　　　CIF Colon

Documents must be presented within 5 days after the date of shipment but within the validity of the credit

DISPATCH/SHIPMENT FROM　　　SHANGHAI TO　　　PANAMA CITY	PARTIAL SHIPMENTS PROHIBITED	TRANSHIPMENTS PROHIBITED

SPECIAL CONDITIONS

1. The documents beneficiary presented should include an inspection certificate signed by applicant or its agent.

2. Each draft accompanying documents must indicate the credit number and name of issuing bank and issuing date.

3. This credit is non-operative unless the name of carrying vessel has been approved by applicant and to be advised by L/C issuing bank in form of an L/C admendment to beneficiary.

4. All charges outside Panama R.P. are for account of beneficiary.

We hereby agree with the drawers endorsers and bona fide holders of drafts drawn under and in compliance with the terms of the terms of this credit that such drafts will be duly honored on due presentation to the drawee if negotiated on or before expiry date and paid on maturity. 　　The advising bank is requested to notify the beneficiary without adding their confirmation. 　　In reimbursement, the drawee bank will debit our account No. 10991266 with our New York Office, making reference to our letter of credit No. Documents are to be airmailed directly to us. Yours faithfully, **CITIBANK. N.A.** CARMEN WILLALGBOS **Authorized Signature**	**Advising Bank Notification**

SPECIMEN

CONTRACT TERMS

COMMODITY & SPECIFICATIONS:

BUTTERFLY BRAND OVERLOCKER SEWING MACHINE JN764

PACKING:

PACKED IN CARTONS OF ONE SET EACH, TOTAL 2200 CARTONS ONLY.

QUANTITY:

2200 SETS

PRICE:

US$164.00 PER SET CFR KUWAIT

TOTAL US DOLLARS THREE HUNDRED AND SIXTY THOUSAND EIGHT HUNDRED ONLY

SHIPMENT:

SHIPMENT TO BE MADE DURING OCT / NOV 2018 FROM SHANGHAI TO KUWAIT WITH PARTIAL SHIPMENTS AND TRANSSHIPMENT ALLOWED

INSURANCE:

INSURANCE TO BE COVERED BY THE BUYER.

PAYMENT:

THE BUYER SHOULD OPEN THROUGH A BANK ACCEPTABLE TO THE SELLER AN IRREVOCABLE LETTER OF CREDIT PAYABLE AT 30 DAYS AFTER SIGHT TO REACH THE SELLER 30 DAYS BEFORE THE MONTH OF SHIPMENT VALID FOR NEGOTIATION IN CHINA UNTIL AT LEAST 15 DAYS AFTER THE DATE OF SHIPMENT.

THE NATIONAL BANK OF DUBAI LTD.
MAIN OFFICE
DEIRA-DUBAI

P.O. Box No. 777 Dubai - United Arav Emirates
Tel:214131 222241 222255 Telex:45421 NATNAL EM
Cable: NATIONAL DUBAI Telefax: 215939

Date: August 15, 2018

To: Shanghai Minghui Import and Export Company
1280 West Yanan Road,
Shanghai, China

Subject to Uniform Customs and Practice for Documentary Credits, 2007 Revision, International Chamber of Commerce Publication No. 600

Dear sir(s):

At the request of: R.T. TRADING AND CONTRACTING CO. W.L.L., P.O.BOX 236565, KUWAIT , we hereby open our irrevocable documentary No. 2173401751 for US$360800.00 ONLY (say U.S.DOLLARS THREE HUNDRED AND SIXTY THOUSAND EIGHT HUNDRED only) favoring yourselves.   Drafts must be in first and second of exchange on OUR BANK payable at 45DAYS' SIGHT and they must be accompanied by the following documents:

- Signed Commercial Invoices in QUAUDRUPLICATE certified to be true and correct stating full name and address of manufactures.
- Packing list in QUAUDRUPLICATE.
- FULL set of clean on board ocean Bills of Lading marked "FREIGHT TO COLLECT" issued by shipping company, made out TO ORDER OF THE SHIPPERS and endorsed IN BLANK.
- SEPARATE CERTIFICATE OF ORIGIN ISSUED BY CHAMBER OF COMMERCE.

The documents must evidence shipment of:
2200 SETS OF BUTTERFLY BRAND OVERLOCKER SEWING MACHINE JN746 AS PER SALES CONFIRMATION NO. SC18-937
from   SHANGHAI CHINA   to   KUWAIT

INSURANCE COVERED IN KUWAIT BY ULTIMATE BUYER

Partial dispatches are   PERMITTED   .   Transshipment is   PERMITTED   .
Shipment(s) to be effected no later than NOVEMBER 30, 2018.

This Credit is valid until NOVEMBER 30, 2018 for presentation documents in KUWAIT

Shipping Marks: R.T. / SC18-937 / KUWAIT / C/NO.1-UP

SPECIAL INSTRUCTIONS:

1) Shipment advice to be sent by fax to the applicant immediately after the shipment stating our L/C No., shipping marks, name of the vessel, goods description and amount as well as the bill of lading No. and date. A copy of such advice must accompany the original documents presented for negotiation.
2) All drafts must be enfaced "Drawn under THE NATIONAL BANK OF DUBAI LTD, DUBAI Credit No. 2173401751 dated August 15, 2018."

We GUARANTEE the payment of drafts drawn in conformity with the terms and conditions stated.   The Negotiating Bank must send all documents including the drafts direct to us, the originals by REGISTERED AIR MAIL and the remainder by SECOND MAIL.

Accountant
Daiel Amy

Yours faithfully
Manager
Albrudula Ali Ebulahim

SALES CONFIRMATION

NO. AN107　　　　　　　　　　　　　　　　　　　　　　**DATE:** MAR. 5, 2018

  This Sales Confirmation is made and entered into by and between **SHANGHAI JINXIU TEXTILES TRADING COMPANY, SHANGHAI, CHINA** hereinafter referred to as **the sellers** and **YICOTAMA CORPORATION, OSAKA, JAPAN** hereinafter referred to as **the buyers**;

  whereby **the sellers** agree to sell and **the buyers** agree to buy the commodity/ies mentioned in this contract subject to the terms and conditions stipulated as follows:

Name Of Commodity & Specifications	Quantity	Unit Price	Amount
100% PURE COTTON APRON		**CIF OSAKA**	
ART. NO.　49394 (014428)	**3,216PCS**	**US$1.00**	**US$3,216.00**
ART. NO.　49393 (014428)	**3,960PCS**	**US$1.00**	**US$3,960.00**
ART. NO.　55306 (014429)	**1,560PCS**	**US$1.25**	**US$1,950.00**
		TOTAL:	**US$9,126.00**
Total Value: SAY US DOLLARS NINE THOUSAND ONE HUNDRED AND TWENTY SIX ONLY.			

Packing: EACH IN A PLASTIC BAG, 12 BAGS TO A CARTON, TOTAL 728 CARTONS.

Shipping Marks: YICOTAMA / OSAKA / NO.1-728

Time of Shipment: Within 45 days of receipt of letter of credit and not later than **MAY 2018** with partial shipments and transshipment allowed.

Port of Loading: **SHANGHAI, CHINA**

Port of Destination: **OSAKA, JAPAN**

Payment Terms: By 100% **CONFIRMED** Irrevocable Letter of Credit payable **AT SIGHT** opened by the Buyer to reach the Seller not later than **APRIL 15, 2018** and to be available for negotiation in China until the 15th day after the date of shipment. In case of late arrival of the L/C, the sellers shall not be liable for any delay in shipment and shall have the right to rescind the contract and or claim for damages.

Insurance: To be effected by the Seller for **110%** of the CIF invoice value covering **WPA RISKS AND WAR RISKS** as per China Insurance Clauses of 1/1/1981.

Confirmed by the sellers　　　　　　　　　　　　　　　　the buyers

SHANGHAI JINXIU TEXTILES TRADING COMPANY　　　YICOTAMA CORPORATION

陈彤　　　　　　　　　　　　　　　　　　Ichilo Hashimoto

18APR05　14:57:32　　　　　　　　　　　　　　　　　　LOGICAL TERMINAL　POO5
MT: S700　　　　　　ISSUE OF A DOCUMENTARY CREDIT　　　PAGE　00001
　　　　　　　　　　　　　　　　　　　　　　　　　　　　FUNC　SWPR3
　　　　　　　　　　　　　　　　　　　　　　　　　　　　UMR　　00182387

MAGACK DWS765I AUTH OK, KEY B19604214FAEA9B2, BKCHCNBJ SAIVJPJT RECORD BASIC
HEADER　　　　　　　　　　F 01 BKCHCNBJA300 8118 157214
APPLICATION HEADER　　　0 700 1547 180405 SAIBJPJTCXXX 3846 992024　180405 1447
　　　　　　　　　　　　　　　　　　　　　　　　　　★ASAHI BANK LTD,
　　　　　　　　　　　　　　　　　　　　　　　　　　★TOKYO

USER HEADER　　　　　　　SERVICE CODE　　103 :
　　　　　　　　　　　　　BANK PRIORITY　113 :
　　　　　　　　　　　　　MSG USER REF　　108 :
　　　　　　　　　　　　　INFO. FROM CI　　115 :

SEQUENCE OF TOTAL　　　★27　　　:　1/1
FORM OF DOC, CREDIT　　★40　　　:　REVOCABLE
DOC, CREDIT NUMBER　　 ★20　　　:　ABL-AN107
DATE OF ISSUE　　　　　★31 C　 :　180405
EXIPRY　　　　　　　　 ★31 D　 :　DATE 180605 AT NEGOTIATING BANK'S COUNTER
APPLICANT　　　　　　　★50　　　:　YICOTAMA CORPORATION, OSAKA, JAPAN
　　　　　　　　　　　　　　　　　　　OSACY SECTION
BENEFICIARY　　　　　　★59　　　:　SHANGHAI JINXIU TEXTILES TRADING COMPANY
　　　　　　　　　　　　　　　　　　　2712 ZHENBEI ROAD,
　　　　　　　　　　　　　　　　　　　SHANGHAI, CHINA
AMOUNT　　　　　　　　 ★32 B　 :　CURRENCY USD AMOUNT 9126,00
MAX. CREDIT AMOUNT　　★39 B　 :　NOT EXCEEDING
AVAILABLE WITH/BY　　 ★41 D　 :　ASAHI BANK LTD, NEW YORK BRANCH
　　　　　　　　　　　　　　　　　　　BY NEGOTIATION
DRAFTS AT ...　　　　 ★42 C　 :　DRAFTS AT 20 DAYS' SIGHT
DRAWEE　　　　　　　　 ★42 A　 :　SAIBJPJT
　　　　　　　　　　　　　　　　　　★ASAHI BANK LTD,
　　　　　　　　　　　　　　　　　　★TOKYO

PARTIAL SHIPMENTS　　 ★43 P　 :　ALLOWED
TRANSSHIPMENT　　　　 ★43 T　 :　PROHIBITED
LOADING IN CHARGE　　 ★44 A　 :　CHINESE PORT(S)
FOR TRANSPORT TO ...　★44 B　 :　OSAKA, JAPAN
LATEST DATE OF SHIP.　★44 C　 :　180531
DESCRIPT. OF GOODS　　★45 A　 :　100% COTTON APRON AS PER S/C NO. AH107

ART NO.	QUANTITY	UNIT PRICE
49394 (014428)	3,216 PIECES	USD1.00
49393 (014428)	3,690 PIECES	USD1.00

55306 (014429)　　1,560 PIECES　　　USD1.25
PRICE TERM　　: CIF OSAKA

DOCUMENTS REQUIRED　　　★46 A　:
+2/3 SET OF ORIGINAL CLEAN ON BOARD OCEAN BILLS OF LADING MADE OUT TO ORDER OF SHIPPER AND BLANK ENDORSED AND MARKED "FREIGHT PREPAID" NOTIFY APPLICANT (WITH FULL NAME AND ADDRESS).

+ORIGINAL SIGNED COMMERCIAL INVOICE AND 4 COPIES INDICATING S/C NO.

+INSURANCE POLICY OR CERTIFICATE IN TWO FOLD ENDORSED IN BLANK, FOR 120PCT OF THE INVOICE VALUE INCLUDING: THE INSTITUTE CARGO CLAUSES (B), THE INSTITUTE WAR CLAUSES, INSURANCE CLAIMS TO BE PAYABLE IN JAPAN IN THE CURRENCY OF THE DRAFTS.

+CERTIFICATE OF ORIGIN GSP FORM A IN 1 ORIGINAL AND 1 COPY.

+PACKING LIST IN 3 FOLD

+BENEFICIARY'S CERTIFICATE STATING THAT ONE SET OF ORIGINAL TRANSPORT DOCUMENT HAS BEEN SENT DIRECTLY TO THE APPLICANT (ATT. OSACY SECTION)

ADDITIONAL COND.　　　★47　　　:
　　　　　　　　　1. T.T. REIMBURSEMENT IS PROHIBITED.
　　　　　　　　　2. THE GOODS TO BE PACKED IN EXPORT STRONG COLORED CARTONS.

DETAILS OF CHARGES　　　★71 B　　:
　　　　　　　　ALL BANKING CHARGES OUTSIDE JAPAN INCLUDING
　　　　　　　　REIMBURSEMENT COMMISSIONS ARE FOR ACCOUNT OF BENEFICIARY.

PRESENTATION PERIOD　　★48　　:
　　　　　　　　DOCUMENTS TO BE PRESENTED WITHIN 5 DAYS AFTER THE DATE OF SHIPMENT, BUT WITHIN THE VALIDITY OF THE CREDIT.

CONFIRMATION　　　　★49　　:　WITHOUT

INSTRUCTIONS　　　　★78　　:
　　　　　　　　THE NEGOTIATION BANK MUST FORWARD THE DRAFTS AND ALL DOCUMENTS BY REGISTERED AIRMAIL DIRECT TO US (INT'L OPERATIONS CENTER MAIL ADDRESS: C.P.O.BOX NO. 800 TOKYO 100-91 JAPAN) IN TWO CONSECUTIVE LOTS, UPON RECEIPT OF THE DRAFTS AND DOCUMENTS IN ORDER, WE WILL REMIT THE PROCEEDS AS INSTRUCTED BY THE NEGOTIATING BANK.

TRAILER:　ORDER IS <MAC:> <PAC:> <ENC:> <CHK:> <TNG:> <PDE:>
　　　　　　MAC: 3CDFF763
　　　　　　CHK: 8A1AA1203070

9. 信用证条款翻译：

1) INSURANCE POLICY OR CERTIFICATE IN DUPLICATE, ENDORSED IN BLANK FOR 110 PCT OF THE INVOICE VALUE, STIPULATING THAT CLAIMS ARE PAYABLE IN THE CURRENCY OF THE DRAFT AND ALSO INDICATING A CLAIM SETTLING AGENT IN SINGAPORE, INSURANCE MUST INCLUDE：ALL RISKS AND WAR RISK AS PER THE RELEVANT OCEAN MARINE CARGO CLAUSES OF PICC DATED 1/1/1981.

2) CERTIFICATE OF ORIGIN IN DUPLICATE ISSUED BY CCPIT STATING THAT THE GOODS ARE OF CHINESE ORIGIN.

3) T.T. REIMBURSEMENT IS NOT ACCEPTABLE.

4) SHIPMENT SAMPLES TO BE SENT DIRECTLY BY COURIER TO APPLICANT FOR APPROVAL BEFORE SHIPMENT AND SUCH APPROVAL WILL BE ADVISED TO BENEFICIARY BY EMAIL. A COPY OF THIS EMAIL MUST ACCOMPANY THE DOCUMENTS FOR NEGOTIATION.

5) IN REIMBURSEMENT，NEGOTIATING BANK MUST DISPATCH ALL DOCUMENTS BY REGISTERED AIRMAIL OR AIR COURIER TO US IN ONE LOT.

10. 根据 OVERSEAS UNION BANK LTD 的信用证（第 191 页）叙述其业务操作的完整流程（说明具体的当事人及每一个业务环节的操作内容）：

1) 签订合同：

2) 申请开证：

3) 开出 L/C：

4) 通知开证：

5) 审核修改：

6) 货物装运：

7) 交单议付：

8) 单据清单：单据名称（用中文写出）　　　单据份数

　　　　a　　　　　　　　　　　　　a

　　　　b　　　　　　　　　　　　　b

　　　　c　　　　　　　　　　　　　c

　　　　…　　　　　　　　　　　　…

9) 审单议付：

10) 寄单索偿：

11) 审单付款：

12) 赎单提货：

OVERSEAS UNION BANK LIMITED
1 Raffles Place, OUB Centre, Singapore 048616.
Telephone: 533 8686 Facsimile: 533 2293
SWIFT: OUBKSGSG Telex: RS 24475 Cable: OVERSUNION

DATE OF ISSUE NOVEMBER 20, 2018
BY COURIER

IRREVOCABLE DOCUMENTARY CREDIT
NO. 5813183050

EXPIRY DATE: JANUARY 15, 2019
IN THE BENEFICIARY'S COUNTRY

APPLICANT
BOLEN TRADING CO (PTE) LTD
42 SG KADUT ST 1
SINGAPORE 729340

BENEFICIARY
SHANGHAI RUIZHI TRADING COMPANY
600 GUBEI ROAD
SHANGHAI CHINA

ADVISING BANK
SHANGHAI PUDONG DEVELOPMENT BANK
INTERNATIONAL DEPT NO: 50
NINGBO ROAD SHANGHAI 200002 CHINA

AMOUNT
USD139,100.00
UNITED STATES DOLLAR ONE HUNDRED THIRTY
NINE THOUSAND ONE HUNDRED ONLY

WE HEREBY ISSUE THIS DOCUMENTARY CREDIT IN YOUR FAVOUR. THIS CREDIT IS AVAILABLE
WITH ADVISING BANK BY NEGOTIATION AGAINST PRESENTATION OF THE FOLLOWING DOCUMENTS
(IN DUPLICATE UNLESS OTHERWISE STATED) AND YOUR DRAFT(S) AT SIGHT DRAWN ON
THE ISSUING BANK.
- SIGNED COMMERCIAL INVOICES IN 4 COPIES.
- FULL SET OF CLEAN ON BOARD MARINE BILLS OF LADING MADE OUT TO
  THE ORDER OF APPLICANT, NOTIFY APPLICANT AND MARKED 'FREIGHT TO COLLECT' AND
  THIS LC NUMBER.
- PACKING LIST AND WEIGHT NOTE SHOWING GOODS PACKED IN SEAWORTHY CARTONS.
- INSURANCE IS TO BE COVERED BY APPLICANT IN WHICH CASE BENEFICIARY IS TO EMAIL
  OR FAX DETAILS OF SHIPMENT INCLUDING QUANTITY, VALUE AND NAME OF VESSEL TO:
  QBE INSURANCE (INTERNATIONAL) PTE LTD
  143 CECIL STREET, NO. 08-01,
  GB BUILDING SINGAPORE 069542
  EMAIL: APPL@QBE.COM.SG   FAX: 2252148
  QUOTING OPEN POLICY NO. EHG 1457941
  A CERTIFICATE TO THIS EFFECT IS REQUIRED.

  SHIPMENT FROM SHANGHAI   TO SINGAPORE
  NOT LATER THAN 31 DECEMBER 2018   PARTIAL SHIPMENT : ALLOWED

DESCRIPTION OF GOODS:
  1 X 20FT CONTAINER OF SILK DETAILS AS PER S/C NO.QICY0593 OF OCTOBER 20, 2018
  TRADE TERM: CFR SHANGHAI

SPECIAL CONDITIONS:
- ALL BANKING CHARGES OUTSIDE SINGAPORE INCLUDING REIMBURSEMENT COMMISSION ARE FOR
  ACCOUNT OF BENEFICIARY.
- DOCUMENTS TO BE PRESENTED WITHIN 15 DAYS AFTER THE DATE OF ISSUANCE OF THE
  TRANSPORT DOCUMENT(S) BUT WITHIN THE VALIDITY OF THE CREDIT.
- WITHOUT ADDING YOUR CONFIRMATION.
- ALL DRAFTS MUST BEAR THIS LC NUMBER.
- NEGOTIATING BANK IS TO FORWARD ALL DOCUMENTS TO US IN ONE LOT BY COURIER.
- UPON RECEIPT OF DOCUMENTS IN COMPLIANCE WITH THIS CREDIT WE SHALL REMIT PROCEEDS
  AS PER NEGOTIATING BANK'S INSTRUCTIONS.
- NEGOTIATING BANK IS TO DEDUCT USD70-00 (OR ITS EQUIVALENT) FROM THE BILL AMOUNT
  CLAIMED FOR EACH PRESENTATION OF DISCREPANT DOCUMENTS UNDER THIS CREDIT;
  NOTWITHSTANDING ANY INSTRUCTIONS TO THE CONTRARY.

THIS DOCUMENTARY CREDIT IS SUBJECT TO 'THE UNIFORM CUSTOMS AND PRACTICE FOR
DOCUMENTARY CREDIT' (2007 REVISION, ICC PUBLICATION NO. 600) AND ENGAGES
US IN ACCORDANCE WITH THE TERMS THEREOF.
THE AMOUNT OF EACH DRAFT MUST BE ENDORSED ON THE REVERSE OF THIS CREDIT
BY THE NEGOTIATING BANK.

OVERSEAS UNION BANK LTD

CHUA SIK KHOON RICKY
A 2090

SPECIMEN

11. 根据以下成交背景资料审核第 10 题中的信用证，说明其存在的问题以及如何进行修改：

出口商：
SHANGHAI RUIZHI IMP & EXP CORPORATION
600 GUBEI ROAD
SHANGHAI CHINA

进口商：
BOLEN TRADING CO
(PTE) LTD
42 SG KADUT ST 1
SINGAPORE

经磋商，双方于 2018 年 10 月 20 日签订了销售合同（S/C NO.QJCY06593）
真丝服装 LADIES' SILK GARMENTS
JFSE 022@USD24.00/PC，JFSF 039@USD6.50/PC
JFSF 040@USD24.00/PC，JFSE 038@USD37.50/PC
每个货号各 1512 PCS
价格条款：CFR
海运出口纸箱包装，集装箱运输，从上海到新加坡
装运时间：2018 年 12 月

双方议定由买方通过新加坡华联银行开立不可撤销即期议付信用证，
通知行为上海浦东发展银行，卖方凭以下单据议付：
—— 即期汇票
—— 商业发票
—— 装箱单
—— 全套正本提单，抬头凭开证银行指示，标注"运费已付"，并通知买方
—— 投保通知

　　　信用证存在的问题　　　　　　　　　　应当如何修改
1)
2)
3)
4)
5)
6)
7)
8)

12. 试翻译以下信开本信用证：

COMMERCIAL BANK OF DUBAI P.S.C

DEIRA BRANCH
P.O.BOX: 1709, DUBAI, U.A.E

IRREVOCABLE DOCUMENTARY	PAGE NO.: [1]	SWIFT:	CBDUAEAD DER
LETTER OF CREDIT NO.:	01DLC077003079	TELEX:	45468 TRBNK EM.
DATE OF ISSUE:	OCTOBER 19, 2018	TELEFAX:	251089 / 254565
DATE OF EXPIRY:	DECEMBER 17, 2018	TELEPHONE:	253222 (10 LINES)
PLACE OF EXPIRY:	CHINA		

BENEFICIARY	APPLICANT
SHANGHAI MINHUA IMP. & EXP. CORPORATION 5/F MINHUA BLDG. 880 HUMING ROAD SHANGHAI CHINA	ALABRA HOME APPL. TRDG CO, LLC. P.O.BOX .21352, DUBAI UAE

ADVISING BANK	CURRENCY AND AMOUNT
BANK OF CHINA SHANGHAI BRANCH 23, CHUNG SHAN ROAD E.1 SHANGHAI CHINA	USD *******49,550.00 UNITED STATES DOLLARS FORTY NINE THOUSAND FIVE HUNDRED AND FIFTY ONLY.

DETAILS OF SHIPMENT		AVAILABLE WITH
TRANSSHIPMENT:	NOT ALLOWED	THE ADVISING BANK ONLY BY NEGOTIATION AGAINST
PARTSHIPMENT:	ALLOWED	PRESENTATION OF DOCUMENTS DESCRIBED HEREIN
SHIPMENT FROM:	CHINA	AND BENEFICIARY'S DRAFT(S) AT SIGHT DRAWN ON
TO:	DUBAI	US.
BY:	VESSEL	**TERMS OF DELIVERY**
NOT LATER THAN:	DECEMBER 02, 2018	CFR DUBAI

DESCRIPTION OF GOODS :

HOUSEHOLD WARES (FOUR ITEMS OF LAMPS)
ALL OTHER DETAILS AS PER INDENT NO. SSTE /363 / CN-9 OF M/S. SALEM SAUD TRADING EST., AND SALES
CONFIRMATION NO. SHMHSC-07210 DATED OCTOBER 03, 2018.
SHIPPING MARKS: ALABRA / SHMHSC-07210 / DUBAI / C/NO.1-UP

DOCUMENTS REQUIRED :

01- SIGNED COMMERCIAL INVOICE IN {THREE } COPIES CERTIFIED TO BE TRUE AND CORRECT MENTIONING
FULL NAME AND ADDRESS OF THE MANUFACTURER AND TERMS OF DELIVERY.

02- CERTIFICATE OF ORIGIN STATING GOODS ARE OF CHINA ORIGIN ISSUED BY CHINA COUNCIL FOR THE
PROMOTION OF INTERNATIONAL TRADE, MENTIONING NAME AND ADDRESS OF THE MANUFACTURER /
PRODUCER & EXPORTER.

03- COMPLETE SET OF (3/3) CLEAN ON BOARD SHIPPING COMPANY'S BILL OF LADING ISSUED TO THE ORDER
OF COMMERCIAL BANK OF DUBAI PSC.[DUBAI] MARKED "FREIGHT PREPAID " AND NOTIFY
APPLICANT.

04- PACKING LIST IN [THREE] COPIES.

05- INSURANCE COVERED IN DUBAI.
SHIPMENT ADVICE MUST BE SENT TO M/S. IRAN INSURANCE CO., P.O.BOX 2004, DUBAI BY REGISTERED POST
OR BY FAX ON FAX NO.217660 QUOTING THEIR OPEN POLICY NO. OMP/ 531 /91 AND STATING OUR L/C NO. ,
AMOUNT, VESSEL NAME AND SHIPPING MARKS THEREIN AND A COPY OF SUCH SHIPMENT ADVICE ALONG
WITH THE ORIGINAL POSTAL RECEIPT / FAX COPY MUST ACCOMPANY THE DOCUMENTS.

CONTINUED ON PAGE NO. 2

COMMERCIAL BANK OF DUBAI P.S.C

بنك دبي التجاري ش.م.ع

DEIRA BRANCH
P.O.BOX: 1709, DUBAI, U.A.E

IRREVOCABLE DOCUMENTARY   PAGE NO.: [2]
LETTER OF CREDIT NO.:   01DLC07003079   DATE OF ISSUE: OCTOBER 19, 2018
USD *******49,550.00

06- A CERTIFICATE FROM THE SHIP OWNER / AGENT STATING THAT THE CARRYING VESSEL IS NOT AN
ISRAELI OWNED VESSEL AND IS NOT SCHEDULED TO CALL AT ANY ISRAELI PORT ON ROUTE TO ITS
DESTINATION AND THE VESSEL IS NOT PROHIBITED TO ENTER ANY ARAB PORT FOR ANY REASON
WHATSOEVER IN ACCORDANCE WITH ITS LOCAL LAWS AND REGULATIONS . [THIS IS NOT REQUIRED IF
SHIPMENT IS EFFECTED BY UNITED ARAB SHIPPING COMPANY'S VESSEL].

OTHER CONDITIONS:
01- CERTIFICATE OF ORIGIN SHOULD INCLUDE THE NAME OF THE COUNTRY FROM WHERE THE GOODS
    ARE EXPORTED.

02- GOODS MUST BE SHIPPED IN 4X20FT CONTAINERS AND B/L MUST EVIDENCE THE COMPLIANCE.

03- COMMISSION @1% OF THE INVOICE VALUE MUST BE DEDUCTED FROM THE PAYMENT TO THE
    BENEFICIARY AT THE TIME OF NEGOTIATION FOR PAYMENT TO MR. C.H.B. MOHD KUNHI, P.O.BOX
    51495, DUBAI WHICH MUST BE CERTIFIED IN THE NEGOTIATING BANK'S COVERING SCHEDULE.

04- B/L SHOULD BEAR VESSEL AGENT'S NAME, ADDRESS AND TELEPHONE NUMBER AT PORT OF
    DESTINATION.

05- SHORT FORM B/L NOT ACCEPTABLE .

06- INVOICE & TRANSPORT DOCUMENTS SHOULD BEAR SHIPPING MARKS AND TOTAL GROSS WEIGHT,
    NET WEIGHT AND MEASUREMENT.

07- THE NUMBER AND THE DATE OF THIS CREDIT AND NAME OF OUR BANK MUST BE
    QUOTED ON ALL DOCUMENTS.

08- ALL DOCUMENTS TO BE ISSUED IN ENGLISH LANGUAGE.

09- ALL CHARGES INCLUDING REIMBURSING CHARGES EXCEPT L/C ISSUING CHARGES ARE ON
    ACCOUNT OF BENEFICIARY.

INSTRUCTIONS TO NEGOTIATION BANK:
- NOTE EACH PRESENTATION ON THE REVERSE OF THIS LETTER OF CREDIT.
- DISPATCH THE FULL SET OF THE NEGOTIATED DOCUMENTS TO US IN ONE LOT BY COURIER SERVICE.
- ON RECEIPT OF CREDIT COMPLIED DOCUMENTS PAYMENT SHALL BE EFFECTED BY US PER CREDIT
   TERMS AS PER NEGOTIATION BANK'S COVERING SCHEDULE.

EXCEPT AS OTHERWISE STATED HEREIN , THIS CREDIT IS SUBJECT TO UNIFORM CUSTOMS AND PRACTICE
FOR DOCUMENTARY CREDITS [2007 REVISION] , INTERNATIONAL CHAMBER OF COMMERCE PUBLICATION
NO. 600.

For COMMERCIAL BANK OF DUBAI P.S.C

Authorised Signature   Authorised Signature

SPECIMEN

13. 试翻译以下 SWIFT 信用证：

```
2018AUG31        13:29:18                        LOGICAL TERMINAL      P005
MT  S700              ISSUE OF A DOCUMENTARY CREDIT          PAGE   00001
                                                             FUNC   SWPR3
                                                             UMR    14635414
MSGACK DWS765I AUTH OK, KEY B6852DT5E5896814, BKCHCNBJ OCBCSGSGBRN RECORD
BASIC HEADER          F    01    BKCHCNBJA300        2514       968514
APPLICATION HEADER    O   700    6814    180831  ROYBANKCNDA  6323 938214    180831   2514  N
                                                 THE ROYAL BANK OF CANADA
                                                 4022 SHIPPARD AVE. E
                                                 SCARBOROUGH TORONTO
                                                 CANADA
USER HEADER           SERVICE CODE       103:
                      BANK. PRIORITY      113:
                      MSG USER REF.       108:
                      INFO. FROM CI       115:
SEQUENCE OF TOTAL    * 27    : 1/1
FORM OF DOC. CREDIT  * 40A   : IRREVOCABLE
DOC. CREDIT NUMBER   * 20    : ROYALBKDLC071501
DATE OF ISSUE         31C    : 180831
EXPIRY               * 31D   : DATE   181121        PLACE    CHINA
APPLICANT            * 50    : PARANDAR INTERNATIONAL INC.,
                              3761 VICTORIA PARK AVE.,
                              UNIT#7,TORONTO,ONTARIO
                              CANADA
BENEFICIARY          * 59    : SHANGHAI MORNING STAR TRADING CO.,LTD.
                              375 DONG DA MING ROAD
                              SHANGHAI 200008
                              P.R.CHINA
AMOUNT               * 32B   : CURRENCY    USD    AMOUNT       80391.40
MAX. CREDIT AMOUNT    39B    : NOT EXCEEDING
AVAILABLE WITH/BY    * 41A   : ADVISING BANK ONLY
                              BY NEGOTIATION
DRAFT AT ...          42C    : 30 DAYS AFTER B/L DATE        FOR FULL INVOICE VALUE
DRAWEE                42A    : THE ROYAL BANK OF CANADA
                              4022 SHIPPARD AVE. E
                              SCARBOROUGH TORONTO
                              CANADA
PARTIAL SHIPMENTS     43P    : NOT ALLOWED
TRANSSHIPMENT         43T    : NOT ALLOWED
LOADING IN CHARGE     44A    : SHANGHAI
FOR TRANSPORT TO...   44B    : TORONTO
LATEST DATE OF SHIP.  44C    : 181031
DESCRIPT. OF GOODS    45A    :
                      PORCELAIN DINNERWARES
                      AS PER SALES CONTRACT NO.SMSC07210 DATED 180819
                      CIF  TORONTO
                      SHIPPING MARKS:      PARANDA
                                           SMSC07210
                                           TORONTO
                                           C/NO.1-UP
DOCUMENTS REQUIRED    46A    :
          1 SIGNED COMMERCIAL INVOICE IN TRIPLICATE SHOWING SHIPPING MARKS AND
            STATING THAT MERCHANDISE IS IN ACCORDANCE WITH APPLICANT'S ORDER NO.
            PARANDAPO-07814 INDICATING FOB VALUE, FREIGHT AND INSURANCE CHARGES.

          2 PACKING LIST IN DUPLICATE INDICATING MEASUREMENT, GROSS WEIGHT AND
            NET WEIGHT OF EACH ARTICLE NO. AS WELL AS EACH PACKAGE.
```

2018AUG31　　　13:29:18　　　　　　　　　　　　　LOGICAL TERMINAL　　P005
MT S700　　　　　　ISSUE OF A DOCUMENTARY CREDIT　　　　PAGE　　00002
　　　　　　　　　　　　　　　　　　　　　　　　　　　　　　　FUNC　　SWPR3
　　　　　　　　　　　　　　　　　　　　　　　　　　　　　　　UMR　　14635414

3 COMPLETE SET OF 4 ORIGINAL CLEAN SHIPPED ON BOARD OCEAN BILLS OF
　LADING MADE OUT TO THE SHIPPER'S ORDER AND ENDORSED TO THE ORDER OF
　ISSUING BANK MARKED 'FREIGHT PREPAID' AND NOTIFY APPLICANT.

4 CERTIFICATE OF ORIGIN GSP FORM A IN DUPLICATE STATING THAT THE GOODS
　ARE OF CHINESE ORIGIN.

5 INSURANCE POLICY OR CERTIFICATE IN DUPLICATE, ENDORSED TO ISSUING BANK'S
　ORDER FOR 110 PCT OF THE INVOICE VALUE, STIPULATING THAT CLAIMS ARE
　PAYABLE IN THE CURRENCY OF THE DRAFT AND ALSO INDICATING A CLAIM
　SETTLING AGENT AT DESTINATION SHOWING THE INSURANCE COVERAGE AS:
　INSTITUTE CARGO CLAUSES (A) AND INSTITUTE CARGO CLAUSES WAR RISKS
　AS PER ICC DATED 1/1/2009.

DETAILS OF CHARGES　　　71B　: ALL BANKING CHARGES INCLUDING
　　　　　　　　　　　　　　　　ADVISING, NEGOTIATION AND REIMBURSEMENT
　　　　　　　　　　　　　　　　ARE FOR THE ACCOUNT OF BENEFICIARY.
PRESENTATION PERIOD　　48　: DOCUMENTS TO BE PRESENTED WITHIN 21 DAYS AFTER
　　　　　　　　　　　　　　　　THE DATE OF SHIPMENT BUT WITHIN THE VALIDITY OF THE CREDIT.
CONFIRMATION　　　　　* 49　: WITHOUT
ADDITIONAL COND.　　　47B　:
　　1 DRAFT SHOULD BEAR A CLAUSE 'DRAWN UNDER DOCUMENTARY CREDIT NO.
　　　ROYALBKDLC071501 OF THE ROYAL BANK OF CANADA DATED 180831.

　　2 TWO ADDITIONAL COPIES/PHOTOCOPIES OF THE RELATIVE INVOICE(S) AND
　　　TRANSPORT DOCUMENT(S) ARE REQUESTED TO BE PRESENTED TOGETHER
　　　WITH THE DOCUMENTS FOR THE ISSUING BANK'S REFERENCE ONLY.

　　3 B/L MUST INDICATE THE FREIGHT AMOUNT AND THE NUMNERS OF THE CONTANIERS BEING
　　　SHIPPED TOGETHER WITH THE CONTAINER AND SEAL NUMBERS.

　　4 BENEFICIARY SHOULD SEND SHIPPING ADVICE TO APPLICANT WITHIN 48 HOURS
　　　AFTER THE SHIPMENT INDICATING VESSEL'S NAME, SHIPMENT DATE, NUMBER
　　　OF PACKAGES, SHIPPING MARKS, LC NO. AND AMOUNT. ONE COPY OF SUCH
　　　ADVICE MUST ACCOMPANY THE DOCUMENTS.

　　5 ALL DOCUMENTS MUST BEAR NAME OF ISSUING BANK AND LC NO. AND SC NO.,
　　　DOCUMENTS ISSUED PRIOR TO THE ISSUANCE OF THIS LC ARE NOT ACCEPTABLE.
INSTRUCTIONS　　　　　78　:
　　　　　　　　　　　T.T. REIMBURSEMENT IS NOT ACCEPTABLE.
　　　　　　　　　　　IN REIMBURSEMENT, NEGOTIATING BANK MUST DISPATCH ALL DOCUMENTS
　　　　　　　　　　　BY REGISTERED AIRMAIL OR AIR COURIER TO US IN ONE LOT.
　　　　　　　　　　　A DISCREPANCY FEE OF USD50.00 WILL BE DEDUCTED FROM THE
　　　　　　　　　　　PROCEEDS IF DOCUMENTS ARE PRESENTED WITH DISCREPANCY(IES) AND
　　　　　　　　　　　ACCEPTANCE OF SUCH DISCREPANT DOCUMENTS WILL NOT IN ANY WAY
　　　　　　　　　　　ALTER THE TERMS AND CONDITIONS OF THIS CREDIT.
　　　　　　　　　　　UPON RECEIPT OF FULL SET OF DOCUMENTS IN ORDER, WE SHALL
　　　　　　　　　　　REIMBURSE YOU ACCORDING TO YOUR INSTRUCTIONS.
SEND. TO REC. INFO.　　72　: SUBJECT TO U.C.P.　　2007 REVISION
　　　　　　　　　　　　　　I.C.C. PUBLICATION　　NO.600
TRAILER　　　　　　　　　ORDER IS <MAC:> <PAC:> <ENC:> <CHK:> <TNG:> <PDE:>
　　　　　　　　　　　　　　MAC:　9KE93827
　　　　　　　　　　　　　　CHK:　975CIE982287

草拟改证函

14. 试代表天宇公司发邮件确认,要求对方修改信用证。

    2018 年 12 月 20 日

    上海天宇贸易公司与韩国 DEASUNG 有限公司签订合同。

    合同号码为 STX-5491。

Shipment to be effected by the end of February 2019 with the relevant L/C reaching the seller by January 15, 2019.

    2019 年 1 月 30 日

    DEASUNG 终于把证开到了。开证行是 Korea Development Bank (KDB) Seoul Branch,证号为 NSW6180,装运期是 2 月份,有效期至 3 月 15 日。

    为避免在交付货物后不能顺利收汇,打电话给客户要求信用证展期,装运期延至 3 月 15 日,有效期延至 3 月底。谨慎起见,同时发信确认。

15.

这两天我去北京出差,下周一回来。

NALABILU BANK YOKOHAMA BRANCH 开来的信用证 No. MMK7664 我已审核完毕,问题如下:

    1.   按合同规定应为空运,但信用证却要求提交海运提单。

    2.   信用证要求提交厂商检验证明,但芒果是农产品,不可能提供。

    3.   信用证禁止分批,但按合同应改为允许。

    4.   信用证未按合同要求加具保兑。

请代我给 Fuji Trading Co., Ltd. 写信,要求改证。谢谢!

试根据下列要求拟写改证函。

16.

信 用 证 预 审 单

本证于 2018 年 10 月 7 日收到

No. 128755

开证行	Australia Commercial Bank Perth Branch		开证日	2018.10.6.	
申请人	Simpson & Kemp Ltd., 34 Madison Street, Perth, Australia		受益人	Shanghai Minjie Imp. & Exp. Co. 343 Guangdong Rd. Shanghai, China	
信用证金额	USD 23454.00 (应为 23554)		信用证号码	EX0127	
汇票付款人	开证行		汇票期限	见票后 30 天 (应为即期)	
可否转运	可以		可否分批	可以	
装运期限	2018.12.15	有效期限	2018.12.31	到期地点	Perth
唛头	未指定		交单日	提单日后 14 天	

单据名称	提单	发票	海关发票	保险单	装箱单	重量单	产地证	普惠制原产地证明	寄单证明	寄单邮据	寄样证明	寄样邮据	检验证明		
银行	2/3	4		2	3		2	3					2		
客户	1/3														

提单或承运单据	抬头	to order	保险	一切险加战争险		
	通知	buyer				
	注意事项	注明运费已付		加成 10%	赔款地点	目的港

备注:

1) 检验证明由申请人指定的人员签发

2) 货物描述中货号 HK778（应为 HP778）

试根据以上信用证预审单拟写改证函,要求对上述阴影条款进行修改。

第六章　出口托运订舱

案　例

2018 年 10 月 15 日,环宇公司接中国银行上海分行通知,收到 F. Van Lan-schot Bankiers N. V. 银行开立的信用证修改书(第 200 页),经审核,符合公司的改证要求。

2018 年 10 月 28 日,环宇公司接供应商——上海普华玩具公司通知货物已备妥,公司向其支付货款,收到增值税发票(第 201 页)。

2018 年 10 月 29 日,环宇公司委托货运代理向船公司订舱。

工作任务

制作订舱文件:出口货物订舱委托书、商业发票、装箱单。

信用证修改书

```
2018OCT15        08:29:35                            LOGICAL TERMINAL 1345
MT S707                      AMENDMENT OF A DOCUMENTARY CREDIT        PAGE  00001
                                                                     FUNC  SWPF
                                                                     UMR   15893

MSGACK DWS765I AUTH OK, KEY B852D12E58D96C34, BKCHCNBJ BOCSUCM RECORD
BASIC HEADER              F 01    BKCHCNBJA300           852    47552
APPLICATION HEADER    O  707  1863  181015   FVLBNL22XXX  3256 124586    18101
                                        F.VAN LANSCHOT BANKIERS N.V.
                                        *ROTTERDAM
                                        *NETHERLANDS
USER HEADER  SERVICE CODE            103:
             BANK. PRIORITY          113:
             MSG USER REF.           108:
             INFO. FROM CI           115:
SENDER'S REFERENCE      * 20    : AM/VA07721SLC
RECEIVER'S REFERENCE    * 21    : NONREF
NUMBER OF AMENDMENT     26E     : 1
DATE OF AMENDMENT       30      : 181015
DATE OF ISSUE           31C     : 181008
BENEFICIARY (BEFORE THIS AMENDMENT)       * 59 :    SHANGHAI UNIVERSAL TRADING CO., LTD.
                                                    MAYING PLAZA, 131 DONGFANG ROAD,
                                                    SHANGHAI 200120, CHINA

NARRATIVE               79      :
    ++     UNDER FIELD 31D
           AMEND "DATE 181130" TO "DATE 181215" AND
           "PLACE NETHERLANDS" TO "PLACE CHINA"
    ++     UNDER FIELD 59
           AMEND "MAYING PLAZA" TO "MAYLING PLAZA"
    ++     UNDER FIELD 42C
           AMEND TO READ:        AT SIGHT FOR FULL INVOICE VALUE
    ++     UNDER FIELD 44C
           AMEND TO READ:        181130
    ++     UNDER FIELD 45A
           AMEND "2088 SETS" TO "2080 SETS"
    ++     UNDER FIELD 46A
           AMEND "2/3 OF ORIGINAL CLEAN ON-BOARD MARINE BILLS OF LADING..." TO "FULL SET 3/3 OF
           ORIGINAL CLEAN ON-BOARD MARINE BILLS OF LADING…"
    ++     UNDER FIELD 46A
           AMEND "FULL SET 3/3 OF MARINE INSURANCE POLICY … FOR 120 PERCENT OF FULL CIF VALUE..."
           TO "FULL SET 3/3 OF MARINE INSURANCE POLICY … FOR 110 PERCENT OF FULL CIF VALUE …"
    ++     UNDER FIELD 46A
           DELETE THE WORDING " THE 1/3 ORIGINAL B/L" IN THE CLAUSE "BENEFICIARY'S CERTIFICATE
           STATING THAT ONE SET OF … WITHIN 72 HOURS AFTER SHIPMENT"
    ++     UNDER FIELD 46A
           DELETE THE CLAUSE "ORIGINAL AND COPY OF QUALITY INSPECTION CERTIFICATE ISSUED
           AND SIGNED BY THE APPLICANT" AND ADD THE CLAUSE " ORIGINAL AND COPY OF QUALITY
           INSPECTION CERTIFICATE ISSUED AND SIGNED BY COMPETENT AUTHORITY AT PORT OF
           LOADING"
    ++     UNDER FIELD 71B
           AMEND TO READ:
           ALL BANKING CHARGES OUTSIDE NETHERLANDS ARE FOR BENEFICIARY'S ACCOUNT
ALL OTHER TERMS AND CONDITIONS REMAIN UNCHANGED
SEND. TO REC. INFO.          72     : /PHONBEN/
```

增值税发票

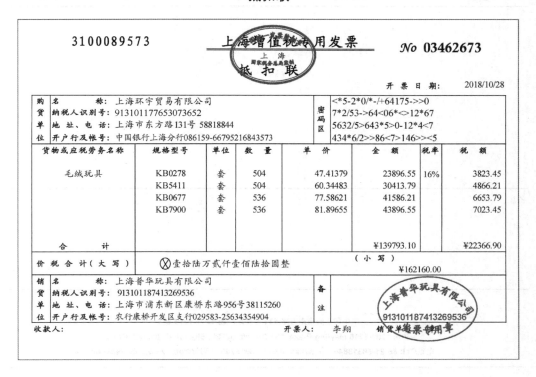

~发票联~

3100089573　　上海增值税专用发票　　No 03462673

开票日期：　2018/10/28

购货单位	名　　称：上海环宇贸易有限公司 纳税人识别号：913101177653073652 地址、电话：上海市东方路131号 58818844 开户行及帐号：中国银行上海分行086159-66795216843573	密码区	<*5-2*0/*-/+64175->>0 7*2/53->64<06*<>12*67 5632/5>643*5>0-12*4<7 434*6/2>>86<7>146>><5

货物或应税劳务名称	规格型号	单位	数量	单价	金额	税率	税额
毛绒玩具	KB0278	套	504	47.41379	23896.55	16%	3823.45
	KB5411	套	504	60.34483	30413.79		4866.21
	KB0677	套	536	77.58621	41586.21		6653.79
	KB7900	套	536	81.89655	43896.55		7023.45
合　　计					¥139793.10		¥22366.90

价税合计（大写）　　⊗壹拾陆万贰仟壹佰陆拾圆整　　（小写）　　¥162160.00

销货单位	名　　称：上海普华玩具有限公司 纳税人识别号：913101187413269536 地址、电话：上海市浦东新区康桥东路956号38115260 开户行及帐号：农行康桥开发区支行029583-25634354904	备注	上海普华玩具有限公司 913101187413269536 销货单位发票专用章

收款人：　　　　　　　　　　　　　　开票人：　李翔

~抵扣联~

3100089573　　上海增值税专用发票　　No 03462673

开票日期：　2018/10/28

购货单位	名　　称：上海环宇贸易有限公司 纳税人识别号：913101177653073652 地址、电话：上海市东方路131号 58818844 开户行及帐号：中国银行上海分行086159-66795216843573	密码区	<*5-2*0/*-/+64175->>0 7*2/53->64<06*<>12*67 5632/5>643*5>0-12*4<7 434*6/2>>86<7>146>><5

货物或应税劳务名称	规格型号	单位	数量	单价	金额	税率	税额
毛绒玩具	KB0278	套	504	47.41379	23896.55	16%	3823.45
	KB5411	套	504	60.34483	30413.79		4866.21
	KB0677	套	536	77.58621	41586.21		6653.79
	KB7900	套	536	81.89655	43896.55		7023.45
合　　计					¥139793.10		¥22366.90

价税合计（大写）　　⊗壹拾陆万贰仟壹佰陆拾圆整　　（小写）　　¥162160.00

销货单位	名　　称：上海普华玩具有限公司 纳税人识别号：913101187413269536 地址、电话：上海市浦东新区康桥东路956号38115260 开户行及帐号：农行康桥开发区支行029583-25634354904	备注	上海普华玩具有限公司 913101187413269536 销货单位发票专用章

收款人：　　　　　　　　　　　　　　开票人：　李翔

⬇ 订舱委托书

上 海 环 宇 贸 易 有 限 公 司
Shanghai Universal Trading Co., Ltd.

出 口 货 物 订 舱 委 托 书

					日期
发货人		装船期限			
		运输方式	☐	BY SEA ☐	BY AIR
		装箱方式	☐	FCL ☐	LCL
		集装箱种类	☐	20'GP ☐	40'GP
		集装箱数量			
收货人		转船运输	☐	YES ☐	NO
		分批装运	☐	YES ☐	NO
		运费交付	☐	PREPAID ☐	COLLECT
被通知人		装运口岸			
		目的港			
		成交条件			
		联系人			
		电话/传真			

标记唛码	货物描述	总件数	总毛重	总尺码

备注

中国上海市东方路 **131** 号美陵广场 **1201-1216** 室
Rm. 1201-1216 Mayling Plaza, 131 Dongfang Rd., Shanghai, 200120, China
电话/Tel: 86-21-58818844　传真/Fax: 86-21-58818766　网址/Web: www.universal.com.cn

商业发票

Shanghai Universal Trading Co., Ltd.

Rm. 1201-1216 Mayling Plaza,
131 Dongfang Rd.,
Shanghai, 200120, China
Tel: 86-21-58818844
Fax: 86-21-58818766

COMMERCIAL INVOICE

TO:

INV. NO. : _____
INV. DATE: _____
S/C NO. : _____

FROM: _____ TO: _____ SHIPPED BY: _____

MARKS & NOS.	DESCRIPTION OF GOODS	QUANTITY	UNIT PRICE	AMOUNT

TOTAL AMOUNT IN WORDS:

TOTAL G.W. / TOTAL N.W.:
TOTAL PACKAGES:

装箱单

Shanghai Universal Trading Co., Ltd.

Rm. 1201-1216 Mayling Plaza,
131 Dongfang Rd.,
Shanghai, 200120, China
Tel: 86-21-58818844
Fax: 86-21-58818766

PACKING LIST

TO:

INV. NO. : _____

INV. DATE: _____

FROM: _____ TO: _____ SHIPPED BY: _____

C/NO.	DESCRIPTION OF GOODS	PKG.	QTY	G.W.	N.W.	MEAS.

TOTAL:

TOTAL PACKAGE IN WORDS:

MARKS & NOS.:

示　范

上 海 环 宇 贸 易 有 限 公 司
Shanghai Universal Trading Co., Ltd.

出 口 货 物 订 舱 委 托 书

日期　2018/10/29

发货人	装船期限	NOV 30, 2018			
SHANGHAI UNIVERSAL TRADING CO., LTD.	运输方式	☒	BY SEA	☐	BY AIR
MAYLING PLAZA,	装箱方式	☒	FCL	☐	LCL
131 DONGFANG ROAD,	集装箱种类	☒	20'GP	☐	40'GP
SHANGHAI 200120, CHINA	集装箱数量	2			
收货人	转船运输	☐	YES	☒	NO
TO ORDER	分批装运	☒	YES	☐	NO
	运费交付	☒	PREPAID	☐	COLLECT
被通知人	装运口岸	SHANGHAI			
TIVOLIAN TRADING B.V.	目的港	ROTTERDAM			
P.O. BOX 1783, HEIMAN DULLAERTOLEIN 3	成交条件	CIF			
3024CA ROTTERDAM, NETHERLANDS	联系人	王凯			
PHONE NUMBER: 0031-10-4767418	电话/传真	021-58818844			

标记唛码	货物描述	总件数	总毛重	总尺码
AS PER INVOICE NO. HY-TIV-INV0373	PLUSH TOYS	386CTNS	3155.000KGS	49.646M3

备注 1)　提单须提交的份数：全套3份正本

　　　2)　提单须标明"FREIGHT PREPAID"

　　　3)　提单须注明承运人在卸货港的代理的名称和地址

　　　4)　提单须注明信用证号码AM/VA07721SLC

　　　5)　承运船只应隶属于班轮公会且船龄不超过20年。船公司还需就此另行出具一份证明。

中国上海市东方路 131 号美陵广场 1201-1216 室
Rm. 1201-1216 Mayling Plaza, 131 Dongfang Rd., Shanghai, 200120, China
电话/Tel: 86-21-58818844　传真/Fax: 86-21-58818766　网址/Web: www.universal.com.cn

Shanghai Universal Trading Co., Ltd.

Rm. 1201-1216 Mayling Plaza,
131 Dongfang Rd.,
Shanghai, 200120, China
Tel: 86-21-58818844
Fax: 86-21-58818766

COMMERCIAL INVOICE

TO:	TIVOLIAN TRADING B.V.	INV. NO. :	HY-TIV-INV0373
	P.O. BOX 1783, HEIMAN DULLAERTOLEIN 3	INV. DATE:	OCT. 29, 2018
	3024CA ROTTERDAM, NETHERLANDS	S/C NO. :	HY-TIV0373

FROM:	SHANGHAI	TO:	ROTTERDAM	SHIPPED BY:

MARKS & NOS.	DESCRIPTION OF GOODS		QUANTITY	UNIT PRICE	AMOUNT
CE/IMP.087 TIV-PO-CSH0873 ROTTERDAM	PLUSH TOYS			CIF ROTTERDAM	
CARTON NO. 1 - 126 KB0278	KB0278	TWIN BEAR	504SETS	US$9.60	US$4,838.40
	KB5411	TWIN BEAR IN BALLET COSTUME	504SETS	US$11.50	US$5,796.00
	KB0677	BROWN BEAR WITH RED BOW	536SETS	US$14.50	US$7,772.00
CE/IMP.087	KB7900	BEAR IN PINK T-SHIRT	536SETS	US$15.40	US$8,254.40
TIV-PO-CSH0873 ROTTERDAM CARTON NO. 1 - 126 KB5411					US$26,660.80
F-TOYS 228 TIV-PO-CSH0873 ROTTERDAM CARTON NO. 1 - 67 KB0677					
F-TOYS 228 TIV-PO-CSH0873 ROTTERDAM CARTON NO. 1 - 67 KB7900					

TOTAL AMOUNT IN WORDS: SAY U.S. DOLLARS TWENTY SIX THOUSAND SIX HUNDRED AND SIXTY AND CENTS EIGHTY ONLY

TOTAL G.W. / TOTAL N.W.: 3155.000KGS / 2190.000KGS
TOTAL PACKAGES: 386CTNS

上 海 环 宇 贸 易 有 限 公 司
SHANGHAI UNIVERSAL TRADING CO., LTD.

李玫师

(SIGNATURE)

Shanghai Universal Trading Co., Ltd.

Rm. 1201-1216 Mayling Plaza,
131 Dongfang Rd.,
Shanghai, 200120, China
Tel: 86-21-58818844
Fax: 86-21-58818766

PACKING LIST

TO: TIVOLIAN TRADING B.V.   **INV. NO. :** HY-TIV-INV0373
        P.O. BOX 1783, HEIMAN DULLAERTOLEIN 3   **INV. DATE:** OCT. 29, 2018
        3024CA ROTTERDAM, NETHERLANDS

FROM: SHANGHAI   TO: ROTTERDAM   SHIPPED BY:

C/NO.	DESCRIPTION OF GOODS	PKG.	QTY	G.W.	N.W.	MEAS.
	PLUSH TOYS					
CE/IMP.087 TIV-PO-CSH0873 ROTTERDAM CARTON NO. 1 - 126 KB0278	KB0278	126CTNS	504SETS	1008.000KGS	693.000KGS	12.474M3
CE/IMP.087 TIV-PO-CSH0873 ROTTERDAM CARTON NO. 1 - 126 KB5411	KB5411	126CTNS	504SETS	1008.000KGS	693.000KGS	12.474M3
F-TOYS 228 TIV-PO-CSH0873 ROTTERDAM CARTON NO. 1 - 67 KB0677	KB0677	67CTNS	536SETS	569.500KGS	402.000KGS	12.349M3
F-TOYS 228 TIV-PO-CSH0873 ROTTERDAM CARTON NO. 1 - 67 KB7900	KB7900	67CTNS	536SETS	569.500KGS	402.000KGS	12.349M3
	TOTAL:	386CTNS	2080SETS	3155.000KGS	2190.000KGS	49.646M3

TOTAL PACKAGES IN WORDS: SAY THREE HUNDRED AND EIGHTY SIX CARTONS ONLY

MARKS & NOS.: AS SHOWN IN C/NO.

上 海 环 宇 贸 易 有 限 公 司
SHANGHAI UNIVERSAL TRADING CO., LTD.

(SIGNATURE)

⬚ 示范评析

1. 订舱委托书上的"发货人"、"收货人"、"通知人"即 Shipper、Consignee、Notify Party，必须按照信用证的提单条款缮制，因为在船公司签发提单时这三项内容将直接复制到提单上面，马虎不得。其次，"装船期限"、"转船运输"、"分批装运"三栏也要根据信用证的规定填写，以便船公司在配船时能符合信用证的规定。信用证对于提单的其他特别规定以及需要船公司、承运人签发的文件，例如本案例中，信用证要求提单须注明承运人在卸货港的代理的名称和地址，并需要承运人证明承运船只隶属于班轮公会、船龄不超过 20 年，这些特殊要求都应该在"备注"栏内写明，以便船公司缮制的提单能符合信用证的要求，或能提供符合信用证规定的其他文件。值得注意的是，这里所说的信用证，泛指信用证及信用证修改书，切勿仅仅参照信用证却忽略了信用证修改书中已作过的变更。

2. 我们注意到，在本案例示范的订舱委托书中并没有将具体的运输标志（唛头）打上去，而是简单地打上了"AS PER INVOICE NO.HY-TIV-INV0373"的字样。这是因为，根据此笔交易信用证的规定，每个货号都有自己独立的唛头，进口商这样的要求通常是便于进口后能快速识别货物，以便分拨给不同的最终买家。所以，如果要在订舱委托书上打上唛头的话，就要打上四种不同的唛头。为了降低单据填制上的难度，我们就打上了"AS PER INVOICE NO. HY-TIV-INV0373"，意即商品的唛头以 HY-TIV-INV0373 号商业发票上显示的为准。由于在委托订舱时除了提交订舱委托书以外同时还有商业发票及装箱单，因此，船公司的经办人员还是可以方便地从相应的发票中了解到商品唛头的情况。

3. 假设本案例中信用证规定四个货号均使用唛头 CE/IMP.087/TIV-PO-CSH0873/ROTTERDAM/CARTON NO.1 AND UP，那么我们在实际刷唛（在纸箱上做运输标志）时，可对装有 KB0278、KB5411、KB0677、KB7900 的四类纸箱依次做以下四种编号：

CE/IMP.087	CE/IMP.087	CE/IMP.087	CE/IMP.087
TIV-PO-CSH0873	TIV-PO-CSH0873	TIV-PO-CSH0873	TIV-PO-CSH0873
ROTTERDAM	ROTTERDAM	ROTTERDAM	ROTTERDAM
CARTON NO.1-126	CARTON NO.127-252	CARTON NO.253-319	CARTON NO.320-386

这样，只要我们看到编号是 1-126 的纸箱，就可以肯定里面装的是 KB0278，凡编号为 127-252 的纸箱装的就是 KB5411。这为收货人搞清每个纸箱内的商品规

格提供了极大的方便。当然,我们也可以在货号 KB0278 的纸箱外刷上 127-252、而在货号 KB5411 的纸箱外刷上 1-126,又或者在货号 KB0677 的纸箱上刷上 1-67、其他的货号随之变更。正因为存在着多种编号的方法,刷唛人(卖方)就必须通过一份文件来告诉收货人(买方)自己所采用的编号方式,这份文件就是“装箱单”,装箱单上的“C/NO.”即指箱号(纸箱编号)。以前面所述的第一种编号方法为例,装箱单上应显示为:

C/NO.	DESCRIPTION OF GOODS	PKG.	QTY	G.W.	N.W.	MEAS.
1-126	KB0278	126CTNS	504SETS	1008.000KGS	693.000KGS	12.474M3
127-252	KB5411	126CTNS	504SETS	1008.000KGS	693.000KGS	12.474M3
253-319	KB0677	67CTNS	536SETS	569.500KGS	402.000KGS	12.349M3
320-386	KB7900	67CTNS	536SETS	569.500KGS	402.000KGS	12.349M3

反过来,我们再来看本案例。由于四个货号的唛头各不相同,所以在 C/NO. 栏目如果只显示纸箱编号(CARTON NO.)部分,将出现“1-126”、“1-126”、“1-67”、“1-67”的情形,所以应将唛头的完整信息显示出来为妥。

Q:办理订舱手续时,应如何填写商业发票和装箱单中“SHIPPED BY”栏?

A:由于此时处于订舱阶段,承运船名、航次尚未确定,故此栏可以“留空”。待取得订舱反馈信息(即:配舱回单)后,可将相关的承运船名、航次填入。

指　南

在国际货物买卖中,如采用 CIF 或 CFR 术语成交,则根据《2010 年国际贸易术语解释通则(INCOTERMS 2010)》的有关规定:出口商必须自负费用与承运人订立运输合同,同时负责租用适航的船舶或向船公司订妥必要的班轮舱位。实际业务中,即便是采用 FOB 术语达成的交易,也常有进口商委托出口商代为向船公司洽订舱位的情况发生。

采用跟单信用证作为支付方式的交易,出口商办理订舱手续的前提是"货妥、证符",又称"货证齐备"。所谓"货妥"指的是出口货物已经备妥待运,而"证符"是指出口商审核信用证(及其修改书)并确认无误。在"货证齐备"的基础上,出口商开始进入出口合同履行的"托运订舱"环节。

由于船公司通常只接受货物运输代理(简称货代)向其提出的订舱申请,因此出口商需要通过货运代理向船公司或其代理办理出口货物的订舱手续,并提供相应的出口货物订舱委托书。订舱委托书是出口商委托货代办理订舱事宜的证明文件,内容包括发货人名称、收货人名称、货物明细、启运港、目的港、信用证规定的装运期限、信用证关于分批装运和转运的规定、对运输的要求以及信用证对运输单据的具体要求等等。除此之外,在委托订舱时,出口商还必须向货代提供与本批货物有关的商业发票和装箱单等。

在实际业务操作时,也有出口商将报检、报关以及货物装船等出运环节一并委托货运代理操办的做法,在此情况下,出口商在委托时还必须向货运代理提供提货单(出仓单)、出口货物报检单、出口货物报关单等。

ⓘ 出口货物托运和订舱的流程

◇ 出口商(货主)缮制"出口货物订舱委托书"、商业发票和装箱单,一并交给货运代理委托其向船公司订舱;

◇ 货运代理收到出口商的委托书后,缮制"集装箱货物海运托运单"(俗称"十联单"),向船公司订舱;

◇ 船公司接受订舱后,在"十联单"上标注船名、航次和 D/R 编号,加盖船公司签单章并做装船日期批注(或电告装船日期),然后将"十联单"第五——十联返还给货运代理；

◇ 货运代理留存"十联单"第八联后,将第五、六、七、九、十联交给出口商。

"集装箱货物海运托运单",一式十联,因而又被称为"十联单",各联的名称分别为:

第一联:集装箱货物托运单(货主留底);

第二联:集装箱货物托运单(船代留底);

第三联:运费通知(1);

第四联:运费通知(2);

第五联:装货单 场站收据副本(SHIPPING ORDER,S/O);
   附页 缴纳出口货物港务申请书;

第六联:场站收据副本 大副联;

第七联:场站收据(DOCK RECEIPT,D/R);

第八联:货代留底;

第九联:配舱回单(1);

第十联:配舱回单(2)。

"十联单"虽有多联,然而对于出口商而言,其核心单据为配舱回单、装货单和场站收据,分别说明如下:

第九联 配舱回单 是对订舱委托的反馈,船公司完成配载后会在配舱回单上注明船名、航次和提单号码返还货运代理。

第五联 装货单(Shipping Order,S/O),又称关单,是船公司或其代理向船上负责人(船长或大副)和集装箱装卸作业区签发的一种通知其接受装货的指示文件。在准备装货前,托运人必须先向海关办理出口报关手续。装货单是报关时必须向海关提交的单据之一。经海关查验后,在装货单上加盖放行章,托运人才能凭此装货单要求装货。这也是装货单习称关单的缘由。

第七联 场站收据(Dock Receipt,D/R)是指承运人委托集装箱堆场、集装箱货运站或内陆站在收到整箱货或拼箱货后签发的收据。场站收据的作用类似于传统运输(件杂货、散货运输)中的大副收据(Mate's Receipt,M/R),托运人可凭经签收的 D/R 向船公司或其代理换取正本提单。"第六联 场站收据副本 大副联"供港区配载使用,由港区或由大副留存。

(i) 托运文件的填制

(一) 出口货物订舱委托书

发货人、收货人、被通知人这三栏应根据信用证对提单的相关规定填写,因为货运代理将参照此填写"集装箱货物海运托运单"、进而船公司将据此缮制提单。

◇　**发货人**
Shipper。如信用证无特别规定,一般填写受益人(即出口商)的名称及地址。

◇　**收货人**
Consignee。根据信用证中对运输单据(提单)收货人的规定填写。
例如:信用证规定:...Bill of Lading consigned to ABC Co. ...
　　　　　　　或...Bill of Lading made out to ABC Co. ...
　　收货人　一栏应填写:ABC Co.或 To ABC Co.
　　这意味着收货人即为 ABC 公司

　　信用证规定:...Bill of Lading consigned to order of shipper...
　　　　　　　或...Bill of Lading made out to order of shipper...
　　收货人　一栏应填写:To order of shipper
　　这意味着具体的收货人由发货人通过背书来指定

　　信用证规定:...Bill of Lading consigned to our order...
　　　　　　　或...Bill of Lading made out to order of the issuing bank...
　　而开证行为 XYZ Bank
　　收货人　一栏应填写:To order of XYZ Bank
　　这意味着由 XYZ 银行通过背书来指定收货人

◇　**被通知人**
Notify Party。根据信用证中对运输单据(提单)被通知方的规定填写。
例如:信用证规定:...Bill of Lading...notify the applicant with fax no...
　　　　　　　或...Bill of Lading...showing applicant as notify party...
　　被通知人　一栏就应填写开证申请人的名称及地址。请注意,填写时必须与信用证中 Applicant 的名称、地址完全一致,若要求注明电话号码、传真号码等,则必须严格相符。

◇ **装船期限**
信用证规定的最迟装运日 latest date of shipment。

◇ **运输方式**
选择实际采用的运输方式。如 By Sea 海运,或 By Air 空运等。

◇ **装箱方式**
选择货物实际采用的装箱方式。如 FCL 整箱,或 LCL 拼箱等。

◇ **集装箱种类　集装箱数量**
选择集装箱种类和集装箱个数。如 20'GP 即 20 英尺普通集装箱,或 40'GP 即 40 英尺普通集装箱。

◇ **转船运输　分批装运**
根据信用证中对转船和分批的规定填写。允许即为 YES。

◇ **运费交付**
参照相关的贸易术语选择。如采用 CFR、CIF 术语时选择 Prepaid(即 Freight prepaid 运费预付),采用 FOB 术语时选择 Collect(即 Freight to collect,运费到付)。这与信用证要求提单上显示的运费条款应是一致的。

◇ **装运口岸　目的港**
信用证规定的装运港和目的港。如信用证未规定具体的港口名称,则按交易实际情况填写。

◇ **成交条件**
成交的贸易术语。如 FOB、CFR、CIF 等。

◇ **联系人　电话/传真**
发货人公司的联系人及联系方式。

◇　**标记唛码**

Shipping marks,也称运输标志。

如信用证中有关于运输标志的规定,则严格按照规定的内容缮制。

例如:信用证规定:Shipping Marks:ABC CO./TR5423/HAMBURG/C/NO.
1-UP.

标记唛码　一栏应填入:

ABC CO.

TR5423

HAMBURG

C/NO.1-370

其中,C/NO.1-UP中的UP则用实际的货物总包装件数来代替。

如信用证和/或合同中没有相关规定,则可由出口商自行设计:

收/发货人的简称

参照号码(如合同号、订单号、信用证号、发票号等)

目的港

件号

如出口货物外包装上没有运输标志,则可填写:N/M(即 No Marks)。

◇　**货物描述**

货物的名称。可以填写货物的总称,但不得与信用证上的货物描述冲突。

◇　**总件数　总毛重　总尺码**

该批出口货物的总的外包装数量、总毛重、总体积。不必按货号分开,只需填写总值即可。请注意,总件数是指外包装件数,例如 240 Cartons,而不是商品的数量。

◇　**备注**

发货人对订舱的特殊要求(如对承运船舶有既定要求)、信用证对提单上显示的信息有特殊要求(如要求加注某些证明文句)或要求船公司除签发提单之外需另行出具某些单据,均可填入此栏。

(二) 商业发票(Commercial Invoice)

商业发票是出口商向进口商开出的载明销售货物详情的单据。它是双方收付货款和记账的凭证,也是出口商办理各项履约手续时对货物的详细说明,同时还是日后缮制其他单据的依据。因此商业发票上显示了该批出口货物较为详细的信息。其他一些单据上往往会出现"as per invoice number…"的表述。

◇ **出具**
在出口商的公司信笺上缮制商业发票表明该发票是由出口商出具的。如果不用公司信笺缮制,也可以在 Seller 一栏注明出口商名称,或是发票最下方打上 issued by 后跟出口商名称。

◇ **TO**
抬头,即买方。也有表述为 Buyer,或是 For account of 的。

◇ **INV.NO. INV. DATE**
发票号码、发票日期。由出口商自行编制。

◇ **S/C NO.**
合同号码。即相关售货合同的号码。

◇ **FROM TO SHIPPED BY**
装运港,目的港,承运船名航次。如不确定,可留空。

◇ **MARKS & NOS.**
运输标志。

◇ **DESCRIPTION OF GOODS QUANTITY UNIT PRICE AMOUNT**
货物描述,即品名规格货号,各货号的数量、单价和金额。注意不要遗漏数量单位、币种和贸易术语,应明确显示发票总金额。

◇ **TOTAL AMOUNT IN WORDS**
发票总金额的大写。

◇　**TOTAL G.W/N.W.　TOTAL PACKAGE**
该批货物的总毛重/总净重和总包装件数。

◇　**签署**
显示出口商的名称并由授权签字人签名。

(三) 装箱单(Packing List)

装箱单是表明出口货物的包装形式、包装内容、唛头、数量、重量、体积或件数的单据。它是商业发票的补充,方便买方了解商品的包装详情、提货及分拣,同时也可供第三方查验核对。

装箱单的部分栏目填制可参照商业发票,我们来重点分析其中间主体部分。这部分应按商品的不同规格(如不同货号),分别列出 C/NO.即 Carton Number 件号,DESCRIPTION OF GOODS 即货物描述,PKG.即 Packages 包装件数,QTY即 Quantity 商品数量,G.W.即 Gross Weight 毛重,N.W.即 Net Weight 净重,MEAS.即 Measurement 尺码。

例如:

C/NO.	DESCRIPTION OF GOODS	PKG.	QTY.	G.W.	N.W.	MEAS.
1-400	CERAMIC DINNERWARE USHJ-4-1	400 CTNS	800PCS	9200KGS	6400KGS	24.992M3
401-843	USKJ-4-A	443 CTNS	443PCS	10632KGS	7974KGS	24.975M3
TOTAL		843 CTNS	1243PCS	19832KGS	14374KGS	49.967M3

需要特别注意的是:

◇　包装件数、数量、毛重、净重和尺码都应有单位,切勿遗漏。其中,包装件数的单位即为包装种类,重量的单位一般是 kg,尺码的单位一般是 m^3。

◇　毛重、净重、尺码一般都保留至小数点后第三位。

◇　C/NO.件号与 PKG.包装件数之间有对应关系。例如 C/NO.1-400,意为第 1箱至第 400 箱,故 PKG.就应为 400(CTNS.)。又如 C/NO.401-843,意为第 401 箱至第 843 箱,故包装件数 PKG.就应为 443(CTNS.)。

◇　不同货号规格之间的件号一般都是首尾相接的,例如 1-100,101-150,151-220,不会出现前后重叠的情况。

◇　除非有特别说明,否则每一行的商品数量、毛重、净重、尺码均指该货号的总数量、总毛重、总净重、总尺码。如需表示单个包装内的数量、毛重、净重、尺码，则应在空白处另行加以说明。

◇　包装件数、数量、毛重、净重、尺码除了分货号列明以外，还应再最后汇总表明总值。如有不同的包装种类，包装件数的总值可以 Packages 为单位，如数量也有不同的计量单位，数量的总值则可以 Units 为单位。

Total Packages in Words 是指大写包装件数，其写法与大写金额相仿，以"Say"开头以"Only"结尾，并注明包装种类。例如：SAY THREE HUNDRED AND FIFTY CARTONS ONLY（计 350 纸箱）。

（i）订舱的反馈文件

从出口托运和订舱流程中，我们可以知道，订舱确认的反馈文件是"十联单"的第 5—7 联和第 9、10 联。其中，第 5—7 联主要用作日后报关，第 9、10 联则为"配舱回单"。

配舱回单上有与提单号码一致的 D/R 编号（即 Dock Receipt 场站收据编号）、承运船名、航次、装船日期，还有船公司的签单章（也有船公司仅盖在第五联装货单上的），即表示船公司已确认了发货人的订舱。

Shipper (发货人) SHANGHAI MINGZHOU TRADING CO.,LTD NO 4516, ZHONG SHAN RD., SHANGHAI, CHINA				D/R No.(编号) PONLSHA01836944		

Consignee (收货人)
TO SHIPPER'S ORDER

配舱回单（1）

第九联

Notify Party (通知人)
NIGROS-GENOSSENSCHAFTS-BUND LIMMATSTRASSE 526
POSTEACH 266 CH-8031 ZURICH SWITZERLAND

Pre-carriage by(前程运输)	Place of Receipt (收货地点)		
Vessel (船名) Voy. No. (航次) **OOCL LONG BEACH V.04W49**	Port of Loading (装货港) **SHANGHAI**		
Port of Discharge(卸货港) **HAMBURG**	Place of Delivery (交货地点)	Final Destination for the Merchant's Reference (目的地)	

Container No. （集装箱号）	Seal No.(封志号) Marks & Nos. （标志与号码）	No. of contai- ners or p'kgs （箱数或件数）	Kind of Packages: Description of Goods （包装种类与货名）	Gross Weight 毛重(公斤)	Measurement 尺码(立方米)
	SCHEKERC **CI-SCH96B** **HAMBURG** **C/NO. 1 - 309**	**309 CARTONS**	**ART CRAFT**	**1527 KGS**	**14.813 CBM**

Particulars Furnished by Merchants（托运人提供详细情况）

TOTAL NUMBER OF CONTAINERS
OR PACKAGES (IN WORDS)　　**SAY THREE HUNDRED AND NINE CARTONS ONLY.**
集装箱数或件数合计(大写)

Container No.(箱号)		Seal No.(封志号)	
装船日期：2018年4月7日	Received(实收)	By Terminal Clerk(场站员签字)	

FREIGHT & CHARGES	Prepaid at (预付地点)	Payable at (到付地点)	Place of Issue (签发地点) **SHANGHAI**
	Total Prepaid (预付总额)	No. of Original B(s)/L (正本提单份数) **THREE**	Booking (订舱确认) APPROVED BY

Service Type on Receiving ☑-CY ☐-CFS ☐-DOOR		Service Type on Delivery ☑-CY ☐-CFS ☐-DOOR		Reefer Temperature Required (冷藏温度)　　　℉ ℃
TYPE OF GOODS （种类）	☑ Ordinary （普通） ☐ Liquid （液体）	☐ Reefer （冷藏） ☐ Live Animal （活动物）	☐ Dangerous ☐ Auto. （危险品） （裸装车辆） ☐ Bulk （散装）	Class Property: IMDG Code UN No.

可否转船：	**NO**	可否分批：	**YES**
装　期：	**April 15, 2018**	效　期：	**April 30, 2018**
金　额：	**US$26,660.80**		
制单日期：	**March 23, 2018**		

练 习

根据以下信息和信用证填制出口订舱文件：

出口商电话：021-54753526　　　　生产厂商：上海日升照明有限公司
出口商传真：021-54753529　　　　　　　　　上海市柳营路340号
发票号码：SHMH07210
发票日期：2018年11月16日

2103S

2203S

AMZ049

ARG108

货 号	品 名	包装方式	包装尺码
2103S	LAMP	4只/纸箱	60×80×65cm
成交数量	成交价格	成交条件	毛/净重
320只(1x20'FCL)	32.2美元/只	CFR	20/17.5kgs

货 号	品 名	包装方式	包装尺码
2203S	LAMP	4只/纸箱	48×52×66cm
成交数量	成交价格	成交条件	毛/净重
604只(1x20'FCL)	25.5美元/只	CFR	22/19.5kgs

货 号	品 名	包装方式	包装尺码
AMZ049	LAMP	4只/纸箱	60×45×52cm
成交数量	成交价格	成交条件	毛/净重
712只(1x20'FCL)	22.8美元/只	CFR	17/15kgs

货 号	品 名	包装方式	包装尺码
ARG108	LAMP	4只/纸箱	50×62×64cm
成交数量	成交价格	成交条件	毛/净重
504只(1x20'FCL)	15.1美元/只	CFR	16/13.2kgs

COMMERCIAL BANK OF DUBAI P.S.C

DEIRA BRANCH
P.O.BOX: 1709, DUBAI, U.A.E

IRREVOCABLE DOCUMENTARY	PAGE NO.: [1]	SWIFT:	CBDUAEAD DER
LETTER OF CREDIT NO.:	01DLC077003079	TELEX:	45468 TRBNK EM.
DATE OF ISSUE:	OCTOBER 19, 2018	TELEFAX:	251089 / 254565
DATE OF EXPIRY:	DECEMBER 17, 2018	TELEPHONE:	253222 (10 LINES)
PLACE OF EXPIRY:	CHINA		

BENEFICIARY	APPLICANT
SHANGHAI MINHUA IMP. & EXP. CORPORATION 5/F MINHUA BLDG. 880 HUMING ROAD SHANGHAI CHINA	ALABRA HOME APPL. TRDG. CO. LLC. P.O.BOX 21352, DUBAI UAE

ADVISING BANK	CURRENCY AND AMOUNT
BANK OF CHINA SHANGHAI BRANCH 23, CHUNG SHAN ROAD E.1 SHANGHAI CHINA	USD *******49,550.00 UNITED STATES DOLLARS FORTY NINE THOUSAND FIVE HUNDRED AND FIFTY ONLY.

DETAILS OF SHIPMENT		AVAILABLE WITH
TRANSSHIPMENT:	NOT ALLOWED	THE ADVISING BANK ONLY BY NEGOTIATION AGAINST
PARTSHIPMENT:	ALLOWED	PRESENTATION OF DOCUMENTS DESCRIBED HEREIN
SHIPMENT FROM:	CHINA	AND BENEFICIARY'S DRAFT(S) AT SIGHT DRAWN ON
TO:	DUBAI	US.
BY:	VESSEL	**TERMS OF DELIVERY**
NOT LATER THAN:	DECEMBER 02, 2018	CFR DUBAI

DESCRIPTION OF GOODS:

HOUSEHOLD WARES (FOUR ITEMS OF LAMPS)
ALL OTHER DETAILS AS PER INDENT NO. SSTE /363 / CN-9 OF M/S. SALEM SAUD TRADING EST., AND SALES
CONFIRMATION NO. SHMHSC-07210 DATED OCTOBER 03, 2018.
SHIPPING MARKS: ALABRA / SHMHSC-07210 / DUBAI / C/NO.1-UP

DOCUMENTS REQUIRED:

01- SIGNED COMMERCIAL INVOICE IN {THREE } COPIES CERTIFIED TO BE TRUE AND CORRECT MENTIONING
FULL NAME AND ADDRESS OF THE MANUFACTURER AND TERMS OF DELIVERY.

02- CERTIFICATE OF ORIGIN STATING GOODS ARE OF CHINA ORIGIN ISSUED BY CHINA COUNCIL FOR THE
PROMOTION OF INTERNATIONAL TRADE, MENTIONING NAME AND ADDRESS OF THE MANUFACTURER /
PRODUCER & EXPORTER.

03- COMPLETE SET OF (3/3) CLEAN ON BOARD SHIPPING COMPANY'S BILL OF LADING ISSUED TO THE ORDER
OF COMMERCIAL BANK OF DUBAI PSC.[DUBAI] MARKED "FREIGHT PREPAID " AND NOTIFY
APPLICANT.

04- PACKING LIST IN [THREE] COPIES.

05- INSURANCE COVERED IN DUBAI.
SHIPMENT ADVICE MUST BE SENT TO M/S IRAN INSURANCE CO. P.C.BOX 2004, DUBAI BY REGISTERED POST
OR BY FAX ON FAX NO.217660 QUOTING THEIR OPEN POLICY NO OMP/531/91 AND STATING OUR L/C NO.,
AMOUNT, VESSEL NAME AND SHIPPING MARKS THEREIN AND A COPY OF SUCH SHIPMENT ADVICE ALONG
WITH THE ORIGINAL POSTAL RECEIPT / FAX COPY MUST ACCOMPANY THE DOCUMENTS.

CONTINUED ON PAGE NO. 2

COMMERCIAL BANK OF DUBAI P.S.C

DEIRA BRANCH
P.O.BOX: 1709, DUBAI, U.A.E

IRREVOCABLE DOCUMENTARY   PAGE NO.: [2]
LETTER OF CREDIT NO.:   01DLC07003079   DATE OF ISSUE: OCTOBER 19, 2018
USD *******49,550.00

06- A CERTIFICATE FROM THE SHIP OWNER / AGENT STATING THAT THE CARRYING VESSEL IS NOT AN
ISRAELI OWNED VESSEL AND IS NOT SCHEDULED TO CALL AT ANY ISRAELI PORT ON ROUTE TO ITS
DESTINATION AND THE VESSEL IS NOT PROHIBITED TO ENTER ANY ARAB PORT FOR ANY REASON
WHATSOEVER IN ACCORDANCE WITH ITS LOCAL LAWS AND REGULATIONS . [THIS IS NOT REQUIRED IF
SHIPMENT IS EFFECTED BY UNITED ARAB SHIPPING COMPANY'S VESSEL].

OTHER CONDITIONS:
01- CERTIFICATE OF ORIGIN SHOULD INCLUDE THE NAME OF THE COUNTRY FROM WHERE THE GOODS
ARE EXPORTED.

02- GOODS MUST BE SHIPPED IN 4X20FT CONTAINERS AND B/L MUST EVIDENCE THE COMPLIANCE.

03- COMMISSION @1% OF THE INVOICE VALUE MUST BE DEDUCTED FROM THE PAYMENT TO THE
BENEFICIARY AT THE TIME OF NEGOTIATION FOR PAYMENT TO MR. C.H.B. MOHD KUNHI, P.O.BOX
51495 ,DUBAI WHICH MUST BE CERTIFIED IN THE NEGOTIATING BANK'S COVERING SCHEDULE.

04- B/L SHOULD BEAR VESSEL AGENT'S NAME , ADDRESS AND TELEPHONE NUMBER AT PORT OF
DESTINATION.

05- SHORT FORM B/L NOT ACCEPTABLE .

06- INVOICE & TRANSPORT DOCUMENTS SHOULD BEAR SHIPPING MARKS AND TOTAL GROSS WEIGHT,
NET WEIGHT AND MEASUREMENT.

07- THE NUMBER AND THE DATE OF THIS CREDIT AND NAME OF OUR BANK MUST BE
QUOTED ON ALL DOCUMENTS.

08- ALL DOCUMENTS TO BE ISSUED IN ENGLISH LANGUAGE

09- ALL CHARGES INCLUDING REIMBURSING CHARGES EXCEPT L/C ISSUING CHARGES ARE
ON ACCOUNT OF BENEFICIARY.

INSTRUCTIONS TO NEGOTIATION BANK:
– NOTE EACH PRESENTATION ON THE REVERSE OF THIS LETTER OF CREDIT.
– DISPATCH THE FULL SET OF THE NEGOTIATED DOCUMENTS TO US IN ONE LOT BY COURIER SERVICE.
– ON RECEIPT OF CREDIT COMPLIED DOCUMENTS PAYMENT SHALL BE EFFECTED BY US PER CREDIT
TERMS AS PER NEGOTIATION BANK'S COVERING SCHEDULE.

EXCEPT AS OTHERWISE STATED HEREIN , THIS CREDIT IS SUBJECT TO UNIFORM CUSTOMS AND PRACTICE
FOR DOCUMENTARY CREDITS [2007 REVISION] , INTERNATIONAL CHAMBER OF COMMERCE PUBLICATION
NO. 600

For COMMERCIAL BANK OF DUBAI P.S.C

Authorised Signature   Authorised Signature

SPECIMEN

海 运 出 口 订 舱 委 托 书

日期

发货人		装船期限				
		运输方式	☐	BY SEA	☐	BY AIR
		装箱方式	☐	FCL	☐	LCL
		集装箱种类	☐	20'GP	☐	40'GP
		集装箱数量				
收货人		转船运输	☐	NO	☐	YES
		分批装运	☐	NO	☐	YES
		运费交付	☐	PREPAID	☐	COLLECT
被通知人		装运口岸				
		目的港				
		成交条件				
		联系人				
		电话/传真				

标记唛码	货物描述	总件数	总毛重	总尺码

备注

COMMERCIAL INVOICE

1) SELLER	3) INVOICE NO.	4) INVOICE DATE
	5) L/C NO.	6) DATE
	7) ISSUED BY	
2) BUYER	8) CONTRACT NO.	9) DATE
	10) FROM	11) TO
	12) SHIPPED BY	13)PRICE TERM

14)MARKS	15)DESCRIPTION OF GOODS	16)QTY.	17)UNIT PRICE	18)AMOUNT

19) ISSUED BY

20) SIGNATURE

PACKING LIST

1) SELLER	3) INVOICE NO.	4) INVOICE DATE
	5) FROM	6) TO
	7) TOTAL PACKAGES(IN WORDS)	
2) BUYER	8) MARKS & NOS.	

9) C/NOS.	10) NOS. & KINDS OF PKGS.	11) ITEM	12)QTY.	13) G.W.	14) N.W.	15) MEAS

16) ISSUED BY

17) SIGNATURE

第七章 出口货物报检

案 例

2018 年 10 月 30 日，货运代理收到环宇公司的订舱委托后，缮制"集装箱货物海运托运单"（又称"十联单"），向船公司订舱。

2018 年 10 月 31 日，环宇公司收到货运代理返还的"配舱回单"等五联（第 226、227 页）。

2018 年 11 月 1 日，向上海海关办理出口商品报检手续。

工作任务

填报出境检验检疫申请：制作出境货物报检单、并连同商业发票和装箱单一起提交上海海关。

第九联 配舱回单

Shipper (发货人) SHANGHAI UNIVERSAL TRADING CO., LTD. MAYLING PLAZA, 131 DONGFANG ROAD, SHANGHAI 200120, CHINA	D/R No.(编号) COSU89302173	
Consignee (收货人) TO ORDER	配舱回单（1）	第九联

Notify Party (通知人)

TIVOLIAN TRADING B.V.

P.O. BOX 1783, HEIMAN DULLAERTOLEIN 3,

3024CA ROTTERDAM, NETHERLANDS

Pre-carriage by(前程运输)	Place of Receipt (收货地点)			
Vessel (船名) Voy. No. (航次) COSCO HELLAS / 013W	Port of Loading (装货港) SHANGHAI			
Port of Discharge(卸货港) ROTTERDAM	Place of Delivery (交货地点)		Final Destination for the Merchant's Reference (目的地)	

Container No. (集装箱号)	Seal No.(封志号) Marks & Nos. (标志与号码)	No. of contai- ners or p'kgs (箱数或件数)	Kind of Packages: Description of Goods (包装种类与货名)	Gross Weight 毛重(公斤)	Measurement 尺码(立方米)
CE/IMP.087 TIV-PO-CSH0873 ROTTERDAM CARTON NO. 1 - 126 KB0278	CE/IMP.087 TIV-PO-CSH0873 ROTTERDAM CARTON NO. 1 - 126 KB5411	386CTNS	PLUSH TOYS	3155.000KGS	49.646CBM
F-TOYS 228 TIV-PO-CSH0873 ROTTERDAM CARTON NO. 1 - 67 KB0677	F-TOYS 228 TIV-PO-CSH0873 ROTTERDAM CARTON NO. 1 - 67 KB7900		FREIGHT PREPAID		

TOTAL NUMBER OF CONTAINERS OR PACKAGES (IN WORDS) 集装箱数或件数合计(大写) SAY THREE HUNDRED AND EIGHTY SIX CARTONS ONLY

Container No.(箱号)		Seal No.(封志号)
装船日期：2018年11月13日	Received(实收)	By Terminal Clerk(场站员签字)

FREIGHT & CHARGES	Prepaid at (预付地点)	Payable at (到付地点)	Place of Issue (签发地点) SHANGHAI
	Total Prepaid (预付总额)	No. of Original B(s)/L (正本提单份数) THREE	Booking (订舱确认) APPROVED BY

Service Type on Receiving ☑-CY ☐-CFS ☐-DOOR	Service Type on Delivery ☑-CY ☐-CFS ☐-DOOR	Reefer Temperature Required (冷藏温度) ℉ ℃
TYPE OF GOODS (种类)	☑Ordinary (普通) ☐Reefer (冷藏) ☐Dangerous (危险品) ☐Auto. (裸装车辆) ☐Liquid (液体) ☐Live Animal (活动物) ☐Bulk (散装)	危险品 Property: IMDG Code UN No. (18)

可否转船	No	可否分批	YES
装 期：	Nov. 30, 2018	效 期：	Dec. 15, 2018
金 额：	US$26,660.80		
制单日期：	Oct. 30, 2018		

第五联 装货单

第六联 场站收据副本 大副联

Shipper (发货人)
SHANGHAI UNIVERSAL TRADING CO., LTD.
MAYLING PLAZA,
131 DONGFANG ROAD,
SHANGHAI 200120, CHINA

D/R No.(编号)
COSU69302173

场站收据副本
大副联

第六联

Consignee (收货人)
TO ORDER

COPY OF DOCK RECEIPT
(FOR CHIEF OFFICER)

Notify Party (通知人)
TIVOLIAN TRADING B.V.
P.O. BOX 1783, HEIMAN DULLAERTOLEIN 3,
3024CA ROTTERDAM, NETHERLANDS

Received by the Carrier the Total number of containers or other packages or units stated below to be transported subject to the terms and conditions of the Carrier's regular form of Bill of Lading (for Combined Transport or port to Port Shipment) which shall be deemed to be incorporated herein.

Date (日期) Oct. 30, 2018

Vessel (船名) Voy. No. (航次)
COSCO HELLAS / 013W

Port of Loading (装货港)
SHANGHAI

场站章

Port of Discharge(卸货港)
ROTTERDAM

Container No. (集装箱号)	Seal No.(封志号) Marks & Nos. (标志与号码)	No. of containers or pkgs (箱数或件数)	Kind of Packages Description of Goods (包装种类与货名)	Gross Weight 毛重(公斤)	Measurement 尺码(立方米)
C8/IMP.087	C8/IMP.087				
TIV-PO-CSH0873	TIV-PO-CSH0873	386CTNS	PLUSH TOYS	3155.000KGS	49.646CBM
ROTTERDAM	ROTTERDAM				
CARTON NO. 1 - 126	CARTON NO. 1 - 126				
KB0278	KB5411				
F-TOYS 228	F-TOYS 228				
TIV-PO-CSH0873	TIV-PO-CSH0873		FREIGHT PREPAID		
ROTTERDAM	ROTTERDAM				
CARTON NO. 1 - 67	CARTON NO. 1 - 67				
KB0677	KB7900				

TOTAL NUMBER OF CONTAINERS
OR PACKAGES (IN WORDS)
集装箱或载货件数合计(大写)

SAY THREE HUNDRED AND EIGHTY SIX CARTONS ONLY

第七联 场站收据

第十联 配舱回单(2)

Shipper (发货人)
SHANGHAI UNIVERSAL TRADING CO., LTD.
MAYLING PLAZA,
131 DONGFANG ROAD,
SHANGHAI 200120, CHINA

D/R No.(编号)
COSU69302173

配舱回单(2)

第十联

Consignee (收货人)
TO ORDER

Notify Party (通知人)
TIVOLIAN TRADING B.V.
P.O. BOX 1783, HEIMAN DULLAERTOLEIN 3,
3024CA ROTTERDAM, NETHERLANDS

Received by the Carrier the Total number of containers or other packages or units stated below to be transported subject to the terms and conditions of the Carrier's regular form of Bill of Lading (for Combined Transport or port to Port Shipment) which shall be deemed to be incorporated herein.

Date (日期) Oct. 30, 2018

Vessel (船名) Voy. No. (航次)
COSCO HELLAS / 013W

Port of Loading (装货港)
SHANGHAI

Port of Discharge(卸货港)
ROTTERDAM

Container No. (集装箱号)	Seal No.(封志号) Marks & Nos. (标志与号码)	No. of containers or pkgs (箱数或件数)	Kind of Packages Description of Goods (包装种类与货名)	Gross Weight 毛重(公斤)	Measurement 尺码(立方米)
C8/IMP.087	C8/IMP.087				
TIV-PO-CSH0873	TIV-PO-CSH0873	386CTNS	PLUSH TOYS	3155.000KGS	49.646CBM
ROTTERDAM	ROTTERDAM				
CARTON NO. 1 - 126	CARTON NO. 1 - 126				
KB0278	KB5411				
F-TOYS 228	F-TOYS 228				
TIV-PO-CSH0873	TIV-PO-CSH0873		FREIGHT PREPAID		
ROTTERDAM	ROTTERDAM				
CARTON NO. 1 - 67	CARTON NO. 1 - 67				
KB0677	KB7900				

TOTAL NUMBER OF CONTAINERS
OR PACKAGES (IN WORDS)
集装箱或载货件数合计(大写)

SAY THREE HUNDRED AND EIGHTY SIX CARTONS ONLY

可否分批:	No	可否分批:	YES
第 Nov. 30, 2018		效 Dec. 15, 2018	
金 US$26,660.80			
制单日期 Oct. 30, 2018			

出境货物报检单

中华人民共和国出入境检验检疫
出境货物报检单

报检单位(加盖公章):					*编 号	
报检单位登记号:	联系人:	电话:		报检日期:	年 月 日	

发货人	(中文)
	(外文)

收货人	(中文)
	(外文)

货物名称(中/外文)	H.S.编码	产地	数/重量	货物总值	包装种类及数量

运输工具名称号码		贸易方式		货物存放地点	
合同号		信用证号		用途	
发货日期		输往国家(地区)		许可证/审批号	
启运地		到达口岸		生产单位注册号	
集装箱规则、数量及号码					

合同、信用证订立的检验检疫条款或特殊要求	标 记 及 号 码	随附单据(划"√"或补填)	
		☐合同	☐包装性能结果单
		☐信用证	☐许可/审批文件
		☐发票	☐
		☐换证凭证	☐
		☐装箱单	☐
		☐厂检单	☐

需要证单名称(划"√"或补填)		*检验检疫费	
☐品质证书 ___正___副	☐植物检疫证书 ___正___副	总金额	
☐重量证书 ___正___副	☐熏蒸/消毒证书 ___正___副	(人民币元)	
☐数量证书 ___正___副	☐出境货物换证凭单 ___正___副		
☐兽医卫生证书 ___正___副	☐出境货物通关单 ___正___副	计费人	
☐健康证书 ___正___副	☐		
☐卫生证书 ___正___副	☐	收费人	
☐动物卫生证书 ___正___副	☐		

报检人郑重声明	领 取 证 单	
1.本人被授权报验		
2.上列填写内容正确属实,货物无伪造或冒用他人的厂名、标志、认证标志,并承担货物质量责任。	日期	
签名:_____	签名	

注:有"*"号栏由出入境检验检疫机关填写

示 范

中华人民共和国出入境检验检疫
出境货物报检单

报检单位(加盖公章): 上海环宇贸易有限公司　　　　　　　* 编　　号　_____

报检单位登记号: 3100916827 3　联系人: 徐立轩　电话: 021-58818844　报检日期: **2018 年 11 月 1 日**

发货人	(中文)	上海环宇贸易有限公司
	(外文)	SHANGHAI UNIVERSAL TRADING CO., LTD.
收货人	(中文)	***
	(外文)	TIVOLIAN TRADING B.V.

货物名称(中/外文)	H.S.编码	产地	数/重量	货物总值	包装种类及数量
毛绒玩具	**9503.0021**	**上海市**	**2080套**	**26660.80美元**	**386纸箱**

运输工具名称号码	**船舶COSCO HELLAS/013W**	贸易方式	**一般贸易**	货物存放地点	***
合同号	**HY-TIV0373**	信用证号	**AM/VA07721SLC**	用途	***
发货日期	***	输往国家(地区)	**荷兰**	许可证/审批号	***
启运地	**上海**	到达口岸	**鹿特丹**	生产单位注册号	***

集装箱规则、数量及号码　　　　　　**2个海运20尺普通箱**

合同、信用证订立的检验检疫条款或特殊要求	标 记 及 号 码	随附单据(划"√"或补填)	
品质检验证书 **须注明下列内容:** **CREDIT NUMBER: AM/VA07721SLC**	**参见发票HY-TIV-INV0373**	☐ 合同 ☐ 信用证 ✓ 发票 ☐ 换证凭证 ✓ 装箱单 ☐ 厂检单	☐ 包装性能结果单 ☐ 许可/审批文件

需要证单名称(划"√"或补填)					* 检验检疫费
✓ 品质证书	1 正 1 副	☐ 植物检疫证书	__正__副	总金额	
☐ 重量证书	__正__副	☐ 熏蒸/消毒证书	__正__副	(人民币元)	
☐ 数量证书	__正__副	☐ 出境货物换证凭单	__正__副		
☐ 兽医卫生证书	__正__副	☐ 出境货物通关单	__正__副	计费人	
☐ 健康证书	__正__副				
☐ 卫生证书	__正__副			收费人	
☐ 动物卫生证书	__正__副				

报检人郑重声明	领 取 证 单	
1.本人被授权报验 2.上列填写内容正确属实,货物无伪造或冒用他人的厂名、标志、认证标志,并承担货物质量责任。 签名: **徐立轩**	日期	
	签名	

注:有"*"号栏由出入境检验检疫机关填写

Shanghai Universal Trading Co., Ltd.

Rm. 1201-1216 Mayling Plaza,
131 Dongfang Rd.,
Shanghai, 200120, China
Tel: 86-21-58818844
Fax: 86-21-58818766

COMMERCIAL INVOICE

TO:	TIVOLIAN TRADING B.V.			INV. NO. :	HY-TIV-INV0373
	P.O. BOX 1783, HEIMAN DULLAERTOLEIN 3			INV. DATE:	OCT. 29, 2018
	3024CA ROTTERDAM, NETHERLANDS			S/C NO. :	HY-TIV0373

| FROM: | SHANGHAI | TO: | ROTTERDAM | SHIPPED BY: | COSCO HELLAS / 013W |

MARKS & NOS.	DESCRIPTION OF GOODS		QUANTITY	UNIT PRICE	AMOUNT
CE/IMP.087	PLUSH TOYS			CIF ROTTERDAM	
TIV-PO-CSH0873					
ROTTERDAM					
CARTON NO. 1 - 126	KB0278	TWIN BEAR	504SETS	US$9.60	US$4,838.40
KB0278	KB5411	TWIN BEAR IN BALLET COSTUME	504SETS	US$11.50	US$5,796.00
	KB0677	BROWN BEAR WITH RED BOW	536SETS	US$14.50	US$7,772.00
CE/IMP.087	KB7900	BEAR IN PINK T-SHIRT	536SETS	US$15.40	US$8,254.40
TIV-PO-CSH0873					US$26,660.80
ROTTERDAM					
CARTON NO. 1 - 126					
KB5411					
F-TOYS 228					
TIV-PO-CSH0873					
ROTTERDAM					
CARTON NO. 1 - 67					
KB0677					
F-TOYS 228					
TIV-PO-CSH0873					
ROTTERDAM					
CARTON NO. 1 - 67					
KB7900					

TOTAL AMOUNT IN WORDS: SAY U.S. DOLLARS TWENTY SIX THOUSAND SIX HUNDRED AND SIXTY AND CENTS EIGHTY ONLY

TOTAL G.W. / TOTAL N.W.: 3155.000 KGS / 2190.000 KGS
TOTAL PACKAGES: 386CTNS

上 海 环 宇 贸 易 有 限 公 司
SHANGHAI UNIVERSAL TRADING CO., LTD.

(SIGNATURE)

Shanghai Universal Trading Co., Ltd.

Rm. 1201-1216 Mayling Plaza,
131 Dongfang Rd.,
Shanghai, 200120, China
Tel: 86-21-58818844
Fax: 86-21-58818766

PACKING LIST

TO: TIVOLIAN TRADING B.V.
P.O. BOX 1783, HEIMAN DULLAERTOLEIN 3
3024 CA ROTTERDAM, NETHERLANDS

INV. NO. : HY-TIV-INV0373
INV. DATE: OCT. 29, 2018

FROM: SHANGHAI   **TO:** ROTTERDAM   **SHIPPED BY:** COSCO HELLAS / 013W

C/NO.	DESCRIPTION OF GOODS	PKG.	QTY	G.W.	N.W.	MEAS.
CE/IMP.087 TIV-PO-CSH0873 ROTTERDAM CARTON NO. 1 - 126 KB0278	KB0278	126CTNS	504SETS	1008.000KGS	693.000KGS	12.474M3
CE/IMP.087 TIV-PO-CSH0873 ROTTERDAM CARTON NO. 1 - 126 KB5411	KB5411	126CTNS	504SETS	1008.000KGS	693.000KGS	12.474M3
F-TOYS 228 TIV-PO-CSH0873 ROTTERDAM CARTON NO. 1 - 67 KB0677	KB0677	67CTNS	536SETS	569.500KGS	402.000KGS	12.349M3
F-TOYS 228 TIV-PO-CSH0873 ROTTERDAM CARTON NO. 1 - 67 KB7900	KB7900	67CTNS	536SETS	569.500KGS	402.000KGS	12.349M3
	TOTAL:	386CTNS	2080SETS	3155.000KGS	2190.000KGS	49.646M3

TOTAL PACKAGE IN WORDS: SAY THREE HUNDRED AND EIGHTY SIX CARTONS ONLY

MARKS & NOS.:   AS SHOWN IN C/NO.

上 海 环 宇 贸 易 有 限 公 司
SHANGHAI UNIVERSAL TRADING CO., LTD.

(SIGNATURE)

示范评析

办理出口货物报检手续时,出口商需登录海关申报系统之"出口检验检疫申请",在申请页面依次录入出境货物检验检疫各栏目,确认无误后,打印生成"出境货物报检单"(即示范中报检单的样式)。

需要特别说明的是,我国对出口玩具及其生产企业实行质量许可制度,因此在报检时,除了常规的"出境货物报检单"、发票、装箱单外,还必须提供生产企业的《出口玩具质量许可证》。

Q:出境货物报检单中"H.S.编码"应如何填写?

A:可查询当年的海关税则表,根据商品的性质归入适当的税目。例如本案例中的商品应归入"95030021 动物玩偶,不论是否着装"。

Q:出境货物报检单中"合同、信用证订立的检验检疫条款或特殊要求"应如何填写?

A:此栏用于填写检验检疫的具体要求以及对检验证书的特殊要求。例如信用证规定:CERTIFICATE OF QUALITY MUST INDICATE THE L/C NO.,DATE AND NAME OF ISSUING BANK.(品质证书上须注明信用证号码、日期和开证行名称),则此栏应填写:

合同、信用证订立的检验 检疫条款或特殊要求
检验证书须注明下列内容: L/C NO.: BHYLC181280 L/C DATE.: NOV.12,2018 NAME OF ISSUING BANK:THE ROYAL BANK OF CANADA

这样,检验检疫机构才会在品质证书上注明相应内容,以满足信用证对单据的要求。

Q:报检单中"需要证单名称"应如何填写?

A:首先,应了解出口货物是否属于法定检验的商品,若是,则在此栏中必须选择"出境货物通关单"。自2018年8月1日起,我国已取消了纸质通关单,但法定检验依旧施行。法定检验商品经检验合格后,海关将提供电子底账数据号,以作原出境货物通关单编号之用。

其次,应仔细查看合同/信用证对检验的规定,若需要出具官方机构签发的检验检疫证书,则应选择相应的证书类型。

也就是说,

对于法定检验的货物,

——相关合同/信用证无官方机构签发的检验证书要求的,则只选择"出境货物通关单"。

——相关合同/信用证要求出具官方机构签发的检验证书的,例如需要品质证书,则选择"出境货物通关单"和"品质证书"。

对于不属于法定检验范围的货物,

——相关合同/信用证要求出具官方机构签发的检验证书的,例如需要数量证书,则选择"数量证书"。

选择相应证单时还必须指明所需的正副本份数。

Q:报检时提交的商业发票和装箱单与委托订舱时提交的是同样的吗?

A:基本相同。只是如果在报检时出口商已经获得订舱反馈的装运船名和航次信息,那么在提交的商业发票和装箱单中宜补充该项内容。

指　南

　　根据我国《商检法》规定,凡是列入《海关实施检验检疫的进出境商品目录》的进出口商品必须由海关按照国家技术规范的要求进行强制性检验,即实行法定检验。

ⓘ 出口货物报检的流程

◇　出口商填制"出境货物报检单",随附商业发票、装箱单,在出口报关前向海关办理货物出境报检手续。

◇　海关受理并收取检验检疫费后,对出口货物实施必要的检验、检疫、消毒等。

◇　出口货物经检验合格后,海关建立电子底账,向出口商反馈电子底账数据号,符合要求的按规定签发检验检疫证书。

ⓘ 出境货物报检单的填制

（一）海关填写项目

◇　**编号**
　　海关受理申报后所作的报检单编号。

◇　**检验检疫费**
　　由海关计费人员核定费用后填写。

（二）报检单位非必填项目

◇　**货物存放地点**
　　须注明具体地点、厂库。

◇　**用途**
　　从 9 个规定选项中选择填写,如"种用或繁殖"、"观赏或演艺"、"试验"等。

◇　**发货日期**

◇　**许可证/审批号**

须办理出境许可证或审批的货物应填写有关许可证号或审批号。

◇　**生产单位注册号**

海关签发的卫生注册证书号或加工厂库注册号等。

◇　**合同、信用证订立的检验检疫条款或特殊要求**

以上栏目,报检单位在报检时若不填写,应用"＊＊＊"表示。

(三) 报检单位必填项目

◇　**报检单位(加盖公章)**

◇　**报检单位登记号**

报检单位在海关的登记代码。

◇　**联系人　电话**

报检员的姓名和联系电话。

◇　**报检日期**

◇　**发货人**

填写发票中所列卖方的中英文名称。

◇　**收货人**

一般填写买方的英文名称即可。

◇　**货物名称(中/外文)**

填写发票中所列名称及规格,可只写中文统称。

◇　**H.S.编码**

填写货物在《商品分类及编码协调制度》(Harmonized Commodity Description & Coding System)中所列编码,即 H.S. Code,以当年海关公布的货物税则编码为准。

◇　**产地**

货物生产/加工的省(自治区、直辖市)以及地区(市)名称。

◇　**数/重量**

填写报验货物的数/重量,重量一般以净重填写,如填写毛重或"以毛作净",则需特别注明。

◇　**货物总值**

填写发票列明的货值,注明币种。

◇　**包装种类及数量**

该批货物的外包装种类及相对应的件数,如:98 纸箱。

◇　**运输工具名称号码**

填写出口货物运输工具的名称及编号,如船名及航次等。如尚未确定,则可只填写运输工具,如"船舶"、"飞机"等。

◇　**贸易方式**

例如"一般贸易"、"三来一补"、"边境贸易"或"其他贸易"等。

◇　**输往国家(地区)**

◇　**启运地　到达口岸**

◇　**集装箱规格、数量及号码**

例如"1个海运20尺普通箱"。若集装箱号码未确定,可不填写。

◇　**标记及号码**

货物的运输标志,注意填写时应与发票等单据保持一致。

◇　**随附单据(划"√"或补填)**

◇　**需要证单名称(划"√"或补填)**

在产地报关的法检商品,应需要通关单1正2副。2018年8月1日起,我国取消了纸质通关单。目前法检商品一经检验合格,海关会提供相应的电子底账数据号,以作原通关单编号之用。是否需要检验证书以及需要哪类检验证书,应根据信用证或买方的要求。

◇　**报检人员郑重声明**

◇　**领取证单**

填写领证日期及领证人姓名。

(i) 报检的反馈文件

出口货物经检验合格后,海关建立电子底账,向出口商反馈电子底账数据号,符合要求的按规定签发检验检疫证书。

中华人民共和国出入境检验检疫

ENTRY-EXIT INSPECTION AND QUARANTINE
OF THE PEOPLE'S REPUBLIC OF CHINA

正 本
ORIGINAL

编号 No.:

QUALITY
INSPECTION CERTIFICATE

发货人
Consignor _____

收货人
Consignee _____

品名
Description of Goods _____

报检数量/重量
Quantity/Weight Declared _____

包装种类及数量
Number and Type of Packages _____

运输工具
Means of Conveyance _____

标记及号码
Mark & No.

检验结果:
RESULTS OF INSPECTION:

从全批货物中，按 *** 标准抽取样品并按 标准规定进行检验，结果如下:

From the whole lot of goods, samples were drawn according to Standard *** and inspected according to the stipulation of Standard with the results as follows:

印章
Official Stamp

签证地点 Place of Issue _____

签证日期 Date of Issue _____

授权签字人 Authorized Officer _____

签 名 Signature _____

练 习

试根据**第六章 出口托运订舱**的**练习**(第 219 页)中的出口货物明细、信用证及以下信息填制出境货物报检单:

报检单位登记号:3100836514
报检单位:上海闵华进出口公司
H.S.编码:9405 2000
报检日期:2018 年 11 月 21 日
随附单据:发票、装箱单
检验性质:法定检验

中 华 人 民 共 和 国 出 入 境 检 验 检 疫
出境货物报检单

报检单位(加盖公章):　　　　　　　　　　　　　　* 编　号 _____

报检单位登记号:　　　　联系人:　　电话:　　　报检日期:　　年　　月　　日

发货人	(中文)					
	(外文)					
收货人	(中文)					
	(外文)					

货物名称(中/外文)	H.S.编码	产地	数/重量	货物总值	包装种类及数量

运输工具名称号码		贸易方式		货物存放地点	
合同号		信用证号		用途	
发货日期		输往国家(地区)		许可证/审批号	
启运地		到达口岸		生产单位注册号	
集装箱规则、数量及号码					

合同、信用证订立的检验 检疫条款或特殊要求	标 记 及 号 码	随附单据(划"√"或补填)
		☐ 合同　　　☐ 包装性能结果单 ☐ 信用证　　☐ 许可/审批文件 ☐ 发票　　　☐ ☐ 换证凭证　☐ ☐ 装箱单　　☐ ☐ 厂检单　　☐

需要证单名称(划"√"或补填)		* 检验检疫费	
☐ 品质证书　　　　__正__副 ☐ 重量证书　　　　__正__副 ☐ 数量证书　　　　__正__副 ☐ 兽医卫生证书　　__正__副 ☐ 健康证书　　　　__正__副 ☐ 卫生证书　　　　__正__副 ☐ 动物卫生证书　　__正__副	☐ 植物检疫证书　　　__正__副 ☐ 熏蒸/消毒证书　　__正__副 ☐ 出境货物换证凭单　__正__副 ☐ 出境货物通关单　　__正__副 ☐ ☐	总金额 (人民币元)	
		计费人	
		收费人	

报检人郑重声明 　1.本人被授权报验 　2.上列填写内容正确属实,货物无伪造或冒用他人的厂名、 标志、认证标志,并承担货物质量责任。 　　　　　　　　签名: _____	领 取 证 单	
	日期	
	签名	

注:有"*"号栏由出入境检验检疫机关填写

第八章　出口货运投保

案　例

2018 年 11 月 4 日,环宇公司收到上海海关签发的品质检验证书(第 241 页)。

2018 年 11 月 5 日,环宇公司向中国人民财产保险股份有限公司上海分公司办理投保手续。

✍ 工作任务

制作投保文件:填制投保单、连同商业发票一起提交给保险公司。

品质检验证书

中华人民共和国出入境检验检疫
ENTRY-EXIT INSPECTION AND QUARANTINE
OF THE PEOPLE'S REPUBLIC OF CHINA

正 本
ORIGINAL

第1页 共1页 Page 1 of 1

编号 No.: 034909628062673

QUALITY
INSPECTION CERTIFICATE

发货人 Consignor	**SHANGHAI UNIVERSAL TRADING CO., LTD.**
收货人 Consignee	**TIVOLIAN TRADING B.V.**

		标记及号码 Mark & No.	
品名 Description of Goods	**PLUSH TOYS**	CE/IMP.087 TIV-PO-CSH0873 ROTTERDAM CARTON NO. 1 - 126 KB0278	CE/IMP.087 TIV-PO-CSH0873 ROTTERDAM CARTON NO. 1 - 126 KB5411
报检数量/重量 Quantity/Weight Declared	**-2080-SETS /-3155-KGS**		
包装种类及数量 Number and Type of Packages	**-368-CTNS**	F-TOYS 228 TIV-PO-CSH0873 ROTTERDAM CARTON NO. 1 - 67 KB0677	F-TOYS 228 TIV-PO-CSH0873 ROTTERDAM CARTON NO. 1 - 67 KB7900
运输工具 Means of Conveyance	**COSCO HELLAS / 013**		

检验结果:
RESULTS OF INSPECTION:

At the request of consignor, our inspectors attended at the warehouse of the consignment on 2008/5/16. In accordance with SN/T 0304–1993 and the relevant state stipulations GB2828, GB6675 and GB9832, 13 cartons were taken and opened at random for visual inspection, from which representative samples were drawn and inspected according to the stipulation mentioned above. The results are as follows:

 Appearance: Pass
 Specifications: Pass
 Quantity: -2080-SETS, -386-CTNS
 Safety: Pass
 Hygienics: Pass

签证地点 Place of Issue **SHANGHAI** 签证日期 Date of Issue **NOV. 4, 2018**

授权签字人 Authorized Officer **XU SAILI** 签 名 Signature *徐赛莉*

我们已尽所知和最大能力实施上述检验,不能因我们签发本证书而免除卖方或其他方面根据合同和法律所承担的产品质量责任和其他责任。
All inspections are carried out conscientiously to the best of our knowledge and ability. This certificate does not in any respect absolve the seller and other related parties from his contractual and legal obligations especiall when product quality is concerned.

投保单

PICC　**中国人民财产保险股份有限公司**　上海市分公司
PICC Property and Casualty Company Limited, Shanghai Branch

地址：　中国上海市中山南路700号 ADD:　No.700 Zhongshan Road (S) Shanghai China 邮编（Post Code）：200010	电话（TEL）：　(021)63773000 传真（FAX）：　(021)63764678

货物运输保险投保单
APPLICATION FORM FOR CARGO TRANSPORTATION INSURANCE

被保险人：
INSURED: _____

发票号（INVOICE NO.）
合同号（CONTRACT NO.）
信用证号（L/C NO.）
发票金额（INVOICE AMOUNT）_____ 投保加成（PLUS）_____ %

兹有下列物品向中国人民财产保险股份有限公司　上海分 公司投保。（INSURANCE IS REQUIRED ON THE FOLLOWING COMMODITIES:）

标　记 MARKS & NOS.	包装及数量 QUANTITY	保险货物项目 DESCRIPTION OF GOODS	保险金额 AMOUNT INSURED

启运日期：　　　　　　　　　　　装载运输工具：
DATE OF COMMENCEMENT _____ PER CONVEYANCE _____

自　　　　　　　　　经　　　　　　　　　至
FROM _____ VIA _____ TO _____

提单号：　　　　　　　　　　　赔款偿付地点：
B/L NO. _____ CLAIM PAYMENT AT _____

投保险别：（PLEASE INDICATE THE CONDITIONS &/OR SPECIAL COVERAGES）

备注：（REMARKS）

请如实告知下列情况：（如'是'在[　]中打'X'）IF ANY, PLEASE MARK 'X':

1、货物种类 GOODS	普通[　] ORDINARY	散装[　] BULK	冷藏[　] REEFER	液体[　] LIQUID	活动物[　] LIVE ANIMAL	机器/汽车[　]　危险品等级[　] MACHINE/AUTO　DANGEROUS CLASS
2、集装箱种类 CONTAINER	普通[　] ORDINARY	开顶[　] OPEN	框架[　] FRAME	平板[　] PLAY	冷藏[　] REFRIGERATOR	
3、转运工具 BY TRANSIT	海轮[　] SHIP	飞机[　] PLANE	驳船[　] BARGE	火车[　] TRAIN	汽车[　] TRUCK	
4、船舶资料 PARTICULAR OF SHIP		船籍 REGISTRY			船龄 AGE	

备注：　被保险人确认本保险合同条款和内容已经完全了解　　　投保人（签名盖章）APPLICANTS SIGNATURE
　　　　THE ASSURED CONFIRMS HEREWITH THE TERMS AND CONDI-
　　　　TIONS OF THESE INSURANCE CONTRACT FULLY UNDER-
　　　　STOOD.

　　　投保日期：(DATE) _____　　　电话　(TEL) _____
　　　　　　　　　　　　　　　　　　　　　地址：(ADD) _____

本公司自用（FOR OFFICE USE ONLY）

经办人　　　　　　　　　　核保人　　　　　　NO.: PICC 0825873
Made By _____　　　　Checked By _____

示 范

PICC 中国人民财产保险股份有限公司 上海市分公司
PICC Property and Casualty Company Limited, Shanghai Branch

地址： 中国上海市中山南路700号
ADD: No.700 Zhongshan Road (S) Shanghai China
邮编（Post Code）：200010

电话（TEL）： (021)63773000
传真（FAX）： (021)63764678

货物运输保险投保单
APPLICATION FORM FOR CARGO TRANSPORTATION INSURANCE

被保险人：
INSURED: **SHANGHAI UNIVERSAL TRADING CO., LTD.**

发票号（INVOICE NO.） **HY-TIV-INV0373**
合同号（CONTRACT NO.） **HY-TIV0373**
信用证号（L/C NO.） **AM/VA07721SLC**
发票金额（INVOICE AMOUNT） **US$26,660.80** 投保加成（PLUS） **10** %

兹有下列物品向中国人民财产保险股份有限公司 **上海分** 公司投保。（INSURANCE IS REQUIRED ON THE FOLLOWING COMMODITIES:）

标 记 MARKS & NOS.	包装及数量 QUANTITY	保险货物项目 DESCRIPTION OF GOODS	保险金额 AMOUNT INSURED
AS PER INVOICE NO. HY-TIV-INV0373	**386CTNS**	**PLUSH TOYS**	**US$29,327.00**

启运日期：
DATE OF COMMENCEMENT **NOV. 13, 2018**
装载运输工具：
PER CONVEYANCE **COSCO HELLAS / 013W**

自 经 至
FROM **SHANGHAI** VIA TO **ROTTERDAM, NETHERLANDS**

提单号：
B/L NO. **COSU89302173**
赔款偿付地点：
CLAIM PAYMENT AT **ROTTERDAM**

投保险别：（PLEASE INDICATE THE CONDITIONS &/OR SPECIAL COVERAGES）

COVERING INSTITUTE CARGO CLAUSES (A) AND INSTITUTE WAR CLAUSES-CARGO

备注： （REMARKS）
1）须三份正本保单
2）保单须注明信用证号码 CREDIT NUMBER: AM/VA07721SLC

请如实告知下列情况：（如'是'在[ ]中打'X'）IFANY, PLEASE MARK 'X':

1、货物种类	普通 [X]	散装 [ ]	冷藏 [ ]	液体 [ ]	活动物 [ ]	机器/汽车 [ ]	危险品等级 [ ]
GOODS	ORDINARY	BULK	REEFER	LIQUID	LIVE ANIMAL	MACHINE/AUTO	DANGEROUS CLASS
2、集装箱种类	普通 [X]	开项 [ ]	框架 [ ]	平板 [ ]	冷藏 [ ]		
CONTAINER	ORDINARY	OPEN	FRAME	PLAY	REFRIGERATOR		
3、转运工具	海轮 [ ]	飞机 [ ]	驳船 [ ]	火车 [ ]	汽车 [ ]		
BY TRANSIT	SHIP	PLANE	BARGE	TRAIN	TRUCK		
4、船舶资料		船籍			船龄		
PARTICULAR OF SHIP		REGISTRY			AGE		

备注： 被保险人确认本保险合同条款和内容已经完全了解
THE ASSURED CONFIRMS HEREWITH THE TERMS AND CONDI-
TIONS OF THESE INSURANCE CONTRACT FULLY UNDER-
STOOD.

投保人（签名盖章）APPLICANT

王凯

投保日期：（DATE） **NOV. 5, 2018**

电话 （TEL） **021-5**　　**8844**
地址 （ADD） **131 DONGFANG ROAD,**
SHANGHAI, CHINA

本公司自用（FOR OFFICE USE ONLY）

经办人
Made By _____

核保人
Checked By _____

NO.: PICC 0825873

Shanghai Universal Trading Co., Ltd.

Rm. 1201-1216 Mayling Plaza,
131 Dongfang Rd.,
Shanghai, 200120, China
Tel: 86-21-58818844
Fax: 86-21-58818766

COMMERCIAL INVOICE

TO: TIVOLIAN TRADING B.V. P.O. BOX 1783, HEIMAN DULLAERTOLEIN 3 3024CA ROTTERDAM, NETHERLANDS	**INV. NO. :**	HY-TIV-INV0373
	INV. DATE:	OCT. 29, 2018
	S/C NO. :	HY-TIV0373

FROM: SHANGHAI	**TO:** ROTTERDAM	**SHIPPED BY :** COSCO HELLAS / 013W

MARKS & NOS.	DESCRIPTION OF GOODS		QUANTITY	UNIT PRICE	AMOUNT
CE/IMP.087 TIV-PO-CSH0873 ROTTERDAM CARTON NO. 1 - 126 KB0278	PLUST TOYS			CIF ROTTERDAM	
	KB0278	TWIN BEAR	504SETS	US$9.60	US$4,838.40
	KB5411	TWIN BEAR IN BALLET COSTUME	504SETS	US$11.50	US$5,796.00
	KB0677	BROWN BEAR WITH RED BOW	536SETS	US$14.50	US$7,772.00
CE/IMP.087 TIV-PO-CSH0873 ROTTERDAM CARTON NO. 1 - 126 KB5411	KB7900	BEAR IN PINK T-SHIRT	536SETS	US$15.40	US$8,254.40
					US$26,660.80
F-TOYS 228 TIV-PO-CSH0873 ROTTERDAM CARTON NO. 1 - 67 KB0677					
F-TOYS 228 TIV-PO-CSH0873 ROTTERDAM CARTON NO. 1 - 67 KB7900	**TOTAL AMOUNT IN WORDS:**	SAY U.S. DOLLARS TWENTY SIX THOUSAND SIX HUNDRED AND SIXTY AND CENTS EIGHTY ONLY			
	TOTAL G.W. / TOTAL N.W.:	3155.000 KGS / 2190.000 KGS			
	TOTAL PACKAGES:	386CTNS			

上 海 环 宇 贸 易 有 限 公 司
SHANGHAI UNIVERSAL TRADING CO., LTD.

(SIGNATURE)

💬 示范评析

Q:CIF 术语下,保险单中的被保险人可以填写进口商吗?

A:一般情况下,被保险人应填写为出口商,信用证结算时即为受益人。这是因为:

第一,根据 CIF 术语对买卖双方风险的划分,只有当货物在指定装运港越过船舷时,其灭失或损坏的风险才自卖方转移至买方。也就是说,在投保时,卖方(而非买方)对即将发运的货物具有保险利益。根据被保险人是保险利益的所有者的原则,保险单上的被保险人应为卖方。

第二,在卖方尚未收妥货款的情况下,以买方作为“被保险人”有较大的风险。一旦碰到买方拒付货款,或是信用证项下出现单证不符而遭到拒付时,恰遇货物在海运途中发生保险范围内的损失,卖方则无法凭该保险单向保险公司提出索赔。不仅如此,由于保险单据的被保险人是买方,卖方想要转让货物另寻买主也比较困难。所以,卖方通常选择将自己作为保险单的被保险人,在向买方交单(或通过银行交单)时,通过在保险单上作必要的背书才将保险利益及索赔权转让给买方。

Q:示范中的投保金额“US \$29327.00”是如何得出的?

A:本案例中,10 月 8 日开来的信用证规定投保金额为“120 percent of full CIF value”,但按照受益人的要求,10 月 15 日开来的信用证修改书已将“120％”降至“110％”,而该笔交易的 CIF 金额(即发票金额,也是信用证金额)为 US \$26660.80,所以保险金额应为 26660.80×110％＝US \$29326.88。通常,保险公司习惯将保险金额按“进一取整”的方法只计算到元(美元),所以最终填写的保险金额就为 US \$29327.00。

指　南

在国际贸易中,货物从卖方到买方手中,通常要经过长途的运输、装卸和存储等流转环节。在这个过程中货物可能遇到各种各样的风险和遭受各种损失。为了在货物受损时能得到经济上的补偿,买方或卖方应在货物启运前,向保险公司办理货物的运输保险。

所谓货物的运输保险是指:投保人(the Insured,在 FOB、CFR 术语下为买方,在 CIF 术语下为卖方)对一批或若干批货物向保险人(the Insurer,即保险公司),按一定的金额投保一定的险别,并缴纳保险费,保险人承保后签发保险单作为承保的凭证。如果所保的货物在运输过程中发生承保风险造成的损失,则保险公司应按其出具的保险单的规定给予被保险人经济上的补偿。

ⓘ 保险条款及险别

(一) 中国保险条款及险别

中国人民保险公司(The People's Insurance Company of China,简称 PICC)参照国际保险市场的一般习惯、结合我国实际,制定了一套"中国保险条款"(China Insurance Clauses,简称 CIC),并于 1981 年 1 月 1 日完成修订。CIC 包括海洋运输货物保险条款(Ocean Marine Cargo Clauses),陆上运输货物保险条款(Overland Transportation Cargo Insurance Clauses),航空运输货物保险条款(Air Transportation Cargo Insurance Clauses)和邮包保险条款(Parcel Post Insurance Clauses)。

海洋货物运输险条款的险别分为基本险别和附加险两种。

基本险别有三种:

◇ 平安险(Free From Particular Average,简称 FPA)

◇ 水渍险(With Average,简称 WA,或 With Particular Average,简称 WPA)

◇ 一切险(All Risks)

这三种险别中,一切险承保范围最大,平安险最小。

附加险分为一般附加险和特殊附加险。

一般附加险(General Additional Risk)即由于外来原因所致的全部或部分损失的风险,它们是主要险别责任范围的扩展,因此不能单独投保。但如投保了一切险,这些附加险也就包括在内了。

特殊附加险(Special Additional Risk)是承保由于特殊风险所造成的全部或部分损失,共有以下八种:

◇　战争险(War Risks)

◇　罢工险(Strike Risks)

◇　黄曲霉素险(Aflatoxin)

◇　交货不到险(Failure to Deliver)

◇　舱面险(On Deck)

◇　进口关税险(Import Duty)

◇　拒收险(Rejection)

◇　货物出口到香港(包括九龙)或澳门,存仓火险责任扩展条款(Flame Risk Retention Clause, F.R.E.C)

被保险人不论已投保何种基本险别,均可以分别加保有关的特殊附加险别。

(二) 协会货物条款及险别

国际上有较大影响且有代表性的保险条款是英国伦敦保险业协会于 1982 年 1 月 1 日完成修订的"协会货物条款"(Institute Cargo Clauses—ICC),2009 年 1 月 1 日再次修订生效。

其中适用于海运货物保险的险别有六种:

◇　Institute Cargo Clauses A,简称 ICC(A)(协会货物 A 险条款)

◇　Institute Cargo Clauses B,简称 ICC(B)(协会货物 B 险条款)

◇　Institute Cargo Clauses C,简称 ICC(C)(协会货物 C 险条款)

◇　Institute War Clauses(Cargo)(协会战争险条款)

◇　Institute Strikes Clauses(Cargo)(协会货物罢工险条款)

◇　Malicious Damage Clauses(恶意损害险条款)

在上述六种险别条款中,除恶意损害险以外,其余五种险别均可以单独投保。

ICC(A)、ICC(B)、ICC(C)的承保范围分别类似于 CIC 的一切险、水渍险和平安险。

ⓘ 出口货运投保的流程

CIF 交易应由卖方办理货物运输的投保事宜。由于 CIF 术语中买卖双方的风险划分是以装运港船舷为界的,也就是说,货物越过装运港船舷起的一切风险要由买方来承担。所以,卖方最迟应在装运前向保险公司投保,相应的,作为保险凭证的保险单据的出单日期也能不迟于装运日期。对此,UCP600 也规定"保险单据日期不得晚于发运日期,除非保险单据表明保险责任不迟于发运日生效"。因此,一般在订妥舱位后,出口商就应及时向保险公司办理出口投保手续。

CIF 条件出口的投保流程为:

◇ 出口商根据合同或信用证的规定,填制"货物运输保险投保单",随附商业发票,向保险公司投保;

◇ 保险公司接受出口商的投保申请后,收取保险费,出具"货物运输保险单"并提供保费发票。

以 FOB 或 CFR 条件成交时,通常在货物装船后,出口商应立即向进口商发出装运通知以便进口商办理投保手续。

ⓘ 货运投保单的填制

各保险公司一般都印就自己的投保单,虽然格式有所差别,但内容基本为:

◇ **被保险人**
除非信用证另有规定,CIF 交易中的被保险人一般为信用证受益人,即出口商。

◇ **发票号　合同号　信用证号码**

◇ **标记**
填写货物的运输标志,也可简单填写为"As per Invoice No..."。

◇ **包装及数量**
一般填写货物的总包装件数和包装种类,例如:285CARTONS。

◇ **保险货物项目**
填写相关交易的货物名称,一般只写货物总称。

◇　**发票金额　投保加成　保险金额**

国际贸易运输货物保险的保险金额一般是以发票金额为基础确定的。但如果出口商仅按发票金额（CIF 价值）投保，那么一旦发生货损，进口商已支付的经营费用，如开证费、电报费、借款利息、税款等和本来可以获得的预期利润，是无法从保险人那里获得补偿的。因此，各国保险法及国际贸易惯例一般都规定进出口货物运输保险的保险金额可在 CIF 价值（即发票金额）基础上适当加成。

对于加成投保的问题，INCOTERMS2010 和 UCP600 都规定，最低的保险金额必须为合同金额/CIF 货物价值的 110%，即投保加成率为 10%（一成）。

当然，保险加成率 10% 并不是一成不变的。进出口双方也完全可以根据不同的货物、不同地区进口价格与当地市价之间不同差价、不同的经营费用和预期利润水平，约定不同的加成率。所以在确定具体保险金额时，必须关注合同中的相关约定，在信用证交易中更应遵照信用证的要求来操作。

例如：发票金额 US $10290.40，投保加成 10%，则

$$保险金额＝发票金额×（1＋保险加成率）$$
$$＝USD10290.4×（1＋10\%）$$
$$＝USD11319.44$$

一般保险公司习惯将保险金额按"进一取整"的方法只计算到元，如将上例按 USD11320 投保。注意不能采取"四舍五入"的方法取整，因为那样可能无法满足最低 110% 的要求。

◇　**启运日期**

填写货物实际出运的日期，也可填写"As per B/L No..."。

◇　**装载运输工具**

海运时填写船名、航次。从配舱回单中可以获知相关信息。

◇　**自　　经　　至**

填写货物实际的装运地、转运地以及目的地。如无转运地，可以留空。

◇　**提单号**

填写相关提单的号码。配舱回单上的 D/R No. 即为日后的提单号码。

◇ **偿付地点**

根据信用证中对保险单据条款的规定填写。一般为目的地或进口国。

◇ **投保险别**

根据信用证中对保险单据条款的规定填写。

◇ **备注**

填写信用证中对保险单据的其他特殊要求,包括份数、证明文句等。

◇ **投保日期　投保人(签名盖章)**

投保日期通常不应迟于实际装运日;由具体经办人签字并盖公章。

(i) 投保的反馈文件

保险公司承保后,出具"货物运输保险单"。

中国平安
PING AN OF CHINA

中国平安财产保险股份有限公司
PING AN PROPERTY & CASUALTY INSURANCE COMPANY OF CHINA, LTD.

总公司地址
中国·深圳
八卦岭八卦三路平安大厦
电话 (Tel): 0755-82262888
图文传真 (Fax): 0755-82414813
邮政编码 (Postcode): 518029
Address of Head Office:
Ping An Building, No.3 Ba Gua Road,
Ba Gua Ling, Shenzhen, China

No. 060500087413　　货 物 运 输 保 险 单
CARGO TRANSPORTATION INSURANCE POLICY

被保险人
Insured:　　**SHANGHAI TIAN YUAN TRADING CO., LTD.**

中国平安财产保险股份有限公司根据被保险人的要求及所交付的约定的保险费，按照本保险单背面所载条款与下列特款，承保下述货物运输保险，特立本保险单。
This Policy of Insurance witnesses that PING AN PROPERTY & CASUALTY INSURANCE COMPANY OF CHINA, LTD., at the request of the Insurance and in consideration of the agreed premium paid by the Insured, undertakes to insure the undermentioned goods in transportation subject to the conditions of Policy as per the clauses printed overleaf and other special clauses attached hereon.

保单号 Policy No.	**PA2008453429238603357 8**	赔款偿付地点 Claim Payable at
发票或提单号 Invoice No. or B/L No.	**INVOICE NO. TR-INVWR59235**	**HAMBURG IN USD**
运输工具 Per Conveyance S.S.	**YU XIANG V.345**	查勘代理人 Survey By.
起运日期 Slg.on or abt	**AS PER B/L** 自 **SHANGHAI, CHINA** From	**PANDI MARINE INSURANCE GMBH**
	至 **HAMBURG, GERMANY** To	**WEIDENALLEE 22, D-20355** **HAMBURG GERMANY** **TEL: +49 40 35008312** **FAX: +49 40 35008315**
保险金额 Amount Insured	**US$19,250.00 SAY US DOLLARS NINETEEN THOUSAND TWO HUNDRED AND FIFTY ONLY**	

保险货物项目、标记、数量及包装:
Description, Marks, Quantity, & Packing of Goods:

承保条件:
Conditions:

PORCELAIN DINNERWARE

TERI
WR59235
HAMBURG
CTN. NO.1-500

500CTNS

COVERING INSTITUTE CARGO CLAUSES (B)
AND INSTITUTE SRIKE CLAUSES - CARGO.

L/C NO. AN-29854 DATED 20 FEBRUARY 2018
ISSUED BY COMMERZBANK AG FRANKFURT AM MAIN

保单正本：2份
Number of Originals: 2

签单日期
Date: MAR 10, 2018

IMPORTANT
PROCEDURE IN THE EVENT OF LOSS OR DAMAGE FOR WHICH
UNDERWRITERS MAY BE LIABLE
LIABILITY OF CARRIERS, BAILEES OR OTHER THIRD PARTIES

It is the duty of the Assured and their Agents, in all cases, to take such measures as may be reasonable for the purpose of averting or minimising a loss and to ensure that all rights against Carriers, Bailees or other third parties are properly preserved and exercised. In particular, the Assured of their Agents are required:
1. To claim immediately on the Carriers, Port Authorities or other Bailees for any missing packages.
2. In no circumstances, except under written protest, to give clean receipts where goods are in doubtful conditions.
3. When delivery is made by Container, to ensure that the Container and its seals are examined immediately by their responsible official. If the Container is delivered damaged or with seals broken or missing or with seals other than as stated in the shipping documents, to clause the delivery receipt accordingly and retain all defective or irregular seals for subsequent identification.
4. To apply immediately for survey by Carriers' or other Bailees' Representatives if any loss or damage be apparent and claim on the Carriers or other Bailees for any actual loss or damage found at such survey.
5. To give notice in writing to the Carriers or other Bailees within 3 days of delivery if the loss or damage was not apparent at the time of taking delivery.

NOTE:- The Consignees or their Agents are recommended to make themselves familiar with the Regulations of the Port Authorities at the port of discharge.

DOCUMENTATION OF CLAIMS
To enable claims to be dealt with promptly, the Assured or their Agents are advised to submit all available supporting documents without delay, including when applicable:
1. Original policies of insurance.
2. Original or certified copy of shipping invoices, together with shipping specification and / or weight notes.
3. Original or certified copy of Bill of Lading and / or other contract of carriage.
4. Survey report or other documentary evidence to show the extent of the loss or damage.
5. Landing account and weight notes at port of discharge and final destination.
6. Correspondence exchanged with the Carriers and other Parties regarding their liability for the loss or damage.

In the event of loss or damage which may involve a claim under this insurance, no claim shall be paid unless immediate notice of such loss or damage has been given to and a Survey Report obtained from this Company's Office or Agents Specified in this Policy.

For and on behalf of
PING AN PROPERTY & CASUALTY INSURANCE
COMPANY OF CHINA, LTD.

Authorized Signature

复核　　　　制单

地址及电话　　**11/F, 12/F, JING AN PLAZA, 8 CHANG SHU ROAD**
Address & Tel.　**SHANGHAI, CHINA 52564888×6395**

注：　未加盖本公司保单专用章，保单无效。

在以 CIF 贸易术语成交的情况下,卖方作为投保人应向保险公司投保货物运输险,并从保险公司处取得以其自身为被保险人(也是保险受益人)的保险单据。在出口商向进口商(或通过银行向进口商)提交货运单据时,出口商要在保险单的背面作必要的背书(Endorsement),以便将保险单项下的保险利益,即在货物发生了承保风险造成的损失时获得保险公司赔偿的权利,转让给进口商。这样,一旦货物在运输途中发生了承保风险造成的损失,进口商就可以向保险单上列明的保险代理要求索赔。

ⓘ 保险单据的种类

保险单据既是保险人对被保险人的承保证明,又是双方之间权利义务的契约。在被保险货物遭受损失时,它是被保险人索赔的主要依据,也是保险人理赔的主要依据。

较为常见的保险单据包括以下几种:

◇　保险单(Insurance Policy)

俗称大保单,是使用最广的一种保险单据。一般详细载明了保险人与被保险人双方约定的主要事项,如承保货物详情、投保险别、保费收取等内容,背面通常还列有保险人与被保险人之间权利和义务等方面的条款,具有法律效力。

◇　保险凭证(Insurance Certificate)

俗称小保单,是一种比较简化的保险单据。它包括了保险单的基本内容,但背面不载明保险人与被保险人之间权利和义务等方面的条款。保险凭证与保险单具有同等的法律效力。

◇　预约保险单(Open Policy)

又称为保险合同(Open Cover),是被保险人与保险人之间订立的总合同,目的是简化保险手续,又可使货物一经装运即可取得保障。实际业务中,承保货物的范围、险别、费率、责任、赔款处理等符合合同条款规定的,在合同有效期内自动承保。预约保险单主要运用于以 FOB 和 CFR 成交的进口交易中。

练　习

试根据以下信用证条款及相关信息填制投保单和保险单：

```
DOC. CREDIT NUMBER    * 20    : 3851L752297
DATE OF ISSUE          31C    : 180624
EXPIRY                * 31D   : DATE  180726        PLACE  BENEFICIARIES' COUNTRY
APPLICANT             * 50    : PROFESSIONAL TRADING CO., LTD.
                                262/10 MOO 3 BOHWIN
                                SRIRACHA, CHONBURI
                                THAILAND
BENEFICIARY           * 59    : SHANGHAI JINGANG TRADING COMPANY
                                17F. JINHANG TOWER
                                NO.880 HUAI HAI ROAD
                                SHANGHAI CHINA
AMOUNT                * 32B   : USD52450.40 FOR 100 PCT OF INVOICE VALUE
PARTIAL SHIPMENTS      43P    : NOT PERMITTED
TRANSSHIPMENT          43T    : NOT PERMITTED
LOADING IN CHARGE      44A    : SHANGHAI
FOR TRANSPORT TO...    44B    : LAEM CHABANG
LATEST DATE OF SHIP.   44C    : 180705
DESCRIPT. OF GOODS     45A    :
                                ROUND PIPE AND SQUARE PIPE
                                AS PER SALES CONFIRMATION NO.JG071405 DATED 180531
                                CIF  LAEM CHABANG
                                SHIPPING MARKS:      P.T.C.L.
                                                     JG071405
                                                     LAEM CHABANG
                                                     C/NO.1-UP
DOCUMENTS REQUIRED     46A    :
     +  INSURANCE POLICY OR CERTIFICATE OR DECLARATION IN TWO  NEGOTIABLE
        FORMS INDICATING "FIRST" OR "SECOND" ORIGINAL PLUS ONE NON-NEGO-
        TIABLE COPY ENDORSED IN BLANK FOR FULL INVOICE VALUE PLUS 10 PER
        CENT WITH CLAIM PAYABLE IN BANGKOK IN THE SAME CURRENCY AS THE
        DRAFT, COVERING INSTITUTE CARGO CLAUSES (A) AND INSTITUTE WAR
        CLAUSES (CARGO) DATED 1/1/2009.
```

保单号码：PYIE2017258972465001482　　　　发票号码：JGINV0725010

货物件数：668 个纸箱　　　　　　　　　　　船名航次：YUN HE V.205

投保日期：2018 年 7 月 2 日　　　　　　　　保单日期：2018 年 7 月 3 日

理赔代理：THE NEW INDIA ASSURANCE CO LTD

CHAMNAN PHENJATI TOWER B，17TH FL

65 RAMA IX RD，HUAYKWANG

BANGKOK 10320

保险单的填制方法请参见**第十二章　　出口交单结汇**的**指南**（第 346 页）。

PICC 中国人民财产保险股份有限公司 上海市分公司
PICC Property and Casualty Company Limited, Shanghai Branch

地址： 中国上海市中山南路700号
ADD: No.700 Zhongshan Road (S) Shanghai China
邮编（Post Code）: 200010

电话（TEL）: (021)63773000
传真（FAX）: (021)63764678

货物运输保险投保单
APPLICATION FORM FOR CARGO TRANSPORTATION INSURANCE

被保险人：
INSURED:

发票号（INVOICE NO.）
合同号（CONTRACT NO.）
信用证号（L/C NO.）
发票金额（INVOICE AMOUNT）   投保加成（PLUS）   %

兹有下列物品向中国人民财产保险股份有限公司 上海分 公司投保。（INSURANCE IS REQUIRED ON THE FOLLOWING COMMODITIES:）

标　记 MARKS & NOS.	包装及数量 QUANTITY	保险货物项目 DESCRIPTION OF GOODS	保险金额 AMOUNT INSURED

启运日期：   装载运输工具：
DATE OF COMMENCEMENT   PER CONVEYANCE

自   经   至
FROM   VIA   TO

提单号：   赔款偿付地点：
B/L NO.   CLAIM PAYMENT AT

投保险别：（PLEASE INDICATE THE CONDITIONS &/OR SPECIAL COVERAGES）

请如实告知下列情况:（如'是'在[ ]中打'X'）IF ANY, PLEASE MARK 'X':

1、货物种类 普通【 】散装【 】冷藏【 】液体【 】活动物【 】机器/汽车【 】危险品等级【 】
GOODS   ORDINARY BULK   REEFER   LIQUID   LIVE ANIMAL MACHINE/AUTO DANGEROUS CLASS

2、集装箱种类 普通【 】开项【 】框架【 】平板【 】冷藏【 】
CONTAINER ORDINARY OPEN   FRAME   PLAY   REFRIGERATOR

3、转运工具 海轮【 】飞机【 】驳船【 】火车【 】汽车【 】
BY TRANSIT SHIP   PLANE   BARGE   TRAIN   TRUCK

4、船舶资料 船籍 船龄
PARTICULAR OF SHIP REGISTRY AGE

备注： 被保险人确认本保险合同条款和内容已经完全了解   投保人（签名盖章）APPLICANT'S SIGNATURE
THE ASSURED CONFIRMS HEREWITH THE TERMS AND CONDI-
TIONS OF THESE INSURANCE CONTRACT FULLY UNDER-
STOOD.

投保日期：(DATE)   电话：（TEL）
地址：（ADD）

本公司自用（FOR OFFICE USE ONLY）

费率   保费   备注：
RATE   PREMIUM

经办人   核保人   负责人
BY

NO.: PICC 0261424

PICC
中国人保财险
北京2008年奥运会保险合作伙伴
OFFICIAL INSURANCE PARTNER OF THE BEIJING 2008 OLYMPIC GAMES

货 物 运 输 保 险 单
CARGO TRANSPORTATION INSURANCE POLICY

总公司设于北京
Head office Beijing

一九四九年创立
Established in 1949

发票号（INVOICE NO.）
合同号（CONTRACT NO.）
信用证号（L/C NO.）
被保险人
INSURED

保单号次
POLICY NO.

中国人民财产保险股份有限公司（以下简称公司）根据被保险人的要求，由被保险人向本公司缴付约定的保险费，按照本保单承保险别和背面所载条款与下列特款承保下述货物运输保险，特立本保险单。
THIS POLICY OF INSURANCE WITNESSES THAT PICC PROPERTY AND CASUALTY COMPANY LIMITED (HEREINAFTER CALLED "THE COMPANY") AT THE REQUEST OF THE INSURED AND IN CONSIDERATION OF THE AGREED PREMIUM PAID TO THE COMPANY BY THE INSURED, UNDERTAKES TO INSURE THE UNDERMENTIONED GOODS IN TRANSPORTATION SUBJECT TO THE CONDITIONS OF THIS POLICY AS PER THE CLAUSES PRINTED OVERLEAF AND OTHER SPECIAL CLAUSES ATTACHED HEREON.

标 记 MARKS & NOS	包装及数量 QUANTITY	保险货物项目 DESCRIPTION OF GOODS	保险金额 AMOUNT INSURED

总保险金额：
TOTAL AMOUNT INSURED：

保费：   启运日期：   装载运输工具：
PREMIUM _____ DATE OF COMMENCEMENT _____   PER CONVEYANCE _____

白   经   至
FROM _____   VIA _____   TO _____

承保险别：
CONDITIONS

所保货物，如发生保险单项下可能引起索赔的损失或损坏，应立即通知本公司下述代理人查勘。如有索赔，应向本公司提交保单止本（本保单共有 ___ 份止本）及有关文件。如一份止本已用于索赔，其余止本自动失效。
IN THE EVENT OF LOSS OR DAMAGE WHICH MAY RESULT IN A CLAIM UNDER THIS POLICY, IMMEDIATE NOTICE MUST BE GIVEN TO THE COMPANY'S AGENT AS MENTIONED HEREUNDER CLAIMS. IF ANY, ONE OF THE ORIGINAL POLICY WHICH HAS BEEN ISSUED IN ___ ORIGINAL(S) TOGETHER WITH THE RELEVENT DOCUMENTS SHALL BE SURRENDERED TO THE COMPANY. IF ONE OF THE ORIGINAL POLICY HAS BEEN ACCOMPLISHED, THE OTHERS TO BE VOID.

中国人民财产保险股份有限公司 上 海 市 分 公 司
PICC Property and Casually Company Limited, Shanghai Branch

赔款偿付地点
CLAIM PAYABLE AT/IN _____

出单日期
ISSUING DATE _____

GENERAL MANAGER

地址： 中国上海中山南路700号
ADD: 700 ZHONGSHAN ROAD (S) SHANGHAI CHINA
邮编（POST CODE）：200010

经办：   复核：

Settling & Customer Service Centre:
(理赔/客户服务中心) 86 21 63674274

保单顺序号 PICC **0794516**

第九章　出口货物原产地认证

案　例

2018 年 11 月 6 日,环宇公司收到中国人民财产保险股份有限公司上海分公司签发的保险单(第 257 页)。

2018 年 11 月 7 日,环宇公司向出入境检验检疫局申请办理普惠制原产地证明格式 A(GSP FORM A)。

✍ 工作任务

填报出境货物原产地申请:制作普惠制原产地证明书申请书、普惠制原产地证明、连同商业发票一并提交给上海海关。

保险单

北京2008年奥运会保险合作伙伴
OFFICIAL INSURANCE PARTNER OF THE BEIJING 2008 OLYMPIC GAMES

货 物 运 输 保 险 单
CARGO TRANSPORTATION INSURANCE POLICY

总公司设于北京
Head office Beijing

一九四九年创立
Established in 1949

发票号（INVOICE NO.）	**HY-TIV0373**
合同号（CONTRACT NO.）	**HY-TIV0373**
信用证号（L/C NO.）	**AM/VA07721SLC**

保单号次
POLICY NO. **PYIE201343958015958273**

被保险人
INSURED **SHANGHAI UNIVERSAL TRADING CO., LTD.**

中国人民财产保险股份有限公司（以下简称公司）根据被保险人的要求，由被保险人向本公司缴付约定的保险费，按照本保单承保险别和背面所载条款与下列特款承保下述货物运输保险，特立本保险单。

THIS POLICY OF INSURANCE WITNESSES THAT PICC PROPERTY AND CASUALTY COMPANY LIMITED (HEREINAFTER CALLED "THE COMPANY") AT THE REQUEST OF THE INSURED AND IN CONSIDERATION OF THE AGREED PREMIUM PAID TO THE COMPANY BY THE INSURED, UNDERTAKES TO INSURE THE UNDERMENTIONED GOODS IN TRANSPORTATION SUBJECT TO THE CONDITIONS OF THIS POLICY AS PER THE CLAUSES PRINTED OVERLEAF AND OTHER SPECIAL CLAUSES ATTACHED HEREON.

标 记 MARKS & NOS	包装及数量 QUANTITY	保险货物项目 DESCRIPTION OF GOODS	保险金额 AMOUNT INSURED
AS PER INVOICE **NO. HY-TIV-INV0373** **CREDIT NUMBER: AM/VA07721SLC**	**386CTNS**	**PLVSH TOYS**	**US$29,327.00**

总保险金额：
TOTAL AMOUNT INSURED: **US DOLLARS TWENTY NINE THOUSAND THREE HUNDRED AND TWENTY SIX ONLY**

保费 PREMIUM **AS ARRANGED**	启运日期： DATE OF COMMENCEMENT **AS PER B/L**		装载运输工具： PER CONVEYANCE **COSCO HELLA / 013W**	
自 FROM **SHANGHAI, CHINA**	经 VIA		至 TO **ROTTERDAM, NETHERLANDS**	

承保险别：
CONDITIONS

COVERING INSTITUTE CARGO CLAUSES (A) AND INSTITUTE WAR CLAUSES - CARGO.

所保货物，如发生保险单项下可能引起索赔的损失或损坏，应立即通知本公司下述代理人查勘。如有索赔，应向本公司提交保单正本（本保单共有 **贰** 份正本）及有关文件。如一份正本已用于索赔，其余正本自动失效。

IN THE EVENT OF LOSS OR DAMAGE WHICH MAY RESULT IN A CLAIM UNDER THIS POLICY, IMMEDIATE NOTICE MUST BE GIVEN TO THE COMPANY'S AGENT AS MENTIONED HEREUNDER CLAIMS. IF ANY ONE OF THE ORIGINAL POLICY WHICH HAS BEEN ISSUED IN **2** ORIGINAL(S) TOGETHER WITH THE RELEVENT DOCUMENTS SHALL BE SURRENDERED TO THE COMPANY. IF ONE OF THE ORIGINAL POLICY HAS BEEN ACCOMPLISHED, THE OTHERS TO BE VOID.

中国人民财产保险股份有限公司 上海市分公司
PICC Property and Casualty Company Limited, Shanghai Branch

赔款偿付地点
CLAIM PAYABLE AT/IN **ROTTERDAM IN USD**

出单日期
ISSUING DATE **NOV. 6, 2018**

GENERAL MANAGER

地址：中国上海中山南路700号 ADD: 700 ZHONGSHAN ROAD (S) SHANGHAI CHINA 邮编（POST CODE）：200010	经办：项钧 复核：廖敏 Settling & Customer Service Centre （理赔/客户服务中心）86 21 63674274

保单顺序号 PICC **1325873**

⬇ 普惠制原产地证明书申请书

普惠制原产地证明书申请书

申请单位(盖章)：　　　　　　　　　　　　　　　　证书号：_____

申请人郑重声明：　　　　　　　　　　　　　　　　注册号：_ _ _ _ _ _ _ _

　　本人是被正式授权代表出口单位办理和签署本申请书的。

　　本申请书及普惠制产地证格式A所列内容正确无误，如发现弄虚作假，冒充格式A所列货物，擅改证书，自愿接受签证机关的处罚及负法律责任。现将有关情况申报如下：

生产单位		生产单位联系人电话	
商品名称 (中英文)		H.S 税目号 (以八位数码计)	

商品(FOB)总值(以美元计)		发 票 号	

最终销售国		证书种类划"√"	（　）加急证书	（　）普通证书
货物拟出运日期				

贸易方式和企业性质(请在适用处划"√")

正常贸易 C	来进料加工 L	补偿贸易 B	其他	中外合资 H	中外合作 Z	外商独资 D	其他

包装数量或毛重或其它数量	

原产地标准：

本项商品系在中国生产，完全符合该给惠国方案规定，其原产地情况符合以下第　　　　条：

　　(1) "P" (完全国产，未使用任何进口原材料)；

　　(2) "W" 其H.S税目号为 _ _ _ _ _ _ _ _ _ (含进口成分)；

　　(3) "F"(对加拿大出口产品，其进口成分不超过产品出厂价值的40%)。

本批产品系：　1. 直接运输从 _____ 到 _____ ；

　　　　　　　2. 转口运输从 _ _ _ _ 中转国（地区） _ _ _ _ 到 _ _ _ _ ；

申请人说明　　　　　　　　　　　　领证人(签名)

　　　　　　　　　　　　　　　　　电　话：

　　　　　　　　　　　　　　　　　日期　　　年　　　月　　　日

　　现提交中国出口商业发票副本一份，普惠制产地证明书格式A(FORM A)一正二副，以及其他附件 *** 份，请予审核签证。

注：凡含有进口成分的商品，必须按要求提交《含进口成分受惠商品成本明细单》。

检验检疫机关联系记录

普惠制原产地证明

ORIGINAL

1. Goods consigned from (Exporter's business name, address, country)	Reference No.
	GENERALIZED SYSTEM OF PREFERENCES **CERTIFICATE OF ORIGIN** **(Combined declaration and certificate)** **FORM A** **Issued in THE PEOPLE'S REPUBLIC OF CHINA** (country) See Notes overleaf
2. Goods consigned to (Consignee's name, address, country)	

3. Means of transport and route (as far as known)	4. For official use

5. Item number	6. Marks and numbers of packages	7. Number and Kind of packages; description of goods	8. Origin criterion (see Notes overleaf)	9. Gross weight or other quantity	10. Number and date of invoices

11. Certification It is hereby certified, on the basis of control carried out, that the declaration by the exporter is correct.	12. Declaration by the exporter The undersigned hereby declares that the above details and statements are correct; that all the goods were produced in _____ (country) and that they comply with the origin requirements specified for those goods in the Generalized System of Preferences for goods exported to _____ (importing country)
Place and date, signature and stamp of certifying authority	Place and date. signature of authorized signatory

示　范

普惠制原产地证明书申请书

申请单位(盖章)：

申请人郑重声明：

证书号：　G183100672730073

注册号：　310067273

本人是被正式授权代表出口单位办理和签署本申请书的。

本申请书及普惠制产地证格式A所列内容正确无误，如发现弄虚作假，冒充格式A所列货物，擅改证书，自愿接受签证机关的处罚及负法律责任。现将有关情况申报如下：

生产单位	上海普华玩具有限公司	生产单位联系人电话		38115260
商品名称 (中英文)	毛绒玩具 / PLUSH TOYS	H.S 税目号 (以八位数码计)		9503.0021
商品(FOB)总值(以美元计)	24450.17美元	发 票 号		HY-TIV-INV0373
最终销售国	荷兰	证书种类划"√"	( ) 加急证书	(√)普通证书
货物拟出运日期		Nov. 13, 2018		

贸易方式和企业性质(请在适用处划"√")

正常贸易 C	来进料加工 L	补偿贸易 B	其他	中外合资 H	中外合作 Z	外商独资 D	其他
√							√

包装数量或毛重或其它数量	386纸箱 / 3155千克 / 2080套

原产地标准：

本项商品系在中国生产，完全符合该给惠国方案规定，其原产地情况符合以下第　（1）　条：

　(1) "P" (完全国产，未使用任何进口原材料)；

　(2) "W" 其H.S税目号为 _____ (含进口成分)；

　(3) "F"(对加拿大出口产品，其进口成分不超过产品出厂价值的40%)。

本批产品系：　1. 直接运输从　中国　　到　荷兰　　　；

　　　　　　　2. 转口运输从 _____ 中转国（地区）_____ 到 _____；

申请人说明	领证人(签名)　薛颖 电 话：021-58818844 日 期　2018 年　11 月　7 日

现提交中国出口商业发票副本一份，普惠制产地证明书格式A(FORM A)一正二副，以及其他附件 *** 份，请予审核签证。

注：凡含有进口成分的商品，必须按要求提交《含进口成分受惠商品成本明细单》。

检验检疫机关联系记录

ORIGINAL

1. Goods consigned from (Exporter's business name, address, country) SHANGHAI UNIVERSAL TRADING CO., LTD. MAYLING PLAZA, 131 DONGFANG ROAD, SHANGHAI 200120, CHINA	Reference No.　G183100672730073 GENERALIZED SYSTEM OF PREFERENCES CERTIFICATE OF ORIGIN (Combined declaration and certificate) FORM A Issued in THE PEOPLE'S REPUBLIC OF CHINA (country) See Notes overleaf
2. Goods consigned to (Consignee's name, address, country) TIVOLIAN TRADING B.V. P.O. BOX 1783, HEIMAN DULLAERTOLEIN 3, 3024CA ROTTERDAM, NETHERLANDS	
3. Means of transport and route (as far as known) FROM SHANGHAI, CHINA TO ROTTERDAM, NETHERLANDS BY SEA	4. For official use

5. Item number	6. Marks and numbers of packages	7. Number and Kind of packages; description of goods	8. Origin criterion (see Notes overleaf)	9. Gross weight or other quantity	10. Number and date of invoices
01	CE/IMP.087 TIV-PO-CSH0873 ROTTERDAM CARTON NO. 1 - 126 KB0278 CE/IMP.087 TIV-PO-CSH0873 ROTTERDAM CARTON NO. 1 - 126 KB5411 F-TOYS 228 TIV-PO-CSH0873 ROTTERDAM CARTON NO. 1 - 67 KB0677 F-TOYS 228 TIV-PO-CSH0873 ROTTERDAM CARTON NO. 1 - 67 KB7900	386(THREE HUNDRED AND EIGHTY SIX) CARTONS OF PLUSH TOYS *** THE GOODS ARE OF CHINESE ORIGIN. CREDIT NUMBER: AM/VA07721SLC	"P"	3155.0KGS	HY-TIV-INV0373 OCT. 29, 2018

11. Certification It is hereby certified, on the basis of control carried out, that the declaration by the exporter is correct.	12. Declaration by the exporter The undersigned hereby declares that the above details and statements are correct; that all the goods were produced in　　CHINA (country) and that they comply with the origin requirements specified for those goods in the Generalized System of Preferences for goods exported to NETHERLANDS (importing country)
SHANGHAI, CHINA NOV. 7, 2018 Place and date, signature and stamp of certifying authority	SHANGHAI, CHINA NOV. 7, 2018 Place and date, signature of authorized signatory

Shanghai Universal Trading Co., Ltd.

Rm. 1201-1216 Mayling Plaza,
131 Dongfang Rd.,
Shanghai, 200120, China
Tel: 86-21-58818844
Fax: 86-21-58818766

COMMERCIAL INVOICE

TO: TIVOLIAN TRADING B.V.	**INV. NO. :** HY-TIV-INV0373
P.O. BOX 1783, HEIMAN DULLAERTOLEIN 3	**INV. DATE:** OCT. 29, 2018
3024CA ROTTERDAM, NETHERLANDS	**S/C NO. :** HY-TIV0373

FROM: SHANGHAI	**TO:** ROTTERDAM	**SHIPPED BY:** COSCO HELLAS / 013W

MARKS & NOS.	DESCRIPTION OF GOODS	QUANTITY	UNIT PRICE	AMOUNT
CE/IMP.087 TIV-PO-CSH0873 ROTTERDAM CARTON NO. 1 - 126 KB0278	PLUSH TOYS		CIF ROTTERDAM	
	KB0278 TWIN BEAR	504 SETS	US$9.60	US$4,838.40
	KB5411 TWIN BEAR IN BALLET COSTUME	504 SETS	US$11.50	US$5,796.00
	KB0677 BROWN BEAR WITH RED BOW	536 SETS	US$14.50	US$7,772.00
CE/IMP.087 TIV-PO-CSH0873 ROTTERDAM CARTON NO. 1 - 126 KB5411	KB7900 BEAR IN PINK T-SHIRT	536 SETS	US$15.40	US$8,254.40
				US$26,660.80
F-TOYS 228 TIV-PO-CSH0873 ROTTERDAM CARTON NO. 1 - 67 KB0677				
F-TOYS 228 TIV-PO-CSH0873 ROTTERDAM CARTON NO. 1 - 67 KB7900				

TOTAL AMOUNT IN WORDS: SAY U.S. DOLLARS TWENTY SIX THOUSAND SIX HUNDRED AND SIXTY AND CENTS EIGHTY ONLY

TOTAL G.W. / TOTAL N.W.: 3155.000 KGS / 2190.000 KGS

TOTAL PACKAGES: 386CTNS

上 海 环 宇 贸 易 有 限 公 司
SHANGHAI UNIVERSAL TRADING CO., LTD.

(SIGNATURE)

🗨 示范评析

Q：CIF 交易中，普惠制原产地证明申请书中的"商品（FOB）总值（以美元计）"应如何计算？

A：此栏的 FOB 总值可通过 CIF 总值减去海洋运费总值和保险费总值来计算。例如本案例中，CIF 总值为 26660.80 美元；从上海港至鹿特丹港的 20 英尺整箱运价为 1010 美元（参见第 14 页**第二章　发盘与出口报价核算**的案例），所以海洋运费总值为 1010×2＝2020 美元；保险金额为 29327.00 美元（参见第 243 页**第八章　出口货运投保**的示范），保险费率为 0.65％（参见第 14 页**第二章　发盘与出口报价核算**的案例），所以保险费 29327×0.65％＝190.63 美元；因此，商品 FOB 总值为 26660.80－2020－190.63＝24450.17 美元。

Q：示范中的普惠制原产地证明上为什么要打上"THE GOODS ARE OF CHINESE ORIGIN"和"CREDIT NUMBER：AM/VA07721SLC"？

A：本案例中的信用证规定：普惠制原产地证明上必须"stating that the goods are of Chinese origin"，尽管证明上印就的文句"all the goods were produced in China"表达了相同的含义，但出于谨慎稳妥的考虑，一般我们还是会按信用证的表述照打一遍。同时，信用证还规定"All documents must indicate this credit number"，所以原产地证明上也应指明相关的信用证号码。

Q：据了解，目前玩具出口到欧盟已不再享受普惠制关税优惠待遇，是否应不再使用普惠制原产地证明而改用一般原产地证明？

A：的确，自欧盟修订普惠制方案以来，我国的服装、鞋帽、玩具、塑料制品、家电等很多产品都已"毕业"，被取消了普惠制优惠。然而，欧盟对毕业制度实行的是动态管理，毕业的产品在一定的条件下可重新获得关税优惠。而且，普惠制产地证明不仅是关税减免的证明文件，同时也是原产地和原产国的证明。多年来，各国进口商对一些毕业产品仍一直要求办理普惠制产地证明，我国出口商也没有必要主动停止申请普惠制产地证。所以，我国出口商应根据进口商的要求办理原产地证明，对毕业的产品，仍可继续申领普惠制产地证明。更重要的是，在信用证交易中，为了符合信用证的条款，出口商更不能擅自变更原产地证明的类型。

指 南

认证的范围很广,所有由可以充分信任的第三方证实某一经鉴定的产品或服务符合特定标准或规范性文件的活动都可以称之为认证。在出口贸易中,可能会涉及产品质量认证,即出口商品必须符合进口国的质量标准,例如欧盟有 CE 认证、GS 安全认证,美国有 FDA 认证、UL 认证等,可能会涉及某些贸易单据(例如商业发票)需经进口国驻华使(领)馆认证后进口商方才接受,即办理"领事认证",或者进口商要求出口商提供原产地证明,即办理原产地认证。在出口交易中,当国外客户提出认证要求时,出口商应当清晰地了解其要求认证的内容、办理此类认证的机构和程序以及所需支付的费用后才能决定是否能够满足客户的要求。

在国际贸易中,各国根据各自的对外贸易政策普遍对进口商品实施差别关税和数量限制,并由海关执行统计,进口国要求出口国出具货物的原产地证明已成为国际惯例,因此在出口贸易中,使用得最为广泛的认证是出口货物的原产地认证,即出口商向官方或权威机构申请签发出口货物的原产地证明。原产地证明相当于货物在国际贸易行为中的"原籍"证书,是进口商保证货物顺利通关的先决条件,也有助于其享受进口的优惠关税。在各种原产地证明中,一般原产地证明(Certificate of Origin,简称 C/O)和普遍优惠制度(普惠制)原产地证明书格式 A(Generalized System of Preferences Certificate of Origin Form A,简称 GSP Form A)是比较常见的两种。

ⓘ 一般原产地证明

一般原产地证明可由中国国际贸易促进委员会(China Council for the Promotion of International Trade,简称 CCPIT,贸促会)签发,也可由海关签发。

(一) 一般原产地证明的申领程序

◇ 出口商须按要求真实完整准确地填制"一般原产地证明书申请书"一份、"原产地证明"(C/O)一套,并随附商业发票、装箱单各一份,至签证机构申请出证。

◇ 签证机构会对出口商提交的申领文件进行审核,确认无误后,在"原产地证明"上签字盖章并退还给出口商。

通常一般原产地证明只签发一正三副,其中一份副本为签证机构留存用。

中国贸促会上海市分会
中国国际商会上海商会

一般原产地证明书/加工装配证明书
申　请　书

申请单位注册号：　**310412181**　　证书号：　**C183104121810036**

全部国产填上P	
	"P"
含进口成分填上W	

申请人郑重声明：　　　　发票号：　**TR-INVWR59235**

　　　本人被授权代表本企业办理和签署本申请书。

　　　本申请书及一般原产地证书/加工装配证明书所列内容正确无误，如发现弄虚作假，

冒充证书所列货物、擅改证书、愿按《中华人民共和国出口货物原产地规则》有关规定接

受惩处并承担法律责任，现将有关情况申报如下：

商品名称	**瓷餐具**	H.S.编码(八位数)	**6911.1010**
商品生产、制造、加工单位、地点	**上海锦铭陶瓷有限公司**		
含进口成分产品主要制造加工工序	***		
商品FOB总值(以美元计)	**16403.75美元**	最终目的地国/地区	**德国**
拟出运日期	**2018年3月10日**	转口国(地区)	***
包装数量或毛重或其它数量	**500纸箱**		

贸易方式和企业性质	
贸易方式	企业性质
一般贸易	**国内合资**

　　　现提交中国出口货物发票一份，一般原产地证明书/加工装配证明书一正三副，

以及其它附件***张，请予以***签证。

申请单位盖章　（上海天源贸易有限公司印章）

申领人（签名）　**徐国良**

电话：　**021-64725124**

日期：　**2018**　年　**2**　月　**28**　日

如有补发，重发或更改C.O.证书，请填写背面申请单。

（二）一般原产地证明书申请书的填制说明

◇ **申请单位注册号　证书号**
填写出口商在签证机构的注册号，并按其规则编制证书号。

◇ **原产地标准**
有两个选项：全部国产的为 P，含进口成分的为 W。

◇ **含进口成分产品主要制造加工工序**
全部国产的产品，此栏应用"＊＊＊"表示。

◇ **商品 FOB 总值（以美元计）**
若出口货物是以 CIF 价格成交的，则按 FOB＝CIF－海洋运费－保险费的方式进行换算。

◇ **拟出运日期**
根据订舱反馈，填写预计的实际装船日。

◇ **转口国（地区）**
若货物买卖不是在生产国与消费国之间直接进行、而是通过第三国转手进行，则此处填写实际转口国国家名称。若无，则用"＊＊＊"表示。

◇ **包装数量或毛重或其他数量**
三项任选其一填写均可。

◇ **贸易方式　企业性质**
贸易方式分为"一般贸易"、"来料加工"、"补偿贸易"等。企业性质可按公司实际组织性质填写。

（三）一般原产地证明的填制

◇ **Certificate No.**
证书号码

◇ **Exporter**
出口人。按信用证填写受益人的名称和详细地址。

◇ **Consignee**
收货人。填写最终收货人（一般为进口商）的名称和详细地址。注意不要与提单上收货人一栏的填写方法混淆。

◇ **Means of transport and route**
运输方式和路线。填写装货港、卸货港及运输方式，如有转运，须注明转运港口。

ORIGINAL

1. Exporter **SHANGHAI TIAN YUAN TRADING CO., LTD.** **ROOM 1105, RUIJIN BLDG.,** **205 SOUTH MAOMING ROAD,** **SHANGHAI CHINA**	Certificate No. **C183104121810036**
2. Consignee **TERI INTERNATIONAL GMBH** **56 KEDENBURGSTRASSE D-758294 HAMBURG** **GERMANY**	**CERTIFICATE OF ORIGIN** **OF** **THE PEOPLE'S REPUBLIC OF CHINA**
3. Means of transport and route **FROM SHANGHAI, CHINA TO HAMBURG GERMANY** **BY SEA**	5. For certifying authority use only
4. Country / region of destination **GERMANY**	

6. Marks and numbers	7. Number and kind of packages; description of goods	8. H.S. Code	9. Quantity	10. Number and date of invoices
TERI **WR59235** **HAMBURG** **CTN. NO.1–500**	**500 (FIVE HUNDRED) CARTONS OF PORCELAIN DINNERWARE** *** **L/C NO. AN-29854 DATED 20 JANUARY 2018** **ISSUED BY COMMERZBANK AG FRANKFURT AM MAIN**	**6911.1010**	**500SETS**	**TR-INVWR59235** **FEB. 15, 2018**

11. Declaration by the exporter	12. Certification
The undersigned hereby declares that the above details and statements are correct; that all the goods were produced in China and that they comply with the Rules of Origin of the People's Republic of China.	It is hereby certified that the declaration by the exporter is correct.
SHANGHAI **FEB. 28, 2018** 徐国良	**SHANGHAI** **FEB. 28, 2018**
Place and date. signature and stamp of authorized signatory	Place and date. signature and stamp of certifying authority

◇ **For certifying authority use only**

签证机构用栏。此栏为签证机构在补发证书或加注其他声明时使用,一般留空。

◇ **Country/region of destination**

目的地国家(地区)。一般应与收货人的国别一致,不能填写转口国国家名称。

◇ **Marks and numbers**

运输标志。应具体填写,并与商业发票保持一致,不能简单填写为"As per Invoice No..."。如货物没有运输标志,则填写"N/M"。如运输标志过多、此栏不够填写,可加注在第 7、8、9、10 栏的空白处。

◇ **Number and kind of packages; description of goods**

包装数量及种类;商品名称。包装件数需同时注明大小写,应填写具体的商品名称,而不要填写商品大类诸如"Machine"、"Garment"等,商标、品牌、货号一般不填写,注意不能与信用证中的货物描述相冲突。填写完毕须在紧跟着的下一行输入结束符号" ＊＊＊＊＊＊＊ ",表示认证货物已描述完毕,不能再添加。

◇ **H.S. Code**

税目号。填写货物在《商品分类及编码协调制度》(Harmonized Commodity Description & Coding System)中所列编码,即 H.S. Code,以当年海关公布的货物税则编码为准。

◇ **Quantity**

填写货物的总数量。

◇ **Number and date of invoices**

发票号码和日期。此栏不得留空。为避免对月份、日期的误解,月份宜用英文表述。

◇ **Declaration by the exporter**

出口人申明。在印就的申明文句下方盖公章、签字确认,并注明签字地点及日期。从履约流程的角度来看,这个日期一般不应早于发票日期,但不会迟于装船日期。

◇　**Certification**

由签证机构签字、盖章认证。实际业务中,很多出口商在填制产地证明时就会一并填好这栏的签署地点和日期。

◇　**信用证要求在原产地证明上加注的内容**

一般加注在单据中间部位的明显处,如填写在 **Number and kind of packages**;**description of goods** 一栏的空白处。

(i) 普惠制原产地证明

普惠制原产证明是受惠国的原产品出口到给惠国时享受普惠制减免关税待遇的官方凭证,适用于一切有资格享受普惠制待遇的产品。在我国,海关是我国政府授权的唯一的普惠制原产地证明格式 A(GSP Form A)签发机构。

(一) 普惠制原产地证明的申领程序

◇　出口商须按要求真实完整准确地填制"普惠制原产地证明书申请书"一份、"普惠制原产地证明"(GSP Form A)一套,并随附商业发票一份,至海关申请出证。

◇　海关对出口商提交的申领文件进行审核,确认无误后,在"普惠制原产地证明"上签字盖章并退还给出口商。

通常普惠制原产地证明只签发一正二副。

(二) 普惠制原产地证明书申请书的填制说明

◇　**证书号　注册号**

填写出口商在签证机构的注册号,并按其规则编制证书号。

◇　**商品 FOB 总值(以美元计)**

若出口货物是以 CIF 价格成交的,则按 FOB＝CIF－海洋运费－保险费的方式进行换算。

◇　**货物拟出运日期**

根据订舱反馈,填写预计的实际装船日。

◇　**贸易方式和企业性质**

在备选栏目内打"√"，如没有合适栏目可选择"其他"。

◇ **包装数量或毛重或其他数量**

三项任选其一填写均可。

◇ **原产地标准**

根据实际情况在"P"、"W"、"F"中选择。

◇ **运输路线**

根据实际情况填写直接运输路线或是转口运输路线。

（三）普惠制原产地证明的填制

◇ **Reference No.**

证书号码。

另外，在证头的横线上也应有"Issued in THE PEOPLE'S REPUBLIC OF CHINA"字样，而且必须是英文全称，不得简化。

◇ **Goods consigned from（Exporter's business name，address，country）**

出口人的名称和详细地址、所在国家，包括街道名、门牌号码等。

◇ **Goods consigned to（Consignee's name，address，country）**

收货人的名称和详细地址、所在国家。一般应填给惠国最终收货人名称，如最终收货人不明确，可填发票抬头人，但不得填写中间转口商的名称。注意不要与提单上收货人一栏的填写方法混淆。

◇ **Means of transport and route（as far as known）**

所知运输方式和路线。填写装货港、卸货港及运输方式，如有转运，应注明转运港口，如输往内陆给惠国，则应注明目的国。例如"FROM SHANGHAI TO HAM-BURG VIA HONGKONG BY VESSEL IN TRANSIT TO SWITZERLAND"。

◇ **For official use**

供官方使用。此栏为签证机构在补发证书或加注其他声明时使用，一般留空。

◇ **Item number**

商品顺序号。若同批出口货物有不同种类（不同税目号），则应分列，并在此栏标注 01、02、03 等。单类商品，此栏则填"1"。

◇　**Marks and numbers of packages**

运输标志。应具体填写，并与商业发票保持一致，不能简单填写为"As per Invoice No ...."。如货物没有运输标志，则填写"N/M"。如运输标志过多、此栏不够填写，可加注在第 7、8、9、10 栏的空白处。

◇　**Number and kind of packages；description of goods**

包装数量及种类；商品名称。包装件数需同时注明大小写，应填写具体的商品名称，而不要填写商品大类诸如"Machine"、"Garment"等，商标、品牌、货号一般不填写，注意不能与信用证中的货物描述相冲突。填写完毕须在紧跟着的下一行输入结束符号"*******"，表示认证货物已描述完毕，不能再添加。

◇　**Origin criterion（see Notes overleaf）**

原产地标准。"P"代表完全自产产品，不含进口成分。其他标准可参阅产地证背面有关条款。

◇　**Gross weight or other quantity**

毛重或其他数量。填写商品的正常计量单位，以重量计算的则填毛重。

◇　**Number and date of invoices**

发票号码和日期。此栏不得留空。为避免对月份、日期的误解，月份宜用英文表述。

◇　**Certification**

由签证机构签字、盖章确认。实际业务中，很多出口商在填制产地证明时就会一并填好这栏的签署地点和日期。

◇　**Declaration by the exporter**

出口人申明。应注明出口国和进口国，并在印就的申明文句下方盖公章、签字确认，注明签字地点及日期。从履约流程的角度来看，这个日期一般不应早于发票日期，但不会迟于装船日期。

◇　**信用证要求在原产地证明上加注的内容**

一般加注在单据中间部位的明显处，如填写在 **Number and kind of packages；description of goods** 一栏的空白处。

练　习

　　试根据**第六章　出口托运订舱**的**练习**（第 219 页）中的出口货物明细、信用证及以下信息填制一般原产地证明及其申请书：

　　申请单位注册号：310075414

　　证书号码：C183100754140524

　　H.S.编码：9405.2000

　　装运日期：2018 年 12 月 1 日

　　贸易方式：一般贸易

　　海运费用：每个 20 英尺集装箱 1000 美元

　　企业性质：国内合资

　　申请日期：2018 年 11 月 23 日

中 国 贸 促 会 上 海 市 分 会
中 国 国 际 商 会 上 海 商 会
一般原产地证明书/加工装配证明书
申 请 书

申请单位注册号：_____ 证书号：_____

| 全部国产填上P | "P" |
| 含进口成分填上W | |

申请人郑重声明： 发票号：_____

本人被授权代表本企业办理和签署本申请书。

本申请书及一般原产地证书/加工装配证明书所列内容正确无误，如发现弄虚作假，

冒充证书所列货物，擅改证书、愿按《中华人民共和国出口货物原产地规则》有关规定接

受惩处并承担法律责任，现将有关情况申报如下：

商品名称		H.S.编码(八位数)	
商品生产、制造、加工单位、地点			
含进口成分产品主要制造加工工序			
商品FOB总值(以美元计)		最终目的地国/地区	
拟出运日期		转口国(地区)	
包装数量或毛重或其它数量			
贸易方式和企业性质			
贸 易 方 式		企业性质	

现提交中国出口货物商业发票一份，一般原产地证明书/加工装配证明书一正三副，

以及其它附件 *** 份，请予审核签证。

申领人（签名）

申请单位盖章： 电话：

日期：

如有补发，重发或更改C.O.证书，请填写背面申请单。

ORIGINAL

1. Exporter	Certificate No.
2. Consignee	**CERTIFICATE OF ORIGIN** **OF** **THE PEOPLE'S REPUBLIC OF CHINA**
3. Means of transport and route	5. For certifying authority use only
4. Country / region of destination	

6. Marks and numbers	7. Number and kind of packages;description of goods	8. H.S. Code	9. Quantity	10. Number and date of invoices

11. Declaration by the exporter	12. Certification
The undersigned hereby declares that the above details and statements are correct;that all the goods were produced in China and that they comply with the Rules of Origin of the People's Republic of China.	It is hereby certified that the declaration by the exporter is correct.
Place and date. signature and stamp of authorized signatory	Place and date. signature and stamp of certifying authority

第十章　出口货物报关

案　例

2018 年 11 月 9 日,环宇公司收到出上海海关签章的普惠制原产地证明(第 276 页)。

2018 年 11 月 10 日,货物运抵港区后,场站根据"集装箱装箱单"(Container Load Plan,简称 CLP)核对实际装箱情况,随后在 CLP 上签收、标注货物的进场日期,将 CLP 装箱人/发货人联(第 277 页)返还给环宇公司。

2018 年 11 月 11 日,环宇公司向上海海关申报货物出口。

工作任务

制作报关文件:填制出口货物报关单、并随附商业发票、装箱单、十联单中第五联装货单等三联,一并提交给上海海关。

普惠制原产地证

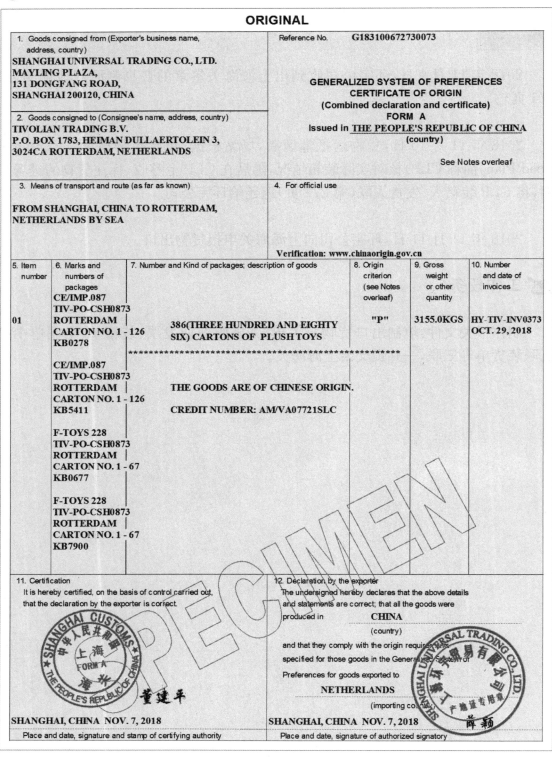

ORIGINAL

1. Goods consigned from (Exporter's business name, address, country) **SHANGHAI UNIVERSAL TRADING CO., LTD.** **MAYLING PLAZA,** **131 DONGFANG ROAD,** **SHANGHAI 200120, CHINA**	Reference No.　**G183100672730073** **GENERALIZED SYSTEM OF PREFERENCES** **CERTIFICATE OF ORIGIN** (Combined declaration and certificate) **FORM A** Issued in **THE PEOPLE'S REPUBLIC OF CHINA** (country) See Notes overleaf
2. Goods consigned to (Consignee's name, address, country) **TIVOLIAN TRADING B.V.** **P.O. BOX 1783, HEIMAN DULLAERTOLEIN 3,** **3024CA ROTTERDAM, NETHERLANDS**	
3. Means of transport and route (as far as known) **FROM SHANGHAI, CHINA TO ROTTERDAM,** **NETHERLANDS BY SEA**	4. For official use Verification: www.chinaorigin.gov.cn

5. Item number	6. Marks and numbers of packages	7. Number and Kind of packages; description of goods	8. Origin criterion (see Notes overleaf)	9. Gross weight or other quantity	10. Number and date of invoices
01	**CE/IMP.087** **TIV-PO-CSH0873** **ROTTERDAM** **CARTON NO. 1 - 126** **KB0278** **CE/IMP.087** **TIV-PO-CSH0873** **ROTTERDAM** **CARTON NO. 1 - 126** **KB5411** **F-TOYS 228** **TIV-PO-CSH0873** **ROTTERDAM** **CARTON NO. 1 - 67** **KB0677** **F-TOYS 228** **TIV-PO-CSH0873** **ROTTERDAM** **CARTON NO. 1 - 67** **KB7900**	**386(THREE HUNDRED AND EIGHTY SIX) CARTONS OF PLUSH TOYS** ** **THE GOODS ARE OF CHINESE ORIGIN.** **CREDIT NUMBER: AM/VA07721SLC**	**"P"**	**3155.0KGS**	**HY-TIV-INV0373** **OCT. 29, 2018**

11. Certification It is hereby certified, on the basis of control carried out, that the declaration by the exporter is correct.	12. Declaration by the exporter The undersigned hereby declares that the above details and statements are correct; that all the goods were produced in　**CHINA** (country) and that they comply with the origin requirements specified for those goods in the Generalized System of Preferences for goods exported to **NETHERLANDS** (importing country)
SHANGHAI, CHINA NOV. 7, 2018 Place and date, signature and stamp of certifying authority	**SHANGHAI, CHINA NOV. 7, 2018** Place and date, signature of authorized signatory

集装箱装箱单 CLP 装箱人/发货人联

Reefer Temperature Required. 冷藏温度				CONTAINER LOAD PLAN 装　箱　单				上海中远海运集装箱船务代理有限公司 COSCO SHIPPING LINES AGENCY (SHANGHAI) CO., LTD

第一联（上）

Reefer Temperature Required. 冷藏温度 ℃. ℉.			
Class 等级	IMDG Page 危规页码	UN No. 联合国编号	Flashpoint 闪点

CONTAINER LOAD PLAN　装　箱　单

上海中远海运集装箱船务代理有限公司
COSCO SHIPPING LINES AGENCY (SHANGHAI) CO., LTD

(5) Shipper's/Packer's Copy
发货人/装箱人联

Ship's Name / Voy No. 船名/航次 COSCO HELLAS / 013W	Port of Loading 装运港 SHANGHAI	Port of Discharge 卸货港 ROTTERDAM	Place of Delivery 交货地 ROTTERDAM	SHIPPER'S / PACKER'S DECLARATIONS: We hereby declare that the container has been thoroughly cleaned without any evidence of cargoes of previous shipment prior to vanning and cargoes has been properly stuffed and secured.

	Bill of Lading No. 提单号	Packages & Packing 件数与包装	Gross Weight 毛重	Measurements 尺码	Description of Goods 货名	Marks & Numbers 唛头
Container No. 箱号 CBHU75989732	COSU89302173	252CTNS	2016KGS	24.948M3	PLUSH TOYS	CE/IMP.087 TIV-PO-CSH0873 ROTTERDAM CARTON NO. 1 - 126 KB0278 CE/IMP.087 TIV-PO-CSH0873 ROTTERDAM CARTON NO. 1 - 126 KB5411
Seal. No. 封号 35737						

Cont.Size	Cont.type.箱类
20' （√）	DC=普通箱(√)OT=开顶箱( )
	HC=高箱( )FR=框架箱( )
40' （ ）	HT=挂衣箱( )PF=平板箱( )
	RE=冷藏箱( )TK=油罐箱( )
45' （ ）	RH=冷藏箱( )高箱LC=45'( )

ISO Code For Container Size/Type.
箱型/箱类 ISO 标准代码
20'GP

Packer's Name/Address.
装箱人名称/地址
上海普华玩具有限公司
上海市浦东新区康桥东路956号

TEL No.　38115260
电话号码

Packing Date. 装箱日期 NOV. 10, 2018	Received By Drayman 驾驶员签收及车号 于振齐 沪AK8456	Total Packages 总件数 252CTNS	Total Cargo Wt. 总货重 2016KGS	Total Meas. 总尺码 24.948M3	Remarks: 备注
Packed BY:	Received By Terminals / Date of Receipt 码头收箱签收和收箱日期 NOV. 10, 2018　张胜辉	Cont Tare. Wt. 集装箱皮重 2200KGS	Cgo/Cont Total Wt. 货/箱总重量 4216KGS		

Reefer Temperature Required. 冷藏温度 ℃. ℉.			
Class 等级	IMDG Page 危规页码	UN No. 联合国编号	Flashpoint 闪点

CONTAINER LOAD PLAN　装　箱　单

上海中远海运集装箱船务代理有限公司
COSCO SHIPPING LINES AGENCY (SHANGHAI) CO., LTD

(5) Shipper's/Packer's Copy
发货人/装箱人联

Ship's Name / Voy No. 船名/航次 COSCO HELLAS / 013W	Port of Loading 装运港 SHANGHAI	Port of Discharge 卸货港 ROTTERDAM	Place of Delivery 交货地 ROTTERDAM	SHIPPER'S / PACKER'S DECLARATIONS: We hereby declare that the container has been thoroughly cleaned without any evidence of cargoes of previous shipment prior to vanning and cargoes has been properly stuffed and secured.

	Bill of Lading No. 提单号	Packages & Packing 件数与包装	Gross Weight 毛重	Measurements 尺码	Description of Goods 货名	Marks & Numbers 唛头
Container No. 箱号 CBHU75989733	COSU89302173	134CTNS	1139KGS	24.698M3	PLUSH TOYS	F-TOYS 228 TIV-PO-CSH0873 ROTTERDAM CARTON NO. 1 - 67 KB0677 F-TOYS 228 TIV-PO-CSH0873 ROTTERDAM CARTON NO. 1 - 67 KB7900
Seal. No. 封号 35738						

Cont.Size	Cont.type.箱类
20' （√）	DC=普通箱(√)OT=开顶箱( )
	HC=高箱( )FR=瓶架箱( )
40' （ ）	HT=挂衣箱( )PF=平板箱( )
	RE=冷藏箱( )TK=油罐箱( )
45' （ ）	RH=冷藏箱( )高箱LC=45'( )

ISO Code For Container Size/Type.
箱型/箱类 ISO 标准代码
20'GP

Packer's Name/Address.
装箱人名称/地址
上海普华玩具有限公司
上海市浦东新区康桥东路956号

TEL No.　38115260
电话号码

Packing Date. 装箱日期 NOV. 10, 2018	Received By Drayman 驾驶员签收及车号 于振齐 沪AK8456	Total Packages 总件数 134CTNS	Total Cargo Wt. 总货重 1139KGS	Total Meas. 总尺码 24.656M3	Remarks: 备注
Packed BY:	Received By Terminals / Date of Receipt 码头收箱签收和收箱日期 NOV. 10, 2018　张胜辉	Cont Tare. Wt. 集装箱皮重 2200KGS	Cgo/Cont Total Wt. 货/箱总重量 3339KGS		

出口货物报关单

中华人民共和国海关出口货物报关单

预录入编号： 海关编号： 页码/页数：

境内发货人	出境关别	出口日期	申报日期			
境外收货人	运输方式	运输工具名称及航次号		提运单号		备案号
生产销售单位	监管方式	征免性质		许可证号		
合同协议号	贸易国（地区）	运抵国（地区）		指运港		
包装种类	件数	毛重（千克）	净重（千克）	成交方式	运费	保费	杂费
随附单证							
标记唛码及备注							

项号	商品编号	商品名称、规格型号	数量及单位	单价/总价/币制	原产国（地区）	最终目的国（地区）	境内货源地	征免

特殊关系确认： 价格影响确认： 支付特许权使用费确认：

兹申明以上内容承担如实申报、依法纳税之法律责任

申报单位（签章）

申报人员	申报人员证号	电话	海关批注及签章	自报自缴
申报单位				

示 范

中华人民共和国海关出口货物报关单

预录入编号：22002018000579756

海关编号：22002018000579756 （上海海关）

境内发货人 上海环宇贸易有限公司	出境关别 上海海关 （2200）	出口日期	申报日期 20181111	备案号
境外收货人 TIVOLIAN TRADING B.V.	运输方式 水路运输 （2）	运输工具名称及航次号 COSCO HELLAS / 013W	提运单号 COSU89302173	
生产销售单位 上海环宇贸易有限公司	监管方式 一般贸易 （0110）	征免性质 一般征税 （101）	许可证号	
合同协议号 HY-TIV0373	贸易国（地区） 荷兰 （NLD）	运抵国（地区） 荷兰 （NLD）	指运港 鹿特丹（荷兰） （NLD066）	
包装种类 纸制或纤维板制盒/箱 （22）	件数 386	毛重（千克） 3155	净重（千克） 2190	成交方式 CIF （1）	运费 USD / 2020 / 3	保费 USD / 190.63 / 3	杂费

随附单证

标记唛码及备注 1：商业发票；装箱单

随附单证 1：

CE/IMP.087
TIV-PO-CSH0873
ROTTERDAM
CARTON NO. 1 - 126
KB0278

CE/IMP.087
TIV-PO-CSH0873
ROTTERDAM
CARTON NO. 1 - 126
KB5411

F-TOYS 228
TIV-PO-CSH0873
ROTTERDAM
CARTON NO. 1 - 67
KB0677

F-TOYS 228
TIV-PO-CSH0873
ROTTERDAM
CARTON NO. 1 - 67
KB7900

项号	商品编号	商品名称、规格型号	数量及单位	单价/总价/币制	原产国（地区）	最终目的国（地区）	境内货源地	征免
01	9503002100101	毛绒玩具	5232只 2190千克 2080套	12.8177 26660.80 USD	中国 （CHN）	荷兰 （NLD）	上海浦东新区 （31222）	照章征税 （1）

3195460018344923 ...系确认：

价格影响确认：

特殊关系确认：

兹申明以上内容承担如实申报、依法纳税之义务并承担相应法律责任

自报自缴：

报关员 沈中良
申报人员证号
申报单位 上海环宇贸易有限公司

电话

海关批注及放行

申报单位（签章）

Shanghai Universal Trading Co., Ltd.

Rm. 1201-1216 Mayling Plaza,
131 Dongfang Rd.,
Shanghai, 200120, China
Tel: 86-21-58818844
Fax: 86-21-58818766

COMMERCIAL INVOICE

TO:	TIVOLIAN TRADING B.V. P.O. BOX 1783, HEIMAN DULLAERTOLEIN 3 3024CA ROTTERDAM, NETHERLANDS	INV. NO. : HY-TIV-INV0373 INV. DATE: OCT. 29, 2018 S/C NO. : HY-TIV0373

FROM:	SHANGHAI	TO:	ROTTERDAM	SHIPPED BY:	COSCO HELLAS / 013W

MARKS & NOS.	DESCRIPTION OF GOODS		QUANTITY	UNIT PRICE	AMOUNT
CE/IMP.087 TIV-PO-CSH0873 ROTTERDAM CARTON NO. 1 - 126 KB0278	PLUSH TOYS			CIF ROTTERDAM	
	KB0278	TWIN BEAR	504SETS	US$9.60	US$4,838.40
	KB5411	TWIN BEAR IN BALLET COSTUME	504SETS	US$11.50	US$5,796.00
	KB0677	BROWN BEAR WITH RED BOW	536SETS	US$14.50	US$7,772.00
CE/IMP.087 TIV-PO-CSH0873 ROTTERDAM CARTON NO. 1 - 126 KB5411	KB7900	BEAR IN PINK T-SHIRT	536SETS	US$15.40	US$8,254.40
					US$26,660.80
F-TOYS 228 TIV-PO-CSH0873 ROTTERDAM CARTON NO. 1 - 67 KB0677					
F-TOYS 228 TIV-PO-CSH0873 ROTTERDAM CARTON NO. 1 - 67 KB7900					

TOTAL AMOUNT IN WORDS: SAY U.S. DOLLARS TWENTY SIX THOUSAND SIX HUNDRED AND SIXTY AND CENTS EIGHTY ONLY

TOTAL G.W. / TOTAL N.W.: 3155.000 KGS / 2190.000 KGS
TOTAL PACKAGES: 386CTNS

上 海 环 宇 贸 易 有 限 公 司
SHANGHAI UNIVERSAL TRADING CO., LTD.

(SIGNATURE)

Shanghai Universal Trading Co., Ltd.

Rm. 1201-1216 Mayling Plaza,
131 Dongfang Rd.,
Shanghai, 200120, China
Tel: 86-21-58818844
Fax: 86-21-58818766

PACKING LIST

TO: TIVOLIAN TRADING B.V.
P.O. BOX 1783, HEIMAN DULLAERTOLEIN 3
3024CA ROTTERDAM, NETHERLANDS

INV. NO. : HY-TIV-INV0373
INV. DATE: OCT. 29, 2018

FROM: SHANGHAI **TO:** ROTTERDAM **SHIPPED BY:** COSCO HELLAS / 013W

C/NO.	DESCRIPTION OF GOODS	PKG.	QTY	G.W.	N.W.	MEAS.
CE/IMP.087 TIV-PO-CSH0873 ROTTERDAM CARTON NO. 1 - 126 KB0278	KB0278	126 CTNS	504 SETS	1008.000 KGS	693.000 KGS	12.474 M3
CE/IMP.087 TIV-PO-CSH0873 ROTTERDAM CARTON NO. 1 - 126 KB5411	KB5411	126 CTNS	504 SETS	1008.000 KGS	693.000 KGS	12.474 M3
F-TOYS 228 TIV-PO-CSH0873 ROTTERDAM CARTON NO. 1 - 67 KB0677	KB0677	67 CTNS	536 SETS	569.500 KGS	402.000 KGS	12.349 M3
F-TOYS 228 TIV-PO-CSH0873 ROTTERDAM CARTON NO. 1 - 67 KB7900	KB7900	67 CTNS	536 SETS	569.500 KGS	402.000 KGS	12.349 M3
	TOTAL:	386 CTNS	2080 SETS	3155.000 KGS	2190.000 KGS	49.646 M3

TOTAL PACKAGE IN WORDS: SAY THREE HUNDRED AND EIGHTY SIX CARTONS ONLY

MARKS & NOS.: AS SHOWN IN C/NO.

上 海 环 宇 贸 易 有 限 公 司
SHANGHAI UNIVERSAL TRADING CO., LTD.

(SIGNATURE)

Shipper (发货人)			
SHANGHAI UNIVERSAL TRADING CO., LTD. MAYLING PLAZA, 131 DONGFANG ROAD, SHANGHAI 200120, CHINA		**D/R No.(编号)** COSU89302173	

装 货 单

第五联

Consignee (收货人)	
TO ORDER	场站收据副本

Notify Party (通知人)	
TIVOLIAN TRADING B.V. P.O. BOX 1783, HEIMAN DULLAERTOLEIN 3, 3024CA ROTTERDAM, NETHERLANDS	Received by the Carrier the Total number of containers or other packages or units stated below to be transported subject to the terms and conditions of the Carrier's regular form of Bill of Lading (for Combined Transport or port to Port Shipment) which shall be deemed to be incorporated herein.

Pre-carriage by(前程运输)	Place of Receipt (收货地点)	**Date** （日期）: Oct. 30, 2018

Vessel (船名) Voy. No. (航次) COSCO HELLAS / 013W	Port of Loading (装货港) SHANGHAI	场站章

Port of Discharge(卸货港) ROTTERDAM	Place of Delivery (交货地点)	Final Destination for the Merchant's Reference (目的地)

Particulars Furnished by Merchants （托运人提供详细情况）

Container No. (集装箱号)	Seal No.(封志号) Marks & Nos. (标志与号码)	No. of containers or p'kgs (箱数或件数)	Kind of Packages: Description of Goods (包装种类与货名)	Gross Weight 毛重(公斤)	Measurement 尺码(立方米)
CE/IMP.087	CE/IMP.087				
	TIV-PO-CSH0873	386CTNS	PLUSH TOYS	3155.000KGS	49.646CBM
ROTTERDAM	ROTTERDAM				
CARTON NO. 1 - 126	CARTON NO. 1 - 126				
KB0278	KB5411				
F-TOYS 228	F-TOYS 228				
	TIV-PO-CSH0873		FREIGHT PREPAID		
ROTTERDAM	ROTTERDAM				
CARTON NO. 1 - 67	CARTON NO. 1 - 67				
KB0677	KB7900				

TOTAL NUMBER OF CONTAINERS
OR PACKAGES (IN WORDS)   SAY THREE HUNDRED AND EIGHTY SIX CARTONS ONLY
集装箱数或件数合计(大写)

Container No.(箱号)	Seal No.(封志号)	Pkgs.(件数)	Container No.(箱号)	Seal No.(封志号)	Pkgs.(件数)

		Received(实收)	By Terminal Clerk(场站员签字)

FREIGHT & CHARGES	Prepaid at (预付地点)	Payable at (到付地点)	Place of Issue (签发地点) SHANGHAI
	Total Prepaid (预付总额)	No. of Original B(s)L (正本提单份数) THREE	Booking (订舱确认) APPROVED BY

Service Type on Receiving			Service Type on Delivery			Reefer Temperature Required 冷藏温度 (18)		°F ℃
☑ -CY	☐ -CFS	☐ -DOOR	☑ -CY	☐ -CFS	☐ -DOOR			
TYPE OF GOODS (种类)	☑ Ordinary (普通)	☐ Reefer (冷藏)	☐ Dangerous (危险品)	☐ Auto. (裸装车辆)	危险品	Class: Property: IMDG Code Page UN No.		
	☐ Liquid (液体)	☐ Live Animal (活动物)	☐ Bulk (散装)					

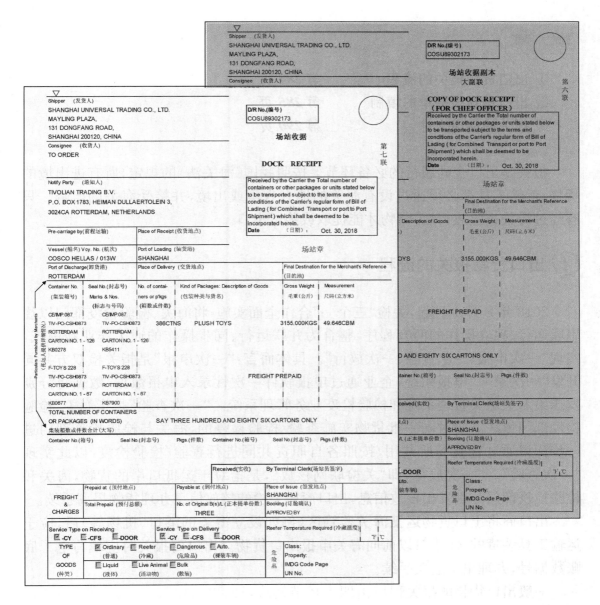

示范评析

Q:出口货物报关单上的要求填写集装箱的自重,何处可以查询?

A:在"集装箱装箱单"CLP上有集装箱的皮重,即自重。

Q:出口货物报关单上的"单价:12.8177"是如何得出的?

A:案例中出口的四个货号属于同一个税则号项下同种类型的商品,在报关时不必按货号分开填报,总价即为实际成交的总价,而单价只需用总价除以总成交数量即可得出。

报关是出口合同履行的必备环节。按照我国《海关法》的规定,所有进出境的货物、运输工具都必须通过设有海关的地方入境或出境,并接受海关的监督。只有经过海关查验放行后,货物才能提取或装运出口。

ⓘ 出口货物报关的流程

2018 年 8 月 1 日起,关检"三个一"合作全面实施,将海关、检验检疫部门以往串联运行、独立操作的两套程序,整合为并联运行、同步操作的通关作业新模式,实现"一次申报、一次查验、一次放行"。具体而言:"一次申报"是指关检双方共同开发"一次录入"申报系统,企业通过申报软件一次性录入申报数据,数据将分别发送给海关通关管理系统和检验检疫业务管理系统。"一次查验"是指海关、检验检疫部门依法需要对同一批货物实施查验/检验检疫的,海关与检验检疫部门进一步探讨通过查验场所共用,按照各自职责共同进行查验/检验检疫,以此实现"一次查验"。"一次放行"即"关检联网核放",是指对于运抵口岸的货物,海关和检验检疫部门分别发出核放信息,出口商凭关检的核放信息办理货物提离手续。

出口商将出口货物运抵海关监管区(例如设立海关的港口、机场等)后,应于运输工具装货的 24 小时以前向海关申报出口货物。出口商报关时应填写电子底账数据号,办理出口通关手续。

一般出口货物的报关程序由四个环节构成,即:出口申报、海关查验、缴纳税费、放行货物。通过海运出口的具体流程如下:

◇ 申报阶段,出口商填制"出口货物报关单",随附"商业发票"、"装箱单",以及十联单的"第五联 装货单"、"第六联 场站收据副本 大副联"和"第七联 场站收据"向海关申报货物出口,同时,数据发送至检验检疫部门。

◇ 查验阶段,海关查验报关文件,核实实际出境货物是否与报关单上申报的内容相符,必要时对货物进行实际查验。

◇ 查验无误后,若属于应缴纳税费的出口货物,海关签发《税、费缴纳通知书》。出口商应在海关规定的期限内,办理税费缴纳手续。

◇ 海关在十联单的"第五联 装货单"上加盖"海关放行章",并将该联及第六、第七联退还出口商,同时,在电子系统中海关放行信息与检验检疫放行信息通过信息系统实现对碰,对碰成功后出口商即可装运放行的货物。

ⓘ 出口报关文件的填制

◇ 预录入编号

该申报项目为系统返填项。

预录入编号指预录入单位录入报关单的编号。一份报关单对应一个预录入编号,由系统自动生成,编号为18位。

◇ 海关编号

该申报项目为系统返填项。

海关编号指海关接受申报时给予报关单的编号。一份报关单对应一个海关编号,编号为18位。

◇ 境内发货人

该申报项目为必填项。

填报在海关备案的对外签订并执行出口贸易合同的中国境内法人、其他组织名称及编码。编码填报18位法人和其他组织统一社会信用代码,没有统一社会信用代码的,填报其在海关备案的10位海关代码或者10位检验检疫编码。

◇ 出境关别

该申报项目为必填项。

根据货物实际出境的口岸海关,填报海关规定的《关区代码表》中相应口岸海关的名称及代码。例如上海海关(2200)、外高桥关(2218)、洋山港区(2248)等。

◇ 出口日期

出口日期指运载出口货物的运输工具办结出境手续的日期,在申报时免予填报,入库后系统自动返填。格式为"YYYYMMDD"。

◇ 申报日期

该申报项目为系统返填项。申报日期指海关接受进出口货物收发货人、受委托的报关企业申报数据的日期。格式为"YYYYMMDD"。

◇ 备案号

该申报项目为选填项。

备案号指应向海关递交的备案审批文件的编号。例如加工贸易成品凭《征免税证明》转为减免税进口货物的,填报《加工贸易手册》编号,涉及征、减、免税审核确认的报关单,填报《征免税证明》编号。

◇　**境外收货人**

该申报项目为必填项。

境外收货人通常指签订并执行出口贸易合同中的买方或合同指定的收货人，名称一般填报英文名称，特殊情况下无境外收发货人的，名称及编码填报"NO"。

◇　**运输方式**

该申报项目为必填项。

按照海关规定的《运输方式代码表》选择填报相应的运输方式。例如水路运输（2）、航空运输（5）、邮件运输（6）等。

◇　**运输工具名称及航次号**

该申报项目为有条件必填项。

填报内容应与运输部门向海关申报的舱单（载货清单）所列相应内容一致。

◇　**提运单号**

该申报项目为有条件必填项。填报出口货物提单或运单的编号。一份报关单只允许填报一个提单或运单号，一票货物对应多个提单或运单时，应分单填报。

◇　**生产销售单位**

该申报项目为必填项。

填报生产销售单位。编码可以选择填报 18 位法人和其他组织统一社会信用代码、10 位海关代码或 10 位检验检疫编码之一。

◇　**监管方式**

该申报项目为必填项。

根据实际对外贸易情况按海关规定的《监管方式代码表》选择填报相应的监管方式简称及代码。例如一般贸易（0110）、来料加工（0214）、展览品（2700）等。一份报关单只允许填报一种监管方式。

◇　**征免性质**

该申报项目为选填项。

根据实际情况，按海关规定的《征免性质代码表》选择填报相应的征免性质简称及代码。例如一般征税（101）、来料加工（802）、港澳 OPA（510）等。

◇　**许可证号**

该申报项目为选填项。

商务部及其授权发证机关签发的出口货物许可证的编号。

◇　**合同协议号**

该申报项目为选填项。

即出口合同号码。

◇　**贸易国(地区)**

该申报项目为必填项。

按海关规定的《国别(地区)代码表》选择填报相应的贸易国(地区)中文名称及代码。例如荷兰(NLD)、美国(USA)、英国(GBR)、日本(JPN)等。

◇　**运抵国(地区)**

该申报项目为必填项。

按海关规定的《国别(地区)代码表》填报货物运抵的国家或地区的中文名称及代码。

◇　**指运港**

该申报项目为必填项。

按海关规定的《港口代码表》选择填报出口货物运往境外的最终目的港的中文名称及代码。例如鹿特丹(荷兰)NLD066、新加坡(新加坡)SGP012、香港(中国香港)HKG003、迪拜(阿联酋)ARE018等。

◇　**包装种类**

该申报项目为必填项。

按照海关规定的《包装种类代码表》选择填报出口货物的所有包装材料,包括运输包装和其他包装。例如纸箱包装填报"纸制或纤维板制盒/箱(22)",木箱包装填报"木制或竹藤等植物性材料盒/箱(23)"等。

◇　**件数**

该申报项目为必填项。

填报出口货物运输包装的件数(按运输包装计)。运输包装指提运单所列货物件数单位对应的包装。不得填报为零,若为散装货物和裸装货物填报为"1"。

◇　**毛重　净重**

该申报项目为必填项。

毛重填报进出口货物及其包装材料的重量之和。净重填报进出口货物的毛重减去外包装材料后的重量,即货物本身的实际重量。计量单位为千克,不足一千克的填报为"1"。

◇　**运费　保费　杂费**

该申报项目为选填项。

运费填报出口货物运至我国境内输出地点装载后的运输费用。运费可按运费单价、总价或运费率三种方式之一填报,注明运费标记(运费标记"1"表示运费率,"2"表示每吨货物的运费单价,"3"表示运费总价),按海关规定的《货币代码表》选择填报相应的币种代码。例如人民币(CNY)、美元(USD)、欧元(EUR)等。

保费填报出口货物运至我国境内输出地点装载后的保险费用。保费可按保险费总价或保险费率两种方式之一填报,注明保险费标记(保险费标记"1"表示保险费率,"3"表示保险费总价),并按海关规定的《货币代码表》选择填报相应的币种代码。

杂费填报成交价格以外的、按照《中华人民共和国进出口关税条例》相关规定应计入完税价格或应从完税价格中扣除的费用。可按杂费总价或杂费率两种方式之一填报,注明杂费标记(杂费标记"1"表示杂费率,"3"表示杂费总价),并按海关规定的《货币代码表》选择填报相应的币种代码。

◇　**随附单证**

该申报项目为系统返填项。

一般有商业发票、装箱单等。填报随附单证信息后,系统自动返填。

◇　**成交方式**

该申报项目为系统必填项。

根据进出口货物实际成交价格条款,按海关规定的《成交方式代码表》选择填报相应的成交方式代码。例如 CIF(1)、CFR(2)、FOB(3)等。

◇　**标记唛码及备注**

该申报项目为必填项。

填报标记唛码中除图形以外的文字、数字,无标记唛码的填报"N/M"。

◇　**项号**

指商品的排列序号,即将出口货物按税则号归类,每一类货物依次对应一个序号。例如该报关单上 N 类货物,分别对应 N 个税则号,则项号依次填 01 02 03 … N。

◇　**商品编号**

该申报项目为必填项。

填报由 13 位数字组成的商品编号。前 8 位为《中华人民共和国进出口税则》和《中华人民共和国海关统计商品目录》确定的编码;9、10 位为监管附加编号,11—13 位为检验检疫附加编号。

◇　**商品名称、规格型号**

该申报项目为必填项。

第一行填报出口货物的中文名称,第二行填报型号规格,应与所提供的商业发票相符。

◇　**数量及单位**

该申报项目为必填项。

填报货物实际成交的数量。分三行填报。第一行按海关法定计量单位填报,第二行按第二法定计量单位填报,如无,则为空,第三行填报成交计量单位及数量。海关通关系统《商品综合分类表》中确定的法定第一计量单位,系统会自动返填计量单位。

◇　**单价　总价　币制**

该申报项目为必填项。

总价为同一项号下的总价,单价为总价除以数量。例如:某出口商品,录入成交数量 1000,成交单位为千克,总价 10000,单价则会自动生成 10。币值填报对照海关规定的《货币代码表》选择相应的货种代码填报。

◇　**原产国(地区)**

该申报项目为必填项。

按海关规定的《国别(地区)代码表》选择填报相应的国家(地区)名称及代码。例如中国(CHN)等。

◇　**最终目的国(地区)**

该申报项目为必填项。

出口货物的最终实际消费、使用或进一步加工制造国家(地区)。

◇　**境内货源地**

该申报项目为必填项。

出口货物在境内的生产地或原始发货地,其名称以海关公布的《国内地区代码表》为准。

◇　**征免**

该申报项目为必填项。

按照海关核发的《征免税证明》或有关政策规定,对报关单所列每项商品选择海关规定的《征减免税方式代码表》中相应的征减免税方式填报。例如照章征税(1)、全免(3)等。

◇　**特殊关系确认　价格影响确认　支付特许权使用费确认**

该申报项目出口货物免予填报。

◇　**申报人员　申报单位**

一般应加盖报关员章、申报单位的报关专用章。

中华人民共和国海关出口货物报关单

| 预录入编号： | | 海关编号： | | | | 页码/页数： |

境内发货人		出境关别		出口日期		申报日期		备案号
境外收货人		运输方式		运输工具名称及航次号		提运单号	
生产销售单位		监管方式		征免性质		许可证号	
合同协议号		贸易国（地区）		运抵国（地区）		指运港	
包装种类		件数	毛重（千克）	净重（千克）	成交方式	运费	保费	杂费
随附单证	

标记唛码及备注

项号	商品编号	商品名称、规格型号	数量及单位	单价/总价/币制	原产国（地区）	最终目的国（地区）	境内货源地	征免

特殊关系确认：　　　价格影响确认：　　　支付特许权使用费确认：　　　　　　自报自缴：

| 申报人员 | 申报人员证号 | 电话 | 兹申明以上内容承担如实申报、依法纳税之法律责任 | 海关批注及签章 |
| 申报单位 | | | 申报单位（签章） | |

报关的反馈文件

　　海关在十联单的"第五联　装货单"上加盖"海关放行章"，以示放行货物，并将该联及第六、第七联退还出口商。

▽

Shipper (发货人)
SHANGHAI TIAN YUAN TRADING CO., LTD.
ROOM 1105, RUIJIN BLDG.,
205 SOUTH MAOMING ROAD,
SHANGHAI CHINA

Consignee (收货人)
TO ORDER

D/R No.(编号)
COSU83465095

装 货 单

场站收据副本

Notify Party (通知人)
TERI INTERNATIONAL GMBH
56 KEDENBURGSTRASSE D-758294 HAMBURG
GERMANY

Received by the Carrier the Total number of
containers or other packages or units stated below
to be transported subject to the terms and conditions
of the Carrier's regular form of Bill of Lading (for
Combined Transport or port to Port Shipment)
which shall be deemed to be incorporated herein.

第五联

Pre-carriage by(前程运输)	Place of Receipt (收货地点)	Date (日期)： FEB. 24, 2018
Vessel (船名) Voy. No. (航次) YU XIANG V.345	Port of Loading (装货港) SHANGHAI	场站章
Port of Discharge(卸货港) HAMBURG	Place of Delivery (交货地点)	Final Destination for the Merchant's Reference (目的地)

Container No. (集装箱号)	Seal No.(封志号) Marks & Nos. (标志与号码)	No. of containers or p'kgs (箱数或件数)	Kind of Packages: Description of Goods (包装种类与货名)	Gross Weight 毛重(公斤)	Measurement 尺码(立方米)
	TERI WR59235 HAMBURG CTN.NO.1-500	500CTNS	PORCELAIN DINNERWARE	9000	24.000

FREIGHT PREPAID

TOTAL NUMBER OF CONTAINERS
OR PACKAGES (IN WORDS)
集装箱数或件数合计(大写)

SAY FIVE HUNDRED CARTONS ONLY

放 行 章

Container No.(箱号)	Seal No.(封志号)	Pkgs.(件数)	Container No.(箱号)	Seal No.(封志号)	Pkgs.(件数)

Received(实收) By Terminal Clerk(场站员签字)

FREIGHT & CHARGES	Prepaid at (预付地点)	Payable at (到付地点)	Place of Issue (签发地点) SHANGHAI
	Total Prepaid (预付总额)	No. of Original B(s)/L (正本提单份数) THREE	Booking (订舱确认) APPROVED BY

Service Type on Receiving ☑ -CY ☐ -CFS ☐ -DOOR	Service Type on Delivery ☑ -CY ☐ -CFS ☐ -DOOR	Reefer Temperature Required (冷藏温度) °F °C
TYPE OF GOODS (种类)	☑ Ordinary (普通) ☐ Reefer (冷藏) ☐ Dangerous (危险品) ☐ Auto. (裸装车辆) ☐ Liquid (液体) ☐ Live Animal (活动物) ☐ Bulk (散装)	危险品 Class: Property: IMDG Code Page UN No.

Particulars Furnished by Merchants (托运人提供详细情况)

练　习

　　试根据**第六章　出口托运订舱**的练习（第 219 页）中的出口货物明细、信用证及以下信息填制出口货物报关单：

　　预录入编号：　220020180006372609
　　海关编号：　　220020180006372609
　　申报海关：　　上海海关
　　申报日期：　　2018 年 11 月 29 日
　　商品编号：　　9405200000　　海关法定计量单位：台（千克）
　　生产厂商：　　上海日升照明有限公司（上海市柳营路 340 号）
　　船　　名：　　DA HE KOU　　航　次：210S
　　提单号码：　　COSU85122784
　　海洋运输：　　装 4 个 20 英尺集装箱
　　海运运费：　　每个 20 英尺集装箱 1000 美元

中华人民共和国海关出口货物报关单

预录入编号：　　　　　　　海关编号：　　　　　　　　　　　　　　　　　　　　　　　　　　页码/页数：

境内发货人	出境关别	出口日期	申报日期	
境外收货人	运输方式	运输工具名称及航次号	提运单号	备案号
生产销售单位	监管方式	征免性质	许可证号	
合同协议号	贸易国（地区）	运抵国（地区）	指运港	
包装种类	件数	毛重（千克）	净重（千克）	成交方式	运费	保费	杂费
随附单证							
标记唛码及备注							

项号	商品编号	商品名称、规格型号	数量及单位	单价/总价/币制	原产国（地区）	最终目的国（地区）	境内货源地	征免

特殊关系确认：　　　　价格影响确认：　　　　支付特许权使用费确认：　　　　自报自缴：

申报人员　　　申报人员证号　　　电话　　　　兹申明以上内容承担如实申报、依法纳税之法律责任　　　海关批注及签章

申报单位　　　　　　　　　　　　　　　　　　　　　申报单位（签章）

第十一章 出口货物装运

案 例

2018 年 11 月 12 日，环宇公司收到上海海关加盖放行章的第五联装货单（第295 页）及第六联场站收据副本大副联、第七联场站收据（第 296 页）。

同日，环宇公司将以上三联提交给堆场。堆场审核无误后，在第七联上签章并退还。

2018 年 11 月 13 日，货物顺利装船。

2018 年 11 月 14 日，向 Tivolian 公司传真发出装运通知。

✍ 工作任务

拟写装运通知（传真格式）。

装货单（第五联）

Shipper （发货人） SHANGHAI UNIVERSAL TRADING CO., LTD. MAYLING PLAZA, 131 DONGFANG ROAD, SHANGHAI 200120, CHINA	D/R No.(编号) COSU89302173

装 货 单

场站收据副本

第五联

| Consignee （收货人）
TO ORDER | |

| Notify Party （通知人）
TIVOLIAN TRADING B.V.
P.O. BOX 1783, HEIMAN DULLAERTOLEIN 3,
3024CA ROTTERDAM, NETHERLANDS | Received by the Carrier the Total number of containers or other packages or units stated below to be transported subject to the terms and conditions of the Carrier's regular form of Bill of Lading (for Combined Transport or port to Port Shipment) which shall be deemed to be incorporated herein. |

Pre-carriage by(前程运输)	Place of Receipt (收货地点)	Date （日期）： Oct. 30, 2018
Vessel (船名) Voy. No. (航次) COSCO HELLAS / 013W	Port of Loading (装货港) SHANGHAI	场站章
Port of Discharge(卸货港) ROTTERDAM	Place of Delivery (交货地点)	Final Destination for the Merchant's Reference (目的地)

Container No. (集装箱号)	Seal No.(封志号) Marks & Nos. (标志与号码)	No. of contai-ners or p'kgs (箱数或件数)	Kind of Packages: Description of Goods (包装种类与货名)	Gross Weight 毛重(公斤)	Measurement 尺码(立方米)
CE/IMP.087 TIV-PO-CSH0873 ROTTERDAM CARTON NO. 1 - 126 KB0278	CE/IMP.087 TIV-PO-CSH0873 ROTTERDAM CARTON NO. 1 - 126 KB5411	386CTNS	PLUSH TOYS	3155.000KGS	49.646CBM
F-TOYS 228 TIV-PO-CSH0873 ROTTERDAM CARTON NO. 1 - 67 KB0677	F-TOYS 228 TIV-PO-CSH0873 ROTTERDAM CARTON NO. 1 - 67 KB7900		FREIGHT PREPAID		

Particulars Furnished by Merchants（毛运人提供的详细情况）

| TOTAL NUMBER OF CONTAINERS
OR PACKAGES (IN WORDS)
集装箱数或件数合计(大写) | SAY THREE HUNDRED AND EIGHTY SIX CARTONS ONLY |

Container No.(箱号)	Seal No.(封志号)	Pkgs.(件数)	Container No.(箱号)	Seal No.(封志号)	Pkgs.(件数)

Received(实收) 放行 Terminal Clerk(场站员签字)

FREIGHT & CHARGES	Prepaid at (预付地点)	Payable at (到付地点)	Place of Issue (签发地点) SHANGHAI
	Total Prepaid (预付总额)	No. of Original B(s)/L (正本提单份数) THREE	Booking (订舱确认) APPROVED BY

Service Type on Receiving ☑ -CY ☐ -CFS ☐ -DOOR	Service Type on Delivery ☑ -CY ☐ -CFS ☐ -DOOR	Reefer Temperature Required (冷藏温度) (18)　　℉　℃
TYPE OF GOODS (种类)	☑ Ordinary (普通)　☐ Reefer (冷藏)　☐ Dangerous (危险品)　☐ Auto. (裸装车辆) ☐ Liquid (液体)　☐ Live Animal (活动物)　☐ Bulk (散装)	危险品	Class: Property: IMDG Code Page UN No.

场站收据副本　大副联(第六联)

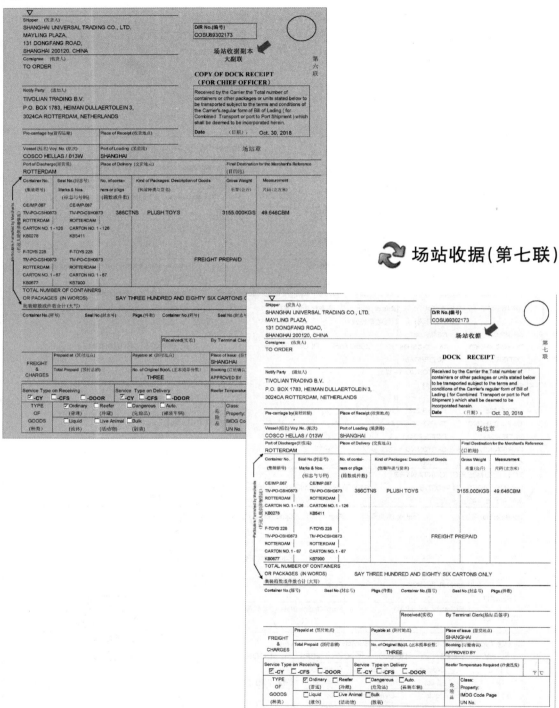

🔽 公司信纸（传真）

上海环宇贸易有限公司
Shanghai Universal Trading Co., Ltd.

FAX

To： _____ **From：** _____

Tel. No.： _____ **Tel. No.：** _____

Page： _____ **Date：** _____

Fax-No.： _____ **Fax-No.：** _____

中国上海市东方路 131 号美陵广场 1201-1216 室

Rm. 1201-1216 Mayling Plaza, 131 Dongfang Rd., Shanghai, 200120, China

电话/Tel: 86-21-58818844　传真/Fax: 86-21-58818766　网址/Web: www.universal.com.cn

示　范

上 海 环 宇 贸 易 有 限 公 司
Shanghai Universal Trading Co., Ltd.

FAX

To:	Tivolian Trading B.V.	**From:**	Shanghai Universal Trading Co., Ltd.
Tel. No.:	+(31)10 4767418	**Tel. No.:**	+(86)21 58818844
Page:	Page 1, Total 1 Page	**Date:**	Nov. 14, 2018
Fax-No.:	+(31)10 4767422	**Fax-No.:**	+(86)21 58818766

SHIPPING ADVICE

CREDIT NUMBER: AM/VA07721SLC

We hereby inform you that the goods under the above credit were shipped on Nov. 13, 2018. The details of shipment are stated below:

Date of Departure:	Nov. 13, 2018			
Shipping Marks:	CE/IMP.087	CE/IMP.087	F-TOYS 228	F-TOYS 228
	TIV-PO-CSH0873	TIV-PO-CSH0873	TIV-PO-CSH0873	TIV-PO-CSH0873
	ROTTERDAM	ROTTERDAM	ROTTERDAM	ROTTERDAM
	CARTON NO. 1 - 126	CARTON NO. 1 - 126	CARTON NO. 1 - 67	CARTON NO. 1 - 67
	KB0278	KB5411	KB0677	KB7900
Number of L/C:	AM/VA07721SLC			
Number of B/L:	COSU89302173			
Number of Contract:	HY-TIV0373			
Number of Order:	TIV-PO-CSH0873			
Number of Cartons:	386 cartons			
Total Gross Weight:	3155 kgs			
Goods Value:	USD26660.80 CIF			
Commodity:	Plush Toys			
Ocean Vessel:	Cosco Hellas / 013W			
From:	Shanghai			
To:	Rotterdam			
ETA:	Dec. 12, 2018			

Yours sincerely,

王凯

David Wang
Shanghai Universal Trading Co., Ltd

中国上海市东方路 131 号美陵广场 1201-1216 室
Rm. 1201-1216 Mayling Plaza, 131 Dongfang Rd., Shanghai, 200120, China
电话/Tel: 86-21-58818844　传真/Fax: 86-21-58818766　网址/Web: www.universal.com.cn

示范评析

本案例信用证规定要求提交的单据中有：

COPY OF BENEFICIARY'S FAX SENT TO APPLICANT（FAX-NO.：＋(31)10 4767422）WITHIN 2 WORKING DAYS AFTER SHIPMENT INDI-CATING DATE OF DEPARTURE, SHIPPING MARKS, NUMBERS OF LC, B/L, CONTRACT AND ORDER AS WELL AS NUMBER OF CARTONS TO-GETHER WITH THE TOTAL GROSS WEIGHT AND GOODS VALUE.

由于装船通知的副本是议付单据之一，所以装船通知本身必须符合信用证的规定，包括在内容上必须包含离港日期、运输标志、信用证号码、提单号码、合同号码、订单号码、总箱数、总毛重和货物价值，在形式上必须是发送给开证申请人的传真，在时间上必须是装运后 2 个工作日内。

当然，除了信用证条款规定的内容以外，出口商还可以再补充一些必要的信息，例如装运港、目的港等，同时也要保证这些信息不会与其他单据上显示的信息相矛盾。

Q：示范中的"ETA"是什么含义？

A：ETA 是 Estimated Time of Arrival 的缩写，意思是"预计达到（目的港）时间"。通常，出口商可以从船公司公布的船期表中查询。另外，如果出口商在实际装船之前就发出了装船通知，通常，还会注明"ETD"，即 Estimated Time of Depar-ture 的缩写，意思是"预计离开（启运港）时间"。

指 南

ⓘ 出口货物装运的流程

◇ 海关在十联单"第五联　装货单"上加盖"海关放行章",连同第六联、第七联退还出口商办理货物装运。
◇ 出口商将以上三联提交给堆场。场站在货物进场、验收无误后,在第七联上签收并退还给出口商。
◇ 货物装船。
◇ 出口商向进口商发出装运通知。
◇ 出口商凭经场站签收的"第七联　场站收据"向船公司换取正本提单。

ⓘ 装运通知

在出口交易中,无论是采用 FOB、CFR 还是 CIF 条件成交,在货物装船后,出口商均有义务向进口商及时发出装运通知。其目的除了通知进口商货物已经发运以便其做好接货准备外,在 FOB 和 CFR 条件下,该通知往往还是进口商办理货物运输投保的依据,因此,在这种条件下的装运通知还被称为投保通知。

实际业务操作时,进口商为了督促出口商履行发送装运通知的义务,常常会在合同或信用证中要求出口商将装运通知或其副本作为其向进口商或银行提交的必要单据之一。因此,在拟写装船通知时必须关注相关文件,除了内容应符合约定和要求以外,其发送的方式(传真、信函或电子邮件等)、发送的时间也必须符合合同或信用证的规定。

一般而言,装运通知的主要内容有:

(一) 基本信息,如:

◇ 提单号码
◇ 船名、航次
◇ 货物品名、数量、金额

◇ 装运港

◇ 目的港

◇ 装运日

◇ 预计到港日

（二）其他信息，如：

◇ 运输标志

◇ 发票号码

◇ 货物原产地

作为投保通知的装运通知，往往还要求注明预约保单号码等。

需要特别注意的是，若装船通知被作为了信用证项下向银行提交的单据，则除了要符合信用证对装船通知本身的规定以外，还必须符合信用证对提交单据的一般要求，例如信用证规定"credit number and date should be shown in all documents"，则装船通知中也必须注明信用证号码和日期。

装运的反馈文件

货物装运后，船公司将签发已装船提单。出口商可凭场站收据向其换领。

SITC SITC CONTAINER LINES CO., LTD.

B/L NO.
SITGSHSVK18021

Port to Port or Combine Transport
BILL OF LADING

1. Shipper
SHANGHAI TIAN YUAN TRADING CO., LTD.
ROOM 1105, RUIJIN BLDG.,
205 SOUTH MAOMING ROAD,
SHANGHAI CHINA

2. Consignee

TO ORDER

3. Notify Party (It is agreed that no responsibility shall attach to the Carrier or his agent for failure to notify)
SENSERA INTERNATIONAL CO., LTD.
220-1058, TAJII, MIHARA-KU SAKAI-SHI, OSAKA
JAPAN
TEL: +816-5835-6175

RECEIVED for shipment in external apparent good order and condition, unless otherwise indicated. The total number of packages or units stuffed in the container, the description of the goods and the weights shown in this Bill of Lading are furnished by the Merchants and the containers are already sealed by the Merchants, and which the carrier has no reasonable means of checking and is not a part of this Bill of Lading contract. The carrier has issued the number of Bills of Lading stated below, all of this tenor and date, one of the original Bills of Lading must be surrendered and endorsed or signed against the delivery of the goods or the delivery order and whereupon any other Bills of Lading shall be void.

NOTE: Notwithstanding any customs or privileges to the contrary, the Merchant's attention is drawn to the fact that the Merchant, in accepting this Bill of Lading, expressly agrees to be bound by all the stipulations, exceptions, limitations, liberties, terms and conditions attached hereto or stated herein, whether written, printed, stamped or otherwise incorporated on the front and/or reverse side hereof as well as the provisions of the Carrier's published Tariff Rules, Regulations and Schedules, without exceptions, as fully as if they were all signed by such Merchant, and the carrier's undertaking to carry the goods is made on the basis of the merchant's acceptance and agreements as aforesaid.

This Bill of Lading is governed by the laws of the People's Republic of China. Any claims and disputes arising under or in connection with this Bill of Lading shall be determined by Shanghai Maritime Court or Qingdao Maritime Court at the exclusion of the Courts of any other country. The printed terms and conditions appearing on the face and reverse side of this Bill of Lading are available at www.sitc.com in SITC's published tariffs.

ORIGINAL

4. Pre-Carriage by*	**5. Place of Receipt***
(Applicable only when this document is used as a Combined Transport Bill of Lading)	(Applicable only when this document is used as a Combined Transport Bill of Lading)
6. Ocean Vessel Voy. No.	**7. Port of Loading**
GLORY FORTUNE V.1910E	SHANGHAI, CHINA
8. Port of Discharge	**9. Place of Delivery***
OSAKA, JAPAN	(Applicable only when this document is used as a Combined Transport Bill of Lading)

Container No./Seal No. Marks and Numbers	Number and Kind of packages: description of goods	Gross Weight Kgs	Measurement
SENSERA SSR18035 OSAKA CTN. NO.1-425 BEAU5623894/20GP/SITE415932	1X20GP FCL CONTAINER 425CARTONS PORCELAIN DINNERWARE CY - CY SHIPPER'S LOAD , COUNT AND SEAL FREIGHT PREPAID L/C NO. 3468053359374 DATED 25 JUNE 2018 ISSUED BY SUMITOMO MITSUI BANKING CORPORATION Above particulars declared by Shipper. Carrier is not responsible. (see clause 12)	8925.000 KGS	24.906 CBM

10. Total No. of Containers Or Packages (in words)	SAY ONE CONTAINER ONLY			
11. Freight & Charges	Rate	Unit	Prepaid	Collect
Prepaid at SHANGHAI	**Payable at**	**Number of Original B(s)/L** THREE		
Place of Issue and Date SHANGHAI 23 JULY 2018		**12. Declared Value/Freight**		
LADEN ON BOARD THE VESSEL		**AS AGENT FOR THE CARRIER**		
DATE 23 JULY 2018	**BY** GLORY FORTUNE V.1910E	SITC CONTAINER LINES CO., LTD SIGN: _____ SITC CONTAINER LINES (SHANGHAI)CO., LTD.		

ING CO., LTD.

D/R No.(编号)
SITGSHSVK18021

场站收据

第七联

DOCK   RECEIPT

Received by the Carrier the Total number of containers or other packages or units stated below to be transported subject to the terms and conditions of the Carrier's regular form of Bill of Lading (for Combined Transport or port to Port Shipment) which shall be deemed to be incorporated herein.

Date (日期):	Jul. 8, 2018	场站章

CO., LTD.
SAKAI-SHI, OSAKA

Place of Receipt (收货地点)

Port of Loading (装货港)
SHANGHAI, CHINA
Place of Delivery (交货地点)

Final Destination for the Merchant's Reference

No. of contai- ners or p'kgs (箱数或件数)	Kind of Packages: Description of Goods (积箱种类及之货名)	Gross Weight 毛重(公斤)	Measurement 尺码(立方米)
425CTNS	PORCELAIN DINNERWARE FREIGHT PREPAID	8925.000	24.906

SAY ONE TWENTY FEET CONTAINER ONLY

(封志号)	Pkgs(件数)	Container No.(箱号)	Seal No.(封志号)	Pkgs(件数)
			Received(实收)	By Terminal Clerk(场站员签字)

	Payable at (到付地点)	Place of Issue (签发地点) SHANGHAI
(运费额)	No. of Original B(s)/L (正本提单份数): THREE	Booking (订舱确认) APPROVED BY

	Service Type on Delivery	Reefer Temperature Required (冷藏温度)	℉ ℃
	☑CY ☐CFS ☐DOOR		
☐ Reefer (冷藏)	☐ Dangerous (危险品)	☐ Auto. (裸装汽车)	Class: Property: MDG Code Page UN No.
☐ Live Animal (活动物)	☐ Bulk (散装)		

练 习

试根据**第六章 出口托运订舱**的**练习**（第 219 页）中的出口货物明细、信用证及以下信息，缮制信用证项下的装运通知和海运提单：

提单编号：COSU85122784
装船日期：2018 年 12 月 1 日
船名：DA HE KOU
航次：210S
海运费用：每个 20 英尺集装箱 1000 美元
集装箱号及封志号：

CBHU57120845	32741
CBHU57120846	32742
CBHU57120847	32743
CBHU57120848	32744

目的地船务代理： SHARAF SHIPPING AGENCY LLC
　　　　　　　　P.O. BOX 576
　　　　　　　　DUBAI
　　　　　　　　UAE
　　　　　　　　TEL：＋971 4 339718

提单的填制方法请参见**第十二章 出口交单结汇**的**指南**（第 341 页）。

上 海 闵 华 进 出 口 公 司
SHANGHAI MINHUA IMP. & EXP. CORPORATION

SHIPPING ADVICE

To: _____ From: _____
Telex. No.: _____ Tel. No.: _____
Page: _____ Date: _____
Fax. No.: _____ Fax. No.: _____

Re: _____

上海闵华进出口公司
SHANGHAI MINHUA IMP. & EXP. CORPORATION

_____
(SIGNATURE)

COSCO SHIPPING 中远海运集装箱运输有限公司
COSCO SHIPPING LINES CO., LTD.

ORIGINAL

TLX: 33057 COSCO SHIPPING
FAX: +86(21) 65458984

PORT TO PORT OR COMBINED TRANSPORT BILL OF LADING

1. Shipper　Insert Name Address and Phone/Fax	Booking No.	Bill of Lading No.

Export References

2. Consignee　Insert Name Address and Phone/Fax	Forwarding Agent and References

Point and Country of Origin

3. Notify Party　Insert Name Address and Phone/Fax　(It is agreed that no responsibility shall attach to the Carrier or his agents for failure to notify)	Also Notify Party-routing & Instructions

4. Combined Transport* Pre-Carriage by	5. Combined Transport* Place of Receipt	
6. Ocean Vessel Voy. No.	7. Port of Loading	Service Contract No.　Commodity Code
8. Port of Discharge	9. Combined Transport* Place of Delivery	Type of Movement

Marks & Nos. Container/Seal No.	No. of Container or Packages	Description of Goods (If Dangerous Goods, See Clause 20)	Gross Weight	Measurement

Declared Cargo Value US$　　Description of Contents for Shipper's use Only (Not part of This B/L Contract)

10. Total Number of Containers and/or Packages (in words)
Subject to Clause 7 Limitation

11. Freight & Charges	Revenue Tons	Rate	Per	Amount	Prepaid	Collect	Freight & Charges Payable at/by

Received in external apparent good order and condition except as otherwise noted. The total number of the packages or units stuffed in the container, the description of the goods and the weights shown in this Bill of Lading are furnished by the merchants, and which the carrier has no reasonable means of checking and is not a part of this Bills of Lading contract. The carrier has issued _____ original Bill of Lading, all of this tenor and date, one of the original Bills of lading must be surrendered and endorsed or signed against the delivery of the shipment and whereupon any other orginal Bills of Lading shall be void. The merchants agree to be bound by the terms and and conditions of this Bill of Lading as if each had personally signed this Bill of lading.
*Applicable Only When Document used as a Combined Transport Bill of Lading.

Date Laden on Board

Signed by:

9805　Date of Issue	Place of Issue	Signed for the Carrier, COSCO SHIPPING LINES CO., LTD

第十二章　出口交单结汇

2018 年 11 月 14 日,环宇公司凭第七联场站收据向船公司换取正本提单(第 309 页)。

2018 年 11 月 15 日,环宇公司将一套装运单据的副本(含商业发票、装箱单、提单、保险单、品质检验证书)和一份正本普惠制原产地证明通过 DHL 寄给 Tivolian 公司。

2018 年 11 月 16 日,根据信用证及信用证修改书,环宇公司缮制并审核所有结汇单据。

2018 年 11 月 23 日,在完成对全套结汇单据的复核及修改后,环宇公司向中国银行上海分行交单。

✍ 工作任务

1. 根据信用证及信用证修改书,审核结汇单据、出具审单意见,并完成尚未缮制单据的填制;

2. 填写《交单委托书》,向银行提交单据。

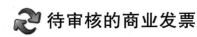 待审核的商业发票

Shanghai Universal Trading Co., Ltd.

Rm. 1201-1216 Mayling Plaza,
131 Dongfang Rd.,
Shanghai, 200120, China
Tel: 86-21-58818844
Fax: 86-21-58818766

COMMERCIAL INVOICE

TO:	TIVOLIAN TRADING B.V.		INV. NO. :	HY-TIV-INV0373
	P.O. BOX 1783, HEIMAN DULLAERTOLEIN 3		INV. DATE:	OCT. 29, 2018
	3024CA ROTTERDAM, NETHERLANDS		S/C NO. :	HY-TIV0373

FROM:	SHANGHAI	TO:	ROTTERDAM	SHIPPED BY:	COSCO HELLAS / 013W

MARKS & NOS.	DESCRIPTION OF GOODS		QUANTITY	UNIT PRICE	AMOUNT
CE/IMP.087	PLUSH TOYS			CIF ROTTERDAM	
TIV-PO-CSH0873					
ROTTERDAM					
CARTON NO. 1 - 126	KB0278	TWIN BEAR	504 SETS	US$9.60	US$4,838.40
KB0278	KB5411	TWIN BEAR IN BALLET COSTUME	504 SETS	US$11.50	US$5,796.00
	KB0677	BROWN BEAR WITH RED BOW	536 SETS	US$14.50	US$7,772.00
CE/IMP.087	KB7900	BEAR IN PINK T-SHIRT	536 SETS	US$15.40	US$8,254.40
TIV-PO-CSH0873					US$26,660.80
ROTTERDAM					
CARTON NO. 1 - 126					
KB5411					

F-TOYS 228
TIV-PO-CSH0873
ROTTERDAM
CARTON NO. 1 - 67
KB0677

F-TOYS 228
TIV-PO-CSH0873
ROTTERDAM
CARTON NO. 1 - 67
KB7900

TOTAL AMOUNT IN WORDS: SAY U.S. DOLLARS TWENTY SIX THOUSAND SIX HUNDRED AND SIXTY AND CENTS EIGHTY ONLY

TOTAL G.W. / TOTAL N.W.: 3155.000 KGS / 2190.000 KGS

TOTAL PACKAGES: 386CTNS

上 海 环 宇 贸 易 有 限 公 司
SHANGHAI UNIVERSAL TRADING CO., LTD.

(SIGNATURE)

待审核的装箱单

Shanghai Universal Trading Co., Ltd.

Rm. 1201-1216 Mayling Plaza,
131 Dongfang Rd.,
Shanghai, 200120, China
Tel: 86-21-58818844
Fax: 86-21-58818766

PACKING LIST

TO: TIVOLIAN TRADING B.V. P.O. BOX 1783, HEIMAN DULLAERTOLEIN 3 3024 CA ROTTERDAM, NETHERLANDS	**INV. NO. :**	HY-TIV-INV0373
	INV. DATE:	OCT. 29, 2018

FROM: SHANGHAI	**TO:** ROTTERDAM	**SHIPPED BY:** COSCO HELLAS / 013W

C/NO.	DESCRIPTION OF GOODS	PKG.	QTY	G.W.	N.W.	MEAS.
CE/IMP.087 TIV-PO-CSH0873 ROTTERDAM CARTON NO. 1 - 126 KB0278	KB0278	126 CTNS	504 SETS	1008.000 KGS	693.000 KGS	12.474 M3
CE/IMP.087 TIV-PO-CSH0873 ROTTERDAM CARTON NO. 1 - 126 KB5411	KB5411	126 CTNS	504 SETS	1008.000 KGS	693.000 KGS	12.474 M3
F-TOYS 228 TIV-PO-CSH0873 ROTTERDAM CARTON NO. 1 - 67 KB0677	KB0677	67 CTNS	536 SETS	569.500 KGS	402.000 KGS	12.349 M3
F-TOYS 228 TIV-PO-CSH0873 ROTTERDAM CARTON NO. 1 - 67 KB7900	KB7900	67 CTNS	536 SETS	569.500 KGS	402.000 KGS	12.349 M3
	TOTAL:	386 CTNS	2080 SETS	3155.000 KGS	2190.000 KGS	49.646 M3

TOTAL PACKAGE IN WORDS:　　SAY THREE HUNDRED AND EIGHTY SIX CARTONS ONLY

MARKS & NOS.:　　AS SHOWN IN C/NO.

上 海 环 宇 贸 易 有 限 公 司
SHANGHAI UNIVERSAL TRADING CO., LTD.

李玫师

(SIGNATURE)

待审核的海运提单

COSCO SHIPPING 中远海运集装箱运输有限公司 COSCO SHIPPING LINES CO., LTD.	**ORIGINAL**	TLX: 33057 COSCO SHIPPING
		FAX: +86(21) 65458984
		PORT TO PORT OR COMBINED TRANSPORT BILL OF LADING

1. Shipper Insert Name Address and Phone/Fax	Booking No.	Bill of Lading No.
SHANGHAI UNIVERSAL TRADING CO., LTD. MAYLING PLAZA, 131 DONGFANG ROAD, SHANGHAI 200120, CHINA	89302173	COSU89302173

Export References

2. Consignee Insert Name Address and Phone/Fax	Forwarding Agent and References
TO ORDER OF SHIPPER	FMC/CHB NO.

Point and Country of Origin

3. Notify Party Insert Name Address and Phone/Fax	(It is agreed that no responsibility shall attach to the Carrier or his agents for failure to notify)	Also Notify Party-routing & Instructions
TIVOLIAN TRADING B.V. P.O. BOX 1783, HEIMAN DULLAERTOLEIN 3, 3024CA ROTTERDAM, NETHERLANDS		

4. Combined Transport* Pre-Carriage by	5. Combined Transport* Place of Receipt

6. Ocean Vessel Voy. No.	7. Port of Loading	Service Contract No.	Commodity Code
COSCO HELLAS / 013W	**SHANGHAI**		

8. Port of Discharge	9. Combined Transport* Place of Delivery	Type of Movement	
ROTTERDAM		**FCL/FCL**	**CY-CY**

Marks & Nos. Container/Seal No.	No. of Container or Packages	Description of Goods (If Dangerous Goods, See Clause 20)	Gross Weight	Measurement
CE/IMP.087 TIV-PO-CSH0873 ROTTERDAM CARTON NO. 1 - 126 KB0278	**386CTNS**	**PLUSH TOYS** SHIPPER'S LOAD, COUNT AND SEAL	2190.000KGS	49.646CBM
ON CY-CY TERM **FREIGHT PREPAID** **CREDIT NUMBER: AM/VA07721S** **THE CARRIER'S AGENT AT THE PORT OF DISCHARGE: CROSS-OCEAN B.V.**				
CBHU75989732 CBHU75989733	/ 35737 / 35738	/ 252CTNS / FCL / FCL / 134CTNS / FCL / FCL	/ 20GP / / 20GP /	

Declared Cargo Value US$	Description of Contents for Shipper's Use Only (Not part of This B/L Contract)

10. Total Number of Containers and/or Packages (in words) Subject to Clause 7 Limitation	**SAY TWO TWENTY FEET CONTAINERS ONLY**

11. Freight & Charges	Revenue Tons	Rate	Per	Amount	Prepaid	Collect	Freight & Charges Payable at/by

Received in external apparent good order and condition except as otherwise noted. The total number of the packages or units stuffed in the container, the description of the goods and the weights shown in this Bill of Lading are furnished by the merchants, and which the carrier has no reasonable means of checking and is not a part of this Bills of Lading contract. The carrier has issued   **THREE** original Bill of Lading, all of this tenor and date, one of the original Bills of lading must be surrendered and endorsed or signed against the delivery of the shipment and whereupon any other original Bills of Lading shall be void. The merchants agree to be bound by the terms and conditions of this Bill of Lading as if each had personally signed this Bill of lading.
*Applicable Only When Document Used as a Combined Transport Bill of Lading.
Demurage and Detention shall be charged according to the tariff pulished on the Home page of LINES.COSCO
SHIPPING.COM. If any ambiguity or query, please search by "Demurrage & Detention Tariff Enquiry", Other services and more details information, pls visit LINES.COSCOSHIPPING.COM.

Date Laden on Board	**NOV. 13, 2018**
Signed by:	

上海中远海运集装箱船务代理有限公司
COSCO SHIPPING LINES AGENCY (SHANGHAI) CO., LTD

9805 Date of Issue **NOV. 13, 2018** Place of Issue **SHANGHAI**	Signed for the Carrier: COSCO SHIPPING LINES CO., LTD
	AS AGENT

待审核的普惠制原产地证明

COPY		
1. Goods consigned from (Exporter's business name, address, country) SHANGHAI UNIVERSAL TRADING CO., LTD. MAYLING PLAZA, 131 DONGFANG ROAD, SHANGHAI 200120, CHINA	Reference No. G183100672730073 **GENERALIZED SYSTEM OF PREFERENCES** **CERTIFICATE OF ORIGIN** **(Combined declaration and certificate)** **FORM A** Issued in THE PEOPLE'S REPUBLIC OF CHINA (country)	
2. Goods consigned to (Consignee's name, address, country) TIVOLIAN TRADING B.V. P.O. BOX 1783, HEIMAN DULLAERTOLEIN 3, 3024CA ROTTERDAM, NETHERLANDS		See Notes overleaf
3. Means of transport and route (as far as known) FROM SHANGHAI, CHINA TO ROTTERDAM, NETHERLANDS BY SEA	4. For official use Verification: www.chinaorigin.gov.cn	

5. Item number	6. Marks and numbers of packages	7. Number and Kind of packages; description of goods	8. Origin criterion (see Notes overleaf)	9. Gross weight or other quantity	10. Number and date of invoices
01	CE/IMP.087 TIV-P O-CSH0873 ROTTERDAM CARTON NO. 1 - 126 KB0278 CE/IMP.087 TIV-P O-CSH0873 ROTTERDAM CARTON NO. 1 - 126 KB5411 F-TOYS 228 TIV-P O-CSH0873 ROTTERDAM CARTON NO. 1 - 67 KB0677 F-TOYS 228 TIV-P O-CSH0873 ROTTERDAM CARTON NO. 1 - 67 KB7900	**386 (THREE HUNDRED AND EIGHTY SIX) CARTONS OF PLUSH TOYS** ** THE GOODS ARE OF CHINESE ORIGIN. CREDIT NUMBER: AM/VA07721SLC	"P"	3155.0KGS	HY-TIV-INV0373 OCT. 29, 2018

| 11. Certification
It is hereby certified, on the basis of control carried out, that the declaration by the exporter is correct.

SHANGHAI, CHINA NOV. 7, 2018
Place and date, signature and stamp of certifying authority | 12. Declaration by the exporter
The undersigned hereby declares that the above details and statements are correct; that all the goods were produced in   **CHINA**
(country)
and that they comply with the origin requirements specified for those goods in the Generalized System of Preferences for goods exported to
NETHERLANDS
(importing country)
SHANGHAI, CHINA NOV. 7, 2018
Place and date, signature of authorized signatory |

待审核的装船通知副本

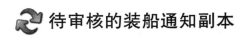

上 海 环 宇 贸 易 有 限 公 司
Shanghai Universal Trading Co., Ltd.

FAX

To:	Tivolian Trading B.V.	**From:**	Shanghai Universal Trading Co., Ltd.
Tel. No.:	+(31)10 4767418	**Tel. No.:**	+(86)21 58818844
Page:	Page 1, Total 1 Page	**Date:**	Nov. 14, 2018
Fax-No.:	+(31)10 4767422	**Fax-No.:**	+(86)21 58818766

SHIPPING ADVICE

CREDIT NUMBER: AM/VA07721SLC

We hereby inform you that the goods under the above credit were shipped on Nov. 13, 2018. The details of shipment are stated below:

Date of Departure:	Nov. 13, 2018			
Shipping Marks:	CE/IMP.087	CE/IMP.087	F-TOYS 228	F-TOYS 228
	TIV-PO-CSH0873	TIV-PO-CSH0873	TIV-PO-CSH0873	TIV-PO-CSH0873
	ROTTERDAM	ROTTERDAM	ROTTERDAM	ROTTERDAM
	CARTON NO. 1 - 126	CARTON NO. 1 - 126	CARTON NO. 1 - 67	CARTON NO. 1 - 67
	KB0278	KB5411	KB0677	KB7900
Number of L/C:	AM/VA07721SLC			
Number of B/L:	COSU89302173			
Number of Contract:	HY-TIV0373			
Number of Order:	TIV-PO-CSH0873			
Number of Cartons:	386 cartons			
Total Gross Weight:	3155 kgs			
Goods Value:	USD26660.80 CIF			
Commodity:	Plush Toys			
Ocean Vessel:	Cosco Hellas / 013W			
From:	Shanghai			
To:	Rotterdam			
ETA:	Dec.12, 2018			

Yours sincerely,

王凯

David Wang
Shanghai Universal Trading Co., Ltd

中国上海市东方路 131 号美陵广场 1201-1216 室
Rm. 1201-1216 Mayling Plaza, 131 Dongfang Rd., Shanghai, 200120, China
电话/Tel: 86-21-58818844 传真/Fax: 86-21-58818766 网址/Web: www.universal.com.cn

待审核的保险单

	货 物 运 输 保 险 单
	CARGO TRANSPORTATION INSURANCE POLICY

北京2008年奥运会保险合作伙伴

	总公司设于北京		一九四九年创立
	Head office Beijing		Established in 1949

发票号（INVOICE NO.） **HY-TIV0373**		
合同号（CONTRACT NO.） **HY-TIV0373**	保单号次	
信用证号（L/C NO.） **AM/VA07721SLC**	POLICY NO. **PYIE201343958015958273**
被保险人		
INSURED **SHANGHAI UNIVERSAL TRADING CO., LTD.**		

中国人民财产保险股份有限公司（以下简称公司）根据被保险人的要求，由被保险人向本公司缴付约定的保险费，按照本保单承保险别和背面所载条款与下列特款承保下述货物运输保险，特立本保险单。

THIS POLICY OF INSURANCE WITNESSES THAT PICC PROPERTY AND CASUALTY COMPANY LIMITED (HEREINAFTER CALLED "THE COMPANY") AT THE REQUEST OF THE INSURED AND IN CONSIDERATION OF THE AGREED PREMIUM PAID TO THE COMPANY BY THE INSURED, UNDERTAKES TO INSURE THE UNDERMENTIONED GOODS IN TRANSPORTATION SUBJECT TO THE CONDITIONS OF THIS POLICY AS PER THE CLAUSES PRINTED OVERLEAF AND OTHER SPECIAL CLAUSES ATTACHED HEREON.

标 记 MARKS & NOS	包装及数量 QUANTITY	保险货物项目 DESCRIPTION OF GOODS	保险金额 AMOUNT INSURED
AS PER INVOICE **NO. HY-TIV-INV0373**	**386CTNS**	**PLVSH TOYS**	**US$29,327.00**
		CREDIT NUMBER: AM/VA07721SLC	

总保险金额： TOTAL AMOUNT INSURED:	**US DOLLARS TWENTY NINE THOUSAND THREE HUNDRED AND TWENTY SIX ONLY**

保费 PREMIUM **AS ARRANGED**	启运日期： DATE OF COMMENCEMENT **AS PER B/L**		装载运输工具： PER CONVEYANCE **COSCO HELLA / 013W**	
自 FROM **SHANGHAI, CHINA**	经 VIA		至 TO **ROTTERDAM, NETHERLANDS**	
承保险别： CONDITIONS				

COVERING INSTITUTE CARGO CLAUSES (A) AND INSTITUTE WAR CLAUSES - CARGO.

所保货物，如发生保险单项下可能引起索赔的损失或损坏，应立即通知本公司下述代理人查勘。如有索赔，应向本公司提交保单正本（本保单共有 **贰** 份正本）及有关文件。如一份正本已用于索赔，其余正本自动失效。

IN THE EVENT OF LOSS OR DAMAGE WHICH MAY RESULT IN A CLAIM UNDER THIS POLICY, IMMEDIATE NOTICE MUST BE GIVEN TO THE COMPANY'S AGENT AS MENTIONED HEREUNDER CLAIMS. IF ANY, ONE OF THE ORIGINAL POLICY WHICH HAS BEEN ISSUED IN **2** ORIGINAL(S) TOGETHER WITH THE RELEVENT DOCUMENTS SHALL BE SURRENDERED TO THE COMPANY. IF ONE OF THE ORIGINAL POLICY HAS BEEN ACCOMPLISHED, THE OTHERS TO BE VOID.

中国人民财产保险股份有限公司 上海市分公司
PICC Property and Casualty Company Limited, Shanghai Branch

赔款偿付地点 CLAIM PAYABLE AT/IN **ROTTERDAM IN USD**	
出单日期 ISSUING DATE **NOV. 6, 2018**	**GENERAL MANAGER**

地址： 中国上海中山南路700号 ADD: 700 ZHONGSHAN ROAD (S) SHANGHAI CHINA 邮编（POST CODE）：200010	经办：项钧 复核：廖敏 Settling & Customer Service Centre （理赔/客户服务中心）86 21 63674274

保单顺序号 PICC **1325873**

待审核的品质检验证书

中华人民共和国出入境检验检疫
ENTRY-EXIT INSPECTION AND QUARANTINE
OF THE PEOPLE'S REPUBLIC OF CHINA

正 本
ORIGINAL
第1页 共1页 Page 1 of 1

编号 No.: 034909628062673

QUALITY
INSPECTION CERTIFICATE

发货人 Consignor	**SHANGHAI UNIVERSAL TRADING CO., LTD.**
收货人 Consignee	**TIVOLIAN TRADING B.V.**

		标记及号码 Mark & No.	
品名 Description of Goods	**PLUSH TOYS**	**CE/IMP.087** **TIV-PO-CSH0873** **ROTTERDAM** **CARTON NO. 1 - 126** **KB0278**	**CE/IMP.087** **TIV-PO-CSH0873** **ROTTERDAM** **CARTON NO. 1 - 126** **KB5411**
报检数量/重量 Quantity/Weight Declared	**-2080-SETS /-3155-KGS**		
包装种类及数量 Number and Type of Packages	**-368-CTNS**	**F-TOYS 228** **TIV-PO-CSH0873** **ROTTERDAM** **CARTON NO. 1 - 67** **KB0677**	**F-TOYS 228** **TIV-PO-CSH0873** **ROTTERDAM** **CARTON NO. 1 - 67** **KB7900**
运输工具 Means of Conveyance	**COSCO HELLAS / 013**		

检验结果:
RESULTS OF INSPECTION:

At the request of consignor, our inspectors attended at the warehouse of the consignment on 2008/5/16. In accordance with SN/T0304-1993 and the relevant state stipulations GB2828, GB6675 and GB9832, 13 cartons were taken and opened at random for visual inspection, from which representative samples were drawn and inspected according to the stipulation mentioned above. The results are as follows:

    Appearance: Pass
    Specifications: Pass
    Quantity: -2080-SETS, -386-CTNS
    Safety: Pass
    Hygienics: Pass

签证地点 Place of Issue	**SHANGHAI**	签证日期 Date of Issue	**NOV. 4, 2018**
授权签字人 Authorized Officer	**XU SAILI**	签 名 Signature	*徐赛莉*

⬇ 汇票

BILL OF EXCHANGE

No. _____

For _____   _____
        (amount in figure)   (place and date of issue)

At _____   of   this   FIRST   Bill of exchange(SECOND being unpaid)

pay to _____ or order the sum of

_____
                                    (amount in words)

Drawn under   _____

L/C No. _____   dated   _____

To: For and on behalf of

        _____   _____
                                                            (Signature)

⬇ 受益人证明

上 海 环 宇 贸 易 有 限 公 司
Shanghai Universal Trading Co., Ltd.

CERTIFICATE

⬇ 交单委托书

中国银行 BANK OF CHINA

出口信用证交单委托书

致： 中国银行 _____ 分行

　　兹随附下列银行正本信用证（修改书）及所属出口单据，请贵行根据国际商会跟单信用证统一惯例（UCP600）予以审核并办理寄单索汇：

开证行：	信用证号：
	通知编号：
发票号码：	发票金额：

单据名称	汇票	发票	提单	副本提单	保险单/投保通知	装箱单	重量单	原产地证明	普惠制原产地证明	品质数量证明	受益人证明	船公司证明	装船通知副本	装船通知	寄单证明
份数															

注： 框内填写"√"以示选择

付款指示：

请将收汇款以 ☐ 原币或者， ☐ 人民币划入我司下列帐户：

开户行： _____ 帐号： _____

特别指示：

1、 邮寄方式： ☐ 快邮 ☐ 普邮 ☐ 指定快邮 _____

2、 本次提交的正本信用证含 _____ 份正本修改书。

公司联系人姓名： _____　　　　　公 司 签 章

电话： _____ 传真： _____　　　　 _____ 年 ___ 月 ___ 日

以下栏目由我行填写

银行签收人：	签收日期
改单/退单记录：	

注：本委托书一式3份，一份于交单时银行签收后退回公司，一份结汇时作回单退公司，一份交由银行留底

示   范

审单意见

信用证号码：AM/VA07721SLC
进口商：Tivolian Trading B.V.

开证银行：F. Van Lanschot Bankiers N.V.
合同号码：HY-TIV0373

商业发票：
1）未按信用证规定显示详细的货物描述
2）未按信用证规定显示 FOB 价值
3）未按信用证规定显示原产地
4）未显示信用证号码

装箱单：
1）单据名称与信用证规定不符
2）未按信用证规定显示详细的货物描述
3）未按信用证规定显示每个纸箱的毛重、尺码
4）未显示信用证号码

海运提单：
1）收货人 Consignee 不符合信用证规定，应为 To Order
2）被通知人 Notify Party 未按信用证规定显示 Phone Numbers
3）运输标志与信用证不符，应显示完整
4）显示的信用证号码与信用证不符，应为 AM/VA07721SLC
5）总毛重错误，应为 3155kgs
6）未按信用证要求显示承运人在卸货港的代理的地址
7）尚未按信用证要求作空白背书

普惠制原产地证： 无误

装船通知副本： 无误

保险单：
1）显示的发票号码与发票不符，应为 HY-TIV-INV0373
2）保险货物项目与其他单据不符，应为 Plush Toys
3）保险金额大写有误，应为 TWENTY SEVEN ONLY
4）装载运输工具（船名）与海运提单不符，应为 COSCO HELLAS
5）正本份数与信用证规定不符，应为 3 份
6）缺少理赔代理
7）尚未按信用证要求作空白背书

品质检验证书：
1）包装数量与其他单据不符，应为 386CTNS
2）运输工具中显示的航次与提单不符，应为 013W
3）未显示信用证号码

漏缺第三方单据： 船公司证明

尚未缮制单据： 汇票和寄单证明

出口信用证交单委托书

致：　中国银行　　　　上海市　　　　分行

　　　兹随附下列银行正本信用证（修改书）及所属出口单据，请贵行根据国际商会跟单信用证统

一惯例（UCP600）予以审核并办理寄单索汇：

开证行： F. VAN LANSCHOT BANKIERS N.V., ROTTERDAM, NETHERLANDS	信用证号： AM/VA07721SLC 通知编号： BP70221563
发票号码： HY-TIV-INV0373	发票金额： US$26,660.80

单据名称	汇票	发票	提单	副本提单	保险单／投保通知	装箱单	重量单	原产地证明	普惠制原产地证明	商检证书	受益人证明	船公司证明	装船通知副本	装船通知	寄单证明
份数	2	5	3	3	3	3			2	2		1	1		1

注：　框内填写"√"以示选择

付款指示：

请将收汇款以 [ ] 原币或者，[√] 人民币划入我司下列帐户：

开户行：　中国银行上海分行　　　　　　　　　账号：086159-66795216843573

特别指示：

1、　邮寄方式：[√] 快邮　[ ] 普邮　[ ] 指定快邮 _____

2、　本次提交的正本信用证含 　1　 份正本修改书。

公司联系人姓名：　*王凯*　　　　　　　　　　公　司　签　章

电话：021-58818844　　传真：021-63753529　　　2018　年　11　月　23　日

以下栏目由我行填写

银行签收人：	签收日期：
改单/退单记录：	

注：本委托书一式3份，一份于交单时银行签收后退回公司，一份结汇时作回单退公司，一份交由银行留底

BILL OF EXCHANGE

No. **HY-TIV130373**

For **US$26,660.80**   **SHANGHAI NOV. 23, 2018**
(amount in figure)   (place and date of issue)

At   ********** SIGHT ************   of this   **FIRST**   Bill of exchange(SECOND being unpaid)

pay to   **BANK OF CHINA , SHANGHAI BRANCH**   or order the sum of

SAY U.S. DOLLARS TWENTY SIX THOUSAND SIX HUNDRED AND SIXTY AND CENTS EIGHTY ONLY
(amount in words)

Drawn under   **F. VAN LANSCHOT BANKIERS N.V., ROTTERDAM, NETHERLANDS**

L/C No.   **AM/VA07721SLC**   dated   **OCT. 8, 2018**

To: **F. VAN LANSCHOT BANKIERS N.V.,**   For and on behalf of
        ROTTERDAM,   **SHANGHAI UNIVERSAL TRADING CO., LTD.**
        NETHERLANDS

                                                     (Signature)

BILL OF EXCHANGE

No. **HY-TIV130373**

For **US$26,660.80**   **SHANGHAI NOV. 23, 2018**
(amount in figure)   (place and date of issue)

At   ********** SIGHT ************   of this   **SECOND**   Bill of exchange(FIRST being unpaid)

pay to   **BANK OF CHINA , SHANGHAI BRANCH**   or order the sum of

SAY U.S. DOLLARS TWENTY SIX THOUSAND SIX HUNDRED AND SIXTY AND CENTS EIGHTY ONLY
(amount in words)

Drawn under   **F. VAN LANSCHOT BANKIERS N.V., ROTTERDAM, NETHERLANDS**

L/C No.   **AM/VA07721SLC**   dated   **OCT. 8, 2018**

To: **F. VAN LANSCHOT BANKIERS N.V.,**   For and on behalf of
        ROTTERDAM,   **SHANGHAI UNIVERSAL TRADING CO., LTD.**
        NETHERLANDS

                                                     (Signature)

Shanghai Universal Trading Co., Ltd.

Rm. 1201-1216 Mayling Plaza,
131 Dongfang Rd.,
Shanghai, 200120, China
Tel: 86-21-58818844
Fax: 86-21-58818766

COMMERCIAL INVOICE

TO:	TIVOLIAN TRADING B.V.		INV. NO. :	HY-TIV-INV0373
	P.O. BOX 1783, HEIMAN DULLAERTOLEIN 3		INV. DATE:	OCT. 29, 2018
	3024CA ROTTERDAM, NETHERLANDS		S/C NO. :	HY-TIV0373

FROM:	SHANGHAI	TO:	ROTTERDAM	SHIPPED BY:	COSCO HELLAS / 013W

MARKS & NOS.	DESCRIPTION OF GOODS		QUANTITY	UNIT PRICE	AMOUNT
CE/IMP.087	4 ITEMS OF TOTAL 2080 SETS OF PLUSH TOYS AS PER APPLICANT'S ORDER				
TIV-PO-CSH0873	NUMBER TIV-PO-CSH0873 AND BENEFICIARY'S CONTRACT NUMBER HY-TIV0373				
ROTTERDAM					
CARTON NO. 1 - 126					CIF ROTTERDAM
KB0278	KB0278	TWIN BEAR	504 SETS	US$9.60	US$4,838.40
	KB5411	TWIN BEAR IN BALLET COSTUME	504 SETS	US$11.50	US$5,796.00
CE/IMP.087	KB0677	BROWN BEAR WITH RED BOW	536 SETS	US$14.50	US$7,772.00
TIV-PO-CSH0873	KB7900	BEAR IN PINK T-SHIRT	536 SETS	US$15.40	US$8,254.40
ROTTERDAM					US$26,660.80
CARTON NO. 1 - 126	LABEL: CE/IMP.087 FOR ARTICLES KB0278, KB5411				
KB5411	LABEL: F-TOYS 228 FOR ARTICLES KB0677, KB7900				
F-TOYS 228	TERMS OF DELIVERY: CIF ROTTERDAM (INCOTERMS 2010)				
TIV-PO-CSH0873					
ROTTERDAM	PACKING IN NEUTRAL SEAWORTHY EXPORT CARTONS SUITABLE FOR LONG				
CARTON NO. 1 - 67	DISTANCE OCEAN TRANSPORTATION				
KB0677					
	CREDIT NUMBER:	AM/VA07721SLC			
F-TOYS 228	ORIGIN OF GOODS:	CHINA			
TIV-PO-CSH0873	FOB VALUE:	US$24,450.17			
ROTTERDAM					
CARTON NO. 1 - 67					
KB7900	TOTAL AMOUNT IN WORDS:	SAY U.S. DOLLARS TWENTY SIX THOUSAND SIX HUNDRED AND SIXTY AND CENTS EIGHTY ONLY			
	TOTAL G.W. / TOTAL N.W.:	3155.000 KGS / 2190.000 KGS			
	TOTAL PACKAGES:	386CTNS			

上 海 环 宇 贸 易 有 限 公 司
SHANGHAI UNIVERSAL TRADING CO., LTD.

(SIGNATURE)

Shanghai Universal Trading Co., Ltd.

Rm. 1201-1216 Mayling Plaza,
131 Dongfang Rd.,
Shanghai, 200120, China
Tel: 86-21-58818844
Fax: 86-21-58818766

PACKING LIST / WEIGHT MEMO

TO:	TIVOLIAN TRADING B.V.		**INV. NO. :**	HY-TIV-INV0373
	P.O. BOX 1783, HEIMAN DULLAERTOLEIN 3		**INV. DATE:**	OCT. 29, 2018
	3024CA ROTTERDAM, NETHERLANDS			

FROM:	SHANGHAI	**TO:**	ROTTERDAM	**SHIPPED BY:**	COSCO HELLAS / 013W

C/NO.	DESCRIPTION OF GOODS	PKG.	QTY	G.W.	N.W.	MEAS.
	4 ITEMS OF TOTAL 2080 SETS OF PLUSH TOYS AS PER APPLICANT'S ORDER NUMBER TIV-PO-CSH0873 AND BENEFICIARY'S CONTRACT NUMBER HY-TIV0373					
	LABEL: CE/IMP.087 FOR ARTICLES KB0278, KB5411 LABEL: F-TOYS 228 FOR ARTICLES KB0677, KB7900					
	TERMS OF DELIVERY: CIF ROTTERDAM (INCOTERMS 2010)					
	PACKING IN NEUTRAL SEAWORTHY EXPORT CARTONS SUITABLE FOR LONG DISTANCE OCEAN TRANSPORTATION					
	CREDIT NUMBER: AM/VA07721SLC					
CE/IMP.087 TIV-PO-CSH0873 ROTTERDAM CARTON NO. 1 - 126 KB0278	KB0278	126 CTNS	504 SETS	1008.000 KGS	693.000 KGS	12.474 M3
CE/IMP.087 TIV-PO-CSH0873 ROTTERDAM CARTON NO. 1 - 126 KB5411	KB5411	126 CTNS	504 SETS	1008.000 KGS	693.000 KGS	12.474 M3
F-TOYS 228 TIV-PO-CSH0873 ROTTERDAM CARTON NO. 1 - 67 KB0677	KB0677	67 CTNS	536 SETS	569.500 KGS	402.000 KGS	12.349 M3

(CONTINUED ON NEXT PAGE)

Shanghai Universal Trading Co., Ltd.

Rm. 1201-1216 Mayling Plaza,
131 Dongfang Rd.,
Shanghai, 200120, China
Tel: 86-21-58818844
Fax: 86-21-58818766

PACKING LIST / WEIGHT MEMO

TO:	TIVOLIAN TRADING B.V.		INV. NO. :	HY-TIV-INV0373
	P.O. BOX 1783, HEIMAN DULLAERTOLEIN 3		INV. DATE:	OCT. 29, 2018
	3024CA ROTTERDAM, NETHERLANDS			

FROM:	SHANGHAI	TO:	ROTTERDAM	SHIPPED BY:	COSCO HELLAS / 013W

C/NO.	DESCRIPTION OF GOODS	PKG.	QTY	G.W.	N.W.	MEAS.
(CONTINUED FROM PREVIOUS PAGE)						
F-TOYS 228	KB7900	67 CTNS	536 SETS	569.500 KGS	402.000 KGS	12.349 M3
TIV-PO-CSH0873						
ROTTERDAM						
CARTON NO. 1 - 67						
KB7900						
	TOTAL:	386 CTNS	2080 SETS	3155.000 KGS	2190.000 KGS	49.646 M3

TOTAL PACKAGES IN WORDS: SAY THREE HUNDRED AND EIGHTY SIX CARTONS ONLY

GROSS WEIGHT AND MEASUREMENTS PER EXPORT CARTON:
KB0278 & KB5411   GROSS WEIGHT: 8KGS.   MEASUREMENTS: 0.099M3 (55*45*40CM)
KB0677 & KB7900   GROSS WEIGHT: 8.5KGS.   MEASUREMENTS: 0.18432M3 (48*64*60CM)

MARKS & NOS.:   SHIPPING MARKS

CE/IMP.087   CE/IMP.087
TIV-PO-CSH0873   TIV-PO-CSH0873
ROTTERDAM   ROTTERDAM
CARTON NO. 1 - 126   CARTON NO. 1 - 126
KB0278   KB5411

F-TOYS 228   F-TOYS 228
TIV-PO-CSH0873   TIV-PO-CSH0873
ROTTERDAM   ROTTERDAM
CARTON NO. 1 - 67   CARTON NO. 1 - 67
KB0677   KB7900

上 海 环 宇 贸 易 有 限 公 司
SHANGHAI UNIVERSAL TRADING CO., LTD.

(SIGNATURE)

						TLX: 33057 COSCO SHIPPING

COSCO SHIPPING 中远海运集装箱运输有限公司
COSCO SHIPPING LINES CO., LTD.

ORIGINAL

FAX: +86(21) 65458984

PORT TO PORT OR COMBINED TRANSPORT BILL OF LADING

1. Shipper Insert Name Address and Phone/Fax	Booking No.	Bill of Lading No.
SHANGHAI UNIVERSAL TRADING CO., LTD. MAYLING PLAZA, 131 DONGFANG ROAD, SHANGHAI 200120, CHINA	89302173	COSU89302173
	Export References	
2. Consignee Insert Name Address and Phone/Fax	Forwarding Agent and References	
TO ORDER		
	Point and Country of Origin	
3. Notify Party Insert Name Address and Phone/Fax (It is agreed that no responsibility shall attach to the Carrier or his agents for failure to notify)	Also Notify Party-routing & Instructions	
TIVOLIAN TRADING B.V. P.O. BOX 1783, HEIMAN DULLAERTOLEIN 3, 3024CA ROTTERDAM, NETHERLANDS PHONE NO.: 0031-10-4767418		

4. Combined Transport* Pre-Carriage by	5. Combined Transport* Place of Receipt		
6. Ocean Vessel Voy. No. **COSCO HELLAS / 013W**	7. Port of Loading **SHANGHAI**	Service Contract No.	Commodity Code
8. Port of Discharge **ROTTERDAM**	9. Combined Transport* Place of Delivery	Type of Movement **FCL/FCL**	**CY-CY**

Marks & Nos. Container/Seal No.	No. of Container or Packages	Description of Goods (If Dangerous Goods, See Clause 20)	Gross Weight	Measurement
CE/IMP.087 TIV-PO-CSH0873 ROTTERDAM CARTON NO. 1 - 126 KB0278	**386CTNS**	**PLUSH TOYS** SHIPPER'S LOAD, COUNT AND SEAL	**3155.000KGS**	**49.646CBM**
CE/IMP.087 TIV-PO-CSH0873 ROTTERDAM CARTON NO. 1 - 126 KB5411		**ON CY-CY TERM** **FREIGHT PREPAID** **CREDIT NUMBER: AM/VA07721SLC**		
F-TOYS 228 TIV-PO-CSH0873 ROTTERDAM CARTON NO. 1 - 67 KB0677		**THE CARRIER'S AGENT AT THE PORT OF DISCHARGE** **NAME: CROSS OCEAN B.V.** **ADDRESS: GROOTHANDEL SGEBOUW ENTRANCE D,** **CONRADSTRAAT 38, NL-3013 AP ROTTERDAM,** **NETHERLANDS**		
F-TOYS 228 TIV-PO-CSH0873 ROTTERDAM CARTON NO. 1 - 67 KB7900	**CBHU75989732** / 35737 / **252CTNS** / **FCL / FCL** / **20GP** / **CBHU75989733** / 35738 / **134CTNS** / **FCL / FCL** / **20GP** /			

Declared Cargo Value US$	Description of Contents for Shipper's Use Only (Not part of This B/L Contract)

10. Total Number of Containers and/or Packages (in words) Subject to Clause 7 Limitation	**SAY TWO TWENTY FEET CONTAINERS ONLY**

11. Freight & Charges	Revenue Tons	Rate	Per	Amount	Prepaid	Collect	Freight & Charges Payable at/by

Received in external apparent good order and condition except as otherwise noted. The total number of the packages or units stuffed in the container, the description of the goods and the weights shown in this Bill of Lading are furnished by the merchants, and which the carrier has no reasonable means of checking and is not a part of this Bills of Lading contract. The carrier has issued **THREE** original Bill of Lading, all of this tenor and date, one of the original Bills of lading must be surrendered and endorsed or signed against the delivery of the shipment and whereupon any other orginal Bills of Lading shall be void. The merchants agree to be bound by the terms and and conditions of this Bill of Lading as if each had personally signed this Bill of lading.
*Applicable Only When Document Used as a Combined Transport Bill of Lading.

Date Laden on Board   **NOV. 13, 2018**
Signed by: 上海中远海运集装箱船务代理有限公司 COSCO SHIPPING LINES AGENCY (SHANGHAI) CO., LTD

9805 Date of Issue **NOV. 13, 2018** Place of Issue	**SHANGHAI**	Signed for the Carrier COSCO SHIPPING LINES CO., LTD **AS AGENT**

货 物 运 输 保 险 单
CARGO TRANSPORTATION INSURANCE POLICY

总公司设于北京　　　　　　一九四九年创立
Head office Beijing　　　　　Established in 1949

发票号（INVOICE NO.）**HY-TIV-INV0373**	保单号次
合同号（CONTRACT NO.）**HY-TIV0373**	POLICY NO. **PYIE200843958015958273**
信用证号（L/C NO.）**AM/VA07721SLC**	

被保险人
INSURED　　**SHANGHAI UNIVERSAL TRADING CO., LTD.**

中国人民财产保险股份有限公司（以下简称本公司）根据被保险人的要求，由被保险人向本公司缴付约定的保险费，按照本保单承保险别和背面所载条款与下列特款承保下述货物运输保险，特立本保险单。

THIS POLICY OF INSURANCE WITNESSES THAT PICC PROPERTY AND CASUALTY COMPANY LIMITED (HEREINAFTER CALLED "THE COMPANY") AT THE REQUEST OF THE INSURED AND IN CONSIDERATION OF THE AGREED PREMIUM PAID TO THE COMPANY BY THE INSURED, UNDERTAKES TO INSURE THE UNDERMENTIONED GOODS IN TRANSPORTATION SUBJECT TO THE CONDITIONS OF THIS POLICY AS PER THE CLAUSES PRINTED OVERLEAF AND OTHER SPECIAL CLAUSES ATTACHED HEREON.

标 记 MARKS & NOS	包装及数量 QUANTITY	保险货物项目 DESCRIPTION OF GOODS	保险金额 AMOUNT INSURED
AS PER INVOICE NO. HY-TIV-INV0373	**386CTNS**	**PLUSH TOYS**	**US$29,327.00**
		CREDIT NUMBER: AM/VA07721SLC	

总保险金额：
TOTAL AMOUNT INSURED: **US DOLLARS TWENTY NINE THOUSAND THREE HUNDRED AND TWENTY SEVEN ONLY**

保费： PREMIUM **AS ARRANGED**	启运日期： DATE OF COMMENCEMENT **AS PER B/L**		装载运输工具： PER CONVEYANCE **COSCO HELLAS　/ 013W**
自 FROM **SHANGHAI, CHINA**	经 VIA		至 TO **ROTTERDAM, NETHERLANDS**

承保险别：
CONDITIONS

COVERING INSTITUTE CARGO CLAUSES (A) AND INSTITUTE WAR CLAUSES - CARGO.

所保货物，如发生保险单项下可能引起索赔的损失或损坏，应立即通知本公司下述代理人查勘。如有索赔，应向本公司提交保单正本（本保单共有 **叁** 份正本）及有关文件。如一份正本已用于索赔，其余正本自动失效。

IN THE EVENT OF LOSS OR DAMAGE WHICH MAY RESULT IN A CLAIM UNDER THIS POLICY, IMMEDIATE NOTICE MUST BE GIVEN TO THE COMPANY'S AGENT AS MENTIONED HEREUNDER CLAIMS. IF ANY ONE OF THE ORIGINAL POLICY WHICH HAS BEEN ISSUED IN **3** ORIGINAL(S) TOGETHER WITH THE RELEVENT DOCUMENTS SHALL BE SURRENDERED TO THE COMPANY. IF ONE OF THE ORIGINAL POLICY HAS BEEN ACCOMPLISHED, THE OTHERS TO BE VOID.

ANCHOR INSURANCE BV
LICHTENAUERLAAN 90, 3062 ME
ROTTERDAM, NETHERLANDS
TEL: +31 10 4587612
FAX: +31 10 4587619

中国人民财产保险股份有限公司 上海市分公司
PICC Property and Casualty Company Limited, Shanghai Branch

赔款偿付地点
CLAIM PAYABLE AT/IN　　**ROTTERDAM IN USD**

出单日期
ISSUING DATE　　**NOV. 6, 2018**

GENERAL MANAGER

地址：中国上海中山南路700号
ADD: 700 ZHONGSHAN ROAD (S) SHANGHAI CHINA
邮编（POST CODE）：200010

经办：项钧　复核：廖敏

Settling & Customer Service Centre:
（理赔/客户服务中心）86 21 63674274

保单顺序号 PICC **1325873**

OCEAN MARINE CARGO CLAUSES

I. Scope of Cover:

This insurance is classified into the following three Conditions - Free From Particular Average (F.P.A.), With Average (W.A.) and All Risks. Where the goods insured hereunder sustain loss or damage, the Company shall undertake to indemnify therefor according to the Insured Condition specified in the Policy and the Provisions of these Clauses:

1. Free From Particular Average (F.P.A)

This insurance covers:

1) Total or Constructive Total Loss of the whole consignment hereby insured caused in the course of transit by natural calamities - heavy weather, lightning, tsunami, earthquake and flood. In case a constructive total loss is claimed for, the Insured shall abandon to the Company the damaged goods and all his rights and title pertaining thereto. The goods on each lighter to or from the seagoing vessel shall be deemed a separate risk.

"Constructive Total Loss" refers to the loss where an actual total loss appears to be unavoidable or the cost to be incurred in recovering or reconditioning the goods together with the forwarding cost to the destination named in the Policy would exceed their value on arrival.

2) Total or Partial Loss caused by accidents - the carrying conveyance being grounded, stranded, sunk or in collision with floating ice or other objects as fire or explosion.

3) Partial loss of the insured goods attributable to heavy weather, lightning and/or tsunami, where the conveyance has been grounded, stranded, sunk or burnt, irrespective of whether the event or events took place before or after such accidents.

4) Partial or total loss consequent on falling of entire package or packages into sea during loading, transhipment or discharge.

5) Reasonable cost incurred by the Insured in salvaging the goods or averting or minimizing a loss recoverable under the Policy, provided that such cost shall not exceed the sum Insured of the consignment so saved.

6) Losses attributable to discharge of the insured goods at a port of distress following a sea peril as well as special charges arising from loading, warehousing and forwarding of the goods at an intermediate port of call or refuge.

7) Sacrifice in and Contribution to General Average and Salvage Charges.

8) Such proportion of losses sustained by the shipowners as is to be reimbursed by the Cargo Owner under the contract of Affreightment "Both to Blame Collision" clause.

2. With Average (W.A.)

Aside from the risks covered under F.P.A. condition as above, this insurance also covers partial losses of the insured goods caused by heavy weather, lightning, tsunami, earthquake and/or flood.

3. All Risks

Aside from the risks covered under the F.P.A. and W.A. conditions as above, this insurance also covers all risks of loss of or damage to the insured goods whether partial or total, arising from external causes in the course of transit.

II. Exclusions:

This insurance dose not cover:

1. Loss or damage caused by the intentional act or fault of the Insured.

2. Loss or damage falling under the liability of the consignor.

3. Loss or damage arising from the inferior quality or shortage of the insured goods prior to the attachment of this insurance.

4. Loss or damage arising from normal loss, inherent vice or nature of the insured goods, loss of market and/or delay in transit and any expenses arising therefrom.

5. Risks and liabilities covered and excluded by the Ocean Marine Cargo War Risks Clauses and Strike, Riot and Civil Commotion Clauses of this Company.

III. Commencement and Termination of Cover:

1. Warehouse to Warehouse Clause:

This insurance attaches from the time the goods hereby insured leave the warehouse or place of storage named in the Policy for the commencement of the transit and continues in force in the ordinary course of transit including sea, land and inland waterway transits and transit in lighter until the insured goods are delivered to the consignee's final warehouse or place of storage at the destination named in the Policy or to any other place used by the Insured for allocation or distribution of the goods or for storage other than in the ordinary course of transit. This insurance shall, however, be limited to sixty (60) days after completion of discharge of the insured goods from the seagoing vessel at the final port of discharge before they reach the above mentioned warehouse or place of storage. If prior to the expiry of the above mentioned sixty (60) days, the insured goods are to be forwarded to a destination other than that named in the Policy, this insurance shall terminate at the commencement of such transit.

2. If owing to delay, deviation, forced discharge, reshipment or transhipment beyond the control of the Insured or any change or termination of the voyage arising from the exercise of a liberty granted to the shipowners under the contract of affreightment, the insured goods arrive at a port or place other than that named in the Policy subject to immediate notice being given to the Company by the Insured and an additional premium being paid, if required, this insurance shall remain in force and shall terminate as hereunder.

1) If the insured goods are sold at port or place not named in the Policy, this insurance shall terminate on delivery of the goods sold, but in no ev shall this insurance extend beyond sixty (60) days after completion of discharge of the insured goods from the carrying vessel at such port or place.

2) If the insured goods are to be forwarded to the final destination named in the Policy or any other destination, this insurance shall terminate in accordance with Section 1 above.

IV. Duty of the Insured:

It is the duty of the Insured to attend to all matters as specified hereunder, failing which the company reserves the right to reject his claim for any loss if and when such failure prejudice the rights of the Company:

1. The Insured shall take delivery of the insured goods in good time upon their arrival at the port of destination named in the Policy. In the event of any damage to the goods, the Insured shall immediately apply for survey to the Survey and/or settling agent stipulated in the Policy. If the insured goods are found short in entire package or packages or to show apparent traces of damage, the Insured shall obtain from the carrier, bailee or other relevent authorities (Customs and Port Authorities etc.) certificate of loss or damage and/or shortlanded memo, Should the carrier, bailee or the other relevent authorities be responsible for such shortage or damage, the Insured shall lodge a claim with them in writing and, if necessary, obtain their confirmation of an extension of the time limit of validity of such claim.

2. The Insured shall, and the Company may also, take reasonable measures immediately in salvaging the goods or preventing or minimizing a loss or damage thereto. The measures so taken by the Insured or by the Company shall not be considered respectively, as a waiver of abandonment hereunder, or as an acceptance thereof.

3. In case of a change of voyage or any omission or error in the description of the interest, the name of the vessel or voyage, this insurance shall remain in force only upon prompt notice to this Company when the Insured becomes aware of the same and payment of an additional premium if required.

4. The following documents shall accompany any claim hereunder made against this Company:

Original Policies, Bill of Lading, Invoice, Packing List, Tally Sheet, Weight Memo, Certificate of Loss or Damage and/or Shortland Memo, Survey Report, Statement of Claim.

If any third party is involved, documents relative to pursuing of recovery from such party should also be included.

5. Immediate notice should be given to the Company when the Cargo Owner's actual responsibility under the Contract of Affreightment "Both to Blame Collision" Clause becomes known.

V. The Time of Validity of A Claim:

The time of validity of a claim under this insurance shall not exceed a period of two years counting from the time of completion of discharge of the insured goods from the seagoing vessel at the final port of discharge.

COPY

1. Goods consigned from (Exporter's business name, address, country) SHANGHAI UNIVERSAL TRADING CO., LTD. MAYLING PLAZA, 131 DONGFANG ROAD, SHANGHAI 200120, CHINA	Reference No. G18310067273073
	GENERALIZED SYSTEM OF PREFERENCES CERTIFICATE OF ORIGIN (Combined declaration and certificate) FORM A Issued in THE PEOPLE'S REPUBLIC OF CHINA (country)
2. Goods consigned to (Consignee's name, address, country) TIVOLIAN TRADING B.V. P.O. BOX 1783, HEIMAN DULLAERTOLEIN 3, 3024CA ROTTERDAM, NETHERLANDS	See Notes overleaf

3. Means of transport and route (as far as known) FROM SHANGHAI, CHINA TO ROTTERDAM, NETHERLANDS BY SEA	4. For official use Verification: www.chinaorigin.gov.cn

5. Item number	6. Marks and numbers of packages	7. Number and Kind of packages; description of goods	8. Origin criterion (see Notes overleaf)	9. Gross weight or other quantity	10. Number and date of invoices
01	CE/IMP.087 TIV-PO-CSH0873 ROTTERDAM CARTON NO. 1 - 126 KB0278 CE/IMP.087 TIV-PO-CSH0873 ROTTERDAM CARTON NO. 1 - 126 KB5411 F-TOYS 228 TIV-PO-CSH0873 ROTTERDAM CARTON NO. 1 - 67 KB0677 F-TOYS 228 TIV-PO-CSH0873 ROTTERDAM CARTON NO. 1 - 67 KB7900	386 (THREE HUNDRED AND EIGHTY SIX) CARTONS OF PLUSH TOYS *** THE GOODS ARE OF CHINESE ORIGIN. CREDIT NUMBER: AM/VA07721SLC	"P"	3155.0KGS	HY-TIV-INV0373 OCT. 29, 2018

11. Certification It is hereby certified, on the basis of control carried out, that the declaration by the exporter is correct. 董建平 SHANGHAI, CHINA NOV. 7, 2018 Place and date, signature and stamp of certifying authority	12. Declaration by the exporter The undersigned hereby declares that the above details and statements are correct; that all the goods were produced in CHINA (country) and that they comply with the origin requirements specified for those goods in the Generalized System of Preferences for goods exported to NETHERLANDS (importing country) 薛颖 SHANGHAI, CHINA NOV. 7, 2018 Place and date, signature of authorized signatory

中华人民共和国出入境检验检疫
ENTRY-EXIT INSPECTION AND QUARANTINE
OF THE PEOPLE'S REPUBLIC OF CHINA

正 本
ORIGINAL
第1页 共1页 Page 1 of 1

编号 No.: 034909628062673

QUALITY
INSPECTION CERTIFICATE

发货人 Consignor	SHANGHAI UNIVERSAL TRADING CO., LTD.
收货人 Consignee	TIVOLIAN TRADING B.V.

		标记及号码 Mark & No.	
品名 Description of Goods	PLUSH TOYS	CE/IMP.087 TIV-PO-CSH0873 ROTTERDAM CARTON NO. 1 - 126 KB0278	CE/IMP.087 TIV-PO-CSH0873 ROTTERDAM CARTON NO. 1 - 126 KB5411
报检数量/重量 Quantity/Weight Declared	-2080-SETS /-3155-KGS		
包装种类及数量 Number and Type of Packages	-386-CTNS	F-TOYS 228 TIV-PO-CSH0873 ROTTERDAM CARTON NO. 1 - 67 KB0677	F-TOYS 228 TIV-PO-CSH0873 ROTTERDAM CARTON NO. 1 - 67 KB7900
运输工具 Means of Conveyance	COSCO HELLAS / 013W		

检验结果:
RESULTS OF INSPECTION:

At the request of consignor, our inspectors attended at the warehouse of the consignment on 2008/5/16. In accordance with SN/T0304-1993 and the relevant state stipulations GB2828, GB6675 and GB9832, 13 cartons were taken and opened at random for visual inspection, from which representative samples were drawn and inspected according to the stipulation mentioned above. The results are as follows:

Appearance: Pass
Specifications: Pass
Quantity: -2080-SETS, -386-CTNS
Safety: Pass
Hygienics: Pass

CREDIT NUMBER: AM/VA07721SLC

印证地点 Place of Issue　**SHANGHAI**　　签证日期 Date of Issue　**NOV. 4, 2018**

Official Stamp　022

授权签字人 Authorized Officer　**XU SAILI**　　签 名 Signature　*徐赛莉*

我们已尽所知和最大能力实施上述检验，不能因我们签发本证书而免除卖方或其他方面根据合同和法律所承担的产品质量责任和其他责任。
All inspections are carried out conscientiously to the best of our knowledge and ability. This certificate does not in any respect absolve the seller and other related parties from his contractual and legal obligations especiall when product quality is concerned.

CERTIFICATE

DATE: NOV. 13, 2018

TO WHOM IT MAY CONCERN

CREDIT NUMBER: AM/VA07721SLC
B/L NO.: COSU89302173
OCEAN VESSEL: COSCO HELLAS / 013W

WE HEREBY CERTIFY THAT THE CARRYING VESSEL BELONGS TO CONFERENCE LINE AND IS NOT MORE THAN TWENTY YEARS OLD.

上海中远海运集装箱船务代理有限公司
COSCO SHIPPING LINES AGENCY (SHANGHAI) CO., LTD

SPECIMEN

AS AGENT
for the Carrier: COSCO SHIPPING LINES CO., LTD

上海环宇贸易有限公司
Shanghai Universal Trading Co., Ltd.

CERTIFICATE

CREDIT NUMBER: AM/VA07721SLC

WE HEREBY CERTIFY THAT ONE SET OF NON-NEGOTIABLE SHIPPING DOCUMENTS TOGETHER WITH ONE ORIGINAL GSP FORM A HAVE BEEN SENT TO THE APPLICANT BY DHL WITHIN 72 HOURS AFTER SHIPMENT.

上 海 环 宇 贸 易 有 限 公 司
SHANGHAI UNIVERSAL TRADING CO., LTD.

(SIGNATURE)

上海环宇贸易有限公司
Shanghai Universal Trading Co., Ltd.

FAX

To：	Tivolian Trading B.V.		**From：**	Shanghai Universal Trading Co., Ltd.
Tel. No.：	+(31)10 4767418		**Tel. No.：**	+(86)21 58818844
Page：	Page 1, Total 1 Page		**Date：**	Nov. 14, 2018
Fax-No.：	+(31)10 4767422		**Fax-No.：**	+(86)21 58818766

SHIPPING ADVICE

CREDIT NUMBER: AM/VA07721SLC

　　We hereby inform you that the goods under the above credit were shipped on Nov. 13, 2018. The details of shipment are stated below:

Date of Departure: Nov. 13, 2018

Shipping Marks:

CE/IMP.087	CE/IMP.087	F-TOYS 228	F-TOYS 228
TIV-PO-CSH0873	TIV-PO-CSH0873	TIV-PO-CSH0873	TIV-PO-CSH0873
ROTTERDAM	ROTTERDAM	ROTTERDAM	ROTTERDAM
CARTON NO. 1 - 126	CARTON NO. 1 - 126	CARTON NO. 1 - 67	CARTON NO. 1 - 67
KB0278	KB5411	KB0677	KB7900

Number of L/C: AM/VA07721SLC
Number of B/L: COSU89302173
Number of Contract: HY-TIV0373
Number of Order: TIV-PO-CSH0873
Number of Cartons: 386 cartons
Total Gross Weight: 3155 kgs
Goods Value: USD26660.80 CIF
Commodity: Plush Toys
Ocean Vessel: Cosco Hellas / 013W
From: Shanghai
To: Rotterdam
ETA: Dec.12, 2018

Yours sincerely,

王凯

David Wang
Shanghai Universal Trading Co., Ltd

中国上海市东方路 131 号美陵广场 1201-1216 室
Rm. 1201-1216 Mayling Plaza, 131 Dongfang Rd., Shanghai, 200120, China
电话/Tel: 86-21-58818844　传真/Fax: 86-21-58818766　网址/Web: www.universal.com.cn

🗨 示范评析

1. 出口商在向银行交单议付前会依据信用证、信用证修改书、《跟单信用证统一惯例》(UCP600)以及出口货物明细(或出口制单明细),对所有的议付单据进行细致严格的审核,本着严格相符的原则,将单据中所有的不符点消灭在交单之前,从而保证信用证项下的安全收汇。作为出口货物的详尽说明,商业发票和装箱单在国内履约环节中曾多次被作为随附单据使用,但出口商在将其作为信用证项下的议付单据提交时还是需要再次对其加以严格审核。案例中经过审单发现的商业发票和装箱单尚存在多处不符点,虽然这些不符点对国内履约并无大碍,但的确会极大地影响受益人获得开证银行的付款保证。

2. 本案例信用证的兑付方式为 Available with any bank by negotiation,所以出口商可以选择在任何银行进行交单议付。由于中国银行上海分行是信用证的通知行,同时也是环宇公司的开户银行,所以环宇公司在该行进行了交单,汇票上的收款人也就填写了该行的名称。

当然,环宇公司向该行提交的是"交单委托书"而非"议付申请书",从这一点我们可以初步判断该笔交易并没有进行出口押汇,中国银行上海分行的角色不是议付行而是交单行、代收行。

3. 如果信用证进行过修改,受益人也接受这些修改,那么在其制单、审单时就应将信用证和信用证修改书结合起来查看,这样才能符合"信用证"的要求。

Q:信用证项下受益人应向银行提交哪些单据?

A:信用证中关于提交单据的要求一般会集中体现在 Documents Required 部分,但有时在 Additional Conditions 或是 Special Conditions 中也会出现对单据的要求。因此我们应全面细致地分析信用证才能保证不遗漏单据。另外,议付信用证项下通常还需要提交汇票,具体要看信用证中是否有 Draft 或是 Bill of Exchange 条款。

Q:为什么在审单意见中说装箱单的名称与信用证规定不符?

A:信用证中规定的单据名称是"PACKING LIST/WEIGHT MEMO",不是指让出口商(受益人)在"装箱单"和"重量单"这两种单据中任选一种提交,而是指要求提交名称为"装箱单和重量单"的单据,因此出口商必须按要求显示正确的单据名称。我们应当注意在信用证中符号"/"往往有多种含义,处理时必须谨慎小心。

指 南

随着贸易术语在国际货物买卖中的普遍采用以及信用证制度的不断发展完善，"一手交钱，一手交货"的交易方式基本已被以单据买卖为核心的"象征性交货"所代替。在这种"象征性交货"条件下，卖方以提交规定的单据作为其履行交货义务的象征和收取货款的依据，而买方则须凭合格的单据履行其付款的义务。因此，结汇单据的作用和地位在国际贸易中就越发显得重要，熟悉它们的基本填制方法和流转程序也成为了从事国际贸易的人员必须具备的业务操作技能。

ⓘ 出口结汇的方式

信用证项下的单据经审核无误后，银行将按信用证规定的付汇条件，将外汇结付给出口商，这就是通常所说的"结汇"。

在我国的出口业务中，议付信用证主要有三种结汇方式：第一种是出口押汇，即银行收取单据作为质押，按汇票面值，扣除从议付日起到估计收到开证行或偿付行票款之日的利息，将货款先行垫付给出口商（即受益人）；第二种是收妥结汇，即银行收到单据后不叙做出口押汇，而是直接将单据寄交开证行，待开证行将货款划给银行后再向出口商结汇；第三种是定期结汇，即银行收到单据后，约定在一定期限内向出口商结汇。

值得注意的是，按照 UCP600 的规定，指定银行在相符交单的情况下，买入汇票及单据，在其获得偿付之前向受益人预付或同意预付款项，才被称之为"议付"。所以在第一种出口押汇方式下，银行所做的就是议付行为，而第二种收妥结汇方式下，银行是不能取得议付行资格的，只能算是交单行、代收行。第三种定期结汇方式下，则要具体看所约定的结汇时间与银行收到开证行货款时间之间的关系。

议付是可以追索的。如开证行拒付，议付行可向出口商追还预付的货款。

ⓘ 常见的出口结汇单据

（一）汇票 Bill of Exchange/Draft

汇票是出票人（drawer）向受票人（drawee）签发的无条件的书面付款命令，要求受票人按照汇票上所列的付款期限、金额向指定的收款人（payee）进行支付。

（二）商业发票 Commercial Invoice

商业发票是卖方向买方开出的载明销售货物详情的单据。其主要功能为：
◇ 收付货款和记账的凭证；
◇ 办理订舱、投保、报关等手续时对货物的说明；
◇ 卖方缮制其他单据的依据。

商业发票是发票（Invoice）的一种类型。发票还有海关发票（Customs Invoice）、税务发票（Tax Invoice）、最终发票（Final Invoice）、领事发票（Consular Invoice）等多种类型。

（三）装箱单 Packing List

装箱单是表明出口货物的包装形式、包装内容、唛头、数量、重量、体积或件数的单据。它一般由卖方出具，是商业发票的补充，目的是便于买方清点、分拣和销售货物，同时也可供第三方查验核对货物。装箱单是包装单据（Packing Document）的一种类型。包装单据还有重量单（Weight List 或 Weight Note 或 Weight Memo）、尺码单（Measurement List）、规格单（Specification List）、搭配单（Assortment List）等多种类型，这些单据根据其具体名称的不同，在记载内容上也各有侧重。

（四）海运提单 Ocean Bill of Lading

海运提单由承运人或其代理人、或船长或其代理人签发，是证明其已收到特定货物，允诺将货物运至特定目的地，并交付给收货人的凭证，也是收货人在目的港据以向承运人或其代理提取货物的凭证。海运提单是运输单据（Transport Document）的一种类型。运输单据还有不可转让的海运单（Non-negotiable Sea

Waybill)、空运单据(Air Transport Document)、承运收据(Cargo Receipt)、多式联运单据(Multi-model Transport Document)等多种类型。

(五) 保险单　Insurance Policy

保险单由保险公司或承保人的代理或代表签发,是承保人根据投保人的要求,表示已经承诺保险责任的凭证,是承保人与投保人之间的正式合同,也是在被保险货物遭受损失时被保险人索赔以及承保人理赔的依据。保险单是保险单据(Insurance Document)的一种类型。保险单据还有保险凭证(Insurance Certificate)、预约保单项下的声明书(Declaration under an Open Cover)等多种类型。

(六) 受益人声明/证明　Beneficiary's Declaration/Beneficiary's Certificate

受益人声明/证明因其由受益人出具而得名,内容通常是受益人声明或证明其已履行某种义务或办理某项工作,例如已发装船通知、已寄单、已寄样等。受益人声明/证明没有固定的格式,一般按信用证要求临时缮制。

(七) 船公司证明　Shipping Company's Certificate

船公司证明的内容通常涉及船龄、船籍、航线、航运组织等。船公司证明必须由船公司出具并签署,内容根据信用证的具体规定。值得注意的是,我们应仔细分析信用证中需要船公司证明的具体内容,如有特殊要求则在出口订舱时就应向船公司提出。

(八) 原产地证明　Certificate of Origin

原产地证明的主要作用是向进口商提供货物原产地或制造地的证明文件。

原产地证明的出具人必须符合信用证规定。例如:信用证规定 certificate of origin issued by Chamber of Commerce,则应由商会,即贸促会签发;信用证规定 certificate of origin issued by competent authority,则可由贸促会或海关签发。如果信用证没有对出具人做出规定,则也可由出口商自行签发。

有时信用证会要求提交一种特殊的原产地证明——普惠制原产地证明格式A(GSP Form A)。普惠制,即普遍优惠制,简称 GSP,是一种关税制度,是发达国家(给惠国)对从发展中国家(受惠国)进口某些适合的产品时给予减免或免税的优惠待遇。也就是说,GSP Form A 除了向进口商证明了货物的原产地或制造地,还能使货物在给惠国享受优惠关税待遇。我国是发展中国家,目前已有欧盟 25 国、瑞士、日本、加拿大、澳大利亚、俄罗斯等多个国家对我国实行普惠制。当然,并不是所有出口到上述国家的货物,进口商都会向我方要求提供 Form A,具体还要看商品类别。在我国 Form A 统一由各地的海关签发。

(九) 检验证书 Inspection Certificate

检验证书是由检验机构或制造厂商等对商品进行检验后出具的关于商品品质、规格、重量、数量等各方面或某方面鉴定的书面证明文件。检验证书的出具人必须符合信用证规定。

ⓘ 信用证项下结汇单据的填制与审核

在信用证交易中,制单审单是整个业务操作中非常重要的环节。如有失误,小则增加费用支出,如不符点处理费,大则失去信用证的付款保证而改为托收,徒增收汇风险。因此出口商在缮制、审核结汇单据时,不仅应考虑到单据的用途、填写必备的内容,而且还必须与信用证条款、UCP600 中的相关条款以及银行实务国际标准(international standard banking practice,ISBP)相吻合,这样才能做到相符交单、顺利收汇。

(一) 结汇单据填制与审核的基本要求

◇ 与信用证条款、UCP600 的相关条款以及银行实务国际标准保持一致

在采用信用证交易的条件下,出口商(即信用证受益人)必须明确:第一,银行处理的是单据,而不是单据可能涉及的货物、服务或履约行为。第二,单据不仅应与信用证条款一致,还必须与 UCP600 的相关条款以及银行实务国际标准保持一致。第三,银行仅基于单据表面判断是否构成相符交单。

这些原则应从两方面去理解。一方面,出口商提交的单据应做到"单证相符、单单一致"。单据的内容首先要符合信用证有关条款的规定,同时单据与单据之间不能互相矛盾。例如:提单上的毛重与装箱单上的毛重应保持一致,不能因为信用证上没有规定具体的货物重量而显示不同的数据。同时还要引起重视的是,"单证一致"不仅指单据的内容要与信用证一致,还包括单据提交的

份数、正副本、出具人、提交的时间和地点等都要符合信用证的要求。另一方面，银行仅审核单据表面是否构成相符交单。也就是说，即使出口商实际履行了某项义务，但如果未在单据上按信用证的规定体现出来，也会被银行视为单证不符而拒付。

尽管 UCP600 相比 UCP500 而言，在一定程度上降低了"单证相符、单单一致"的标准，在一些地方不要求"完全一致"而改用"不冲突、不矛盾"的原则，但在判断相符交单的标准中加入了银行实务国际标准，而银行实务国际标准却是灵活的，不确定的，从而给受益人和审单银行都带来了一定程度的不确定性。因此在实践中，出口商往往还是执行严格的标准来对待信用证单据，以保证安全收汇。

◇　与出口合同保持一致

信用证是买方（开证申请人）依照买卖合同及有关贸易惯例向银行申请开立的，作为银行审核单据以决定是否付款的依据。因此，一般买方都会要求开证银行在信用证中加列一些关于货物描述的条款，以便约束受益人单据上所列的货物与买卖双方在合同中约定的一致。但是，信用证毕竟不能代替买卖合同。特别是对于一些比较复杂的货物买卖，比如，大型的成套设备，信用证中没有也不可能详细规定货物的具体规格型号、技术指标、单价，以及包装情况。对于这些内容，受益人在制单时只能按照合同的有关规定缮制，但须注意，这些内容不能与信用证的规定相抵触。

◇　内容完整，符合有关法规及商业习惯

虽然结汇单据的填制有信用证的规范以及买卖合同的制约，但就单据制作本身而言，信用证和合同的规定不可能是面面俱到的。制单时必须符合国家的法律法规以及商业习惯、业务流程，能提供主要功能。例如，信用证中一般不会规定汇票必须由出票人签署，但一般各国的票据法都规定"汇票要由出票人签署，否则视为无效"，因此出口商不能因为信用证没有相关条款而不在汇票上签字。又如，信用证没有规定发票要显示大写金额，但发票作为一种销售单据，其大写金额作为一种常规信息应予记载，出口商一般应规范在商业发票上显示其大写及小写金额。再如，检验证书的日期一般都早于装船日期，因为出口商的检验通常应该在货物装船前完成，尽管在信用证没有明确规定的情况下，银行也有可能拒绝签发日期晚于提单日的装船前检验证书。

◇ 及时制单审单

结汇单据的种类繁多,不仅单据与单据之间有联系,而且制单工作本身也是一项和发货装运联系在一起的综合性的工作。首先,在办理各项履约手续时提供给有关部门的单据中有一些单据就是结汇单据,例如办理原产地认证时提交的原产地证书,其本身一般就是信用证项下要求的结汇单据,所以在制作该单据时就应注意要符合信用证要求,而不应待到装运后准备结汇单据时才意识到信用证要求其加注证明文句。又如,办理投保时就应按信用证的要求确定保险金额,而不应等到要交单时才发现投保加成率不符合信用证规定。再如,商业发票在很多业务环节如托运、报检、报关时都需要提交,尽管在上述业务环节时受理机构不会在意信用证对商业发票的特殊要求,但出口商必须在最后交单结汇前对其进行认真的审核、修改,因为银行将以信用证为标准进行审单。另外,结汇单据中的部分单据并非由出口商自行缮制,例如提单、保险单等,对于这些第三方单据,除了在办理相关手续时应事先告知特殊要求,还必须在收到单据后及时审核,以便在发现问题后能及时联系修改。

(二) 结汇单据的填制与审核

◇ 汇票

从汇票的定义上讲,汇票是出票人签发的,命令付款人在见票时或者在指定日期无条件支付确定的金额给收款人的票据。而在以议付信用证结算的交易中,就通常表现为受益人按照信用证的规定签发汇票,指示开证行在信用证规定的付款时间支付信用证金额给议付行。

汇票原则上可以由出口商自行缮制,但在实际业务中,出口商往往向交单银行领取印就的汇票格式进行填制。各银行的汇票格式略有不同,但通常都是一式两联,第一联印有"First Bill of exchange(SECOND being unpaid)"字样,第二联印有"Second Bill of exchange(FIRST being unpaid)"字样。

汇票的主要栏目有:

汇票号码　No.

可自行编制,通常与发票号码相一致。

BILL OF EXCHANGE

No. **TR-INVWR59235**

For **US$17,500.00**   **SHANGHAI, CHINA** , **15 APRIL 2018**

                                                        (Date)

At ***********45 DAYS AFTER********** sight of this **FIRST** Bill of Exchange (second being unpaid)

Pay to **CHINA CONSTRUCTION BANK, SHANGHAI BRANCH**

or order the sum of **SAY UNITED STATES DOLLARS SEVENTEEN THOUSAND AND FIVE**

HUNDRED ONLY   Value received and charge the same

to account of

Drawn under **COMMERZBANK AG FRANKFURT AM MAIN**

L/C No. **AN-29854**   dated **20 FEBRUARY 2018**

To: **COMMERZBANK AG**
      FRANKFURT AM MAIN   **SHANGHAI TIANYUAN TRADING COMPANY**

                                                          季立君

小写金额 For

一般与信用证金额一致，包括其币种。

出票地点、日期

即签发汇票的地点和日期，一般在出口地，由受益人在交单议付当天签发。汇票的出票日期无论如何不能迟于信用证的交单到期日。

付款期限 At...sight

根据信用证的汇票条款（Draft at...）填写。

例如：

信用证规定 Drafts at sight，即见票即付，

则在"At"与"sight"之间的横线上打上" *** "或"——"，或直接打上"At Sight"。

信用证规定 Drafts at 30 days after sight，即见票后 30 天付款，

则在"At"与"sight"之间的横线上打上"30 days after"。

信用证规定 Drafts at 30 days after date，即出票后 30 天付款，

则在"At"与"sight"之间的横线上打上"30 days after date"。

信用证规定 Drafts at 30 days after B/L date,即提单日后 30 天付款,
则在"At"与"sight"之间的横线上打上"30 days after B/L date"。

收款人　Pay to...or order

通常直接填写议付行的名称。

值得注意的是,Pay to...or order 的含义是"付给……或其指定人",这意味着这种汇票的收款人还可以通过一定的方式将收款权指定给其他人。因此在实际业务中,也有出口商在"Pay to"和"or order"之间打上自己的名称,在向银行交单议付时,再通过背书指定议付银行为收款人。

大写金额　the sum of...

出票条款　Drawn under...L/C No. ...dated...

即开立汇票的依据。在信用证交易中,开立汇票的依据当然就是信用证,即根据××银行于×年×月×日开立的号码为××的信用证开立汇票,所以一般就填写开证行名称、信用证号码和信用证日期。如信用证有规定,则按信用证的要求填写。

受票人　To

即付款人。根据信用证的汇票条款填写。

例如:信用证规定 Drawee:ABC Bank,则付款人即填写 ABC Bank。

信用证规定 draft(drawn/value) on us/ourselves,则付款人即填写开证行。

值得注意的是,信用证规定的汇票的付款人并非一定是开证行,也有可能是另一家银行,这家银行在信用证业务中就被称为"付款行"。汇票的付款人填写另一家银行,并不会免除开证行在信用证项下的付款责任。在填写银行名称时,同时还要注明分行名称或是地址。

出票人签署

在汇票上通常没有栏目名称,只是由出票人签署在汇票的右下角填写公司名称并签署。也有公司在签署前面加上"For and on behalf of"来表示出票人身份。在信用证交易中,出票人一般为受益人。

背书

汇票背书是指汇票的收款人在汇票的背面写上自己的名称并签字,再把汇票交付给受让人的行为。汇票背书的目的是转让收款权,也就是说汇票原先指定的收款人可以通过背书的方式将自己的收款权利转让给受让人。汇票背书有多种方式,例如记名背书,即指定受让人,写明"付给××或其指定人"。

若受益人在开具的汇票中将自己指定为收款人,当其向议付银行交单时,他便会将汇票记名背书给议付行,如:

Pay to CHINA CONSTRUCTION BANK, SHANGHAI BRANCH

SHANGHAI TIANYUAN TRADING COMPANY

季立君

◇ 发票

发票的基本填制方法在**第六章 出口托运订舱的指南**(第 215 页)中已有介绍,这里主要以 UCP600 为依据,分析发票作为信用证项下结汇单据时的缮制和审核要点。

名称

发票的具体名称应与信用证要求相符。

如信用证仅要求提交"Invoice"而未做进一步界定,发票的名称可以是"Invoice",也可以是 Commercial Invoice(商业发票),Tax Invoice(税务发票),Final Invoice(最终发票)等,但是不能提交 Provisional Invoice(临时发票)、Pro-forma Invoice(预开发票)或类似发票。所以,最直接也是最稳妥的方法就是始终保持发票的具体名称与信用证的规定完全一致。

出具和签名

除可转让信用证以外,发票通常由受益人出具。在受益人的公司信笺上缮制商业发票即表明该发票是由受益人出具的。如果不用公司信笺缮制,也可以在 Seller 一栏注明受益人名称,或是发票最下方打上 issued by 后跟受益人名称。

根据 UCP600 的规定,除非信用证有明确要求,否则发票可以不经签署。

抬头

除可转让信用证以外,发票通常以申请人为抬头。可以表示为"To:××",也可以表示为"For account of ××",或者直接打上"Buyer:××"。

运输标志

若信用证规定的运输标志的件号未明确,例如"…/C/NO 1-UP",则应以实际出运货物的总件数来替代 UP。

货物描述

发票中的货物描述(Description of Goods)必须与信用证中的货物描述(Description of Goods and/or Services)一致。货物细节可以在发票的若干处显示,但合并在一起时必须与信用证中的完全一致。如果某贸易术语是货物描述的一部分,则表示发票必须显示信用证指明的贸易术语,而且如果货物描述提供了贸易术语的出处,则表示发票也必须标明该出处。例如信用证货物描述中显示 C&F,而发票上显示为 CFR,则被视为未满足信用证要求,又如信用证货物描述中显示 CIF Rotterdame Incoterms 2000,而发票上如仅显示为 CIF Rotterdam,则也被视为未满足信用证要求。

金额和币种

发票显示的单价和币种必须与信用证中的一致。一般情况下,不允许分批装运的信用证中,发票金额应与信用证金额一致。

数量、重量和尺码

发票显示的货物数量、重量和尺码不得与其他单据显示的相应数值相矛盾。

信用证要求在发票上加注的内容

一般加注在单据中间部位的明显处,如填写在 **Description of Goods** 一栏的空白处。

正本

在受益人原始信笺上出具的或是经签署的商业发票,均可被视为正本,也可直接在其名称下方标注"Original"字样。

◇　装箱单

装箱单的基本填制方法在**第六章　出口托运订舱**的指南(第 216 页)中已有介绍,这里主要以 UCP600 为依据,分析装箱单作为信用证项下结汇单据时的缮制和审核要点。

名称

装箱单的具体名称应与信用证要求相符。例如信用证仅要求提交"Packing

List"而装箱单显示为"Weight Memo",则视为不符。

若信用证要求提交详细包装单据(Detailed Packing List),则除了一般将单据名称显示为"Detailed Packing List",更重要的是必须在内容上列出每件包装的内容及重量、尺码等其他相关资料。

货物描述

装箱单中的货物描述(Description of Goods)可使用统称,而不必像商业发票那样详尽,但不得与信用证中的货物描述冲突。

数量、毛重、净重和尺码

一般地,装箱单上显示的数量、毛重、净重和尺码总是每个货号的数量、毛重、净重和尺码的小计总量。如果信用证要求装箱单上要显示单件包装的内含数量(composition)、毛重、净重和尺码,则需要在装箱单中间的空白部分另行填制。

需要注意的是,当信用证需要显示单件包装的体积时,通常我们会用该货号的总体积除以该货号的包装件数来计算单件包装的体积,这样可以避免因四舍五入保留小数的缘故而导致表面上看"单件体积×件数≠总体积"的问题。

以上这些信息不得与其他单据显示的相应数值相矛盾。

运输标志

若信用证规定的运输标志的件号未明确,例如"…/C/NO 1-UP",则应以实际出运货物的总件数来替代 UP。

信用证要求在装箱单上加注的内容

一般加注在单据中间部位的明显处,如填写在 **Description of Goods** 一栏的空白处。

正本

在受益人原始信笺上出具的或是经签署的装箱单,均可被视为正本,也可直接在其名称下方标注"Original"字样。

◇　提单

B/L No.

提单号码。一般与十联单上的 D/R No.保持一致。

 **SITC CONTAINER LINES CO., LTD.**

	B/L NO. **8SHADUB3EH011**

Port to Port or Combined Transport
BILL OF LADING

1. Shipper

SHANGHAI TIAN YUAN TRADING CO., LTD.
ROOM 1105, RUIJIN BLDG.,
205 SOUTH MAOMING ROAD,
SHANGHAI CHINA

2. Consignee

TO ORDER

3. Notify Party (It is agreed that no responsibility shall attach to the Carrier or his agent for failure to notify)

TERI INTERNATIONAL GMBH
56 KEDENBURGSTRASSE D-758294 HAMBURG
GERMANY

RECEIVED for shipment in external apparent good order and condition, unless otherwise indicated. The total number of packages or units stuffed in the container, the description of the goods and the weights shown in this Bill of Lading are furnished by the Merchants and the containers are already sealed by the Merchants, and which the carrier has no reasonable means of checking and is not a part of this Bill of Lading contract. The carrier has issued the number of Bills of Lading stated below, all of this tenor and date, one of the original Bills of Lading must be surrendered and endorsed or signed against the delivery of the goods or the delivery order and whereupon any other Bills of Lading shall be void.

NOTE: Notwithstanding any customs or privileges to the contrary, the Merchant's attention is drawn to the fact that the Merchant, in accepting this Bill of Lading, expressly agrees to be bound by all the stipulations, exceptions, limitations, liberties, terms and conditions attached hereto or stated herein, whether written, printed, stamped or otherwise incorporated on the front and/or reverse side hereof as well as the provisions of the Carrier's published Tariff Rules, Regulations and Schedules, without exceptions, as fully as if they were all signed by such Merchant, and the carrier's undertaking to carry the goods is made on the basis of the merchant's acceptance and agreements as aforesaid.

This Bill of Lading is governed by the laws of the People's Republic of China. Any claims and disputes arising under or in connection with this Bill of Lading shall be determined by Shanghai Maritime Court or Qingdao Maritime Court at the exclusion of the Courts of any other country.

The printed terms and conditions appearing on the face and reverse side of this Bill of Lading are available at www.sitc.com in SITC's published tariffs.

4. Pre-Carriage by*	5. Place of Receipt*
(Applicable only when this document is used as a Combined Transport Bill of Lading)	(Applicable only when this document is used as a Combined Transport Bill of Lading)
6. Ocean Vessel Voy. No.	**7. Port of Loading**
YUXIANG V.345	SHANGHAI
8. Port of Discharge	**9. Place of Delivery***
HAMBURG	
	(Applicable only when this document is used as a Combined Transport Bill of Lading)

ORIGINAL

Container No./Seal No. Marks and Numbers	Number and Kind of packages: description of goods	Gross Weight	Measurement
TERI WR59235 HAMBURG CTN. NO.1-500 CCLU2356117/20GP/SITE47113	1X20GP CONTAINER FCL/FCL 500 CARTONS PORCELAIN DINNERWARE CY - CY SHIPPER'S LOAD , COUNT AND SEAL FREIGHT PREPAID L/C NO. AN-29854 DATED 20 FEBURARY 2018 ISSUED BY COMMERZBANK AG FRANKFURT AM MAIN Above particulars declared by shipper. Carrier is not responsible. (see clause 12)	9000.000 KGS	24.000 CBM

PARTICULAR FURNISHED BY THE MERCHANT

10. Total No. of Containers Or Packages (in words)	SAY ONE CONTAINER ONLY				
11. Freight & Charges	Rate	Unit	Prepaid	Collect	

Prepaid at SHANGHAI	Payable at	Number of Original B(s)/L THREE
Place of issue and Date SHANGHAI 13 MAR 2018		12. Declared Value Charge

LADEN ON BOARD THE VESSEL		AS AGENT FOR THE CARRIER SITC CONTAINER LINES CO., LTD
DATE	**BY**	SIGN:
13 MAR 2018	YU XIANG V.345	SITC CONTAINER LINES (SHANGHAI) CO., LTD.

SPECIMEN

Shipper Consignee Notify Party

这三栏的填制方法在**第六章 出口订舱**的指南"出口货物订舱委托书"(第212页)中已有介绍。在审核提单时,就应特别注意与信用证中提单条款的对应。

例如:信用证规定 consigned to ABC Co.,提单的 Consignee 就必须打上 ABC Co.,而不能写成 To order of ABC Co.。前者被称为记名收货人,后者就是指示收货人。

又如:信用证规定 made out to order of shipper,提单就必须打上 To order of shipper,而不能写成 To order。前者被称为记名指示,后者就是不记名指示。

注意在记名指示抬头中,必须显示具体指示人的名称。例如,信用证规定提单收货人为 to order of issuing bank,则在提单的 Consignee 中必须显示具体 issuing bank 的名称,如 to order of ABC Bank。唯一的例外是 to order of shipper,鉴于提单上已显示 shipper 的具体名称,填写收货人时便可以简单地写上 to order of shipper。

被通知人 Notify Party 也应按照信用证的规定填写有关方,并注明要求的联系信息。有时,信用证可能规定两个被通知人,提单也应按此缮制。

Ocean Vessel Voy. No.

填写货物实际装船的船名、航次。

Port of Loading Port of Discharge

填写实际装运的装货港和卸货港。注意须与信用证规定的装运港和目的港一致。但若信用证规定为笼统的区域或范围,如 port of loading:China Ports,则提单必须显示具体的港口名称,而且该港口应位于信用证规定的地理区域或范围之内。

如有转运,可在 Port of Discharge 中注明,例如 Hamburg via Hongkong。

Pre-Carriage by Place of Receipt Place of Delivery

前程运输,接货地,交货地。这三栏适用于多种运输方式联合运输的情况。

Container No./Seal No. Marks & Nos.

集装箱号码/封志号,运输标志。运输标志应与信用证规定一致,如有多个运输标志,则应逐个列明。但若信用证规定的运输标志的件号未明确,例如"…/C/NO 1-UP",则应以实际出运货物的总件数来替代 UP。

Number and Kind of packages：Description of Goods

包装件数和包装种类,货物描述。此处的货物描述可使用统称,不必像商业发票那样详尽,但不得与信用证中的货物描述冲突。在此栏的空白处,一般还会显示以下内容:

Freight Prepaid

运费条款。根据不同的运费交付安排,一般有 Freight Prepaid 或 Freight to Collect 两种。如信用证对此作出了具体规定,则词句用语应与信用证一致。例如信用证规定"Freight to collect",则提单就不宜显示为"Freight Collected"。

FCL/FCL

集装箱运输方式。一般有 FCL/FCL(整箱交、整箱接)、LCL/LCL(拼箱交、拼箱接)、LCL/FCL(拼箱交、整箱接)、FCL/LCL(整箱交、拼箱接)等多种方式。

CY-CY

集装箱运输交接地点,即集装箱在发货人、承运人和收货人之间的交接方式,具体分为"CY to CY"(集装箱堆场到集装箱堆场)、"CFS to CFS"(集装箱货运站到集装箱货运站)、"DOOR to DOOR"(门到门,即发货人的货仓到收货人的货仓)等多种方式。

Shipper's load, count and seal

货主装箱、计数和加封。此类条款称为"船方免责条款"。通常适用于 FCL/FCL 运输方式下,由于货物一般由货主自行装箱封箱的,加上了船方免责条款,在箱体没有损坏的前提下,如果箱内货物有货损或者短装,船方可以免责。也有船方在货物描述前加上"Said to contain"(据称装有)。

Gross Weight   Measurement

货物的总毛重、总尺码,一般保留三位小数,通常不必按货号分开计算。

Total No. of Containers or Packages(in words)

集装箱个数或货物包装件数的大写。

Number of Original B(s)/L

船公司签发的正本提单的份数。若信用证规定了提交的正本提单份数,例如

"Full set of two original B/L"、"2/2 Marine bills of lading…",则应要求船公司照此份数签发,此栏填写"Two"。若信用证未作具体规定,只是要求提交全套正本提单,则可按船公司惯常操作,一般签发三份,此处填写"Three"。

Place and Date of Issue

提单签发地点和日期。

Laden On Board the Vessel

已装船批注。其他类似的用语还有:On Board, Shipped on board 等。

用已装船批注的方式来注明货物的装运日期,就满足了信用证规定提交已装船提单(shipped on board bill of lading)的要求。也可以通过在提单表面预先印就"On Board"或类似字样来表示该提单是已装船提单。

Signed

签发。按 UCP600 的要求,提单必须表明承运人的名称,必须由承运人(carrier)或具名代理人,或者由船长(master 或 captain)或其具名代理人签发。任何签字都必须标明其具体身份。

例如:

```
AS AGENT FOR THE CARRIER SITC CONTAINER LINES CO., LTD
SIGN:        夏任宁
        SITC CONTAINER LINES (SHANGHAI) CO., LTD.
```

此签署表明提单是由承运人的代理人签发的(as agent for the carrier),承运人的名称是 SITC Container Lines Co., Ltd,代理人的名称为 SITC Container Lines(Shanghai) Co., Ltd。

信用证要求在提单上加注的内容

一般加注在单据中间部位的明显处,如填写在 **Description of Goods** 一栏的空白处。

背书

提单背书的目的是转让收货权,所以当提单原先的收货人为指示收货人时,无论是记名指示还是不记名指示,都可以通过背书来转让收货权。

例如,信用证规定提单收货人为　　ABC Co.

则提单不需要也不能背书,因为收货人是指定的某个人,不能转让收货权。

又如,信用证规定提单收货人为　　　To order of issuing bank

或　　　To order of applicant

则提单应分别由开证行、开证申请人背书。受益人无权背书。

再如,信用证规定提单收货人为　　　To order of shipper

或　　　To order

则提单应由托运人,通常为受益人背书。

背书形式有两种:空白背书和记名背书。空白背书是指不指定被背书人,仅由背书人签章,记名背书则是先指定被背书人,然后由背书人签章。

例如,空白背书:

SHANGHAI TIANYUAN TRADING COMPANY

季立君

记名背书:

Delivered to SUMITOMO MITSUI BANKING CORPORATION

SHANGHAI TIANYUAN TRADING COMPANY

季立君

对提单的背书形式一般信用证会作具体规定,例如"blank endorsed"或者"endorsed to our order",缮制时应据此填制。如信用证没有具体规定,一般作空白背书,当然作记名背书,银行也可以接受。

清洁

银行只接受清洁的运输单据,信用证提单条款大都明示 clean on board bill of lading。但"clean"一词并不需要在提单上出现,只要提单表面没有记载明确宣称货物或包装有缺陷的条款或批注,例如 packaging is not sufficient for the sea journey.

正本

在提单名称的部分标注着"Original"字样表示正本。

◇　保险单

Insured

被保险人。除非信用证另有规定,一般为信用证受益人。

Policy No.

保单号次。填写本张保险单的号码。

中国平安
PING AN OF CHINA

中国平安财产保险股份有限公司
PING AN PROPERTY & CASUALTY INSURANCE COMPANY OF CHINA, LTD.

总公司地址：
中国·深圳
八卦岭八卦三路平安大厦
电话（Tel）：0755-82262888
图文传真（Fax）：0755-82414813
邮政编码（Postcode）：518029

Address of Head Office:
Ping An Building, No.3 Ba Gua Road.
Ba Gua Linq, Shenzhen, China

No. 060501287413

货 物 运 输 保 险 单
CARGO TRANSPORTATION INSURANCE POLICY

被保险人
Insured: **SHANGHAI TIAN YUAN TRADING CO., LTD.**

中国平安财产保险股份有限公司根据被保险人的要求及所交付约定的保险费，按照本保险单背面所载条款与下列特款，承保下述货物会运输保险，持立本保险单。
This Policy of Insurance witnesses that PING AN PROPERTY & CASUALTY INSURANCE COMPANY OF CHINA, LTD., at the request of the Insurance and in consideration of the agreed premium paid by the Insured, undertakes to insure the undermentioned goods in transportation subject to the conditions of Policy as per the clauses printed overleaf and other special clauses attached hereon.

保单号： Policy No. **PA20134534292386033578**	赔款偿付地点 Claim Payable at
发票或提单号 Invoice No. or B/L No. **INVOICE NO. TR-INVWR59235**	**HAMBURG IN USD**
运输工具 Per Conveyance S.S. **YU XIANG V. 345**	查勘代理人 Survey By: **PANDI MARINE INSURANCE GMBH**
起运日期 Slg.on or abt **AS PER B/L** 自 From **SHANGHAI, CHINA**	**WEIDENALLEE 22, D-20355,** **HAMBURG GERMANY**
至 To **HAMBURG, GERMANY**	**TEL: +49 40 35008312** **FAX: +49 40 35008315**

保险金额
Amount Insured **US$19,250.00　SAY US DOLLARS NINETEEN THOUSAND TWO HUNDRED AND FIFTY ONLY**

保险货物项目、标记、数量及包装：
Description, Marks, Quantity, & Packing of Goods:

承保条件：
Conditions:

PORCELAIN DINNERWARE

TERI
WR59235
HAMBURG
CTN. NO. 1-500

500CTNS

COVERING INSTITUTE CARGO CLAUSES (B)
AND INSTITUTE SRIKE CLAUSES - CARGO.

L/C NO. AN-29854 DATED 20 FEBRUARY 2018
ISSUED BY COMMERZBANK AG FRANKFURT AM MAIN

保单正本：2份
Number of Originals：2

签单日期
Date: MAR 10, 2018

IMPORTANT
PROCEDURE IN THE EVENT OF LOSS OR DAMAGE FOR WHICH UNDERWRITERS MAY BE LIABLE
LIABILITY OF CARRIERS, BAILEES OR OTHER THIRD PARTIES

It is the duty of the Assured and their Agents, in all cases, to take such measures as may be reasonable for the purpose of averting or minimising a loss and to ensure that all rights against Carriers, Bailees or other third parties are property preserved and exercised. In particular, the Assured of their Agents are required.
1. To claim immediately on the Carriers. Port Authorities or other Bailees for any missing package.
2. In no circumstances, except under written protest, to give clean receipts when goods are in doubtful conditions.
3. When delivery is made by Container, to ensure that the Container and its seals are examined immediately by their responsible official. If the Container is delivered damaged or with seals broken or missing or with seals other than as stated in the shipping documents, to clause the delivery receipt accordingly and retain all defective or irregular seals for subsequent identification.
4. To apply immediately for survey by Carriers' on other Bailees' Representatives if any loss or damage be apparent and claim on the Carriers or other Bailees for any actual loss or damage found at such survey.
5. To give notice in writing to the Carriers or other Bailees within 3 days of delivery if the loss or damage was not apparent at the time of taking delivery.
NOTE: the Consignee or their Agents are recommended to make themselves familiar with the Regulations of the Port, Authorities at the port of discharge.

DOCUMENTATION OF CLAIMS
To enable claims to be dealt with promptly, the Assured or their Agents are advised to submit all available supporting documents without delay, including when applicable.
1. Original policies of insurance.
2. Original or certified copy of shipping invoices, together with shipping specification and / or weight notes.
3. Original or certified copy of Bill of Lading and / or other contract of carriage.
4. Survey report or other documentary evidence to show the extent of the loss or damage.
5. Landing account and weight notes at port of discharge and final destination.
6. Correspondence exchanged with the Carriers and other Parties regarding their liability for the loss or damage.

In the event of loss or damage which may involve a claim under this insurance, no claim shall be paid unless immediate notice of such loss or damage has been given to and a Survey Report obtained from this Company's Office or Agents specified in this Policy.

For and on behalf of
PING AN PROPERTY & CASUALTY INSURANCE
COMPANY OF CHINA, LTD.

Authorized Signature

复核：　　　　　　制单：

地址及电话
Address & Tel. **11/F, 12/F, JING AN PLAZA, 8 CHANG SHU ROAD**
SHANGHAI, CHINA 52564888×6395

注：　未加盖本公司保单专用章，保单无效。

Invoice No. or B/L No.

发票号码或提单号码。

Per Conveyance S.S.

填写运输工具名称。海运方式下一般填写相应的船名、航次。

Slg on or abt

Sailing on or about, 启运日期。可以填写货物的实际装运日期, 也可填写为
"As per B/L No. ×××"。

From…To…

自……至……。填写货物实际的启运地和目的地。有些保险单上还会出现
Via 一栏, 表示转运地, 如未发生转运, 留空即可。

Claim payable at

赔款偿付地点。按信用证中的保险单条款填写, 通常是进口国/进口地, 或者
是货物的最终目的地。一般还同时注明赔付的币种, 例如 Claim payable at Hamburg in USD.

Survey By/Settling Agent

填写保险公司在赔款偿付地代理机构的名称及联系信息。

Amount Insured

保险金额。通常信用证对于保险金额的约定, 都是以货物 CIF 价值或发票金
额的某一比例为基准。这个比例被视为信用证对最低保额的要求。

当按这一比例计算得出的保险金额出现小数时, 保险公司通常习惯采取"进
一取整"的方法只按整数承保。例如: 发票金额 US $10290.40, 信用证规定按发票
金额的 110% 投保, 则

$$保险金额＝发票金额×(1＋保险加成率)$$
$$＝USD10290.4×(1＋10\%)$$
$$＝USD11319.44$$

通常我们会按 USD11320.00 投保, 当然也可以按 USD11319.44 投保, 但不能
按 USD11319.00 投保。

如果信用证（或者合同）对此未作具体规定，则可按 10％的投保加成率操作。

在小写保险金额之后，通常还会跟上大写保险金额，大小写必须一致。

Description, Marks, Quantity, & Packing of Goods

保险货物项目、标记、数量及包装。

保险货物可使用统称，而不必像商业发票一般详尽，但不得与信用证中的货物描述冲突。

标记必须与其他单据一致，也可简单地填写为"As per Invoice No. ×××"。

数量及包装可选择填写一项，数量或包装件数，但应写明单位，如 500SETS 或 500CTNS，不能仅写 500。

Conditions

承保险别，一般应注明保险险别和保险条款，具体文句应与信用证中的保险单条款一致。

Premium　Rate

保费、费率。有些保险单上会出现此栏目，除非信用证有特殊规定，一般填写 as arranged。

No. of Originals

保险公司签发的正本保险单的份数。若信用证规定了提交的正本保单份数，例如"Full set of three original insurance policy"、"3/3 Marine Insurance Policy…"，则应要求保险公司照此份数签发，此处填写"Three"或"3"。若信用证未作具体规定，只是要求提交全套正本保单，则可按保险公司惯常操作。

Issuing Date

出单日期。根据 UCP600 规定，保险单据日期不得晚于发运日期，除非保险单据表明保险责任不迟于发运日生效。也就是说，除非保险单据表面有类似 "This insurance policy is effective from the date of shipment."的文句，否则，保险单的出单日期不应晚于提单日期。

Signed

签发。按 UCP600 的要求，保险单必须必须由保险公司（insurance company）或承保人（underwriter）或他们的代理人或代表出具并签署。

信用证要求在保单上加注的内容

一般加注在单据中间部位的明显处,如填写在 **Description of Goods** 或 **Conditions** 一栏的空白处。

背书

保单背书的目的是转让保险利益,即在货物发生承保风险并造成损失时,可获得保险公司赔偿的权利。所以,当被保险人为受益人的情况下,受益人在向银行交单时,必须对保单进行背书,以便将索赔权转让给相关方。

背书形式有二种:空白背书和记名背书。空白背书是指不指定被背书人,仅由背书人签章,记名背书则是先指定被背书人,然后由背书人签章。

例如,空白背书:

SHANGHAI TIANYUAN TRADING COMPANY

季立君

记名背书:

To COMMERZBANK AG, FRANKFURT AM MAIN

SHANGHAI TIANYUAN TRADING COMPANY

季立君

对保单的背书形式一般信用证会作具体规定,例如"blank endorsed"或者"endorsed to our order",缮制时应据此填制。如信用证没有具体规定,一般作空白背书。

正本

一般在保险单上印就"Original"水印字样表示正本。还有一些保险单的第一份正本用"Original"或"First Original"表示,第二份正本用"Duplicate"或"Second Original"表示,第三份正本用"Triplicate"或"Third Original"表示。

◇　受益人证明

通常,受益人会采用公司信笺缮制受益人证明,也可在空白纸上缮制然后由受益人签章。其内容主要包括以下几点:

名称

单据名称位于单据的正上方,应按信用证规定的名称缮制,例如:Certificate

（证明），Statement（申明），Declaration（声明）等。

日期

可根据需证明的内容而定，例如寄单证明的日期不应早于单据寄出的日期。但必须符合信用证的规定，如无要求，也可不注明日期。

DECLARATION

ORIGINAL

MAR. 15, 2018

TO WHOM IT MAY CONCERN

L/C NO.:　　　AN-29854
INVOICE NO.:　TR-INVWR59235
S/C NO.:　　　WR59235

WE HEREBY DECLARE THAT EACH COPY OF SHIPPING DOCUMENTS HAS BEEN FAXED TO THE APPLICANT WHITHIN 48 HOURS AFTER SHIPMENT.

APPLICANT:　　TERI INTERNATIONAL GMBH

L/C NO. AN-29854 DATED 20 FEBRUARY 2018
ISSUED BY COMMERZBANK AG FRANKFURT AM MAIN

SHANGHAI TIAN YUAN TRADING CO., LTD.

季立君

抬头

抬头通常填写为"TO WHOM IT MAY CONCERN"。信用证有特殊要求的，按信用证填写。信用证如无要求，也可不填写抬头。

事由

事由通常填写信用证号码和发票号。信用证有特殊要求的，按信用证填写。信用证如无要求，也可不填写事由。

证明文句

按照信用证规定的文句书写。通常可以"We hereby certify/state/declare

that…"开头。需注意,在信用证规定的文句中出现"prompt""immediately""as soon as possible"等形容性词语时,缮制证明时也必须原样显示。

信用证要求在受益人证明上加注的内容

一般加注在单据中间部位的明显处,如填写在证明文句的下方空白处。

签章

在证明的右下方注明受益人公司名称,并盖章或签名。

正本

在受益人原始信笺上出具的或是经签章的受益人证明,均可被视为正本,也可直接在其名称下方标注"Original"字样。

◇ 船公司证明

通常,船公司证明应采用船公司的信笺缮制,也可在空白纸上缮制然后由船公司签章。其内容主要包括以下几点:

名称

单据名称位于单据的正上方,应按信用证规定的名称缮制,例如:Certificate (证明),Statement(申明),Declaration(声明)等。

日期

可根据需证明的内容而定,但必须符合信用证的规定,如无要求,也可不注明日期。

抬头

抬头通常填写为"TO WHOM IT MAY CONCERN"。信用证有特殊要求的,按信用证填写。信用证如无要求,也可不填写抬头。

事由

事由通常填写信用证号码、承运船名和航次及提单号码。信用证有特殊要求的,按信用证填写。信用证如无要求,也可不填写事由。

CERTIFICATE

DATE: MAR 13, 2018

TO WHOM IT MAY CONCERN

B/L NO: 8SHADUB3EH011
VESSEL NAME: YU XIANG
VOYAGE NO.   V. 345

THIS IS TO CERTIFY THAT THE SHIPMENT IS MADE BY A SEAWORTHY VESSEL WHICH
IS CLASSIFIED 100 A1 ISSUED BY LLOYDS OR EQUIVALENT CLASSIFICATION SOCIETY.

L/C NO. AN-29854 DATED 20 FEBRUARY 2018
ISSUED BY COMMERZBANK AG FRANKFURT AM MAIN

AS AGENT FOR THE CARRIER SITC CONTAINER LINES CO., LTD
SIGN:
SITC CONTAINER LINES (SHANGHAI) CO., LTD.

证明文句

按照信用证规定的文句书写。通常可以"We hereby certify/state/declare that..."开头或"This is to certify/state/declare that..."。

例如,信用证条款要求:Shipping Company's certificate in triplicate issued by the shipping co. or their agents certifying that the vessel is a fully classified regular liner vessel under 15 operating years of age and is not owned by any Israeli national or resident and will not call at or pass through any Israeli port in route to Yemen republic.

那么,船公司证明中的文句描述为:

This is to certify that the vessel is a fully classified regular liner vessel under 15 operating years of age and is not owned by any Israeli national or resident and will not call at or pass through any Israeli port in route to Yemen republic.

信用证要求在船公司证明上加注的内容

一般加注在单据中间部位的明显处,如填写在证明文句的下方空白处。

签章

在证明的右下方注明船公司名称,并签名。由承运人或船长的签字,须表明"承运人"或"船长"的身份,如为代理人代表承运人或船长签字,则须表明代理人名称,并注明其系代表承运人还是船长签字。

正本

在船公司原始信笺上出具的或是经签章的船公司证明,均可被视为正本,也可直接在其名称下方标注"Original"字样。

◇ 原产地证明

原产地证明的基本填制方法在**第九章　出口货物原产地认证**的**指南**(第 264 页)中已有介绍,这里主要以 UCP600 为依据,分析原产地证明作为信用证项下结汇单据时的缮制和审核要点。

名称　签发人

原产地证明的具体名称应与信用证要求相符。在我国,普通原产证明 Certificate of Origin,可以由出口商自行签发(缮制方法与受益人证明类似),也可以由中国国际贸易促进委员会签发,或由海关签发。若信用证用"qualified"、"independent"、"official"、"competent"等词描述出单人时,则不应由受益人自行签发。而普惠制原产地证明 GSP Form A 则只能由海关统一签发。因此缮制时必须首先明确信用证需要提交的原产地证明的种类。

信用证要求在原产地证明上加注的内容

一般加注在单据中间部位的明显处,如填写在 **Number and Kind of packages；description of goods** 一栏结束符 ***************** 的下方空白处。

正本

在原产地证明的最上方印就"Original"字样表示正本。副本最上方印就

"Copy"字样。

◇ 检验证书

检验证书 Certificate of Inspection,可以由出口商自行签发(缮制方法与受益人证明类似),也可以由生产厂商签发,或由专门的检验机构签发。若信用证用"first class"、"well known"、"qualified"、"independent"、"official"、"competent"、"local"等词描述出单人时,则不应由受益人自行签发。当然,如果信用证已明确指出检验证书的签发人或检验证书名称,则应照此办理。

名称 项目

检验证书的种类繁多,因此必须注意检验项目和证书名称都必须与信用证要求相符。例如信用证要求提交"Quality and Weight Inspection Certificate",则除了在检验项目上应有质量和重量两个项目,证书的名称也必须从表面上符合信用证要求。

Consignor Consignee

一般填写信用证受益人和申请人的名称。

Description of Goods

货物描述。可使用统称,而不必像商业发票一般详尽,但不得与信用证中的货物描述冲突。

Quantity/Weight Declared Number and Type of Packages

报检数量/重量。包装种类和数量。一般在数字前后会加上"—"符号,以防更改。

Means of Conveyance

运输工具。如不明确,也可填写运输方式,如 By Sea。但所填内容不能与其他单据相矛盾。

Mark & No.

运输标志。

中华人民共和国出入境检验检疫
ENTRY-EXIT INSPECTION AND QUARANTINE
OF THE PEOPLE'S REPUBLIC OF CHINA

正 本
ORIGINAL
第1页 共1页 Page 1 of 1

编号 No.:   0349096280957976

QUALITY AND WEIGHT
INSPECTION CERTIFICATE

发货人 Consignor	SHANGHAI TIAN YUAN TRADING CO., LTD.
收货人 Consignee	***

品名 Description of Goods	ELECTROLYTIC MANGANESE METAL	标记及号码 Mark & No.	N/M
报检数量/重量 Quantity/Weight Declared	-150-DRUMS /-15000-MT		
包装种类及数量 Number and Type of Packages	IRON DRUM -150-DRUMS		
运输工具 Means of Conveyance	BY SEA		

检验结果:
RESULTS OF INSPECTION:

According to Standard No.YB / T051-2003, respective samples were drawn from this lot of goods, and inspected according to Standard No. GB/T8654·1-2007 with results as follows:

Spe.	Mn	99.87%	C	0.025%
	S	0.036%	P	0.0010%
	Fe-Si-Se	0.0662%		

Size in Flake

From the whole lot of said goods, representative samples of sound appearance were drawn at random and weighed on tested scales, and the weight of whole cargo was ascertained as follows:
Weight: Total net weight -15000-MT.
Packing: In iron drums of 100KGS net each on pallets
Lot No.: H43453490-2008-0462
Conclusion: This lot of goods is in comformity with the requirements Standard No. YB/T051-2003 and the Contract No.7235445CB.

印章 Official Stamp 签证地点 Place of Issue   SHANGHAI   签证日期 Date of Issue   Feb. 09, 2018

授权签字人 Authorized Officer ZHOU XIAOYU   签 名 Signature   周筱瑜

我们已尽所知和最大能力实施上述检验,不能因我们签发本证书而免除卖方或其他方面根据合同和法律所承担的产品质量责任和其他责任。
All inspections are carried out conscientiously to the best of our knowledge and ability. This certificate does not in any respect absolve the seller and other related parties from his contractual and legal obligations especial when product quality is concerned.

Results of Inspection

检验结果。如信用证对此有文句上的要求，也必须符合。

Place of Issue　Date of Issue

签发地点、签发日期。一般而言，签发日期不应迟于提单日期。

Official Stamp　Authorized Officer　Signature

公章、签发人姓名、签字。

信用证要求在检验证书上加注的内容

一般加注在单据中间部位的明显处，如填写在 **Results of Inspection** 一栏的空白处。

正本

在检验证书的右上角标注着"Original"字样表示正本。

出口商审核结汇单据的目的是做到相符交单，保证安全收汇。因此，出口商审核单据的标准往往比银行更为严格。另一方面，出口商还掌握着合同和货物实际装运情况等多种数据，也比银行更容易判断单据制作中是否存在问题。

出口商在完成结汇单据的缮制和审核后，即向银行交单，填写"交单委托书"，或填写"议付申请书"办理议付。议付行审核单据、认为单证相符后，将向出口商预付货款，并将单据寄往开证行指定的银行索偿。

练 习

1. 根据以下出口成交及货运相关信息和信用证,缮制全套出口结汇单据:

买方: PARANDAR INTERNATIONAL INC.   卖方: SHANGHAI MORNING STAR TRADING CO., LTD.

3761 VICTORIA PARK AVE.,   375 DONG DA MING ROAD

UNIT#7,TORONTO,ONTARIO   SHANGHAI 200008

CANADA   P.R.CHINA

SHD12-P213

SHD12-P214

SHD16-P541

SHD16-P545

货 号	品 名	包装方式	包装尺码
SHD12-P213	12PC DINNERWARE SET	4套装1个纸箱	62×48×52cm
成交数量	成交单价（美元）	成交条件	货物毛/净重
644套	47.5	CIF	21/18kgs

货 号	品 名	包装方式	包装尺码
SHD12-P214	12PC DINNERWARE SET	4套装1个纸箱	60×48×50cm
成交数量	成交单价（美元）	成交条件	货物毛/净重
692套	42.3	CIF	21/18kgs

货 号	品 名	包装方式	包装尺码
SHD16-P541	16PC DINNERWARE SET	2套装1个纸箱	55×46×44.5cm
成交数量	成交单价（美元）	成交条件	货物毛/净重
222套	48.2	CIF	18/16kgs

货 号	品 名	包装方式	包装尺码
SHD16-P545	16PC DINNERWARE SET	2套装1个纸箱	52×48×42cm
成交数量	成交单价（美元）	成交条件	货物毛/净重
238套	41.3	CIF	18/16kgs

（SHD12-P213及SHD12-P214各装一个20英尺整箱；SHD16-P541和SHD16-P545拼装一个20英尺整箱）

保险理赔代理：	ROYALTON INSURANCE COMPANY	承运船名：	GLORY OCEAN
	3470 LAIRD RD.	航次：	V. 190E
	UNIT 6-9 MISSISSAUGA	海运费率：	每个20英尺集装箱1230美元
	ONTARIO, CANADA		
发票号码：	SMSCINV07210	提单号码：	SITGSHSVK18267
发票日期：	2018年10月10日	提单日期：	2018年10月26日
保险单号码：	2051880130202080915		
保单日期：	2018年10月24日	集装箱号：	封志号码：
海运保险费：	575美元	CCLU2356117	47113
产地证号码：	G183100386150056	CCLU2356118	47114
产地证日期：	2018年10月23日	CCLU2356119	47115

```
2018AUG31        13:29:18                    LOGICAL TERMINAL    P005
MT S700                  ISSUE OF A DOCUMENTARY CREDIT    PAGE   00001
                                                          FUNC   SWPR3
                                                          UMR    14635414

MSGACK DWS765I AUTH OK, KEY B6852DT5E5896814, BKCHCNBJ OCBCSGSGBRN RECORD
BASIC HEADER       F   01   BKCHCNBJA300      2514    962365
APPLICATION HEADER O 700   6814   180831 ROYBANKCNDA  6323 938214 180831  2514  N
                                    THE ROYAL BANK OF CANADA
                                    4022 SHIPPARD AVE. E
                                    SCARBOROUGH TORONTO
                                    CANADA
USER HEADER         SERVICE CODE     103:
                    BANK PRIORITY    113:
                    MSG USER REF.    108:
                    INFO. FROM CI    115:
SEQUENCE OF TOTAL  * 27    : 1/1
FORM OF DOC. CREDIT * 40A  : IRREVOCABLE
DOC. CREDIT NUMBER * 20    : ROYAOBKDLC621501
DATE OF ISSUE        31C   : 180831
EXPIRY             * 31D   : DATE  181121      PLACE    CHINA
APPLICANT          * 50    : PARANDAR INTERNATIONAL INC.
                             3761 VICTORIA PARK AVE.
                             UNIT#7, TORONTO, ONTARIO
                             CANADA
BENEFICIARY        * 59    : SHANGHAI MORNING STAR TRADING CO.,LTD.
                             375 DONG DA MING ROAD
                             SHANGHAI 200008
                             P. R. CHINA
AMOUNT             * 32B   : CURRENCY    USD   AMOUNT      80391.40
MAX. CREDIT AMOUNT   39B   : NOT EXCEEDING
AVAILABLE WITH/BY  * 41A   : ADVISING BANK ONLY
                             BY NEGOTIATION
DRAFT AT ...         42C   : 30 DAYS AFTER B/L DATE       FOR FULL INVOICE VALUE
DRAWEE               42A   : THE ROYAL BANK OF CANADA
                             4022 SHIPPARD AVE. E
                             SCARBOROUGH TORONTO
                             CANADA
PARTIAL SHIPMENTS    43P   : NOT ALLOWED
TRANSSHIPMENT        43T   : NOT ALLOWED
LOADING IN CHARGE    44A   : SHANGHAI
FOR TRANSPORT TO...  44B   : TORONTO
LATEST DATE OF SHIP. 44C   : 181031
DESCRIPT. OF GOODS   45A   :
                     PORCELAIN DINNERWARES
                     AS PER SALES CONTRACT NO. SMSC-07210 DATED 180819
                     CIF  TORONTO
                     SHIPPING MARKS:   PARANDA
                                       SMSC-07210
                                       TORONTO
                                       C/NO.1-UP

DOCUMENTS REQUIRED   46A  :
           1 SIGNED COMMERCIAL INVOICE IN TRIPLICATE SHOWING SHIPPING MARKS AND
             STATING THAT MERCHANDISE IS IN ACCORDANCE WITH APPLICANT'S ORDER NO.
             PARANDAPO-18814 INDICATING FOB VALUE, FREIGHT AND INSURANCE CHARGES.
           2 PACKING LIST IN DUPLICATE INDICATING MEASUREMENT, GROSS WEIGHT AND
             NET WEIGHT OF EACH ARTICLE NO. AS WELL AS OF EACH PACKAGE.
           3 COMPLETE SET OF 4 ORIGINAL CLEAN SHIPPED ON BOARD OCEAN BILLS OF
             LADING MADE OUT TO THE SHIPPER'S ORDER AND ENDORSED TO THE ORDER OF
             ISSUING BANK MARKED 'FREIGHT PREPAID' AND NOTIFY APPLICANT.
```

4 CERTIFICATE OF ORIGIN GSP FORM A IN DUPLICATE STATING THAT THE GOODS
ARE OF CHINESE ORIGIN.
5 INSURANCE POLICY OR CERTIFICATE IN DUPLICATE, ENDORSED TO ISSUING BANK'S
ORDER FOR 110 PCT OF THE INVOICE VALUE, STIPULATING THAT CLAIMS ARE
PAYABLE IN THE CURRENCY OF THE DRAFT AND ALSO INDICATING A CLAIM
SETTLING AGENT AT DESTINATION SHOWING THE INSURANCE COVERAGE AS:
INSTITUTE CARGO CLAUSES (A) AND INSTITUTE CARGO CLAUSES WAR RISKS
AS PER ICC DATED 1/1/2009.

DETAILS OF CHARGES   71B : ALL BANKING CHARGES INCLUDING
                                ADVISING, NEGOTIATION AND REIMBURSEMENT
                                ARE FOR THE ACCOUNT OF BENEFICIARY.

PRESENTATION PERIOD   48   : DOCUMENTS TO BE PRESENTED WITHIN 21 DAYS AFTER
                                THE DATE OF SHIPMENT BUT WITHIN THE VALIDITY OF THE CREDIT

CONFIRMATION   * 49   : WITHOUT

ADDITIONAL COND.   47B :

    1 DRAFT SHOULD BEAR A CLAUSE 'DRAWN UNDER DOCUMENTARY CREDIT NO.
      ROYAOBKDLC621501 OF THE ROYAL BANK OF CANADA DATED 180831.
    2 TWO ADDITIONAL COPIES/PHOTOCOPIES OF THE RELATIVE INVOICE(S) AND
      TRANSPORT DOCUMENT(S) ARE REQUESTED TO BE PRESENTED TOGETHER
      WITH THE DOCUMENTS FOR THE ISSUING BANK'S REFERENCE ONLY.
    3 B/L MUST INDICATE THE FREIGHT AMOUNT AND NUMBER OF CONTAINERS BEING
      SHIPPED TOGETHER WITH THE CONTAINER AND SEAL NO(S).
    4 BENEFICIARY SHOULD SEND SHIPPING ADVICE TO APPLICANT WITHIN 48 HOURS
      AFTER THE SHIPMENT INDICATING VESSEL'S NAME, SHIPMENT DATE, NUMBER
      OF PACKAGES, SHIPPING MARKS, NUMBER OF CREDIT AND AMOUNT. ONE COPY OF
      SUCH ADVICE MUST ACCOMPANY THE DOCUMENTS.
    5 ALL DOCUMENTS MUST BEAR NAME OF ISSUING BANK, NUMBER AND DATE OF CREDIT
      AND S/C NO. DOCUMENTS ISSUED PRIOR TO THE ISSUANCE OF THIS CREDIT ARE NOT
      ACCEPTABLE.

INSTRUCTIONS   78
                        T.T. REIMBURSEMENT IS NOT ACCEPTABLE.
                        IN REIMBURSEMENT, NEGOTIATING BANK MUST DISPATCH ALL DOCUMENTS
                        BY REGISTERED AIRMAIL OR AIR COURIER TO US IN ONE LOT.
                        A DISCREPANCY FEE OF USD70.00 WILL BE DEDUCTED FROM THE
                        PROCEEDS IF DOCUMENTS ARE PRESENTED WITH DISCREPANCY(IES) AND
                        ACCEPTANCE OF SUCH DISCREPANT DOCUMENTS WILL NOT IN ANY WAY
                        ALTER THE TERMS AND CONDITIONS OF THIS CREDIT.
                        UPON RECEIPT OF FULL SET OF DOCUMENTS IN ORDER, WE SHALL
                        REIMBURSE YOU ACCORDING TO YOUR INSTRUCTIONS.

SEND. TO REC. INFO.   72   : SUBJECT TO U.C.P.   2007 REVISION
                               I.C.C. PUBLICATION   NO.600

TRAILER   ORDER IS < MAC:> < PAC:> < ENC:> < CHK:> < TNG:> < PDE:>
                               MAC: 7KM48205
                               CHK: 852FHS035824

BILL   OF   EXCHANGE

No. _____

For _____   _____

     (amount in figure)   (place and date of issue)

At _____   of   this   FIRST   Bill of exchange(SECOND being unpaid)

pay to_____ or order the sum of

_____

                         (amount in words)

Value received for _____   of   _____

              (quantity)   (name of commodity)

Drawn under _____

L/C No. _____   dated   _____

To: For and on behalf of

_____   _____

                                         (Signature)

提交份数：

上海晨星贸易有限公司
Shanghai Morning Star Trading Co.,Ltd.

COMMERCIAL INVOICE

TO:

INV. NO. : _____

INV. DATE: _____

S/C NO. : _____

FROM: _____　TO: _____　SHIPPED BY: _____

MARKS & NOS.	DESCRIPTION OF GOODS	QUANTITY	UNIT PRICE	AMOUNT

TOTAL AMOUNT IN WORDS:

TOTAL G.W. / TOTAL N.W.:

TOTAL PACKAGES:

19) ISSUED BY

20) SIGNATURE

上海市东大名路375号(200080) 电话/Tel:86-21-65960332 传真/Fax:86-21-65960328　No.375, Dong Da Ming Rd., Shanghai, P.R.C.

提交份数：

上海晨星贸易有限公司
Shanghai Morning Star Trading Co.,Ltd.

PACKING LIST

TO:

INV. NO. :

DATE:

FROM:　　　　　　　　　　TO:　　　　　　　　　　　SHIPPED BY :

C/NO.	DESCRIPTION OF GOODS	PKG.	QTY	G.W.	N.W.	MEAS.

TOTAL:

TOTAL PACKAGES IN WORDS:

MARKS & NOS.

19) ISSUED BY

20) SIGNATURE

上海市东大名路375号(200080) 电话/Tel:86-21-65960332 传真/Fax:86-21-65960328　　No.375, Dong Da Ming Rd., Shanghai, P.R.C.

提交份数:

SITC CONTAINER LINES CO., LTD.

B/L NO.

1. Shipper	**Port to Port or Combine Transport**

BILL OF LADING

RECEIVED for shipment in external apparent good order and condition, unless otherwise indicated. The total number of packages or units stuffed in the container, the description of the goods and the weights shown in this Bill of Lading are furnished by the Merchants and the containers are already sealed by the Merchants, and which the carrier has no reasonable means of checking and is not a part of this Bill of Lading contract. The carrier has issued the number of Bills of Lading stated below, all of this tenor and date, one of the original Bills of Lading must be surrendered and endorsed or signed against the delivery of the goods or the delivery order and whereupon any other Bills of Lading shall be void.

NOTE: Notwithstanding any customs or privileges to the contrary，the Merchant's attention is drawn to the fact that the Merchant, in accepting this Bill of Lading, expressly agrees to be bound by all the stipulations, exceptions, limitations, liberties, terms and conditions attached hereto or stated herein, whether written, printed, stamped or otherwise incorporated on the front and/or reverse side hereof as well as the provisions of the Carrier's published Tariff Rules, Regulations and Schedules, without exceptions, as fully as if they were all signed by such Merchant, and the carrier's undertaking to carry the goods is made on the basis of the merchant's acceptance and agreements as aforesaid.

This Bill of Lading is governed by the laws of the People's Republic of China. Any claims and disputes arising under or in connection with this Bill of Lading shall be determined by Shanghai Maritime Court or Qingdao Maritime Court at the exclusion of the Courts of any other country.

The printed terms and conditions appearing on the face and reverse side of this Bill of Lading are available at www.sitc.com in SITC's published tariffs.

2. Consignee

3. Notify Party (It is agreed that no responsibility shall attach to the Carrier or his agent for failure to notify)

4.Pre-Carriage by*	5.Place of Receipt*
(Applicable only when this document is used as a Combined Transport Bill of Lading)	(Applicable only when this document is used as a Combined Transport Bill of Lading)
6.Ocean Vessel Voy. No.	7.Port of Loading
8.Port of Discharge HAMBURG	9.Place of Delivery* (Applicable only when this document is used as a Combined Transport Bill of Lading)

ORIGINAL

PARTICULAR FURNISHED BY THE MERCHANT

Container No./Seal No. Marks and Numbers	Number and Kind of packages: description of goods	Gross Weight	Measurement
	Above particulars declared by shipper. Carrier is not responsible. (see clause 12)		

10. Total No. of Containers
Or Packages (in words)

11. Freight & Charges	Rate	Unit	Prepaid	Collect
Prepaid at	Payable at	Number of Original B(s)/L		
Place of issue and Date		12. Declared Value/Charge		

LADEN ON BOARD THE VESSEL
DATE   BY

提交份数：

中国平安 PING AN OF CHINA

中国平安财产保险股份有限公司
PING AN PROPERTY & CASUALTY INSURANCE COMPANY OF CHINA, LTD.

总公司地址：
中国·深圳
八卦岭八卦三路平安大厦
电话 (Tel)：0755-82262888
图文传真 (Fax)：0755-82414813
邮政编码 (Postcode)：518029

Address of Head Office:
Ping An Building, No.3 Ba Gua Road.
Ba Gua Ling, Shenzhen, China

No. 060500087415

货物运输保险单
CARGO TRANSPORTATION INSURANCE POLICY

被保险人
Insured:

中国平安财产保险股份有限公司根据被保险人的要求及所交付约定的保险费，按照本保险单背面所载条款与下列特款，承保下述货物运输保险，特立本保险单.

This Policy of Insurance witnesses that PING AN PROPERTY & CASUALTY INSURANCE COMPANY OF CHINA, LTD., at the request of the Insurance and in consideration of the agreed premium paid by the Insured, undertakes to insure the undermentioned goods in transportation subject to the conditions of Policy as per the clauses printed overleaf and other special clauses attached hereon.

保单号： Policy No.	赔款偿付地点 Claim Payable at
发票或提单号 Invoice No. or B/L No.	
运输工具： Per Conveyance S.S.	查勘代理人 Survey By:
起迄日期　　　　　　　自 Slg. on or abt　　　　　From 　　　　　　　　　　　至 　　　　　　　　　　　To	

保险金额
Amount Insured

保险货物项目、标记、数量及包装：
Description, Marks, Quantity, & Packing of Goods:

承保条件：
Conditions:

ORIGINAL

保单正本：
Number of Originals:

签单日期
Date:

For and on behalf of
PING AN PROPERTY & CASUALTY INSURANCE COMPANY OF CHINA, LTD

Authorized Signature

复核：　　　　　　制单：

地址及电话　　11/F, 12/F, JING AN PLAZA, 8 CHANG SHU ROAD
Address & Tel.　SHANGHAI, CHINA 52564888×6395

注：　未加盖本公司保单专用章，保单无效。

提交份数：

ORIGINAL

1. Goods consigned from (Exporter's business name, address, country)	Reference No.
	GENERALIZED SYSTEM OF PREFERENCES **CERTIFICATE OF ORIGIN** **(Combined declaration and certificate)** **FORM A** **Issued in THE PEOPLE'S REPUBLIC OF CHINA** (country) See Notes overleaf
2. Goods consigned to (Consignee's name, address, country)	
3. Means of transport and route (as far as known)	4. For official use

5. Item number	6. Marks and numbers of packages	7. Number and Kind of packages; description of goods	8. Origin criterion (see Notes overleaf)	9. Gross weight or other quantity	10. Number and date of invoices

11. Certification
It is hereby certified, on the basis of control carried out, that the declaration by the exporter is correct.

Place and date, signature and stamp of certifying authority

12. Declaration by the exporter
The undersigned hereby declares that the above details and statements are correct; that all the goods were produced in

.... (country)

and that they comply with the origin requirements specified for those goods in the Generalized System of Preferences for goods exported to

_____
(importing country)

Place and date. signature of authorized signatory

提交份数：

上海晨星贸易有限公司
Shanghai Morning Star Trading Co.,Ltd.

SHIPPING ADVICE

To:　_____　　　From:　_____

Tel. No.:　_____　　　Tel. No.:　_____

Page:　_____　　　Date:　_____

Fax. No.:　_____　　　Fax. No.:　_____

上海晨星贸易有限公司
SHANGHAI MORNING STAR TRADING CO.,LTD.

_____

(SIGNATURE)

上海市东大名路375号(200080) 电话/Tel:86-21-65960332　传真/Fax:86-21-65960328　No.375, Dong Da Ming Rd., Shanghai, P.R.C.

提交份数：

2. 试根据以下信用证审核全套结汇单据，指出单据存在的问题并说明应当如何修改。

COMMERCIAL BANK OF DUBAI P.S.C

DEIRA BRANCH
P.O.BOX: 1709, DUBAI, U.A.E

IRREVOCABLE DOCUMENTARY	PAGE NO.: [1]	SWIFT:	CBDUAEAD DER
LETTER OF CREDIT NO.:	01DLC077003079	TELEX:	45468 TRBNK EM.
DATE OF ISSUE:	OCTOBER 19, 2018	TELEFAX:	251089 / 254565
DATE OF EXPIRY:	DECEMBER 17, 2018	TELEPHONE:	253222 (10 LINES)
PLACE OF EXPIRY:	CHINA		

BENEFICIARY	*APPLICANT*
SHANGHAI MINHUA IMP. & EXP. CORPORATION 5/F MINHUA BLDG. 880 HUMING ROAD SHANGHAI CHINA	ALABRA HOME APPL. TRDG CO. LLC. P.O. BOX 21352 DUBAI UAE

ADVISING BANK	*CURRENCY AND AMOUNT*
BANK OF CHINA SHANGHAI BRANCH 23, CHUNG SHAN ROAD E.1 SHANGHAI CHINA	USD *******49,550.00 UNITED STATES DOLLARS FORTY NINE THOUSAND FIVE HUNDRED AND FIFTY ONLY

DETAILS OF SHIPMENT		*AVAILABLE WITH*
TRANSSHIPMENT:	NOT ALLOWED	THE ADVISING BANK ONLY BY NEGOTIATION AGAINST
PARTSHIPMENT:	ALLOWED	PRESENTATION OF DOCUMENTS DESCRIBED HEREIN
SHIPMENT FROM:	CHINA	AND BENEFICIARY'S DRAFT(S) AT SIGHT DRAWN ON
TO:	DUBAI	US.

		TERMS OF DELIVERY
BY:	VESSEL	CFR DUBAI
NOT LATER THAN:	DECEMBER 02, 2018	

DESCRIPTION OF GOODS :

HOUSEHOLD WARES (FOUR ITEMS OF LAMPS)
ALL OTHER DETAILS AS PER INDENT NO. SSTE/363/CN-9 OF M/S. SALEM SAUD
TRADING EST., AND SALES CONFIRMATION NO. SHMHSC-07210 DATED OCTOBER 03, 2018
SHIPPING MARKS: ALABRA / SHMHSC-07210 / DUBAI / C/NO.1-UP

DOCUMENTS REQUIRED :

01- SIGNED COMMERCIAL INVOICE IN { THREE } COPIES CERTIFIED TO BE TRUE AND CORRECT MENTIONING
　　FULL NAME AND ADDRESS OF THE MANUFACTURER AND TERMS OF DELIVERY.

02- CERTIFICATE OF ORIGIN STATING GOODS ARE OF CHINESE ORIGIN ISSUED BY CHINA COUNCIL FOR THE
　　PROMOTION OF INTERNATIONAL TRADE, MENTIONING NAME AND ADDRESS OF THE MANUFACTURER /
　　PRODUCER & EXPORTER.

03- COMPLETE SET OF (3/3) CLEAN ON BOARD SHIPPING COMPANY'S BILL OF LADING ISSUED TO THE ORDER
　　OF COMMERCIAL BANK OF DUBAI PSC. [DUBAI] MARKED "FREIGHT PREPAID " AND NOTIFY
　　APPLICANT.

04- PACKING LIST IN { THREE } COPIES.

05- INSURANCE COVERED IN DUBAI.
　　SHIPMENT ADVICE MUST BE SENT TO M/S . IRAN INSURANCE CO., P.O.BOX 2004, DUBAI BY REGISTERED
　　POST/TELEX ON TELEX NO.46215 BIMEH EM OR BY FAX ON FAX NO.217660 QUOTING THEIR OPEN POLICY
　　NO. OMP/ 531 /91 AND STATING OUR L/C NO., AMOUNT , VESSEL NAME AND SHIPPING MARKS THEREIN
　　AND A COPY OF SUCH SHIPMENT ADVICE MUST ACCOMPANY THE THE DOCUMENTS.

CONTINUED ON PAGE NO. 2

بنك دبي التجاري ش.م.ع
COMMERCIAL BANK OF DUBAI P.S.C

DEIRA BRANCH
P.O.BOX: 1709, DUBAI, U.A.E

IRREVOCABLE DOCUMENTARY   PAGE NO.: [2]
LETTER OF CREDIT NO.:   01DLC07003079   DATE OF ISSUE: OCTOBER 19, 2018
USD *******49,550.00

06- A CERTIFICATE FROM THE SHIP OWNER / AGENT STATING THAT THE CARRYING VESSEL IS NOT AN
ISRAELI OWNED VESSEL AND IS NOT SCHEDULED TO CALL AT ANY ISRAELI PORT ON ROUTE TO ITS
DESTINATION AND THE VESSEL IS NOT PROHIBITED TO ENTER ANY ARAB PORT FOR ANY REASON
WHATSOEVER IN ACCORDANCE WITH ITS LOCAL LAWS AND REGULATIONS . [THIS IS NOT REQUIRED IF
SHIPMENT IS EFFECTED BY UNITED ARAB SHIPPING COMPANY'S VESSEL].

OTHER CONDITIONS :
01- CERTIFICATE OF ORIGIN SHOULD INCLUDE THE NAME OF THE COUNTRY FROM WHERE THE GOODS
ARE EXPORTED.

02- GOODS MUST BE SHIPPED IN 4X20FT CONTAINERS AND B/L MUST EVIDENCE THE COMPLIANCE.

03- COMMISSION @1% OF THE INVOICE VALUE MUST BE DEDUCTED FROM THE PAYMENT TO THE
BENEFICIARY AT THE TIME OF NEGOTIATION FOR PAYMENT TO MR. C.H.B. MOHD KUNHI, P.O. BOX
51495, DUBAI WHICH MUST BE CERTIFIED IN THE NEGOTIATING BANK'S COVERING SCHEDULE.

04- B/L SHOULD BEAR VESSEL AGENT'S NAME, ADDRESS AND TELEPHONE NUMBER AT PORT OF
DESTINATION.

05- SHORT FORM B/L NOT ACCEPTABLE .

06- INVOICE & TRANSPORT DOCUMENTS SHOULD BEAR SHIPPING MARKS AND TOTAL GROSS WEIGHT,
NET WEIGHT AND MEASUREMENT.

07- THE NUMBER AND THE DATE OF THIS CREDIT AND NAME OF OUR BANK MUST BE
QUOTED ON ALL DOCUMENTS.

08- ALL DOCUMENTS TO BE ISSUED IN ENGLISH LANGUAGE

09- ALL CHARGES INCLUDING REIMBURSING CHARGES EXCEPT L/C ISSUING CHARGES ARE
ON ACCOUNT OF BENEFICIARY.

INSTRUCTIONS TO NEGOTIATION BANK :
– NOTE EACH PRESENTATION ON THE REVERSE OF THIS LETTER OF CREDIT.
– DISPATCH THE FULL SET OF THE NEGOTIATED DOCUMENTS TO US IN ONE LOT BY COURIER SERVICE.
– ON RECEIPT OF CREDIT COMPLIED DOCUMENTS PAYMENT SHALL BE EFFECTED BY US PER CREDIT
TERMS AS PER NEGOTIATION BANK'S COVERING SCHEDULE.

EXCEPT AS OTHERWISE STATED HEREIN , THIS CREDIT IS SUBJECT TO UNIFORM CUSTOMS AND PRACTICE
FOR DOCUMENTARY CREDITS [2007 REVISION] , INTERNATIONAL CHAMBER OF COMMERCE PUBLICATION
NO. 600.

For COMMERCIAL BANK OF DUBAI P.S.C.

Authorised Signature   Authorised Signature

BILL OF EXCHANGE

No. SHMH07210

For US$49,550.00   SHANGHAI   DEC. 18, 2018

(amount in figure)   *(place and date of issue)*

At *********************   sight of this   **FIRST**   Bill of exchange (SECOND being unpaid)

pay to OURSELVES   or order the sum of

SAY U.S. DOLLARS FORTY NINE THOUSAND FIVE HUNDRED AND FIVE ONLY

(amount in words)

Value received for   585 CARTONS   of   HOUSEHOLD WARES (FOUR ITEMS OF LAMPS)

(quantity)   *(name of commodity)*

Drawn under   COMMERCIAL BANK OF DUBAI P.S.C.

L/C No.   01DLC077003070   dated   OCT. 19, 2018

To: ALABRA HOME APPL. TRDG. CO. LLC.   For and on behalf of

P.O. BOX 21352,   SHANGHAI MINHUA IMP. & EXP. CORPORATION

DUBAI

UAE

(Signature)

提交份数：一式两联

COMMERCIAL INVOICE

1) SELLER	3) INVOICE NO.	4) INVOICE DATE
SHANGHAI MINHUA IMP. & EXP. CORPORATION	SHMH07210	NOV. 16, 2018
5/F MINHUA BLDG.	5) L/C NO.	6) DATE
880 HUMING ROAD	01DLC077003079	OCT. 03, 2018
SHANGHAI CHINA	7) ISSUED BY	
	COMMERCIAL BANK OF DUBAI P.S.C.	
2) BUYER	8) CONTRACT NO.	9) DATE
ALABRA HOME APPL. TRDG. CO. LTD.	SHMHSC-07210	OCT. 19, 2018
P.O.BOX 21352	10) FROM	11) TO
DUBAI	SHANGHAI	DUBAI
UAE	12) SHIPPED BY	13) PRICE TERM
	DA HE KOU V. 210S	CFR DUBAI

14) MARKS	15) DESCRIPTION OF GOODS		16) QTY.	17) UNIT PRICE	18) AMOUNT
	HOUSEHOLD WARES (FOUR ITEMS OF LAMPS)				
ALABRA	2103S	LAMP	320 PCS.	US$32.20	US$10,300.00
SHMNSC-07210	2203S	LAMP	604 PCS.	US$25.50	US$15,402.00
DUBAI	AMZ049	LAMP	700 PCS.	US$22.80	US$16,233.60
C/NO.1-535	ARG108	LAMP	504 PCS.	US$15.10	US$7,610.40
					US$49,550.00

TOTAL AMOUNT IN WORDS:
SAY U.S.DOLLARS FORTY NINE THOUSAND FIVE HUNDRED AND FIFTY ONLY

ALL OTHER DETAILS AS PER INDENT NO.SSTB/363/CN-9 OF M/S. SALEM SAUD
TRADING EST., AND SALES CONFIRMATION NO. SHMHSC-07210 DATED
OCTOBER 03, 2018.

TOTAL PACKAGES: 535CARTONS
TOTAL GROSS WEIGHT: 9964KGS.
TOTAL MEASUREMENT: 99.748M3

NAME AND ADDRESS OF THE MANUFACTURER:
SHANGHAI RISHENG LIGHTING CO.,LTD.
340 LIU YING RD.,
SHANGHAI CHINA

19) ISSUED BY

SHANGHAI MINHUA IMP. & EXP. CORPORATION

20) SIGNATURE

提交份数：3 份

PACKING LIST

1) SELLER	3) INVOICE NO.	4) INVOICE DATE
SHANGHAI MINHUA IMP. & EXP. CORPORATION 15/F MINHUA BLDG. 880 HUMING ROAD SHANGHAI CHINA	SHMH07210	NOV. 16, 2018
	5) FROM	6) TO
	SHANGHAI	DUBAI
	7) TOTAL PACKAGES(IN WORDS)	
	SAY FIVE HUNDRED AND THIRTY FIVE CARTONS ONLY	
2) BUYER	8) MARKS & NOS.	
ALABRA HOME APPL. TRDG. CO. LLC. P.O. BOX 21352 DUBAI UAE	ALABRA SHMHSC-07210 DUBAI C/NO.1-535	

9) C/NOS.	10) NOS. & KINDS OF PKGS	11) ITEM	12)QTY.	13) G.W.	14) N.W.	15) MEAS
	HOUSEHOLD WARES (FOUR ITEMS OF LAMPS)					
1 - 80	80 CARTONS	2103S	320 PCS.	1600.00KGS.	1400.00KGS.	24.960M3
80 - 231	151 CARTONS	2203S	604 PCS.	3322.00KGS.	2944.50KGS.	24.915M3
232 - 409	178 CARTONS	AMZ409	712 PCS.	3026.00KGS.	2670.00KGS.	24.920M3
410 - 535	126 CARTONS	ARG108	504 PCS.	2016.00KGS.	1663.20KGS.	24.948M3
TOTAL:	535 CARTONS			9960.00KGS.	8677.70KGS.	99.743M3

```
L/C NO.:        01DLC077003079
S/C NO.:        SHMHSC-07210
ISSUING BANK:   DUBAI COMMERCIAL BANK
```

19) ISSUED BY

SHANGHAI MINHUA EXP. & IMP. CORPORATION

20) SIGNATURE

提交份数:2份

			TLX: 33057 COSCO SHIPPING
COSCO SHIPPING 中远海运集装箱运输有限公司 COSCO SHIPPING LINES CO., LTD	**ORIGINAL**		FAX: +86(21) 65458984
			PORT TO PORT OR COMBINED TRANSPORT BILL OF LADING

1. Shipper Insert Name Address and Phone/Fax	Booking No.	Bill of Lading No.
SHANGHAI MINHUA IMP. & EXP. CORPORATION **5/F MINHUA BLDG.** **880 HUMING ROAD** **SHANGHAI CHINA**		**COSU85122784**

2. Consignee Insert Name Address and Phone/Fax	Forwarding Agent and References
TO ORDER	
	Point and Country of Origin

3. Notify Party Insert Name Address and Phone/Fax (It is agreed that no responsibility shall attach to the Carrier or his agents for failure to notify)	Also Notify Party-routing & Instructions
ALABRA HOME APPL. TRDG. CO. LLC. **P.O. BOX 21325** **DUBAI** **UAE**	

4. Combined Transport* Pre-Carriage by	5. Combined Transport* Place of Receipt	
6. Ocean Vessel Voy. No. **DA HE KOU V. 210S**	7. Port of Loading **SHANGHAI**	Service Contract No. / Commodity Code
8. Port of Discharge **DUBAI**	9. Combined Transport* Place of Delivery	Type of Movement **FCL/FCL CY-CY**

Marks & Nos. Container/Seal No.	No. of Container or Packages	Description of Goods (If Dangerous Goods, See Clause 20)	Gross Weight	Measurement
ALABRA **SHMHSC-07210** **DUBAI** **C/NO. 1-585**	**535CTNS**	**HOUSE WARES (FOUR ITEMS OF LAMPS)**	**9964KGS**	**99.743M3**
ON CY-CY TERM **FREIGHT PREPAID** **SAY FIVE HUNDRED AND THIRTY CARTONS ONLY**				
L/C NO.:	**01DLC077003079**			
L/C DATE:	**OCTOBER 19, 2018**			
ISSUING BANK:	**COMMERCIAL BANK OF DUBAI P.S.C.**			
WE EVIDENCE THAT GOODS ARE SHIPPED IN 4X20FT CONTAINERS				
CBHU57120845	**/ 32741**	**/ 80CTNS**	**/ FCL / FCL**	**/ 20GP /**
CBHU57120846	**/ 32742**	**/ 151CTNS**	**/ FCL / FCL**	**/ 20GP /**
CBHU57120847	**/ 32743**	**/ 178CTNS**	**/ FCL / FCL**	**/ 20GP /**
CBHU57120848	**/ 32744**	**/ 126CTNS**	**/ FCL / FCL**	**/ 20GP /**
		SHIPPER'S LOAD, COUNT AND SEAL		

Declared Cargo Value US$	Description of Contents for Shipper's use Only (Not part of This B/L Contract)
10. Total Number of Containers and/or Packages (in words) Subject to Clause 7 Limitation	**SAY TOTAL FOUR 20 FEET CONTAINERS ONLY.**

11. Freight & Charges	Revenue Tons	Rate	Per	Amount	Prepaid	Collect	Freight & Charges Payable at/by

Received in external apparent good order and condition except as otherwise noted. The total number of the packages or units stuffed in the container, the description of the goods and the weights shown in this Bill or Lading are furnished by the merchants, and which the carrier has no reasonable means of checking and is not a part of this Bill of Lading contract. The carrier has issued **THREE** original Bill of Lading, all of this tenor and date, one of the original Bills of Lading must be surrendered and endorsed or signed against the delivery of the shipment and whereupon any other original Bills of Lading shall be void. The merchants agree to be bound by the terms and conditions of this Bill of Lading as if each had personally signed this Bill of Lading.
* Applicable Only When Document used as a Combined Transport Bill of Lading.

Date Laden on Board	**DEC 5, 2018**
Signed by:	上海中远海运集装箱务代理有限公司 COSCO SHIPPING LINES AGENCY (SHANGHAI) CO., LTD

9805 Date of Issue **DEC 5, 2018** Place of Issue **SHANGHAI**	Signed for the Carrier, COSCO SHIPPING LINES CO., LTD **AS AGENT**

提单背书:

SHANGHAI MINHUA IMP. & EXP. CORPORATION

提交份数:3份正本

ORIGINAL

1. Exporter	Certificate No. C183100754240081

1. Exporter

SHANGHAI MINHUA IMP. & EXP. CORPORATION
5/F MINHUA BLDG.
880 HUMING ROAD
SHANGHAI CHINA

Certificate No. C183100754240081

CERTIFICATE OF ORIGIN

OF

THE PEOPLE'S REPUBLIC OF CHINA

2. Consignee

ALABRA HOME APPL. TRDG. CO. LLC.
P.O. BOX 21352
DUBAI
UAE

3. Means of transport and route

FROM SHANGHAI CHINA TO DUBAI UAE BY SEA

5. For certifying authority use only

4. Country / region of destination

UAE

6. Marks and numbers	7. Number and kind of packages;description of goods	8. H.S. Code	9. Quantity	10. Number and date of invoices
ALABRA **SHMHSC-07210** **DUABI** **C/NO. 1-535**	**535 (FIVE HUNDRED AND THIRTY) CARTONS OF LAMPS** ** ISSUING BANK'S NAME: **COMMERCIAL BANK OF DUBAI P.S.C.** LETTER OF CREDIT NUMBER: **01DLC077003079** DATE OF ISSUE: **OCTOBER 19, 2018** **WE STATE THAT THE GOODS ARE OF CHINESE ORIGIN.**	**9405.2000**	**2140PCS.**	**SHMH072010** **NOV. 16, 2018**

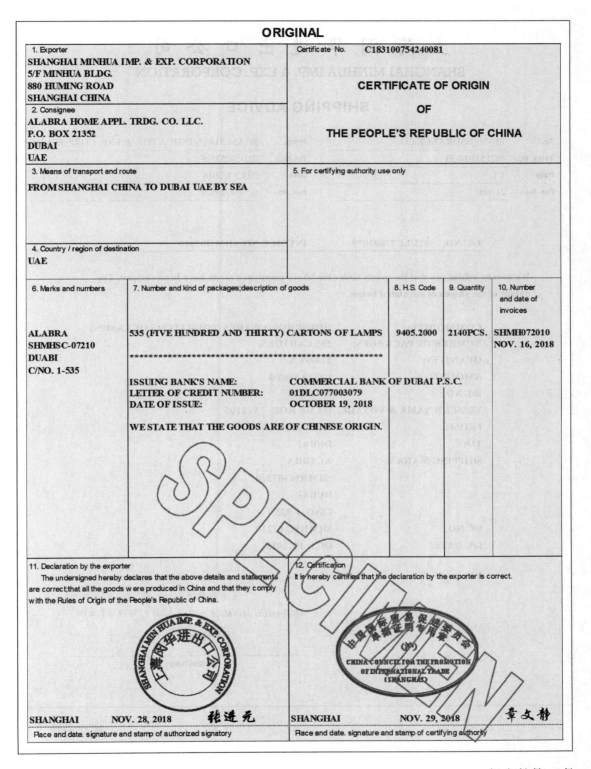

11. Declaration by the exporter	12. Certification
The undersigned hereby declares that the above details and statements are correct;that all the goods were produced in China and that they comply with the Rules of Origin of the People's Republic of China.	It is hereby certified that the declaration by the exporter is correct.
SHANGHAI NOV. 28, 2018	**SHANGHAI** NOV. 29, 2018
Place and date, signature and stamp of authorized signatory	Place and date, signature and stamp of certifying authority

提交份数:2 份

上 海 闵 华 进 出 口 公 司
SHANGHAI MINHUA IMP. & EXP. CORPORATION

SHIPPING ADVICE

To:	IRAN INSURANCE CO.	**From:**	SHANGHAI MINHUA IMP. & EXP. CORPORATION
Telex. No.:	46215 BIMEH	**Tel. No.:**	021-54753526
Page:	1/1	**Date:**	DEC. 5, 2018
Fax. No.:	217660	**Fax. No.:**	021-54753529

L/C NO.　01DLC77003079　　INVOICE NO. SHMH07210

We hereby inform you that the goods under the above mentioned credit have been shipped. The details of the shipment are stated below.

COMMODITY:	HOUSEHOLD WARES (FOUR ITEMS OF LAMPS)
NUMBER OF PACKAGES:	535 CARTONS
QUANTITY:	2140PCS.
AMOUNT:	US$49,550.00
B/L NO.:	85122784
VESSEL'S NAME & VOYAGE:	DA HE KOU　V. 210S
FROM:	SHANGHAI
TO:	DUBAI
SHIPPING MARKS:	ALABRA
	SHMHSC-07210
	DUBAI
	C/NO. 1-535
S/C NO.:	SHMHSC-07210
L/C DATE:	OCT. 19, 2018

上海闵华进出口公司
SHANGHAI MINHUA IMP. & EXP. CORPORATION

(SIGNATURE)

提交份数：1 份

出口单据审核记录

存在问题 修改意见

汇票

1

2

3

商业发票

1

2

3

装箱单

1

2

3

海运提单

1

2

3

原产地证明

1

2

3

装运通知

1

2

3

其他单据

1

2

3

第十三章　出口业务善后

案　例

2018 年 12 月 10 日,环宇公司收到中国银行上海分行开具的"涉外收入申报单"(即银行水单,第 379 页),获知开证行 F.Van Lanschot Bankiers N.V.已付款,此笔交易顺利结汇。

2018 年 12 月 11 日,环宇公司向 Tivolian 公司去函、圆满结束本次交易。

2018 年 12 月 15 日,环宇公司向税务局办理出口退税手续。

工作任务

拟写业务善后函。

涉外收入申报单(又称"银行水单")

<table>
<tr><td colspan="2">涉外收入申报单（对公）</td><td>日期：</td><td>2018/12/10</td></tr>
<tr><td></td><td></td><td>时间：</td><td>16:35:12</td></tr>
<tr><td></td><td></td><td>页数：</td><td>1</td></tr>
</table>

根据《国际收支统计申报办法》（1995年8月30日由国务院批准），特制发本申报单。　　　　制表机关：国家外汇管理局
国家外汇管理局和有关银行为您的申报内容保密

出口收汇核销专用联

申报号码：	310000　0003　31　130525　N073		申报日期：	2018/12/10
申报银行：	310000000331　中国银行上海分行国际业务部（营业）		企业注册所在地：	310000
收款人编码：	761256738　分公司代号：000　收款人名称：		上海环宇贸易有限公司	
人民币账号：		外汇账号：	086159-66795216843573	
结算方式：	信用证	付款人名称：	F. VAN LANSCHOT BANKIERS N.V., ROTTERDAM, NETHERLANDS	
收入款金额：	USD　美元	其中	结汇金额：	0
	26,660.80		现汇金额：	26,559.47
收款日期：	2018/12/9	是否已收入收款帐户：是	其他金额：	0
银行业务编号：	BP70221563			

扣费信息　　出口收汇核销项下扣费明细

项　目		银行费用	回扣	佣金	运费	保费
国内	币种	USD				
扣费	金额	101.33	0	0	0	0
国外	币种	USD				
扣费	金额	0	0	0	0	0
项　目		还贷款	租赁款	退款	赔款	其他
国内	币种					
扣费	金额	0	0	0	0	0
国外	币种					
扣费	金额	0	0	0	0	0

以下内容请企业根据本笔交易如实填写

付款人国别/地区：	NL　荷兰	发票或合同号码：	HY-TIV-INV0373 / HY-TIV0373
国际收支交易编码：	0TON	交易附言：	一般贸易毛绒玩具出口
报关单号码：22002018000579375G		填报人电话：021-58818844	
		报关日期　　　　币种　　　　报关金额	
		2018/11/11　　　USD　　　　26,660.80	
收汇核销号码：		如果本笔收入款为退款，请填写该笔收入对应的原对外付款申报号码：	
核销号码		申报号码　　　　　　　　完全退款	
银行柜员信息	银行操作人：卢敏华		操作日期：2018/12/9
	银行复核人：卢敏华		复核日期：2018/12/10
企业人员信息	填报人：761256736		
	企业操作员：761256736		操作日期：2018/12/10
	企业复核人：761256736		复核日期：2018/12/10
外管局信息	审批编号：		
	查复性申报原因：		
	是否查复性申报：　　　否		

报表结束

中国银行上海分行
★ 2018.12.10 ★
业　务　清　讫

示 范

Payment received and thank you

发件人： David Wang <d.wang@universal.com.cn>
日 期： 2018年12月11日
收件人： Chila Trooborg <chtrooborg@tivolian.nl>

上海环宇贸易有限公司
Shanghai Universal Trading Co., Ltd.

Dear Mr. Trooborg

We are glad to receive the proceeds under L/C No. AM/VA07721SLC against S/C No. HY-TIV0373.

We appreciate your cooperation during the past months and are pleased to see the first transaction going through smoothly.

We trust that the goods will arrive at Rotterdam safe and sound and give you complete satisfaction.

We look forward to the pleasure of doing further business with you in the near future.

Best wishes

David Wang
Sales Manager
Shanghai Universal Trading Co., Ltd.
Tel: +86 21 58818863
Email: d.wang@universal.com.cn

中国上海市东方路 131 号美陵广场 1201-1216 室
Rm. 1201-1216 Mayling Plaza, 131 Dongfang Rd., Shanghai, 200120, China
电话/Tel: 86-21-58818844　传真/Fax: 86-21-58818766　网址/Web: www.universal.com.cn

指　南

当出口商向开证行（通过议付行）提交整套结汇单据后，业务就进入了善后阶段。开证行将对所提交的单据进行审核，以确定是否构成相符交单（complying presentation）。如果开证行对单据没有提出异议，说明出口商已得到开证行的付款保证，即在即期信用证项下得到付款，而在远期信用证项下得到付款承诺。进口方在目的港接收货物后，本笔交易就可视为顺利完成。但如果开证行认为单证不一致，就可能会拒付。这对于出口商来讲，就意味着以银行信用为基础的信用证付款方式的失效。收到银行的拒付通知后，出口商一定先要确定遭到拒付的原因，与国内议付行、交单行相配合，做好应变工作，尽可能降低无法正常收汇而产生的风险和损失，同时还应迅速与进口方联络，寻求解决办法，尽量说服进口方付款并接受货物。在业务善后阶段，出口商在收汇后，还应按照国家的相关规定办理收汇核销手续和出口退税手续。

ⓘ 业务善后函的基本结构

拟写业务善后函是出口商在本阶段的一个重要步骤。它是对整笔业务的回顾和对日后合作的展望，这对于确立买卖双方之间长期的业务关系是非常有帮助的。由于可能面临的情形不同，业务善后函又可分为以下两大类：

（一）开证行付款（或承兑付款）时的业务善后函

由于整笔交易进展得非常顺利，业务善后函在写法上就显得相对比较简单。出口商可以回顾该笔交易中值得肯定的地方，诸如感谢对方所做的努力，对交易增进了双方的了解表示高兴等，也可以展望未来，如希望能继续扩大合作，收到更多的订单，建立长期业务往来关系，或借此推荐新产品等等。例如：

◇　We are pleased to receive the proceeds under L/C No. YKE5395.

◇　We are glad to know that the issuing bank has honored our draft against L/C No. ET673.

◇　We hope this deal will be the basis of the further development of our business relationship.

◇　We are sure that you will find the consignment to your entire satisfaction and looking forward to your repeat orders.

◇　We trust that through our joint efforts, we will have a more prospective future.

◇　We would like to take this opportunity to recommend to you our new products.

(二) 遭到开证行拒付时的善后函

虽然这类业务善后函会因单证不符的内容不同而写法各异,但总的来说,出口商应当首先分析拒付的原因是否对进口方履约(如进口报关等)造成了障碍,并采取相应的措施尽力弥补,同时也可以强调单证不符点是细微的,并不影响实际商品的品质,不会对进口方的实际利益造成损害。当然,由于出口商此时处于极不利的地位,语气应当诚恳、委婉,并且具有说服力,以赢得买方的谅解,比如对由此造成的不便表示抱歉,回顾双方以往的愉快合作等。有时作出一些具体的让步或适当的补偿,也是必要和明智的。例如:

◇　We are very concerned to receive the Notification of Dishonor from the issuing bank for L/C No. WER2651.

◇　We feel deeply sorry for the mistake in our negotiation documents, which is made as a result of our clerk's carelessness.

◇　After investigation of the matter, we found it was a typing mistake made by our new clerk.

◇　We are really sorry for the inconvenience we have brought to you.

◇　You may rest assured that such a mistake will never occur again.

◇　We really hope this incident will not affect negatively our friendly cooperation.

◇　We can guarantee that the quantity of the goods is exactly in line with the stipulations of the relative contract.

◇　Since our goods have been shipped on time, would you be kind to make the payment through your bank?

◇　Could you kindly instruct your banker to accept the documents?

◇　We would greatly appreciate it if you could help us in consideration of our long-term trade relations.

(i) 出口退税的业务流程

在货物报关出口之日起至次年 4 月 30 日前最后一个增值税纳税申报期截至日前，出口商可向税务机关申请办理出口退税手续：

（一）登录"外贸企业出口退税申报系统"进行出口退税网上申报，采集或录入出口明细数据、进货明细数据，数据检查无误后确认，汇总后生成申报数据向税务机关进行报送。

（二）如企业被认定为需要提供收汇资料的企业，则在申报出口退税时，还需要提供收汇凭证。未被认定为提供收汇资料的企业则可先申报出口退税再收汇，但须在退税申报截止之日内收汇并按规定提供收汇资料。

（三）税务机关审核无误后，将出口货物的退税款项拨付出口商。

（四）出口商应存留备查"增值税专用发票 抵扣联"的原始凭证，以及"出口明细申报表"、"进货明细申报表"、"退税汇总申报表"及其电子数据。

练 习

1.

　　上海飞龙工贸公司与南非老客户 The Laseys' International Co. Ltd. 上月达成一笔交易（合同号码为 18-G668），今早已顺利收到货款。

　　试以飞龙公司业务员的身份拟写善后函，并随寄最新商品目录。

2.

　　收到银行拒付通知如下：

BANQUE INDOSUEZ
东 方 汇 理 银 行
SHANGHAI BRANCH P.R.C.

DATE: MARCH 15, 2019

BENEFICIARY	L/C NO.
SHANGHAI RAINBOW TRADING COMPANY 906 XIANXIA ROAD SHANGHAI 200336 CHINA TEL: 62765723 FAX: 62779800	18-CS155
	DATE OF ISSUANCE DECEMBER 18, 2018
ISSUING BANK CREDIT AGRICOLE INDOSUEZ DUBAI BRANCH	AMOUNT USD79,569.20
	OUR REFERENCE NO. SHG1291622

Dear Sirs,

We hereby advise you that we have received from the a/m bank a(n) Notification of Dishonor reads:

WE FIND THE DOCUMENTS UNDER CAPTIONED L/C CONTAINING FOLLOWING DISCREPANCIES:

*THE ON BOARD DATE IN THE B/L IS THREE DAYS LATER THAN THE LATEST SHIPMENT DATE SPECIFIED IN THE L/C.

Please contact the Buyer and we hold your documents at your disposal.

Yours faithfully,

for **BANQUE INDOSUEZ**

Shanghai Branch

　　经查，此次延误是由于工厂仓库遭火灾，烧毁了部分制成品，耽误了生产计划而造成的。请向客户去函致歉，希望其尽早付款赎单。

附 录 练习答案

第一章 建立业务关系

1.

Shanghai Zhengyuan Imp. & Exp. Co., Ltd.

14 Floor, 975 Hongqiao Road, Shanghai 200337, China

Tel: 86-21-62747799   Fax: 86-21-62747800

Sep. 23, 2018

Toneveal Products Corp.
17 Mayfield Road，Copenhagen, Denmark

Dear Sirs,

We have your name and address from the CCPIT and learned that you are interested in the household electric appliances. We wish to inform you that we specialize in this line, and would be pleased to enter into business relations with you.

Our company is a Top-50 trading company in Shanghai in terms of export volume and we have the most experienced sales team and qualified technical support in the industry. Our superior service and outstanding performance have won sound reputation in the circle. We are also dealing in the electronics for entertainment and communications. Almost all of the products have met a warm reception in the European countries.

To give you a general idea of our products, we enclose a complete set of leaflets showing various products with detailed specifications and means of packing. Quotations and samples will be sent upon receipt of your specific inquiries.

In case you need more information about our business status, we shall be only too glad to provide at any time.

Looking forward to your early reply.

Yours faithfully,
Wendy Zhao
Shanghai Zhengyuan Imp. & Exp. Co., Ltd.

2.

ULTRA International Trading Company

Room 901 Loyal Mansion, 455 Taojiang Road, Shanghai, China

Tel: (021) 62142222　Fax: (021) 62142233　www.ultra.com.cn

To:　　MPE Enterprise UK Ltd.　（Fax No. 44-20-7739 6565）
From: Ultra International Trading Company　（Fax No. 86-21-6234 1133）
Date:　Sep. 23, 2018

Dear Sir or Madam,

We have come to know your name and address from Mr. Cooper of Barrison Bros. Ltd., who is one of our old clients. We wish to inform you that we specialize in exporting arts and crafts and have satisfied customers throughout the world. We shall be very pleased to enter into business with you.

We are sending you separately one copy of our illustrated price list for your reference. This is of the first half this year, so some prices are not in line with current market. But you may acquaint yourselves with usual items we are handling.

For instance, our wooden decorations on Page 15-21 include carving animals, photo frames, vases, candle holders, and a great variety of pendants which are beautifully designed and especially ideal for Christmas hanging and decoration. They have enjoyed a high popularity in the international market.

Due to lack of time and space, we have not been able to include all the commodities we can offer and therefore ask you to make your enquiries for any items no matter whether they appear on the list. Our latest one will be forwarded to you when finished.

We are looking forward to your specific enquiry.

Best regards,
James Wang
Ultra International Trading Company

3.

SHANGHAI WANTONG MACHINERY IMPORT & EXPORT COMPANY

231 EAST BEIJING ROAD, SHANGHAI, CHINA

Tel: 0086-21-63293536　　Fax: 0086-21-63293636

Freemen & Co., Ltd,
2378 Flee Street, Lagos, Nigeria

23 Sept. 2018

Dear Sir or Madam,

We write to introduce ourselves as one of leading exporters from China, of a wide range of machinery and equipment.

We enclose a copy of our latest catalogue covering the details of all the items available at present, and hope that some of these will interest you. It will be a great pleasure to receive your enquiries for any of the items against which we will send you our favorable quotations.

Should, by chance, your corporation not deal with the import of the goods mentioned above, we would be most grateful if this letter could be forwarded to your friend, or a firm, who may be interested.

We hope to hear from you soon.

Yours faithfully,
Anthon Li
Shanghai Wantong Machinery Import & Export Company

4.

上海新际贸易公司

Shanghai Xinji Trading Company
330 Anqing Rd, Shanghai, China
Tel: 86-21-67554321 Fax:86-21-67554344

Wit Co., Ltd.
Seosomun-Dong, 2-gu, Chung-gu
Seoul, Korea

23 Sep. 2018

Dear Sir or Madam

We learned from the Bank of China that you are a reputable distributor with extensive sales connections in your area. We are writing to you with a view to getting into business with you in the near future.

Our company was established in 2006 with a registered capital of RMB two million. We have been focusing on the exporting of light industrial products. With more than a decade of efforts, we have expanded our business scope impressively and now we deal in nearly one hundred kinds of merchandise. We have successfully set up firm cooperation relations with many advanced manufacturers in China and have introduced a lot of excellent products abroad. Enclosed please find our latest catalogue.

You might be interested to know that we recently launched a new kind of table lighter, as a novelty decoration or a practical gift, which is of supreme quality and fine workmanship. Its exceptional material and unique style have evoked a good reaction in Japan. We have airmailed some samples to you and expect your kind comments.

We look forward to working with you.

Yours faithfully
Richard Luo
Shanghai Xinji Trading Company Limited

5.

上海捷信贸易公司
SHANGHAI JIEXIN TRADING COMPANY

地址：中国上海上南路739号   739 SHANGNAN ROAD, SHANGHAI, P.R.C.
电话：86-21-68528852   TEL: 86-21-68528852
传真：86-21-68528850   FAX: 86-21-68528850

Warlaka Al-Adasani Ent.
PO Box 55825, Hawalli, 32063, Kuwait

Sep 23, 2018

Dear Mr. Al-Subeeh,

How are you? It is almost a year since we concluded our last transaction. During this long period, I believe you have been going smoothly in a profitable way, while our company has been developing fast as well. Now we have set up more factories and the capacity of our manufacturers has been doubled, so we can do business more flexibly.

Looking back on the past cooperation between us, I appreciate the sound friendship and joint efforts though some shipments were not to your satisfaction. You may be interested to know that we have established a comprehensive monitoring system to ensure the quality and improve our after-sales service programs all-round. I assure you if I receive your new enquiry I would give the best price for the high-quality goods in strict conformity with the delivery date.

In particular, I would like to recommend our new products, 100% table cloths and napkins, which receive a positive reaction in some other western Asian countries because of their fashionable designs, elaborate craftsmanship and excellent materials. The latest catalogue is enclosed.

I will be appreciated if you would inform your comments on these items as well as the market situation in your region. It is obviously to our mutual benefit if we can meet the demand of your country.

I look forward to hearing from you.

Yours sincerely,
William Yu
Shanghai Jiexin Trading Company

第二章 发盘与出口报价核算

1.

1）发票金额为 158472.00 元,其中,货款为 136613.79 元,税款为 21858.21 元。

2）158472÷(1+16%)×11%＝15027.52 元

3）158472－15207.52＝143444.48 元或 158472÷(1+16%)×(1+16%－11%)＝143444.48 元

2.

1）24500÷25 取整×30＝29400 套

2）55÷(0.68×0.355×0.86)取整×30＝7920 套

3）总运费 890 美元;每套运费 890÷7920＝0.11237 美元

4）61.5÷1000＝0.0615 吨

5）(30×44×44)÷1000000＝0.05808 立方米

6）总运费 0.0615×(300÷2)×72＝664.2 美元;每台运费 0.0615×72÷2＝2.214 美元

7）17500÷61.5 取整×2＝568 台

8）25÷(0.3×0.44×0.44)取整×2＝860 台

9）总运费 1300 美元;每台运费 1300÷568＝2.29 美元

10）17500÷28 取整×16＝10000 打

11）25÷(0.62×0.48×0.385)取整×16＝3488 打

12）总运费 1100 美元;每打运费 1100÷3488＝0.31537 美元

3.

1）55－55÷(1+17%)×11%＝49.829 元/件

2）(49.829＋2.24＋2.75)÷(1－3%)÷6.7＝8.435 美元/件

3）(49.829＋2.24＋55×8%)÷(1－3%)÷6.7＝8.689 美元/件;55×8%＝4.4 元/件

4）(49.829＋2.24)÷(1－3%－8%)÷6.7＝8.732 美元/件;8.732×8%×6.7＝4.68 元/件

4.

采购成本：   240 元/套

退税收入：   240÷(1+16%)×13%＝26.8966 元/套

垫款利息：   240×6%÷12×1＝1.2 元/套

出口定额费：   240×3%＝7.2 元/套

出口 300 套时：

每个纸箱的尺码为：66×48×52÷1000000＝0.16474 立方米；重量为：21÷1000＝0.021 吨；鉴于 0.16474＞0.021；故海洋运费应按货物的尺码计；

国内包干费：　　　0.16474×55÷4＝2.2652 元/套

海洋运费：　　　（0.16474×62÷4）×7＝17.8743 元/套

所以，

FOBC3＝（240－26.8966＋1.2＋7.2＋2.2652）÷（1－0.25％－3％－10％）÷7
　　　＝36.85 美元/套；

CFRC3＝（240－26.8966＋1.2＋7.2＋2.2652＋17.8743）÷（1－0.25％－3％
　　　－10％）÷7＝39.79 美元/套；

CIFC3＝（240－26.8966＋1.2＋7.2＋2.2652＋17.8743）÷（1－0.25％－3％－10％
　　　－1.1×0.3％）÷7＝39.95 美元/套；

出口 1 个 20 英尺整箱时：

25÷（0.66×0.48×0.52）取整＝151 箱，17500÷21 取整＝833 箱，取较小值，数量151×4＝604 套，

国内包干费：　　　800÷604＝1.3245 元/套

海洋运费：　　　1000×7÷604＝11.5894 元/套

所以，

FOBC3＝（240－26.8966＋1.2＋7.2＋1.3245）÷（1－0.25％－3％－10％）÷7
　　　＝36.69 美元/套；

CFRC3＝（240－26.8966＋1.2＋7.2＋1.3245＋11.5894）÷（1－0.25％－3％
　　　－10％）÷7＝38.60 美元/套；

CIFC3＝（240－26.8966＋1.2＋7.2＋1.3245＋11.5894）÷（1－0.25％－3％－10％
　　　－1.1×0.3％）÷7＝38.75 美元/套；

出口 1 个 40 英尺整箱时：

55÷（0.66×0.48×0.52）取整＝333 箱，24500÷21 取整＝1166 箱，取较小值，数量333×4＝1332 套，

国内包干费：　　　1300÷1332＝0.97598 元/套

海洋运费：　　　1600×7÷1332＝8.4084 元/套

所以，

FOBC3＝（240－26.8966＋1.2＋7.2＋0.97598）÷（1－0.25％－3％－10％）÷7
　　　＝36.64 美元/套；

CFRC3＝（240－26.8966＋1.2＋7.2＋0.97598＋8.4084）÷（1－0.25％－3％
　　　－10％）÷7＝38.02 美元/套；

CIFC3＝（240－26.8966＋1.2＋7.2＋0.97598＋8.4084）÷（1－0.25％－3％－10％
　　　－1.1×0.3％）÷7＝38.17 美元/套

5.

拼箱报价核算：

	计算过程	计算结果	
退税收入	185/(1+16%)*9%	14.3534	人民币/辆
实际成本	185-14.3534	170.6466	人民币/辆
定额费	185*4%	7.4000	人民币/辆
贷款利息	185*6%*30/360	0.9250	人民币/辆
海洋运费	(48*40*80)/1000000*60*6.6	60.8256	人民币/辆
海运保险费	42.415*(1+10%)*0.8%*6.6	2.4635	人民币/辆
FOBC报价	(170.6466+0.925+7.4+5.5+80*6.6/100+185*10%)/(1-3%)/6.6	32.5291	美元/辆
CFRC报价	(170.6466+0.925+7.4+5.5+80*6.6/100+185*10%+60.8256)/(1-3%)/6.6	42.0302	美元/辆
CIFC报价	(170.6466+0.925+7.4+5.5+80*6.6/100+185*10%+60.8256)/(1-3%-(1+10%)*0.8%)/6.6	42.4150	美元/辆

20 英尺整箱报价核算：

	计算过程	计算结果	
装箱数量	25/(0.48*0.4*0.8) 取整*1	162	辆
包干费	800/162	4.9383	人民币/辆
海洋运费	1200/162*6.6	48.8889	人民币/辆
海运保险费	40.1263*(1+10%)*0.8%*6.6	2.3305	人民币/辆
FOBC报价	(170.6466+0.925+7.4+4.9383+80*6.6/162+185*10%)/(1-3%)/6.6	32.1258	美元/辆
CFRC报价	(170.6466+0.925+7.4+4.9383+80*6.6/162+185*10%+48.8889)/(1-3%)/6.6	39.7623	美元/辆
CIFC报价	(170.6466+0.925+7.4+4.9383+80*6.6/162+185*10%+48.8889)/(1-3%-(1+10%)*0.8%)/6.6	40.1263	美元/辆

40 英尺整箱报价核算：

	计算过程	计算结果	
装箱数量	55/(0.48*0.4*0.8) 取整*1	358	辆
包干费	1400/358	3.9106	人民币/辆
海洋运费	2100/358*6.6	38.7151	人民币/辆
海运保险费	38.0793*(1+10%)*0.8%*6.6	2.2116	人民币/辆
FOBC报价	(170.6466+0.925+7.4+3.9106+80*6.6/358+185*10%)/(1-3%)/6.6	31.6865	美元/辆
CFRC报价	(170.6466+0.925+7.4+3.9106+80*6.6/358+185*10%+38.7151)/(1-3%)/6.6	37.7339	美元/辆
CIFC报价	(170.6466+0.925+7.4+3.9106+80*6.6/358+185*10%+38.7151)/(1-3%-(1+10%)*0.8%)/6.6	38.0793	美元/辆

6.

拼箱（LCL）报价核算			
TY-12/JH012	计算过程	核算单位：　**set**	计算结果
实际成本(¥)	320-320/(1+16%)*13%		284.1379
公司定额费(¥)	320*3%		9.6000
垫款利息(¥)	320*5.22%*45/360		2.0880
海洋运费(¥)	0.62*0.48*0.52*76*6.5/4		19.1119
FOB (US$)	(284.1379+5.2+9.6+2.088)/(1-15%-0.3%)/6.5		54.6773
CFR (US$)	(284.1379+5.2+9.6+2.088+19.1119)/(1-15%-0.3%)/6.5		58.1487
CIF (US$)	(284.1379+5.2+9.6+2.088+19.1119)/(1-(1+10%)*0.65%-15%-0.3%)/6.5		58.6438

TY-12/JH015	计算过程	核算单位：　**set**	计算结果
实际成本(¥)	290-290/(1+16%)*13%		257.5000
公司定额费(¥)	290*3%		8.7000
垫款利息(¥)	290*5.22%*45/360		1.8923
海洋运费(¥)	0.6*0.48*0.5*76*6.5/4		17.7840
FOB (US$)	(257.5+5.2+8.7+1.8923)/(1-15%-0.3%)/6.5		49.6399
CFR (US$)	(257.5+5.2+8.7+1.8923+17.784)/(1-15%-0.3%)/6.5		52.8701
CIF (US$)	(257.5+5.2+8.7+1.8923+17.784)/(1-(1+10%)*0.65%-15%-0.3%)/6.5		53.3202

SP-16/MY005	计算过程	核算单位：　**set**	计算结果
实际成本(¥)	310-310/(1+16%)*13%		275.2586
公司定额费(¥)	310*3%		9.3000
垫款利息(¥)	310*5.22%*45/360		2.0228
海洋运费(¥)	0.55*0.46*0.445*76*6.5/2		27.8085
FOB (US$)	(275.2586+5.2+9.3+2.0228)/(1-15%-0.3%)/6.5		52.9982
CFR (US$)	(275.2586+5.2+9.3+2.0228+27.8085)/(1-15%-0.3%)/6.5		58.0492
CIF (US$)	(275.2586+5.2+9.3+2.0228+27.8085)/(1-(1+10%)*0.65%-15%-0.3%)/6.5		58.5434

CL-16/MY007	计算过程	核算单位：　**set**	计算结果
实际成本(¥)	280-280/(1+16%)*13%		248.6207
公司定额费(¥)	280*3%		8.4000
垫款利息(¥)	280*5.22%*45/360		1.8270
海洋运费(¥)	0.52*0.48*0.42*76*6.5/2		25.8935
FOB (US$)	(248.6207+5.2+8.4+1.827)/(1-15%-0.3%)/6.5		47.9607
CFR (US$)	(248.6207+5.2+8.4+1.827+25.8935)/(1-15%-0.3%)/6.5		52.6639
CIF (US$)	(248.6207+5.2+8.4+1.827+25.8935)/(1-(1+10%)*0.65%-15%-0.3%)/6.5		53.1123

20英尺整箱（20'FCL）报价核算

TY-12/JH012　　计算过程　　　　　　　　　　　　　　　核算单位：　set　　计算结果

	计算过程	计算结果
出口退税额(¥)	320/(1+16%)*13%	35.8621
海洋运费(¥)	1230*6.5/644 【装箱数量:25÷(0.62×0.48×0.52)取整×4＝644套】	12.4146
包干费(¥)	920/644	1.4286
FOB (US$)	(320-35.8621+1.4286+9.6+2.088)/(1-15%-0.3%)/6.5	53.9923
CFR (US$)	(320-35.8621+1.4286+9.6+2.088+12.4146)/(1-15%-0.3%)/6.5	56.2472
CIF (US$)	(320-35.8621+1.4286+9.6+2.088+12.4146)/(1-(1+10%)*0.65%-15%-0.3%)/6.5	56.7261

TY-12/JH015　　计算过程　　　　　　　　　　　　　　　核算单位：　set　　计算结果

	计算过程	计算结果
出口退税额(¥)	290/(1+16%)*13%	32.5000
海洋运费(¥)	1230*6.5/692 【装箱数量:25÷(0.6×0.48×0.5)取整×4＝692套】	11.5535
包干费(¥)	920/692	1.3295
FOB (US$)	(290-32.5+1.3295+8.7+1.8923)/(1-15%-0.3%)/6.5	48.9368
CFR (US$)	(290-32.5+1.3295+8.7+1.8923+11.5535)/(1-15%-0.3%)/6.5	51.0354
CIF (US$)	(290-32.5+1.3295+8.7+1.8923+11.5535)/(1-(1+10%)*0.65%-15%-0.3%)/6.5	51.4699

SP-16/MY005　　计算过程　　　　　　　　　　　　　　　核算单位：　set　　计算结果

	计算过程	计算结果
出口退税额(¥)	310/(1+16%)*13%	34.7414
海洋运费(¥)	1230*6.5/444 【装箱数量:25÷(0.55×0.46×0.445)取整×2＝444套】	18.0068
包干费(¥)	920/444	2.0721
FOB (US$)	(310-34.7414+2.0721+9.3+2.0228)/(1-15%-0.3%)/6.5	52.4300
CFR (US$)	(310-34.7414+2.0721+9.3+2.0228+18.0068)/(1-15%-0.3%)/6.5	55.7007
CIF (US$)	(310-34.7414+2.0721+9.3+2.0228+18.0068)/(1-(1+10%)*0.65%-15%-0.3%)/6.5	56.1749

CL-16/MY007　　计算过程　　　　　　　　　　　　　　　核算单位：　set　　计算结果

	计算过程	计算结果
出口退税额(¥)	280/(1+16%)*13%	31.3793
海洋运费(¥)	1230*6.5/476 【装箱数量:25÷(0.52×0.48×0.42)取整×2＝476套】	16.7962
包干费(¥)	920/476	1.9328
FOB (US$)	(280-31.3793+1.9328+8.4+1.827)/(1-15%-0.3%)/6.5	47.3673
CFR (US$)	(280-31.3793+1.9328+8.4+1.827+16.7962)/(1-15%-0.3%)/6.5	50.4181
CIF (US$)	(280-31.3793+1.9328+8.4+1.827+16.7962)/(1-(1+10%)*0.65%-15%-0.3%)/6.5	50.8473

40英尺整箱（40'FCL）报价核算

TY-12/JH012

	计算过程	核算单位： set	计算结果
海洋运费(¥)	2130*6.5/1420 【装箱数量:55÷(0.62×0.48×0.52)取整×4＝1420套】		9.7500
包干费(¥)	1550/1420		1.0915
FOB (US$)	(320-35.8621+1.0915+9.6+2.088)/(1-15%-0.3%)/6.5		53.9311
CFR (US$)	(320-35.8621+1.0915+9.6+2.088+9.75)/(1-15%-0.3%)/6.5		55.7020
CIF (US$)	(320-35.8621+1.0915+9.6+2.088+9.75)/(1-(1+10%)*0.65%-15%-0.3%)/6.5		56.1762

TY-12/JH015

	计算过程	核算单位： set	计算结果
海洋运费(¥)	2130*6.5/1524 【装箱数量:55÷(0.6×0.48×0.5)取整×4＝1524套】		9.0846
包干费(¥)	1550/1524		1.0171
FOB (US$)	(290-32.5+1.0171+8.7+1.8923)/(1-15%-0.3%)/6.5		48.8801
CFR (US$)	(290-32.5+1.0171+8.7+1.8923+9.0846)/(1-15%-0.3%)/6.5		50.5302
CIF (US$)	(290-32.5+1.0171+8.7+1.8923+9.0846)/(1-(1+10%)*0.65%-15%-0.3%)/6.5		50.9604

SP-16/MY005

	计算过程	核算单位： set	计算结果
海洋运费(¥)	2130*6.5/976 【装箱数量:55÷(0.55×0.46×0.445)取整×2＝976套】		14.1855
包干费(¥)	1550/976		1.5881
FOB (US$)	(310-34.7414+1.5881+9.3+2.0228)/(1-15%-0.3%)/6.5		52.3421
CFR (US$)	(310-34.7414+1.5881+9.3+2.0228+14.1855)/(1-15%-0.3%)/6.5		54.9187
CIF (US$)	(310-34.7414+1.5881+9.3+2.0228+14.1855)/(1-(1+10%)*0.65%-15%-0.3%)/6.5		55.3863

CL-16/MY007

	计算过程	核算单位： set	计算结果
海洋运费(¥)	2130*6.5/1048 【装箱数量:55÷(0.52×0.48×0.42)取整×2＝1048套】		13.2109
包干费(¥)	1550/1048		1.4790
FOB (US$)	(280-31.3793+1.479+8.4+1.827)/(1-15%-0.3%)/6.5		47.2848
CFR (US$)	(280-31.3793+1.479+8.4+1.827+13.2109)/(1-15%-0.3%)/6.5		49.6844
CIF (US$)	(280-31.3793+1.479+8.4+1.827+13.2109)/(1-(1+10%)*0.65%-15%-0.3%)/6.5		50.1074

出口报价核算汇总

货号	TY-12/JH012	TY-12/JH015	SP-16/MY005	CL-16/MY007
品名	12pc Dinnerware Set	12pc Dinnerware Set	16pc Dinnerware Set	16pc Dinnerware Set
拼箱（LCL）报价				
FOB	US$ 54.68 PER SET	US$ 49.64 PER SET	US$ 53.00 PER SET	US$ 47.96 PER SET
CFR	US$ 58.15 PER SET	US$ 52.87 PER SET	US$ 58.05 PER SET	US$ 52.66 PER SET
CIF	US$ 58.64 PER SET	US$ 53.32 PER SET	US$ 58.54 PER SET	US$ 53.11 PER SET
20英尺整箱（20'FCL）报价				
FOB	US$ 53.99 PER SET	US$ 48.94 PER SET	US$ 52.43 PER SET	US$ 47.37 PER SET
CFR	US$ 56.25 PER SET	US$ 51.04 PER SET	US$ 55.70 PER SET	US$ 50.42 PER SET
CIF	US$ 56.73 PER SET	US$ 51.47 PER SET	US$ 56.17 PER SET	US$ 50.85 PER SET
40英尺整箱（40'FCL）报价				
FOB	US$ 53.93 PER SET	US$ 48.88 PER SET	US$ 52.34 PER SET	US$ 47.28 PER SET
CFR	US$ 55.70 PER SET	US$ 50.53 PER SET	US$ 54.92 PER SET	US$ 49.68 PER SET
CIF	US$ 56.18 PER SET	US$ 50.96 PER SET	US$ 55.39 PER SET	US$ 50.11 PER SET

7.

Shanghai Tianyuan Trading Company

No. 451 Zunyi Road, Shanghai, China

Tel: (86) 21 62598822   Fax: (86) 21 62598825   Zip: 200335

G Wood & Sons Trading Company
36 Castle Street,
Bristol, BS1 ABO, U.K.

Sept. 6, 2018

Dear Ms. Marji,

We are very pleased to receive your inquiry of Sept. 5.

Enclosed are our illustrated catalogue and price list, which can give the details you asked for. Also by separate post we are sending you a full range of samples and, when you have had a chance to examine them, we feel confident that you will agree that the goods are excellent in quality and competitive in price.

On regular purchases in quantity of no less than five thousand of individual items, we would offer you a special discount of 3% of the listed price. For your information, we do business on the basis of sight L/C.

Polyester cotton products are rapidly becoming popular because they are strong, warm and light. After studying our prices you will not be surprised to learn that we are finding it difficult to meet the demand. But if you place your order not later than the end of this month, we would guarantee delivery within 30 days from receipt of the relevant L/C.

We invite your attention to our other products, details of which you will find in the catalogue, and look forward to receiving your first order.

Yours sincerely,
Lilian Xu
Shanghai Tianyuan Trading Company

8.

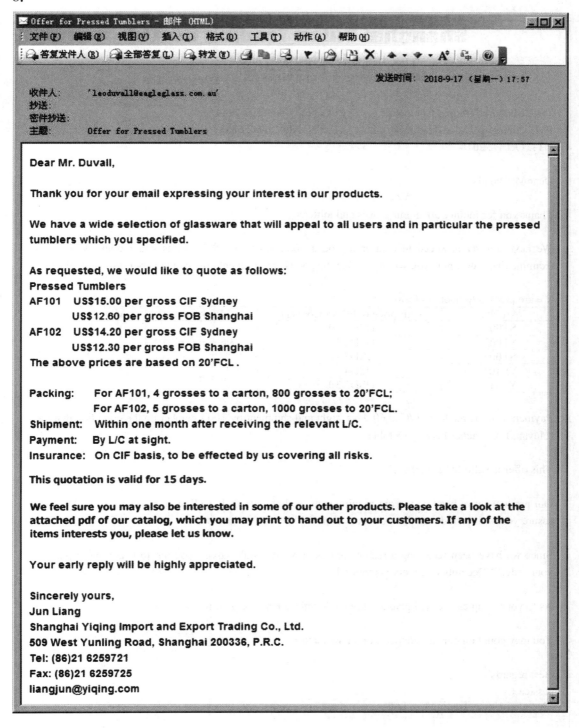

Offer for Pressed Tumblers – 邮件 (HTML)

文件(F)　编辑(E)　视图(V)　插入(I)　格式(O)　工具(T)　动作(A)　帮助(H)

答复发件人(R)　全部答复(L)　转发(W)

发送时间：　2018-9-17（星期一）17:57

收件人：　'leoduvall@eagleglass.com.au'
抄送：
密件抄送：
主题：　Offer for Pressed Tumblers

Dear Mr. Duvall,

Thank you for your email expressing your interest in our products.

We have a wide selection of glassware that will appeal to all users and in particular the pressed tumblers which you specified.

As requested, we would like to quote as follows:
Pressed Tumblers
AF101　US$15.00 per gross CIF Sydney
　　　　US$12.60 per gross FOB Shanghai
AF102　US$14.20 per gross CIF Sydney
　　　　US$12.30 per gross FOB Shanghai
The above prices are based on 20'FCL .

Packing:　　For AF101, 4 grosses to a carton, 800 grosses to 20'FCL;
　　　　　　For AF102, 5 grosses to a carton, 1000 grosses to 20'FCL.
Shipment:　Within one month after receiving the relevant L/C.
Payment:　By L/C at sight.
Insurance:　On CIF basis, to be effected by us covering all risks.

This quotation is valid for 15 days.

We feel sure you may also be interested in some of our other products. Please take a look at the attached pdf of our catalog, which you may print to hand out to your customers. If any of the items interests you, please let us know.

Your early reply will be highly appreciated.

Sincerely yours,
Jun Liang
Shanghai Yiqing Import and Export Trading Co., Ltd.
509 West Yunling Road, Shanghai 200336, P.R.C.
Tel: (86)21 6259721
Fax: (86)21 6259725
liangjun@yiqing.com

9.

Shanghai Union Trading Co. Ltd.

9 Floor, Xiehe Plaza, 202 West Beijing Road, Shanghai, China

Tel: 86-21-64568930　　Fax: 86-21-64568932　　wwww.union.sh.cn

TO：Margaret Trading Company　　　（Fax No. 1-604-507 2944）
FM：Shanghai Union Trading Co. Ltd.　（Fax No. 86-21-64568932）
DT：Oct 11, 2018

Dear Ms Woods,

Thank you for inquiry about our gloves and mittens.

We have already arranged to courier to you a good selection of the items you require. When you examine them, we know you will agree that the goods are excellent quality and very reasonable pirced.

We are pleased to quote as follows:

Art No.	Unit price (CFR Vancouver)	Packing	Min Quantity
ST001	USD3.80		
ST002	USD4.50	96 pairs/ctn	4800 pairs per Art. No.
ST003	USD5.10		
YE101	USD4.70	60 pairs/ctn	
YE115	USD5.30		

Payment is to be made by L/C at 60 days' sight and shipment by 10 December on the condition that the relevant L/C reaches here by October.

This offer is valid for 2 weeks.

Our products have been up to your requirements, selling extremely well in other countries, and we can assure you with confidence that your customers will be much impressed.

Since we have been receiving a rush of orders now, we would advise you not to lose time in placing your order if December delivery is required.

As to your samples, we will give our favorable offer upon receipt of them.

You may count on our full cooperation in the matter.

Best regards,
Jessica Li
Shanghai Union Trading Co. Ltd.

10.

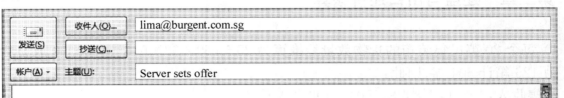

Dear Sir or Madam

We learned your name and address from *alibaba.com* and are writing to inform you that we can provide a December supply of server sets and more importantly, to seek possibilities to establish long-term business relationship with you.

We are one of leading Imp. & Exp. companies in China specializing in light industrial products. Extensive connections with manufacturers guarantee us a stable and adequate stock as well as the market-tailored products. Our commodities enjoy a high popularity in Middle East, Europe and America. As to the server sets, they are our best sellers reputable for their excellent quality and fashionable designs.

To be specific, we would like to quote as follows:
Stainless Steel Server Sets
Art. No. S9420	USD 18.60 per set CIF Singapore	5 sets to a carton
Art. No. S9320	USD 23.00 per set CIF Singapore	4 sets to a carton
Art. No. S9411	USD 28.50 per set CIF Singapore	3 sets to a carton

Min. Order Qty :	200 cartons each item
Payment:	by L/C at 30 days after B/L date.
Shipment:	in December with the relative L/C reaching us by the end of October.
Insurance:	for 110% CIF value against All Risks.

Our illustrated catalogue is attached, which may be helpful in making your choices. Upon receipt of your specific requirement, we would be happy to offer you samples.

Looking forward to your favorable reply.

Yours faithfully
Linda Mei
Shanghai Meigu Imp. & Exp. Company

第三章　还盘与出口还价核算

1.

1）每个 20 英尺集装箱的货物数量经推算为 $25÷(50×62×64)÷1000000$ 取整后为 126 箱计 504 盏；因此：

销售收入：	$14.5×6.8×504＝49694.4$ 元
退税收入：	$81÷(1＋16\%)×13\%×504＝4575.1034$ 元
采购成本：	$81×504＝40824$ 元
包干费：	750 元
海洋运费：	$1200×6.8＝8160$ 元
银行费用：	$49694.4×0.25\%＝124.236$ 元
垫款利息：	$40824×5.8\%×30÷360＝197.316$ 元
定额费用：	$40824×3.5\%＝1428.84$ 元
获利总额：	销售收入＋退税收入－采购成本－各项费用
	$49694.4＋4575.1034－40824－750－8160－124.236－197.316－$
	$1428.84＝2785.11$ 元
销售利润率：	$2785.11÷49694.4×100\%＝5.60\%$
成本利润率：	$2785.11÷40824×100\%＝6.82\%$

2）每个 40 英尺集装箱的货物数量经推算为 $55÷(50×62×64)÷1000000$ 取整后为 277 箱计 1108 盏；因此：

销售收入：	$14.3×6.8×1108＝107741.92$ 元
退税收入：	$81÷(1＋16\%)×13\%×1108＝10057.9655$ 元
采购成本：	$81×1108＝89748$ 元
包干费：	1250 元
海洋运费：	$2100×6.8＝14280$ 元
海运保险费：	$107741.92×110\%×0.35\%＝414.8064$ 元
银行费用：	$107741.92×0.25\%＝269.3548$ 元
垫款利息：	$89748×5.8\%×30÷360＝433.782$ 元
定额费用：	$89748×3.5\%＝3141.18$ 元
获利总额：	销售收入＋退税收入－采购成本－各项费用
	$107741.92＋10057.9655－89748－1250－14280－414.8064－$
	$269.3548－433.782－3141.18＝8262.76$ 元
销售利润率：	$8262.76÷107741.92×100\%＝7.67\%$
成本利润率：	$8262.76÷89748×100\%＝9.21\%$

3)

销售收入：　　14.5×6.8×504＝49694.4 元

退税收入：　　81÷(1＋16％)×13％×504＝4575.1034 元

采购成本：　　81×504＝40824 元

包干费：　　　750 元

银行费用：　　49694.4×0.25％＝124.236 元

垫款利息：　　40824×5.8％×30÷360＝197.316 元

定额费用：　　40824×3.5％＝1428.84 元

预期利润：　　49694.4×10％＝4969.44 元

海洋运费：　　销售收入＋退税收入－采购成本－各项费用(除海洋运费外)－预期利润

　　　　　　　49694.4＋4575.1034－40824－750－124.236－197.316－1428.84－4969.44＝5975.6714 元人民币＝878.78 美元

4)

销售收入：　　14.3×6.8＝97.24 元

退税收入：　　采购成本÷(1＋16％)×13％

包干费：　　　1250÷1108＝1.1282 元

海洋运费：　　2100×6.8÷1108＝12.8881 元

海运保险费：　97.24×110％×0.35％＝0.37437 元

银行费用：　　97.24×0.25％＝0.2431 元

垫款利息：　　采购成本×5.8％×30÷360

定额费用：　　采购成本×3.5％

预期利润：　　97.24×12％＝11.6688 元

采购成本：　　销售收入＋退税收入－采购成本－各项费用

　　　　　　　＝97.24＋采购成本÷(1＋16％)×13％

　　　　　　　－1.1282－12.8881－0.37437－0.2431

　　　　　　　－采购成本×5.8％×30÷360－采购成本×3.5％－11.6688

采购成本－采购成本÷(1＋16％)×13％＋采购成本×5.8％×30÷360＋采购成本×3.5％

　　　　　　　＝97.24－1.1282－12.8881－0.37437－0.2431－11.6688

采购成本×(1－13％÷(1＋16％)＋5.8％×30÷360＋3.5％)＝70.9374

采购成本　　　＝70.9374÷(1－13％÷(1＋16％)＋5.8％×30÷360＋3.5％)

　　　　　　　＝76.46 元/盏

2.

还价后的利润总额核算:(核算单位为 4 个 20 英尺整箱)

	计算过程	核算单位:	**4*20'FCL**	计算结果
销售收入总额(¥)	(53.8*644+48.1*692+52.5*444+47*476)*6.2			704409.2800
退税收入总额(¥)	(320*644+290*692+310*444+280*476)*11%/(1+16%)			64262.7586
采购成本总额(¥)	320*644+290*692+310*444+280*476			677680.0000
海洋运费总额(¥)	1230*6.2*4			30504.0000
保险费(¥)	(53.8*644+48.1*692+52.5*444+47*476)*6.2*(1+10%)*0.5%			3874.2510
包干费总额(¥)	900*4			3600.0000
公司定额费总额(¥)	(320*644+290*692+310*444+280*476)*4%			27107.2000
垫款利息总额(¥)	(320*644+290*692+310*444+280*476)*8%*1/12			4517.8667
银行手续费总额(¥)	(53.8*644+48.1*692+52.5*444+47*476)*6.2*0.5%			3522.0464
利润总额(¥)	704409.28+64262.7586-677680-30504-3874.2510-3600-27107.2-4517.8667-3522.0464			17866.6745
销售利润率(%)	17866.6745/704409.28			2.54%

还价后的采购成本核算:(销售利润率保持在 8%)

TY-12/JH012

	计算过程	核算单位:	**set**	计算结果
销售收入(¥)	53.8*6.2			333.5600
海洋运费(¥)	1230*6.2/644			11.8416
包干费(¥)	900/644			1.3975
保险费(¥)	53.8*6.2*(1+10%)*0.5%			1.8346
银行手续费(¥)	53.8*6.2*0.5%			1.6678
利润(¥)	53.8*6.2*8%			26.6848
采购成本(¥)	(333.56-11.8416-1.3975-1.8346-1.6678-26.6848)/(1-11%/(1+16%)+4%+8%*1/12)			304.8138

TY-12/JH015

	计算过程	核算单位:	**set**	计算结果
销售收入(¥)	48.1*6.2			298.2200
海洋运费(¥)	1230*6.2/692			11.0202
包干费(¥)	900/692			1.3006
保险费(¥)	48.1*6.2*(1+10%)*0.5%			1.6402
银行手续费(¥)	48.1*6.2*0.5%			1.4911
利润(¥)	48.1*6.2*8%			23.8576
采购成本(¥)	(298.22-11.0202-1.3006-1.6402-1.4911-23.8576)/(1-11%/(1+16%)+4%+8%*1/12)			272.0106

SP-16/MY005	计算过程	核算单位： **set**	计算结果
销售收入(¥)	52.5*6.2		325.5000
海洋运费(¥)	1230*6.2/444		17.1757
包干费(¥)	900/444		2.0270
保险费(¥)	52.5*6.2*(1+10%)*0.5%		1.7903
银行手续费(¥)	52.5*6.2*0.5%		1.6275
利润(¥)	52.5*6.2*8%		26.0400
采购成本(¥)	(325.5-17.1757-2.027-1.7903-1.6275-26.04)/(1-11%/(1+16%)+4%+8%*1/12)		290.8470

CL-16/MY007	计算过程	核算单位： **set**	计算结果
销售收入(¥)	47*6.2		291.4000
海洋运费(¥)	1230*6.2/476		16.0210
包干费(¥)	900/476		1.8908
保险费(¥)	47*6.2*(1+10%)*0.5%		1.6027
银行手续费(¥)	47*6.2*0.5%		1.4570
利润(¥)	47*6.2*8%		23.3120
采购成本(¥)	(291.4-16.021-1.8908-1.6027-1.457-23.312)/(1-11%/(1+16%)+4%+8%*1/12)		259.6200

还价采购成本汇总

货号	TY-12/JH012	TY-12/JH015	SP-16/MY005	CL-16/MY007
品名	12pc Dinnerware Set	12pc Dinnerware Set	16pc Dinnerware Set	16pc Dinnerware Set
原采购成本(¥)	320元/套	290元/套	310元/套	280元/套
还价后采购成本(¥)	304.8138元/套	272.0106元/套	290.847元/套	259.62元/套
降价幅度(%)	4.75%	6.20%	6.18%	7.28%

3.

Shanghai Jinyuan Import & Export Co., Ltd.

224 East Jinling Road, Shanghai 200001, China　Tel: 86 21 6755 3427　Fax: 86 21 6755 2215

F & A Telephone Supplies Co., Ltd.
128 Taiyoun Road,
Kuala Lumpur, Malaysia

Jun. 22, 2018

Dear Mr. Wahid,

Thank you for your letter of Jun. 20, 2018.

We have inspected other brands as mentioned by you and found although they look alike, there are several features not included in their products.

1. We use DECT6.0 technology for interference free performance with superior clarity and range, while other 2.4G phones may conflict with WiFi.
2. Our phones have personalized ringers to individualize ring tones for different callers, while others don't.
3. Our phones are incredibly tough and meet the JIS7 waterproof standard, so they can handle any environment indoors or outdoors.

Because of the above advantages our costs are more expensive and our quality is far better than others.

However, in order to assist you to compete with other dealers in the market, we are prepared to make a 1.5% reduction if your order reaches USD50,000.

We hope to receive your order soon, and if you have any questions just let us know.

Yours sincerely,
Eric Zhao
Shanghai Jinyuan Import & Export Co., Ltd.

4.

SHANGHAI KANGJIAN TRADING CO., LTD.

510 Guangzhou Road Shanghai 200021, China
Tel: +86 21 56332421   Fax: +86 21 56783325

August 21, 2018

ACE Bro. Co., Ltd.
P.O. Box 263 Sentrum, N-0845 Oslo, Norway

Dear Mr. Donald,

We have carefully considered your letter of August 18. However, we are unable to change our quotation for these tyre chains.

You think only at a competitive price can a new product enter into a market, on which we share the similar view. The price we quoted leaves us with only small margin. The fact that we have had many orders at this price is in itself evidence of the good value of our products.

There are various reasons whether a new product could be well received or not. We believe you will do successful business with the present price by proper sales promotion. We can guarantee the punctuate delivery.

So we hope you will consider ordering our goods. If you then still feel you cannot accept our offer, we hope it will not prevent you from contacting us again in the future.

We look forward to hearing from you soon.

Yours sincerely,

Linda Xiao

Shanghai Kangjian Trading Co., Ltd.

5.

Shanghai Tengyue Shoes Industrial Co., Ltd.

719 Wuning Road, Shanghai 200244, China

Tel:86 21 64234510　Fax: 86 21 64234466　www.tengyue.sh.cn

ACME Footwear Company Limited
64 Spray St, Elwood, Melbourne, Australia

12 Sept. 2018

Dear Mr. Smith,

Thank you for your letter of 10 Sept. 2018. We note that you feel our prices not competitive enough and request a discount of 5%.

However, we have already cut our profit to the minimum so it is hard to reduce the prices any further without sacrificing the quality. We do not wish to offer you a product that you will find difficult to sell or later have complaints about. In order to keep the long-term reputation for manufacturing footwear of superb quality, we employ only the most skilled craftsmen and use only the finest materials. Our production costs have increased very considerably over the last few years, and yet we have been able to avoid raising the selling prices. We are willing to keep our prices as low as possible for the consumers, but, as we have said, we find it impossible to reduce them.

We know that cheaper models are marketed by our competitors, but we are very proud of our shoes and they have been very well received, with good sales reported regularly from many areas, such as the United States and Western Europe.

We look forward to receiving at least a trial order from you, and we would be glad to include your name in our list of cherished customers.

Yours sincerely,

Adson Lin

Shanghai Tengyue Shoes Industrial Co., Ltd.

6.

Re: MOQ and payment of Ornamental Cloth
发件人：huyiwen@yongjin.sh.com.cn
时　间：2018 年 10 月 26 日 15:28
收件人：m.lacona@softee.com.ar

 Shanghai Yongjin Trading Co., Ltd.

Hello Marcelo

Thanks for your email of yesterday.

We are sorry to say to reduce the quantity so much will result in a rise in the cost, which our current prices cannot cover. So we have to raise the price by 1% for each item. But we believe even with such adjustment, our products remain competitive for their excellent quality, fresh colors and fashionable designs.

As we have been working together for many years, we wish we could grant your request to switch to D/P. However, it is our usual practice to do business on the L/C basis either with old friends or new customers. I hope you can understand our situation. However, bearing in mind the very pleasant cooperation we have had, we agree to payment by L/C at 30 days' sight. I trust this concession will cause a considerable increase of your orders and assure you that I shall always do my utmost to execute them to your complete satisfaction.

Look forward to continuing to work with you.

All the best
Yiwen

Yiwen Hu
Sales Manager
Shanghai Yongjin Trading Co., Ltd.
15F Yinhai Manshion, 450 Fujian Road, Shanghai, China
Tel: 0086-21-56967500　56967412　Fax: 0086-21-56967403
www.yongjin.com.cn

7.

Shanghai Huixiang International Trade Co., Ltd.

344 Hubei Road, Shanghai 200017, China
Tel: (86) 21 6733 5621　Fax: (86) 21 6733 5788

SAMEIM International SARL
Quai François-Mauriac 639851 Paris Cedex 13 France

Nov. 4, 2018

Dear Mr. Daladier,

Your letter of Nov. 2 has been duly received.

As you know, our fountain pens are of excellent quality. They are beautiful in design and fluent in writing, which make them enjoy a good reputation in Asian and American market. We believe the current price is quite reasonable according to the quality. But in order to conclude the first transaction between us, we will allow you a 2% discount if the quantity of your order reaches 2,000 dozens. This is the greatest concession we can make.

As to the terms of payment, I'm sorry that we are not able to use D/A terms with new clients. After more smooth transactions, I think there will be a better time for us to dicuss the issue again. You can always rest assured of punctual shipment as long as we receive your L/C in time.

I hope that you will agree to this suggestion and look forward to having your initial order.

Yours sincerely,
Jane Xue
Sales Manager
Shanghai Huixiang International Trade Co., Ltd.

第四章　接受与出口合同签订

1.

成交核算			
收入：	计算过程	核算单位：**3x20'FCL**	计算结果
销售收入总额(¥)	(52.2*644+48*692+56.5*222+51.7*238)*6.5		595922.60
退税收入总额(¥)	(300*644+275*692+315*222+285*238)/(1+16%)*13%		58417.07
支出：			
采购成本总额(¥)	300*644+275*692+315*222+285*238		521260.00
海洋运费总额(¥)	2760*3*6.5		53820.00
包干费总额(¥)	1200*3		3600.00
公司定额费总额(¥)	(300*644+275*692+315*222+285*238)*3%		15637.80
垫款利息总额(¥)	(300*644+275*692+315*222+285*238)*6%*90/360		7818.90
银行手续费总额(¥)	(52.2*644+48*692+56.5*222+51.7*238)*6.5*0.3%		1787.77
保险费总额(¥)	(52.2*644+48*692+56.5*222+51.7*238)*6.5*(1+10%)*0.65%		4260.85
利润：			
利润总额(¥)	595922.6+58417.07-521260-53820-3600-15637.8-7818.9-1787.77-4260.85		46154.35
销售利润率(%)	46154.35/595922.6		7.75%

2.

成交核算			
收入：	计算过程	核算单位：**4x20'FCL**	计算结果
销售收入总额(¥)	(32.2*320+25.5*604+22.8*712+15.1*504)*6.6		327030.00
退税收入总额(¥)	(160*320+140*604+125*712+76*504)/(1+16%)*9%		20410.14
支出：			
采购成本总额(¥)	160*320+140*604+125*712+76*504		263064.00
海洋运费总额(¥)	1420*4*6.6		37488.00
包干费总额(¥)	1000*4		4000.00
公司定额费总额(¥)	(160*320+140*604+125*712+76*504)*4.5%		11837.88
垫款利息总额(¥)	(160*320+140*604+125*712+76*504)*4.9%*60/360		2148.36
银行手续费总额(¥)	(32.2*320+25.5*604+22.8*712+15.1*504)*6.6*0.25%		817.58
客户佣金总额(¥)	(32.2*320+25.5*604+22.8*712+15.1*504)*6.6*3%		9810.90
利润：			
利润总额(¥)	327030+20410.14-263064-37488-4000-11837.88-2148.36-817.58-9810.9		18273.42
销售利润率(%)	18273.42/327030		5.59%

3.

1）C708　中国灰鸭绒　含绒量90％，允许1％上下

2）蝴蝶牌缝纫机　型号JA-1　直驱式电脑平缝机

3）S836　白兔毛绒玩具　品质同卖方在2018年7月底之前提供的样品

4）品质和技术数据与所附技术协议相符，该技术协议视为本合同不可分割的一部分。

5）81000R　印花布(经树脂处理)　30支×36支　72×69　89/91厘米×38.4米

6）买方的花样须于装运月份前60天送达卖方，经厂方接受和稍予修改/调整为准，并允许合理色差。

7）对于由买方提供设计、商标、牌号、标识和/或印记的商品，如发生对第三者工业产权的侵害，将由买方负责。

4.

1）铁桶装，每桶净重 185～190 千克。（化工原料）

2）纸箱装，每箱四盒，每盒约 9 磅，每只涂蜡并包纸。（水果）

3）新单层麻袋装，每袋约 100 千克。（大米）

4）纸箱装，每箱 50 打，尺码搭配。（汗衫）

5）货物采用中性包装，买方提供的标签须于装运月份前 45 天运抵卖方。（轻纺产品）

6）用牢固的新木箱或纸箱包装，适合长途的海运或空运，防湿、防潮、防震、防锈并耐粗暴搬运。凡因由于包装不良所产生的任何费用和损失将由卖方负担。（仪器）

5.

DESIGN NO. 款式	QUANTITY 数量	CARTON NO 件号/箱号	NOS OF PKGS. 件数
93-13	1260 PCS.	（1）1-21	（5）21 CARTONS
93-14	1260 PCS.	（2）22-42	（6）21 CARTONS
93-15	1200 PCS.	（3）43-62	（7）20 CARTONS
93-16	1680 PCS.	（4）63-90	（8）28 CARTONS

以上出口商品的总数量是 5400 PCS，包装总件数为 90 箱。

6.

1）价格中包括 5％的佣金

QUANTITY　数量	UNIT PRICE　单价	AMOUNT　总值
350 PCS.	US $125.00/PC. CIFC5％ NEW YORK	US $43,750.00 CIFC5％ NEW YORK
TOTAL VALUE(IN WORDS)总金额（大写）： SAY US DOLLARS FORTY THREE THOUSAND SEVEN HUNDRED AND FIFTY ONLY.		

2) 再给予 5% 的折扣

QUANTITY　数量	UNIT PRICE　单价	AMOUNT　总值
		CIF NEW YORK
350 PCS.	US $ 125.00/PC.	US $ 43,750.00
	LESS 5% DISCOUNT	US $ 2,187.50
	TOTAL	US $ 41,562.50

TOTAL VALUE(IN WORDS)总金额(大写)：
SAY US DOLLARS FORTY ONE THOUSAND FIVE HUNDRED SIXTY TWO AND CENTS FIFTY ONLY.

7.

1) 货物于 2018 年 7 月间由上海海运至汉堡并允许分批装运和转运。

2) 2018 年 7、8 月间分两批由上海运至旧金山并允许转运。

3) 2018 年 7、8 月间分为数量相等的两批自上海运至旧金山并允许转运。

4) 货物在 2018 年 7、8 月间每月各装一批自上海运往旧金山并允许转运。

5) 2018 年 7、8 月间由上海装运至旧金山,每月各装一批,每批数量相等并允许转运。

6) 收到信用证后 30 天内装运,信用证必须在 2018 年 6 月底之前开抵卖方,否则卖方有权不经通知而取消本合同或者对由此造成的直接损失向买方提出索赔。

8.

1) 保险由卖方按发票金额的 110% 投保水渍险和战争险,根据 1981 年 1 月 1 日中国人民保险公司的海运货物保险条款办理。

2) 凡是以 CIF 条件达成的交易,根据合同规定的险别按发票金额的 110% 投保。如果要求加大投保金额或扩大险别,新增的保险费将由买方负担。

3) 保险自装船起由买方自理,但卖方应按本合同第 11 条的规定通知买方。如未能按此办理,买方因此而遭受的一切损失全由卖方负担。(第 11 条:卖方在货物装船后,立即将合同号、品名、包装件数、毛重、净重、发票金额、载货船名及装船日期用电报、传真或电传通知买方。)

9.

TERMS & CONDITIONS OF PAYMENT

1) All the payment to be made under this contract will be effected in US Dollars by L/C or T/T.

2) Technical Support for US Dollars 25,000.00(Say Twenty Five Thousand) shall be paid by T/T against the certificate issued by the end-user stating that the technical support is successfully completed.

3) 90% of the balance of the total contract value is to be paid by irrevocable sight L/C which is opened one month prior to the delivery of the goods.

4) 10% of the balance shall be paid by a banker's draft issued by Bank of China against the certificate stating that the technical assistance, installation and trial test are finished and this certificate should be duly signed by the end-user.

10.

除另有规定者外,付款采用信用证方式。买方应通过为卖方所接受的一流银行,开立金额为 100% 合同金额的不可撤销即期信用证。

买方应保证信用证最迟在本合同规定装运月份前 30 天送达卖方,否则因此不能按期装运者,卖方不负责任;如超过装运期仍未开到者,卖方有权取消合同并向买方提出索赔。

买方信用证内,请勿指定航线、船名及承保保险公司的名称。

为方便卖方交单议付,信用证有效期应规定在最后装运日后至少 10 天,在中国到期。信用证的金额应允许有 5% 的增减。

为保证按期装运,买方应通过银行以全电开立信用证,并在证内注明允许分批装和转运,同时注明本合同号码。

11.

买方应通过卖方所接受的银行于装运月份前 30 天之前开立并送达卖方不可撤销见票后 45 天付款的远期信用证,规定 50% 发票金额凭见票后 45 天付款之远期光票支付,余下 50% 的货款以见票后 45 天付款交单支付。100% 发票金额的全套装运单据随附于托收项下,于买方付清发票的全部金额后交单。如买方不付清全部发票金额,则货运单据须由开证行掌握凭卖方指示处理。以上条款须在信用证中明确表述。

本条款如此订立主要是为了防止在进口商仅付清信用证项下 50% 货款即可取得全部货运单据情况的发生,使出口商安全收到 100% 的合同款项更有保障。

12.

上 海 远 大 进 出 口 公 司
SHANGHAI YUANDA IMPORT & EXPORT COMPANY
上海市溧阳路 1088 号龙邸大厦 16 楼
16th Floor, Dragon Mansion, 1088 Liyang Road, Shanghai 200081 China
电话(Tel):0086-21-56666624　　传真(Fax):0086-21-56666698

正本

ORIGINAL

销 货 合 约
SALES CONTRACT

编号 No.:　YD-YYSC0827

日期 Date:　Aug.27, 2018

买方
Buyers:　Hong Sheng (Hongkong) Co., Ltd.

地址
Address:　17/F, One Kowloon, 1 Wang Yuen Street, Kowloon Bay, Hong Kong

电话　　　　　　　　　　　　　　传真
Tel:　852- 2893-1521　　　　　Fax:　852- 2893-1525

兹经买卖双方同意成交下列商品订立条款如下：
The Undersigned Sellers and Buyers have agreed to close the following transaction according to the terms and conditions stipulated below.

货物名称及规格 Name of commodity and Specifications	数　量 Quantity	单　价 Unit Price	金　额 Amount
Chinese Rice　F.A.Q. 　Broken Grains (max.) 20% 　Admixture (max.) 0.2% 　Moisture (max.) 10%	2000 tons	CIF US$360.00	Singapore US$720,000.00
5% more or less both in Amount and Quantity allowed at the Sellers' Option	总　值 Total Amount	Say US Dollars Seven Hundred and Twenty Thousand Only	

包装
Packing:　50kg in a new gunny bag. Total 40,000 bags.

装运
Shipment:　To be effected during Dec. 2018 / Jan. 2019 in two equal lots from Shanghai to Singapore, allowing partial shipments and transshipment.

保险
Insurance:　To cover 110% of invoice value against All Risks as per and subject to the Ocean Marine Cargo Clauses of P.I.C.C. dated 1/1/1981.

付款
Payment:　The buyer shall open through a bank acceptable to the seller an irrevocable L/C payable at sight for 100% of contract valve to reach the seller by Oct. 15, 2018 and valid for negotiation in China until the 15th day after the date of shipment.

卖方 SELLERS
Shanghai Yuanda Import & Export Company

买方 BUYERS

13.

SALES CONTRACT

NO. STEP-08BS02

DATE MAR. 9, 2018

SELLER SHANGHAI LIHUA TRADING COMPANY

856 HUTAI ROAD

SHANGHAI

CHINA

BUYER STEPS GENERAL TRADING EST.,

P.O.BOX. 1240

DUBAI

U.A.E.

ART. NO.	NAME OF COMMODITY & SPECIFICATIONS	QUANTITY	UNIT PRICE	AMOUNT
				CFR DUBAI
SIT4958	BABY STROLLER	200SETS	US$80.50	US$16,100.00
SIT3455	BABY STROLLER	720SETS	US$46.60	US$33,552.00
LIE1476	BABY STROLLER	170SETS	US$105.00	US$17,850.00
			TOTAL	US$67,502.00
TOTAL AMOUNT IN WORDS	SAY UNITED STATES DOLLARS SIXTY SEVEN THOUSAND FIVE HUNDRED AND TWO ONLY.			

PACKING:

SIT4958　　　PACKED IN CARTONS OF 1 SET EACH, TOTAL 200 CARTONS

SIT3455　　　PACKED IN CARTONS OF 2 SETS EACH, TOTAL 360 CARTONS

LIE1476　　　PACKED IN CARTONS OF 1 SET EACH, TOTAL 170 CARTONS

TOTAL 730 CARTONS IN THREE 20 FEET CONTAINERS.

SHIPMENT:

TO BE SHIPPED FROM SHANGHAI, CHINA TO DUBAI, U.A.E.

BY SEA TRANSPORTATION

NO LATER THAN MAY 31, 2018

WITH PARTIAL SHIPMENTS ALLOWED AND TRANSSHIPMENT PROHIBITED.

INSURANCE:

INSURANCE TO BE COVERED BY THE BUYER.

PAYMENT:

THE BUYER SHOULD OPEN THROUGH A BANK ACCEPTABLE TO THE SELLER

AN IRREVOCABLE L/C AT 30 DAYS' SIGHT

FOR 100% OF TOTAL CONTRACT VALUE

TO REACH THE SELLER BY THE END OF MAR. 2018

AND VALID FOR NEGOTIATION IN CHINA

UNTIL THE 15TH DAY AFTER THE DATE OF SHIPMENT.

14.

SHANGHAI XINRONG TRADING CORPORATION

SUITE 1202 YINXIN TOWER, 444 JINLING ROAD, SHANGHAI 200002, CHINA
TEL: (86) 21 62144562　FAX: (86) 21 62144667

23 March 2018

Kiddie Korner Inc
Vancouver Canada

Dear Mr. Kidman

Thank you for your order No.C008 of 21 March. We are glad to confirm that all the items required are in stock. It is our pleasure to supply you again and we are sure that you will be also satisfied with the shipment this time.

We have sent to you by express mail our Sales Confirmation No. CA02 in duplicate. Please countersign it and return one copy to us for filing.

Please kindly open the relative L/C without delay, on receipt of which we will make up your order. You may rest assured that we will send shipping advice as soon as the shipment is completed.

The said order and your further orders will always have our best attention.

Yours sincerely
Lilly GAO
Shanghai Xinrong Trading Corporation

15.

Shanghai Yongsheng Potteries & Porcelain Co. Ltd.

Suite 1115, 555 Taopu Road, Shanghai 200302, China　Tel: (86) 21 5922 1021　Fax: (86) 21 5922 0111

March 24, 2018

Dilimin Co., Ltd
28 Victory Street
Manila, the Philippines

Dear Ms. Chilenian,

Thank you for your order No. JM341 for porcelain wares after our friendly negotiation. This order shows again your confidence on us.

We can assure you of the high quality and the punctuate delivery so long as the relative L/C reaches us in time. We believe the conclusion of this transaction will lead to more business in future.

Enclosed is our Sales Confirmation No. EX345 in duplicate. Please countersign it and return one copy for our file.

In addition, we would like to take this opportunity to recommend to you our new series—the Great Wall Brand Porcelain, which is celebrated for its fine quality, elegant design and typical Chinese style packaging. We have also enclosed its illustrated catalogue and price-list for your reference. Please let us know if any item interests you.

We really appreciate any comments on our products.

Yours sincerely,
David Liu
Shanghai Yongsheng Potteries & Porcelain Co., Ltd.

第五章　信用证审核与修改

1.

托收的利弊

付款交单方式最不令人满意的特点是买方或其银行可能拒绝付款赎单,尤其在行市下跌的时候,其危害性更大。在这种情况下,卖方虽然仍旧是货主,但他有可能收不到货款。

在付款交单方式下,付款之前,买方不能取得代表货物所有权的单据和提取货物,货物所有权仍在卖方手中。假如买方拒付,卖方仍可把货物出售给他人。

在承兑交单项下,会出现进一步的困难:买方承兑汇票以后,代表所有权的单据就交到他手里。因此,如果他在付款前破产或无力支付,卖方就要蒙受损失。

因此,卖方很少接受付款交单或承兑交单,除非买方具有无可置疑的信誉或买卖双方有特殊的关系。出口商采用信用证就比采用付款交单或承兑交单好得多。然而,在某些场合或为了某种目的,付款交单或承兑交单仍然是必要的,例如:

1) 为了贯彻对外贸易政策,尤其为了促进与发展中国家的贸易。

2) 为了扩大出口,特别是推销我们的新产品和难销产品。

3) 通过向小企业提供信用以发展同他们的贸易往来。

4) 在与分公司做生意时为了简化付款手续。

2. 即期付款交单(D/P at sight)的结算流程

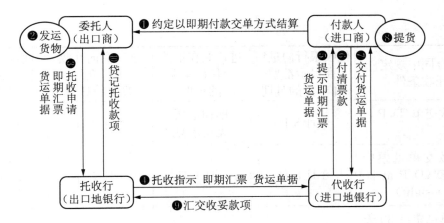

3. 远期付款交单(D/P at ×××days after sight)的结算流程

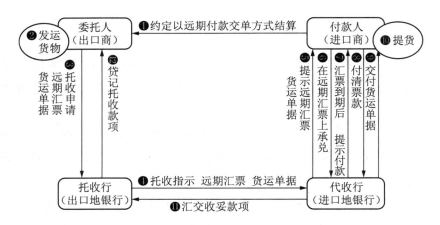

4. 承兑交单(D/A at ×××days after sight)的结算流程

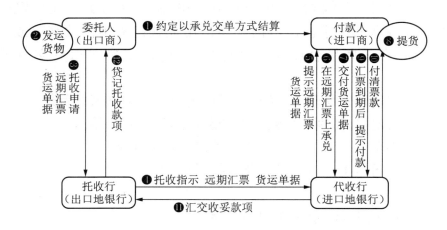

5.

交易合同中规定的托收条件	代收银行向进口商提示汇票和单据的日期	进口商在汇票上作出承兑的日期	进口商向代收银行支付票款的日期	代收银行向进口商提交货运单据的日期
即期付款交单(D/P at sight)	8月8日	即期汇票无需承兑	8月8日	8月8日
远期付款交单见票后30天付款(D/P at 30 days after sight)	8月8日	8月8日	9月7日	9月7日
承兑交单见票后30天付款(D/A at 30 days after sight)	8月8日	8月8日	9月7日	8月8日

6.
致：中国工商银行上海分行
自：TOKAIBANK TOKYO
2018 年 6 月 15 日　　　　编号　SRL 91388
开立跟单信用证
请予通知：
我行于 2018 年 6 月 15 日开立不可撤销信用证 LC635-38564，在中国有效至 2018
年 7 月 30 日。
开证申请人：　DAITO TSUSHO CO.，LTD. 504，18-18，2-CHOME
　　　　　　　TATSUNUMA，ADACHI-KU，TOKYO，121，JAPAN
受益人：　　　上海晨星公司　中国上海东大名路 375 号

金额：　　　　186,400.00 美元

本证在任何银行凭受益人开具的按发票全额以 THE TOKAI BANK 纽约分行为
付款人的即期汇票议付。

允许分批，不准转运。
装运自中国上海至日本名古屋不迟于 2018 年 7 月 15 日
出运商品为 8000 套服装
详见 2018 年 4 月 6 日之订单 DAITO3746 成本加运费、保险费至名古屋

所需单据：
＋　经签署的商业发票一式三份注明信用证号。
＋　全套清洁已装船海运提单做成凭托运人指示抬头并作空白背书，注明运费已
　　预付并通知申请人。
＋　装箱单一式三份。
＋　海运保险单或保险凭证一式两份，作空白背书，按发票金额的 110％投保海运
　　战争险和一切险，依据中国人民保险公司中国保险条款办理。索赔在日本用
　　汇票币种支付。
＋　普惠制原产地证明格式 A 一份。
＋　品质数量证明一份。

所有单据必须于运输单据签发日后的 15 天内提交，且在信用证的有效期内。

其他条件：

+ 全套上述装运单据的副本及正本原产地证明格式 A 须于装运后 48 小时内用快件寄给申请人；
+ 保险由托运人办理；
+ 禁止电汇索偿；
+ 日本以外所有银行费用将由受益人承担；
+ 凡凭本证所出具的汇票必须列有信用证号码和日期；
+ 议付银行须将汇票寄交付款行，同时将其他所有单据用航空挂号邮件分两次寄交我行。

凡符合本证条款所开立的汇票，本行保证承担履行承兑付款责任。

本证受《跟单信用证统一惯例》2007 年修订本（国际商会第 600 号出版物）的约束。

7.

1）凭受益人开具的即期汇票并随附注明本证号码的下列单据。

2）本证项下的所有汇票上必须注明："凭××银行×月×日开立的××号信用证出具"之条款。

3）经签署的商业发票一式五份，注明开证申请人进口许可证号码和本信用证号码。

4）全套清洁已装船海运提单，做成凭托运人指示抬头并作"交付给中国银行新加坡分行或其指定人"的背书，注明"运费付讫"并通知上述开证申请人。

5）做成可转让格式的海运保险单或保险凭证按 CIF 发票金额的 110％投保中国人民保险公司 1981 年 1 月 1 日的海运货物保险条款中一切险和战争险，保险至吉隆坡为止并按汇票所用货币在目的地赔付。

6）装箱单一式三份，详细注明货物内包装的各项规格以及每件包装内的具体货物内容。

7）表明装运 1500 箱运动球类，由中国口岸于 2018 年 7 月 20 日之前海运至科威特港，不允许分批装运和转运。

8）本证项下汇票须于 2018 年 8 月 30 日或之前在中国提交议付。

9）所有单据必须在运输单据签发以后 15 日内提交议付银行，但不得迟于信用证的到期日。

10）凡根据本证开具的与本证条款相符的汇票；并能按时提交本证所规定的单据（如果在规定的期限内开具并议付），我行保证对出票人、背书人和善意持有人承担付款责任。

11）本信用证根据《跟单信用证统一惯例》（2007 年修订法国巴黎国际商会第 600

号出版物)办理并遵守该惯例中的各项条款,特别是第 7 和第 8 条的规定。信用证所要求的汇票须注明我行名称、开证日期和本证号码。议付银行须将每一次议付的金额及日期批注在本信用证背面。

8.

1) 大米交易信用证审核结果:

— APPLICANT 名称错误,Maurlcio 应改为 Mauricio;

— APPLICANT 地址错误,45 V 应改为 45 B;

— BENEFICIARY 名称错误,Export & Import 应改为 Import & Export;

— 信用证到期地在国外,开证行柜台前应改为通知行柜台前;

— 汇票付款期限推迟了,30 days after sight 应改为 30 days after B/L date;

— 装运期提前了,12 月 15 日应改为 12 月 31 日;

— 提单条款中运费规定有误,Freight to be collected 应改为 Freight prepaid;

— 提单条款中正本份数不妥,2/3 应改为 3/3,并同时删除寄单证明条款(单据条款第 4 款);

— 装箱单条款中包装种类有误,new gunny bags 应改为 gunny bags;

— 保险条款中加成率有误,plus 110 PCT 应改为 plus 10 PCT;

— 货物描述中没有数量的溢短装规定,应明确规定数量可以上下浮动 5%;

— 货物描述中合同日期有误,11 月 18 日应改为 11 月 8 日;

— 交单日太紧,应按合同约定,将 5 天修改为 15 天;

— 目的港有误,Panama City 应改为 Colon R.P.;

— 分批装运和转运规定与合同不符,应改为均允许;

— 特别条款 Special conditions 第 1 款要求检验证书由开证申请人签发,不妥,建议改为由中国官方机构签发;

— 特别条款 Special conditions 第 3 款限制了信用证生效,应删除;

(备注:若合同金额有上下浮动的范围,则信用证应据此作相同规定,或者按合同金额的上限开立;若合同金额含佣金,则信用证可按含佣金额开立,也可扣除佣金按净价开立。该信用证的金额虽与合同不一致,但其实是以合同金额的浮动上限、扣除佣金后得出的,即 72000×(1+5%)×(1-3%)=73332.00,因此不作修改)

2) 缝纫机交易信用证审核结果:

— 付款期限为"at 45 days' sight"(见票后 45 天),与合同规定不符,应为见票后 30 天;

—　提单上要求标注运费"freight to collect"（运费到付），与合同交易条件 CFR
　有矛盾，应改为运费已付；
—　货物描述中商品货号为"JN746"，与合同规定不符，应为 JN764；
—　到期日"2018 年 11 月 30 日"与合同支付条款中信用证至装运日后第 15 天到
　期的规定不符，应改为 2018 年 12 月 15 日（以最迟装运日 11 月 30 日起算加
　15 天）；
—　到期地点在"Kuwait"（科威特），与合同支付条款中信用证在中国议付的规定
　不符，应改为在中国到期。

3) 纺织品交易信用证审核结果：
—　信用证的性质不符合合同要求，应将 revocable 改为 Irrevocable（不可撤销）；
—　信用证 Confirmation：without（没有保兑），应按合同规定加具保兑；
—　到期日不符合合同要求，6 月 5 日应改为 6 月 15 日；
—　议付行在纽约，与合同规定"在中国议付"不符，应改为在中国的银行议付；
—　汇票的付款期限不符，应为见票即付；
—　转运规定与合同不符，应改为允许转运；
—　合同号码错误，应为 AN107 而不是 AH107；
—　货号 49393(014428) 的数量不符，应为 3960pcs 而非 3690pcs；
—　提交的正本提单份数有误，应为 3/3 而非 2/3，同时应删去有关寄送正本单据
　的证明条款；
—　投保金额与合同不符，应为发票金额的 110％而非 120％；
—　信用证附加条款的第 2 条，对货物包装的要求与合同不符，应删除彩印 Col-
　ored 的要求；
—　交单时间太紧，应按合同支付条款规定，将装运日后 5 天内交单改为 15 天内
　提交。

9.
1) 保险单或保险凭证一式两份，做成空白背书，按发票金额的 110％投保，规定赔
　付货币与汇票币种一致并且标注新加坡理赔代理信息，投保中国人民保险公司
　1981 年 1 月 1 日生效的海洋货物运输保险条款的一切险及战争险。
2) 由中国国际贸易促进委员会签发的原产地证明一式两份，声明货物原产自中国。
3) 电汇索偿方式将不予接受。
4) 船样须于装船前直接快递至开证申请人认可。认可书将通过电子邮件的方式
　通知受益人。该电子邮件的副本须随附其他单据一并提交议付。

5）索偿时,议付行须将全套单据通过航空挂号信或航空快递的形式一次性寄至我行。

10.

1）签订合同：2018 年 10 月 20 日,上海 RUIZHI 贸易公司与新加坡 BOLEN 贸易公司签订编号为 QICY0593 的销售合同;

2）申请开证：合同签订后,新加坡 BOLEN 贸易公司向新加坡华联银行(Overseas Union Bank)申请开立信用证;

3）开出 L/C：2018 年 11 月 20 日,新加坡华联银行开出了号码为 5813183050 号信用证,金额为 139100 美元;

4）通知开证：随后,上海浦东发展银行向上海 RUIZHI 贸易公司通知了该信用证;

5）审核修改：收到国外来证后,上海 RUIZHI 贸易公司审核信用证,如发现有问题则联系新加坡 BOLEN 贸易公司通过新加坡华联银行修改信用证;

6）货物装运：2018 年 12 月 31 日前,上海 RUIZHI 贸易公司须在上海港将信用证项下的货物装船运往新加坡;

7）交单议付： 2019 年 1 月 15 日前,并且在运输单据签发后 15 天内,上海 RUIZHI 贸易公司须将下列单据提交上海浦发银行议付:

8）单据清单：

单据名称	单据份数
a　汇票	a　一式两联
b　商业发票	b　一式四份
c　海运提单	c　全套(一式两份/两份正本)
d　装箱重量单	d　一式两份
e　受益人证明(发送投保通知)	e　一份

9）审单议付：上海浦东发展银行审核单据,确认符合信用证后,将款项垫付给上海 RUIZHI 贸易公司;

10）寄单索偿：上海浦东发展银行将信用证项下的单据用快递方式一次性寄往新加坡华联银行要求偿付;

11）审单付款：新加坡华联银行审核单据,确认交单相符后,向上海浦东发展银行作出偿付;

12）赎单提货：新加坡 BOLEN 贸易公司审单确认相符后向新加坡华联银行付款,并取得单据,待货物到港后办理提货手续。

11.

信用证存在的问题	应当修改为
1）受益人公司名称（Trading Company）有误	Imp. & Exp. Corporation
2）金额（USD139,100.00）有误	USD139,104.00（大写金额一并修改）
3）提单抬头（To the order of Applicant）有误	To Order of issuing bank
4）提单标注的运费条款（Freight To Collect）有误	Freight Prepaid
5）货物描述中的商品名称（Silk）有误	Silk Garments
6）货物描述中的销售合同号码（QICY0593）有误	QJCY06593
7）货物描述中贸易术语（CFR Shanghai）有误	CFR Singapore

12.

<table>
<tr><td colspan="2" align="center">迪拜商业银行 德拉分行
阿拉伯联合酋长国 迪拜 1709 邮政信箱</td></tr>
<tr><td>不可撤销跟单信用证号码：01DLC077003079
开证日期：2018 年 10 月 19 日
到期日：2018 年 12 月 17 日
到期地点：中国</td><td>页码：第 1 页　SWIFT：CBDUAEAD DER
电传号码：45468 TRBNK EM.
传真号码：251089/254565
电话号码：253222（10 线）</td></tr>
<tr><td>受益人：
上海闵华进出口公司
中国上海沪闵路 880 号闵华大厦 5 楼</td><td>申请人：
ALABRA 家用品贸易有限公司
阿拉伯联合酋长国迪拜邮政信箱 21352</td></tr>
<tr><td>通知行：
中国银行上海分行
中国上海中山东一路 23 号</td><td>币种和金额：
49,550.00 美元
计肆万玖仟伍佰伍拾美元整</td></tr>
<tr><td>装运细节：
转运：　　　　　　禁止
分批装运：　　　　允许
装运港：　　　　　中国港口
目的港：　　　　　迪拜
运输方式：　　　　船运
装运不得迟于：　　2018 年 12 月 2 日</td><td>指定银行及付款方式：
凭向通知银行提交由受益人签发的以我行为付款人的即期汇票及本信用证项下列明的单据议付

交货术语：
成本加运费至迪拜港</td></tr>
<tr><td colspan="2">货物描述：
家居用品（四个品种的灯具）</td></tr>
</table>

续表

其他细节参照 SALEM SAUD 公司的编号为 SSTE97/363/CN-9 订单以及 2018 年 10 月 3 日的第 SHMHSC-07210 号销售确认书。
运输标志:ALABRA/SHMHSC-07210/DUBAI/C/NO.1-UP

单据要求:
01- 经签署的商业发票一式三份,声明真实正确,显示制造商的全名和地址以及交货术语。
02- 中国国际贸易促进委员会(贸促会)签发的原产地证明,声明货物产自中国并显示制造商/生产商以及出口商的名称和地址。
03- 全套三份正本清洁已装船的船公司提单,收货人做成凭迪拜商业银行指示,标注运费预付并通知开证申请人。
04- 装箱单一式三份。
05- 投保在迪拜办理
装运通知必须通过挂号信件或传真(217660)发送给迪拜的伊朗保险公司,邮政信箱为2004,装运通知须注明预约保险单号码 OMP/531/91、信用证号码、货物金额、船名及运输标志,该通知的副本以及挂号信的邮局收据或传真的副本必须作为议付单据一并提交议付。
06- 船主或船代的证明一份,声明承运船只非以色列船籍,不在其前往目的地途中停靠任何以色列港口且不会因依据阿拉伯地方法律法规的规定,以任何理由被禁止进入阿拉伯港口。(如果货物由阿拉伯联合海运公司的船舶承运则无需提交上述证明)

其他条款:
01- 原产地证明必须注明货物出口国名称。
02- 提单必须显示货物由四个 20 英尺集装箱装运。
03- 1‰ 的发票金额将从给受益人的议付款项中扣除作为支付给迪拜 51495 邮政信箱 C.H.B.MOHD KUNHI 先生的佣金,上述扣款须明确标注在议付银行的面函上。
04- 提单必须注明目的地船代的名称、地址和电话号码。
05- 简式提单不予接受。
06- 发票以及运输单据必须标注运输标志以及货物的总毛重、净重和尺码。
07- 所有单据必须显示本信用证号码、开证日期以及我行的名称和地址。
08- 所有单据须用英语填具。
09- 受益人将承担除信用证开证费之外的包括偿付费在内的一切费用。

对议付银行的指示:
- 每一次交单均需在信用证背面注明。
- 全套议付单据须通过快递一次寄送我方。
- 凡收到符合本信用证规定的单据,我行将根据信用证条款及议付行面函的指示履行付款责任。
除非另有规定,本信用证遵循国际商会出版的第 600 号跟单信用证统一惯例(2007 年修订版)的相关规定。

开证行授权签署

13.

合计次序：	*27：	本证共 1 页
跟单信用证类别：	*40A：	不可撤销信用证
跟单信用证号码：	*20：	ROYALBKLC071501
开证日期：	31C：	2018 年 8 月 31 日
到期日及地点：	*31D：	日期：2018 年 11 月 21 日，地点：中国
开证申请人：	*50：	PARANDAR 国际公司
		加拿大安大略省多伦多市
		维多利亚公园大街 3761 号
受益人：	*59：	上海晨星贸易有限公司
		中国上海
		东大名路 375 号　邮政编码 200008
金额：	*32B：	币种：美元　　金额：80,391.40
最高信用证金额：	39B：	不超过上述金额
兑付银行及兑付方式：	*41A：	仅由通知行议付
汇票期限：	42C：	按发票全额提单日后 30 天支付
汇票受票人：	42A：	加拿大皇家银行
分批装运：	43P：	不允许
转运：	43T：	不允许
起运港：	44A：	上海
目的港：	44B：	多伦多
最迟装运日：	44C：	2018 年 10 月 31 日
货物描述：	45A：	

陶瓷餐具
参照 2018 年 8 月 19 日签订的号码为
SMSC07210 合同
成本、运费加保险费至多伦多
运输标志：PARANDA/SMSC07210/
TORONTO/C/NO.1-UP

单据要求：

1. 经签署的商业发票一式三份，注明运输标志，并表明货物符合开证申请人出具的号码为 PARANDAPO-07814 订单的规定，发票须显示 FOB 价值以及运费和保险费金额。

2. 装箱单一式两份，注明每个货号以及每件货物的体积、毛重和净重。

3. 全套(四份正本)清洁已装船海运提单,做成凭发货人指示,背书为"凭开证银行指示交付",注明"运费已付",通知开证申请人。

4. 普惠制原产地证明格式 A 一式两份,声明货物原产自中国。

5. 保险单或保险凭证一式两份,做成凭开证银行指示的背书,按发票金额的 110% 投保,规定赔付货币与汇票币种一致并注明目的港理赔代理人信息。注明的投保险别为:2009 年 1 月 1 日的协会货物 A 险和协会战争险。

费用条款:　　　　　71B:　所有的银行费用,包括信用证通知费、议付费、偿付费均由受益人承担。

交单期限:　　　　　48:　单据须在装船后的 21 天内且在信用证有效期内提交。

保兑:　　　　　＊49:　无须保兑

附加条款:　　　　　47B:

1. 汇票须注明"根据加拿大皇家银行于 2018 年 8 月 31 日开立的号码为 ROYALBKDLC071501 的信用证出具"。

2. 交单时,须额外提交商业发票及运输单据的副本或影印本各两份供开证行参考。

3. 提单上须显示运费额以及所装运货物的集装箱数量和集装箱号码及封志号码。

4. 受益人须在装运日后 48 小时内向开证申请人发送装运通知,其内容包括:船名、装船日期、货物总包装件数、运输标志、信用证号码及金额。该装运通知副本须随附其他单据一并提交议付。

5. 所有单据必须注明我行名称、信用证号码及售货确认书号码。早于信用证开证日出具的单据将不予接受。

指示:　　　　　78:

电汇索偿不接受。

偿付办法:议付行须将全套单据通过航空挂号信或航空快递一次性寄交我行。

对于每套含有不符点的单据,我行将向受益人收取 50 美元。接受含有不符点的单据并不意味着改变本信用证的条款。

凡收到符合信用证条款规定的全套单据,我行将按你行指示进行偿付。

银行间的通知:　　72:　本信用证遵循国际商会第 600 号出版物《跟单信用证统一惯例》(2007 年修订本)的相关规定

14.

Amending L/C No. NSW6180
发件人：peterying@tianyu.com.cn
时 间：2019 年 1 月 30 日 10:06
收件人：choiyongwoo@deasung.co.kr

 SHANGHAI TIANYU INTERNATIONAL TRADING CO., LTD.

Dear Mr Choi

This is to confirm what we have discussed over the telephone as to amending L/C No. NSW6180 issued by Korea Development Bank (KDB) Seoul Branch.

As stipulated in S/C No. STX-5491, shipment can be made by the end of February 2019 provided your L/C reaches us not later than January 15. However, we received your L/C only today and it is hardly possible for us to ship the goods in the specified time. Under this scenario, we regret to ask you to extend the above L/C to March 15, 2019 and March 31, 2019 for shipment and negotiation respectively. The amendment shall reach us by February 5, 2019; otherwise shipment will be further postponed.

We look forward to receiving the relevant L/C amendment at an early date and thank you for your kind cooperation.

Yours truly
Peter Ying
Shanghai Tianyu International Trading Co., Ltd.

Shanghai Tianyu International Trading Co., Ltd.
138 Guangxin Road, Shanghai 210006, China
Phone: (86) 21 6270 1242
Fax: (86) 21 6270 1250
www.tianyu.com.cn

15.

Shanghai Hanxiang Foodstuff Trading Company

67 Guangyuan West Road, Shanghai, China
Tel: 86 21 62849675   Fax: 86 21 62849676

August 4, 2018

Fuji Trading Co. Ltd.
Yamashita-cho, Naka-ku
Yokohama, Japan

Dear Mr. Keshihoto,

Thank you for your L/C No. MMK7664 issued by Nalabilu Bank Yokohama Branch.

But when we checked its clauses we found your L/C calls for Bill of Lading, which we are of course unable to obtain, for it is agreed in the contract that the goods will be dispatched by air cargo as so to ensure freshness.

Furthermore, your L/C requires Manufacturer's Certificate, which is not included in the contract. In fact, the contracted commodity is a kind of agricultural produce. It is impossible to for us to present a manufacturer's certificate.

As to partial shipments, it would be to our mutual benefit if we can ship immediately whatever is ready instead of waiting for the whole shipment to be completed. So we request you to amend L/C as "partial shipments allowed".

In addition, as this is the first time we do business with clients in your country, we hope the L/C can be confirmed by the advising bank, which is also clearly stated in the contract. We will appreciate it if you can cooperate with us in this regard.

Since the first lot of goods is now ready for shipment, we hope you can instruct your bank to amend the L/C as soon as possible.

Yours sincerely,
Richard Sun
Shanghai Hanxiang Foodstuff Trading Company

16.

SHANGHAI **MINJIE** IMPORT & EXPORT CO.

343 Guangdong Road   Shanghai   China

Tel: (86-21) 6478 1212   Fax: (86-21) 6478 4532

October 7, 2018

Simpson & Kemp Ltd.,
34 Madison Street,
Perth, Australia

Dear Mr. Beckon,

We are pleased to have received your L/C No.EX0127 issued by the Australia Commercial Bank, Perth Branch. However, on examining its clauses, we regret to find certain points are not in conformity with the terms stipulated in the contract.

The discrepancies are as follows:
1. The expiry place should be in China, not in Perth.
2. The total amount should be USD23554.00 instead of USD23454.00.
3. The draft should be at sight, not 30 days after sight.
4. The covering goods should be Art. No. HP778 instead of HK778.
5. Amend the clause" 2/3 original B/L made out to order marked freight prepaid notify the buyer" to "3/3 original B/L made out to order marked freight prepaid notify the buyer". And, delete the wording " Certificate in 3 copies certifying 1/3 original B/L has been sent directly to the buyer."
6. The inspection clause should read as "Inspection certificates are required to be issued by China Customs."

We shall appreciate it if you will modify promptly the L/C as requested.

Yours sincerely,
Jeff Gao
Shanghai Minjie Import & Export Co.

第六章　出口托运订舱

海运出口订舱委托书

日期　Nov. 16, 2018

发货人	装船期限		DEC.2, 2018		
SHANGHAI MINHUA IMP. & EXP. CORPORATION	运输方式	☑	**BY SEA**	☐	**BY AIR**
5/F. MINHUA BLDG.	装箱方式	☑	**FCL**	☐	**LCL**
880 HUMING ROAD	集装箱种类	☑	**20'GP**	☐	**40'GP**
SHANGHAI CHINA	集装箱数量		4		
收货人	转船运输	☑	**NO**	☐	**YES**
TO THE ORDER OF COMMERCIAL BANK OF DUBAI PSC.(DUBAI)	分批装运	☐	**NO**	☑	**YES**
	运费交付	☑	**PREPAID**	☐	**COLLECT**
被通知人	装运口岸		SHANGHAI		
ALABRA HOME APPL. TRDG. CO. LLC.	目的港		DUBAI		
P.O.BOX 21352,	成交条件		CFR		
DUBAI	联系人		何培民		
UAE	电话/传真		021-54753526　/　021-54753529		

标记唛码	货物描述	总件数	总毛重	总尺码
ALABRA SHMHSC-07210 DUBAI C/NO.1-535	HOUSEHOLD WARES (FOUR ITEMS OF LAMPS)	535 CARTONS	9964.00KGS	99.743M3

备注　1　全套提单（三份）注明"运费预付"；

　　　2　货物系由四个二十英尺集装箱装运，提单需做相应的标注；

　　　3　提单上须注明目的地船代理的名称、地址和电话号码；

　　　4　提单上须显示运输标志、货物的总毛重、净重和体积以及开证行名称、信用证号码和开证日期；

　　　5　船东或船代的证明一份，声明承运船只不是以色列船籍，不会在其前往目的地前在任何以色列港口停靠且不会由于阿拉伯地方法律的规定而被禁止进入阿拉伯港口。

COMMERCIAL INVOICE

1) SELLER	3) INVOICE NO.	4) INVOICE DATE
SHANGHAI MINHUA IMP. & EXP. CORPORATION	SHMH07210	NOV.16, 2018
5/F. MINHUA BLDG.	5) L/C NO.	6) DATE
880 HUMING ROAD	01DLC077003079	OCT.19, 2018
SHANGHAI CHINA	7) ISSUED BY	
	COMMERCAIL BANK OF DUBAI P.S.C.	
2) BUYER	8) CONTRACT NO.	9) DATE
ALABRA HOME APPL. TRDG. CO. LLC.	SHMHSC-07210	OCT.3, 2018
P.O.BOX 21352,	10) FROM	11) TO
DUBAI	SHANGHAI	DUBAI
UAE	12) SHIPPED BY	13)PRICE TERM
		CFR DUBAI

14)MARKS	15)DESCRIPTION OF GOODS		16)QTY.		17)UNIT PRICE	18)AMOUNT
	HOUSEHOLD WARES (FOUR ITEMS OF LAMPS)					
ALABRA	2103S	LAMP	320	PCS.	US$32.20	US$10,304.00
SHMHSC-07210	2203S	LAMP	604	PCS.	US$25.50	US$15,402.00
DUBAI	AMZ049	LAMP	712	PCS.	US$22.80	US$16,233.60
C/NO.1-535	ARG108	LAMP	504	PCS.	US$15.10	US$7,610.40
						US$49,550.00

TOTAL AMOUNT IN WORDS:
SAY U.S.DOLLARS FORTY NINE THOUSAND FIVE HUNDRED AND FIFTY ONLY

TOTAL PACKAGES: 535CARTONS
TOTAL GROSS WEIGHT: 9964KGS.
TOTAL MEASUREMENT: 99.743M3

19) ISSUED BY
SHANGHAI MINHUA IMP. & EXP. CORPORATION

20) SIGNATURE

PACKING LIST

1) SELLER	3) INVOICE NO.	4) INVOICE DATE
SHANGHAI MINHUA IMP. & EXP. CORPORATION	SHMH07210	NOV.16, 2018

5) FROM	6) TO
SHANGHAI	DUBAI

5/F. MINHUA BLDG.
880 HUMING ROAD
SHANGHAI CHINA

7) TOTAL PACKAGES(IN WORDS)
SAY FIVE HUNDRED AND THIRTY FIVE CARTONS ONLY

2) BUYER	8) MARKS & NOS.
ALABRA HOME APPL. TRDG. CO. LLC. P.O.BOX 21352, DUBAI UAE	ALABRA SHMHSC-07210 DUBAI C/NO.1-535

9) C/NOS.	10) NOS. & KINDS OF PKG	11) ITEM	12)QTY.	13) G.W.	14) N.W.	15) MEAS
HOUSEHOLD WARES (FOUR ITEMS OF LAMPS)						
1 - 80	80 CARTONS	2103S	320 PCS.	1600.00KGS.	1400.00KGS.	24.960M3
81 - 231	151 CARTONS	2203S	604 PCS.	3322.00KGS.	2944.50KGS.	24.915M3
232 - 409	178 CARTONS	AMZ049	712 PCS.	3026.00KGS.	2670.00KGS.	24.920M3
410 - 535	126 CARTONS	ARG108	504 PCS.	2016.00KGS.	1663.20KGS.	24.948M3
TOTAL:	535 CARTONS			9964.00KGS.	8677.70KGS.	99.743M3

16) ISSUED BY
SHANGHAI MINHUA IMP. & EXP. CORPORATION

17) SIGNATURE

第七章 出口货物报检

中华人民共和国出入境检验检疫
出境货物报检单

报检单位(加盖公章):	上海闵华进出口公司			*编 号	
报检单位登记号: 3100836514	联系人:汤梅	电话:021-54753536		报检日期:	2018 年 11 月 21 日

发货人	(中文)	上海闵华进出口公司
	(外文)	SHANGHAI MINHUA IMP. & EXP. CORPORATION
收货人	(中文)	***
	(外文)	ALABRA HOME APPL. TRDG. CO. LLC.

货物名称(中/外文)	H.S.编码	产地	数/重量	货物总值	包装种类及数量
灯具	9405.2000	上海市	2140只	49550美元	535纸箱

运输工具名称号码	船舶	贸易方式	一般贸易	货物存放地点	***
合同号	SHMHSC-07210	信用证号	01DLC077003079	用途	***
发货日期	***	输往国家(地区)	阿拉伯联合酋长国	许可证/审批号	***
启运地	上海	到达口岸	迪拜	生产单位注册号	***
集装箱规则、数量及号码		海运20尺普通箱4个			

合同、信用证订立的检验 检疫条款或特殊要求	标 记 及 号 码	随附单据(划"√"或补填)	
***	ALABRA SHMHSC-07210 DUBAI C/NO.1-535	☐ 合同 ☐ 信用证 ☑ 发票 ☐ 换证凭证 ☑ 装箱单 ☐ 厂检单	☐ 包装性能结果单 ☐ 许可/审批文件 ☐ ☐ ☐ ☐

需要证单名称(划"√"或补填)				*检验检疫费	
☐ 品质证书 ___正___副 ☐ 重量证书 ___正___副 ☐ 数量证书 ___正___副 ☐ 兽医卫生证书 ___正___副 ☐ 健康证书 ___正___副 ☐ 卫生证书 ___正___副 ☐ 动物卫生证书 ___正___副		☐ 植物检疫证书 ___正___副 ☐ 熏蒸/消毒证书 ___正___副 ☐ 出境货物换证凭单 ___正___副 ☑ 出境货物通关单 _1_正_2_副		总金额 (人民币元)	
				计费人	
				收费人	

报检人郑重声明 1.本人被授权报验 2.上列填写内容正确属实,货物无伪造或冒用他人的厂名、 标志、认证标志,并承担货物质量责任。 签名: 汤梅	领 取 证 单	
	日期	
	签名	

注:有"*"号栏由出入境检验检疫机关填写

第八章 出口货运投保

PICC 中国人民财产保险股份有限公司 上海市分公司
PICC Property and Casualty Company Limited, Shanghai Branch

地址: 中国上海市中山南路700号
ADD: No.700 Zhongshan Road (S) Shanghai China

电话（TEL）: (021)63773000

邮编（Post Code）: 200010

传真（FAX）: (021)63764678

货物运输保险投保单
APPLICATION FORM FOR CARGO TRANSPORTATION INSURANCE

被保险人:
INSURED: **SHANGHAI JINGANG TRADING COMPANY**

发票号（INVOICE NO.）   **JGINV0725010**
合同号（CONTRACT NO.）   **JG071405**
信用证号（L/C NO.）   **3851L752297**
发票金额（INVOICE AMOUNT）   **US$52,450.40**

投保加成（PLUS）   **10** %

兹有下列物品向中国人民财产保险股份有限公司 **上海分** 公司投保。 （INSURANCE IS REQUIRED ON THE FOLLOWING COMMODITIES:）

标 记 MARKS & NOS.	包装及数量 QUANTITY	保险货物项目 DESCRIPTION OF GOODS	保险金额 AMOUNT INSURED
P.T.C.L. **JG071405** **LAEM CHABANG** **C/NO.1-668**	**668CARTONS**	**ROUND PIPE AND SQUARE PIPE**	**US$57,696.00**

启运日期:
DATE OF COMMENCEMENT   **AS PER BILL OF LADING**

装载运输工具:
PER CONVEYANCE   **YUN HE**   **V. 205**

自   经
FROM **SHANGHAI**   VIA

至
TO **LAEM CHABANG**

提单号:
B/L NO. **AS PER BILL OF LADING**

赔款偿付地点:
CLAIM PAYMENT AT **BANGKOK**

投保险别: （PLEASE INDICATE THE CONDITIONS &/OR SPECIAL COVERAGES）

COVERING INSTITUTE CARGO CLAUSES (A) AND INSTITUTE WAR CLAUSES (CARGO) DATED 1/1/2009

请如实告知下列情况: （如'是'在[ ]中打'X'） IF ANY, PLEASE MARK 'X':

1、货物种类 普通 [X] 散装 [ ] 冷藏 [ ] 液体 [ ] 活动物 [ ] 机器/汽车 [ ] 危险品等级 [ ]
  GOODS ORDINARY BULK REEFER LIQUID LIVE ANIMAL MACHINE/AUTO DANGEROUS CLASS

2、集装箱种类 普通 [X] 开顶 [ ] 框架 [ ] 平板 [ ] 冷藏 [ ]
  CONTAINER ORDINARY OPEN FRAME PLAY REFRIGERATOR

3、转运工具 海轮 [ ] 飞机 [ ] 驳船 [ ] 火车 [ ] 汽车 [ ]
  BY TRANSIT SHIP PLANE BARGE TRAIN TRUCK

4、船舶资料 船籍 船龄
  PARTICULAR OF SHIP REGISTRY AGE

备注: 被保险人确认本保险合同条款和内容已经完全了解
THE ASSURED CONFIRMS HEREWITH THE TERMS AND CONDI-
TIONS OF THESE INSURANCE CONTRACT FULLY UNDER-
STOOD.

投保日期: （DATE） **Jul. 02, 2018**

投保人（签名盖章）THE INSURER'S SIGNATURE

电话: （TEL） 021-64715305
地址: （ADD） **17F JINHANG TOWER**
NO.800 HUAI HAI ROAD
SHANGHAI CHINA

本公司自用（FOR OFFICE USE ONLY）

费率
RATE

保费
PREMIUM

备注:

经办人
BY

核保人

负责人

NO.: PICC 0261424

货 物 运 输 保 险 单
CARGO TRANSPORTATION INSURANCE POLICY

总公司 设于北京
Head office Beijing

一九四九年创立
Established in 1949

发票号（INVOICE NO.）　**JGINV0725010**	
合同号（CONTRACT NO.）　**JG071405**	保单号次
信用证号（L/C NO.）　**3851L752297**	POLICY NO. **PYIE2017258972465001482**

被保险人
INSURED　**SHANGHAI JINGANG TRADING COMPANY**

中国人民财产保险股份有限公司（以下简称公司）根据被保险人的要求，由被保险人向本公司缴付约定的保险费，按照本保单承保险别和背面所载条款与下列特款承保下述货物运输保险，特立本保险单。

THIS POLICY OF INSURANCE WITNESSES THAT PICC PROPERTY AND CASUALTY COMPANY LIMITED (HEREINAFTER CALLED "THE COMPANY") AT THE REQUEST OF THE INSURED AND IN CONSIDERATION OF THE AGREED PREMIUM PAID TO THE COMPANY BY THE INSURED, UNDERTAKES TO INSURE THE UNDERMENTIONED GOODS IN TRANSPORTATION SUBJECT TO THE CONDITIONS OF THIS POLICY AS PER THE CLAUSES PRINTED OVERLEAF AND OTHER SPECIAL CLAUSES ATTACHED HEREON.

标 记 MARKS & NOS	包装及数量 QUANTITY	保险货物项目 DESCRIPTION OF GOODS	保险金额 AMOUNT INSURED
P.T.C.L. JG071405 LAEM CHABANG C/NO.1-668	**668CARTONS**	**ROUND PIPE AND SQUARE PIPE**	**US$57,696.00**

总保险金额：
TOTAL AMOUNT INSURED: **SAY U.S.DOLLARS FIFTY SEVEN THOUSAND SIX HUNDRED NINETY SIX ONLY**

保费： PREMIUM　**AS ARRANGED**	启运日期： DATE OF COMMENCEMENT　**AS PER B/L**	装载运输工具： PER CONVEYANCE　**YUN HE**	**V. 205**
自 FROM　**SHANGHAI**	经 VIA	至 TO **LAEM CHABANG**	

承保险别：
CONDITIONS

COVERING INSTITUTE CARGO CLAUSES (A) AND INSTITUTE WAR CLAUSES (CARGO) DATED 1/1/2009

所保货物，如发生保险单项下可能引起索赔的损失或损坏，应立即通知本公司下述代理人查勘。如有索赔，应向本公司提交保单正本（本保单共有**贰**份正本）及有关文件。如一份正本已用于索赔，其余正本自动失效。

IN THE EVENT OF LOSS OR DAMAGE WHICH MAY RESULT IN A CLAIM UNDER THIS POLICY, IMMEDIATE NOTICE MUST BE GIVEN TO THE COMPANY'S AGENT AS MENTIONED HEREUNDER CLAIMS. IF ANY, ONE OF THE ORIGINAL POLICY WHICH HAS BEEN ISSUED IN **TWO** ORIGINAL(S) TOGETHER WITH THE RELEVENT DOCUMENTS SHALL BE SURRENDERED TO THE COMPANY. IF ONE OF THE ORIGINAL POLICY HAS BEEN ACCOMPLISHED, THE OTHERS TO BE VOID.

THE NEW INDIA ASSURANCE CO LTD
CHAMNAN PHENJATI TOWER B,17TH FL
65 RAMA IX RD, HUAYKWANG
BANGKOK 10320

中国人民财产保险股份有限公司 上 海 市 分 公 司
PICC Property and Casualty Company Limited, Shanghai Branch

赔款偿付地点
CLAIM PAYABLE AT/IN　**BANGKOK IN US DOLLARS**

出单日期
ISSUING DATE　**Jul 03, 2018**

GENERAL MANAGER

地址：中国上海中山南路700号 ADD: 700 ZHONGSHAN ROAD (S) SHANGHAI CHINA 邮编（POST CODE）：200010	经办：　复核：　Settling & Customer Service Centre: （理赔/客户服务中心）86 21 63674274

保单顺序号　PICC　**0794516**

保单背书：

第九章 出口货物原产地认证

中 国 贸 促 会 上 海 市 分 会

中 国 国 际 商 会 上 海 商 会

一般原产地证明书/加工装配证明书
申 请 书

申请单位注册号： **310075414** 证书号： **C183100754140524**		全部国产填上P 含进口成分填上W **"P"**

申请人郑重声明： 发票号： **SHMH07210**

　　本人被授权代表本企业办理和签署本申请书。

　　本申请书及一般原产地证书/加工装配证明书所列内容正确无误，如发现弄虚作假，

　　冒充证书所列货物，擅改证书、愿按《中华人民共和国出口货物原产地规则》有关规定接

　　受惩处并承担法律责任，现将有关情况申报如下：

商品名称	**灯具**	H.S.编码(八位数)	**9405.2000**
商品生产、制造、加工单位、地点		**上海**	
含进口成分产品主要制造加工工序		※※※	
商品FOB总值(以美元计)	**US$45,550.00** 最终目的地国/地区	**阿联酋**	
拟出运日期	**2018年12月1日** 转口国(地区)	※※※	
包装数量或毛重或其它数量	**535纸箱** **9964千克/公斤**	**2140只**	

贸易方式和企业性质

贸 易 方 式	企业性质
一般贸易	**国内合资**

　　现提交中国出口货物商业发票一份，一般原产地证明书/加工装配证明书一正三副，

　　以及其它附件 ※※※ 份，请予审核签证。

申请单位盖章：

领领人（签名） **秦立华**

电话： 021-63753526

日期： **2018年11月23日**

如有补发，重发或更改C.O.证书，请填写背面申请单。

ORIGINAL

1. Exporter	Certificate No.　C183100754140524
SHANGHAI MINHUA IMP. & EXP. CORPORATION **5/F. MINHUA BLDG.** **880 HUMING ROAD** **SHANGHAI CHINA**	**CERTIFICATE OF ORIGIN** **OF** **THE PEOPLE'S REPUBLIC OF CHINA**
2. Consignee **ALABRA HOME APPL. TRDG. CO. LLC.** **P.O. BOX 21352,** **DUBAI** **UAE**	

3. Means of transport and route	5. For certifying authority use only
FROM SHANGHAI CHINA TO DUBAI U.A.E. BY SEA	

4. Country / region of destination
UAE

6. Marks and numbers	7. Number and kind of packages; description of goods	8. H.S. Code	9. Quantity	10. Number and date of invoices
ALABRA **SHMHSC-07210** **DUBAI** **C/NO.1-535**	**535 (FIVE HUNDRED AND THIRTY FIVE) CARTONS OF LAMPS** *** **ISSUING BANK'S NAME:**　　　**COMMERCAIL BANK OF DUBAI P.S.C.** **LETTER OF CREDIT NUMBER:**　**01DLC077003079** **DATE OF ISSUE:**　　　　　　**OCT. 19, 2018** **NAME AND ADDRESS OF THE MANUFACTURER:** **SHANGHAI RISHENG LIGHTING CO.,LTD.** **340 LIU YING RD.,** **SHANGHAI, CHINA** **THE NAME OF EXPORTING COUNTRY:CHINA** **WE CERTIFY THAT THE GOODS ARE OF CHINESE ORIGIN.**	**9405.2000**	**2140PCS.**	**SHMH07210** **NOV. 16, 2018**

11. Declaration by the exporter	12. Certification
The undersigned hereby declares that the above details and statements are correct; that all the goods were produced in China and that they comply with the Rules of Origin of the People's Republic of China	It is hereby certified that the declaration by the exporter is correct.
SHANGHAI　　　**NOV. 23, 2018**	**SHANGHAI**　　　**NOV. 23, 2018**
Place and date. signature and stamp of authorized signatory	Place and date. signature and stamp of certifying authority

第十章 出口货物报关

页码/页数：

中华人民共和国海关出口货物报关单 （上海海关）

预录入编号：220020180003372609

海关编号：220020180006372609

境内发货人	出境关别	出口日期	申报日期	备案号
上海闵华进出口公司	上海海关 （2200）		20181129	
境外收货人	运输方式	运输工具名称及航次号	提运单号	
ALABRA HOME APPL. TRDG. CO. LLC.	水路运输 （2）	DA HE KOU/210S	COSU85122784	
生产销售单位	监管方式	征免性质	许可证号	
上海闵华进出口公司	一般贸易 （0110）	一般征税 （101）		
合同协议号	贸易国（地区）	运抵国（地区）	指运港	最终目的国（地区）
SHMHSC-07210	阿联酋 （ARE）	阿联酋 （ARE）	迪拜（阿联酋）	阿联酋 （ARE018）
包装种类	件数	毛重（千克）	净重（千克）	成交方式	运费	保费	杂费
纸制或纤维板制盒/箱 （22）	535	9964	8678	CFR （1）	USD/4000/3		

随附单证 1：商业发票；装箱单

随附单证 1：

标记唛码及备注：
ALABRA
SHMHSC-07210
DUBAI
C/NO.1-535

项号	商品编号	商品名称；规格型号	数量及单位	单价/总价/币制	原产国（地区）	境内货源地	征免
01	9405200000	灯具	2140台 8677.7千克 2140台	23.1542 49550.00 USD	中国 （CHN）	静安 （31069）	照章征税 （1）

特殊关系确认： 价格影响确认： 支付特许权使用费确认：

特许权证号：

兹申明以上内容承担如实申报、依法纳税之法律责任并承担相应法律责任

报关人员 李静
报关员 3122280097213214

申报人员 电话 申报单位 上海闵华进出口公司

申报单位（签章）

海关批注及签章
自报自缴：

第十一章 出口货物装运

上海闵华进出口公司
SHANGHAI MINHUA IMP. & EXP. CORPORATION

SHIPPING ADVICE

To:	IRAN INSURANCE CO.,	**From:**	SHANGHAI MINHUA IMP. & EXP. CORPORATION
Telex. No.:		**Tel. No.:**	021-54753526
Page:	1/1	**Date:**	Dec. 01, 2018
Fax. No.:	217660	**Fax. No.:**	86-21-54753529

L/C NO.: 01DLC077003079　　**INVOICE NO.:** SHMH07210

We hereby inform you that the goods under the above mentioned credit have been shipped. The details of the shipment are stated below.

COMMODITY:	HOUSEHOLD WARES (FOUR ITEMS OF LAMPS)
NUMBER OF PACKAGES:	535CARTONS
QUANTITY:	2140PCS.
AMOUNT:	US$49,550.00
B/L NO.:	COSU85122784
VESSEL'S NAME & VOYAGE:	DA HE KOU　V. 210S
SHIPMENT DATE:	Dec. 01, 2018
FROM:	SHANGHAI
TO:	DUBAI
SHIPPING MARKS:	ALABRA
	SHMHSC-07210
	DUBAI
	C/NO. 1-535
NAME OF ISSUING BANK:	COMMERCAIL BANK OF DUBAI P.S.C.
L/C DATE:	Oct. 19, 2018
S/C NO.:	SHMHSC-07210
OPEN POLICY NO.:	OMP/531/91

上海闵华进出口公司
SHANGHAI MINHUA IMP. & EXP. CORPORATION

(SIGNATURE)

COSCO SHIPPING 中远海运集装箱运输有限公司 COSCO SHIPPING LINES CO., LTD.	**ORIGINAL**	TLX: 33057 COSCO SHIPPING
		FAX: +86(21) 65458984
		PORT TO PORT OR COMBINED TRANSPORT BILL OF LADING

1. Shipper　Insert Name Address and Phone/Fax	Booking No.	Bill of Lading No.
SHANGHAI MINHUA IMP. & EXP. CORPORATION 5/F. MINHUA BLDG. 880 HUMING ROAD SHANGHAI CHINA	Export References	COSU85122784

2. Consignee　Insert Name Address and Phone/Fax	Forwarding Agent and References
TO THE ORDER OF COMMERCIAL BANK OF DUBAI PSC.(DUBAI)	
	Point and Country of Origin

3. Notify Party Insert Name Address and Phone/Fax	(It is agreed that no responsibility shall attach to the Carrier or his agents for failure to notify)	Also Notify Party-routing & Instructions
ALABRA HOME APPL. TRDG. CO. LLC. P.O.BOX 21352, DUBAI UAE		

4. Combined Transport* Pre-Carriage by	5. Combined Transport* Place of Receipt	

6. Ocean Vessel Voy. No.	7. Port of Loading	Service Contract No.	Commodity Code
DA HE KOU　V. 210S	SHANGHAI		

8. Port of Discharge	9. Combined Transport* Place of Delivery	Type of Movement	
DUBAI		FCL / FCL　　CY-CY	

Marks & Nos. Container/Seal No.	No. of Container or Packages	Description of Goods (If Dangerous Goods, See Clause 20)	Gross Weight	Measurement
ALABRA SHMHSC-07210 DUBAI C/NO.1-535	535CTNS	HOUSEHOLD WARES (FOUR ITEMS OF LAMPS) SHIPPER'S LOAD, COUNT AND SEAL	9964.000KGS	99.743CBM

VESSEL AGENT AT PORT OF DESTINATION:
 NAME:　　　　SHARAF SHIPPING AGENCY LLC
 ADDRESS:　　P.O. BOX 576, DUBAI, UAE
 TELEPHONE NUMBER: +971 4 339718

L/C NO.:	01DLC077003079
L/C DATE:	OCT.19, 2018
ISSUING BANK:	COMMERCAIL BANK OF DUBAI P.S.C.

ON CY-CY TERM

FREIGHT PREPAID

TOTAL NET WEIGHT: 8677.7KGS

WE EVIDENCE THAT GOODS ARE SHIPPED IN 4X20FT CONTAINERS

CBHU57120845	/ 32741	/	80CTNS	/	FCL / FCL	/	20GP	/
CBHU57120846	/ 32742	/	151CTNS	/	FCL / FCL	/	20GP	/
CBHU57120847	/ 32743	/	178CTNS	/	FCL / FCL	/	20GP	/
CBHU57120848	/ 32744	/	126CTNS	/	FCL / FCL	/	20GP	/

Declared Cargo Value US$	Description of Contents for Shipper's use Only (Not part of This B/L Contract)

10. Total Number of Containers and/or Packages (in words) 　　 Subject to Clause 7 Limitation	SAY FIVE HUNDRED AND THIRTY FIVE CARTONS ONLY

11. Freight & Charges	Revenue Tons	Rate	Per	Amount	Prepaid	Collect	Freight & Charges Payable at/by

Received in external apparent good order and condition except as otherwise noted. The total number of the packages or units stuffed in the container, the description of the goods and the weights shown in this Bill of Lading are furnished by the merchants, and which the carrier has no reasonable means of checking and is not a part of this Bill of Lading contract. The carrier has issued **THREE** original Bill of Lading, all of this tenor and date, one of the original Bills of Lading must be surrendered and endorsed or signed against the delivery of the shipment and whereupon any other orginal Bills of Lading shall be void. The merchants agree to be bound by the terms and and conditions of this Bill of Lading as if each had personally signed this Bill of Lading.
*Applicable Only When Document used as a Combined Transport Bill of Lading.

Date Laden on Board	**Dec. 01 , 2018**
Signed by:	

9805　Date of Issue **Dec. 01 , 2018**　　Place of Issue　　**SHANGHAI**　Signed for the Carrier, COSCO SHIPPING LINES CO., LTD

第十二章　出口交单结汇

1.

BILL OF EXCHANGE

No.　SMSCINV07210

For　US$80,391.40　　　　　　　　　　　　　　SHANGHAI　　NOV. 4, 2018

　　　(amount in figure)　　　　　　　　　　　　　(place and date of issue)

At　30 DAYS AFTER B/L DATE　　　　of　this　　　FIRST　　Bill of exchange(SECOND being unpaid)

pay to　　BANK OF CHINA, SHANGHAI BRANCH　　　　　　　　　　　or order the sum of

SAY U.S.DOLLARS EIGHTY THOUSAND THREE HUNDRED AND NINETY ONE AND CENTS FORTY ONLY

　　　　　　　　　　　　　(amount in words)

Value received for　　　　564CARTONS　　　　of　　　PORCELAIN DINNERWARES

　　　　　　　　　　(quantity)　　　　　　　　(name of commodity)

Drawn under　THE ROYAL BANK OF CANADA

L/C No.　　ROYAOBKDLC621501　　　　　dated　　　　　AUG. 31, 2018

To:　THE ROYAL BANK OF CANADA　　　　　　For and on behalf of
　　4022 SHIPPARD AVE. E　　　　　SHANGHAI MORNING STAR TRADING CO., LTD.
　　SCARBOROUGH TORONTO
　　CANADA

S/C NO.:　SMSC-07210　　　　　　　　　　　　　(Signature)

提交份数：一式两联

上海晨星贸易有限公司
Shanghai Morning Star Trading Co.,Ltd.

COMMERCIAL INVOICE

TO:　PARANDAR INTERNATIONAL INC.
3761 VICTORIA PARK AVE.
UNIT#7, TORONTO, ONTARIO
CANADA

INV. NO. :　SMSCINV07210
INV. DATE:　OCT. 10, 2018
S/C NO. :　SMSC-07210

FROM:　SHANGHAI　　TO:　TORONTO　　SHIPPED BY: GLORY OCEAN　V. 190E

MARKS & NOS.	DESCRIPTION OF GOODS	QUANTITY	UNIT PRICE	AMOUNT
	PORCELAIN DINNERWARES			
	AS PER SALES CONTRACT NO. SMSC-07210 DATED 180819		CIF TORONTO	
PARANDA	SHD12-P213　12PC DINNERWARE SET	644 SETS	US$47.50	US$30,590.00
SMSC-07210	SHD12-P214　12PC DINNERWARE SET	692 SETS	US$42.30	US$29,271.60
TORONTO	SHD16-P541　16PC DINNERWARE SET	222 SETS	US$48.20	US$10,700.40
C/NO.1-564	SHD16-P545　16PC DINNERWARE SET	238 SETS	US$41.30	US$9,829.40
				US$80,391.40

WE STATE THAT MERCHANDISE IS IN ACCORDIANCE WITH APPLICANT'S
ORDER NO. PARANDAPO-18814

TOTAL AMOUNT IN WORDS:　SAY U.S. DOLLARS EIGHTY THOUSAND THREE HUNDRED AND NINETY ONE AND
CENTS FORTY ONLY.

TOTAL G.W. / TOTAL N.W.:　11154KGS.　/　9692KGS.

TOTAL PACKAGES:　564CTNS.

NAME OF ISSUING BANK:　THE ROYAL BANK OF CANADA
NUMBER OF CREDIT:　ROYAOBKDLC621501
DATE OF CREDIT:　AUG. 31, 2018

FOB VALUE:　US$76,126.40
FREIGHT:　US$3,690.00
INSURANCE CHARGES:　US$575.00

19) ISSUED BY
SHANGHAI MORNING STAR TRADING CO., LTD.

20) SIGNATURE

上海市东大名路375号(200080) 电话/Tel:86-21-65960332 传真/Fax:86-21-65960328　No.375, Dong Da Ming Rd., Shanghai, P.R.C.

提交份数:5份

上海晨星贸易有限公司
Shanghai Morning Star Trading Co.,Ltd.

PACKING LIST

TO:　PARANDAR INTERNATIONAL INC.
3761 VICTORIA PARK AVE.
UNIT#7, TORONTO, ONTARIO
CANADA

INV. NO. :　SMSCINV07210
DATE:　OCT. 10, 2018

FROM:　SHANGHAI　　TO:　TORONTO　　SHIPPED BY:　GLORY OCEAN V. 190E

C/NO.	DESCRIPTION OF GOODS	PKG.	QTY	G.W.	N.W.	MEAS.
	PORCELAIN DINNERWARES					
1-161	SHD12-P213	161CTNS	644 SETS	3381 KGS.	2898 KGS.	24.955 M3
162-334	SHD12-P214	173CTNS	692 SETS	3633 KGS.	3114 KGS.	24.912 M3
335-445	SHD16-P541	111CTNS	222 SETS	1998 KGS.	1776 KGS.	12.543 M3
446-564	SHD16-P545	119CTNS	238 SETS	2142 KGS.	1904 KGS.	12.495 M3
	TOTAL:	564CTNS		11154 KGS.	9692 KGS.	74.905 M3

TOTAL PACKAGES IN WORDS:　SAY FIVE HUNDRED AND SIXTY FOUR CARTONS ONLY

MARKS & NOS.
PARANDA
SMSC-07210
TORONTO
C/NO.1-564

NAME OF ISSUING BANK:　THE ROYAL BANK OF CANADA
NUMBER OF CREDIT:　ROYAOBKDLC621501
DATE OF CREDIT:　AUG. 31, 2018
S/C NO.:　SMSC-07210

GROSS WEIGHT, NET WEIGHT AND MEASUREMENT OF EACH PACKAGE:

ART. NO.	G.W.	N.W.	MEAS.
SHD12-P213	21.0 KGS.	18.0 KGS.	0.155 M3
SHD12-P214	21.0 KGS.	18.0 KGS.	0.144 M3
SHD16-P541	18.0 KGS.	16.0 KGS.	0.113 M3
SHD16-P545	18.0 KGS.	16.0 KGS.	0.105 M3

19) ISSUED BY
SHANGHAI MORNING STAR TRADING CO., LTD.

20) SIGNATURE

上海市东大名路375号(200080) 电话/Tel:86-21-65960332 传真/Fax:86-21-65960328　　No.375, Dong Da Ming Rd , Shanghai, P.R.C.

提交份数：2 份

SITC CONTAINER LINES CO., LTD.

B/L NO. SITGSHSVK18267

1. Shipper

SHANGHAI MORNING STAR TRADING CO., LTD.
375 DONG DA MING ROAD
SHANGHAI 200008
P.R. CHINA

2. Consignee

TO THE SHIPPER'S ORDER

Port to Port or Combine Transport
BILL OF LADING

RECEIVED for shipment in external apparent good order and condition, unless otherwise indicated. The total number of packages or units stuffed in the container, the description of the goods and the weights shown in this Bill of Lading are furnished by the Merchants and the containers are already sealed by the Merchants, and which the carrier has no reasonable means of checking and is not a part of this Bill of Lading contract. The carrier has issued the number of Bills of Lading stated below, all of this tenor and date, one of the original Bills of Lading must be surrendered and endorsed or signed against the delivery of the goods or the delivery order and whereupon any other Bills of Lading shall be void.

NOTE: Notwithstanding any customs or privileges to the contrary, the Merchant's attention is drawn to the fact that the Merchant, in accepting this Bill of Lading, expressly agrees to be bound by all the stipulations, exceptions, limitations, liberties, terms and conditions attached hereto or stated herein, whether written, printed, stamped or otherwise incorporated on the front and/or reverse side hereof as well as the provisions of the Carrier's published Tariff Rules, Regulations and Schedules, without exceptions, as fully as if they were all signed by such Merchant, and the carrier's undertaking to carry the goods is made on the basis of the merchant's acceptance and agreements as aforesaid.

This Bill of Lading is governed by the laws of the People's Republic of China. Any claims and disputes arising under or in connection with this Bill of Lading shall be determined by Shanghai Maritime Court or Qingdao Maritime Court at the exclusion of the Courts of any other country.
The printed terms and conditions appearing on the face and reverse side of this Bill of Lading are available at www.sitc.com in SITC's published tariffs.

3. Notify Party (It is agreed that no responsibility shall attach to the Carrier or his agent for failure to notify)

PARANDAR INTERNATIONAL INC.
3761 VICTORIA PARK AVE.
UNIT#7, TORONTO, ONTARIO
CANADA

4. Pre-Carriage by*	5. Place of Receipt*
(Applicable only when this document is used as a Combined Transport Bill of Lading)	(Applicable only when this document is used as a Combined Transport Bill of Lading)
6. Ocean Vessel Voy. No.	7. Port of Loading
GLORY OCEAN V. 190E	SHANGHAI
8. Port of Discharge	9. Place of Delivery*
TORONTO	(Applicable only when this document is used as a Combined Transport Bill of Lading)

ORIGINAL

Container No./Seal No. Marks and Numbers	Number and Kind of packages: description of goods	Gross Weight	Measurement
PARANDA	564 CARTONS	11154.000	74.905
SMSC-07210	PORCELAIN DINNERWARES	KGS	CBM
TORONTO	CY - CY FCL/FCL		
C/NO. 1-564			
	SHIPPER'S LOAD, COUNT AND SEAL		
	FREIGHT PREPAID	FREIGHT AMOUNT: US$3690.00	
CCLU2356117 / 47113	NUMBER OF CONTAINERS BEING SHIPPED: THREE 20 FEET CONTAINERS		
CCLU2356118 / 47114	NAME OF ISSUING BANK: THE ROYAL BANK OF CANADA		
CCLU2356119 / 47115	NUMBER OF CREDIT: ROYAOBKDLC621501		
	DATE OF CREDIT: AUG. 31, 2018		
	S/C NO.: SMSC-07210		
	Above particulars declared by shipper. Carrier is not responsible. (see clause 12)		

PARTICULAR FURNISHED BY THE MERCHANT

10. Total No. of Containers Or Packages (in words)	SAY THREE CONTAINERS ONLY			
11. Freight & Charges	Rate	Unit	Prepaid	Collect

Prepaid at SHANGHAI	Payable at	Number of Original B(s)L FOUR
Place of Issue and Date SHANGHAI OCT. 26, 2018		12. Declared Value/Charge

LADEN ON BOARD THE VESSEL

DATE   BY
OCT. 26, 2018   GLORY OCEAN V. 190E

AS AGENT FOR THE CARRIER SITC CONTAINER LINES CO., LTD
SIGN: _____
SITC CONTAINER LINES (SHANGHAI) CO., LTD.

提单背书: **TO THE ORDER OF THE ROYAL BANK OF CANADA**
SHANGHAI MORNING STAR TRADING CO., LTD.

提交份数: 4 份正本、2 份副本

中国平安 PING AN OF CHINA

中国平安财产保险股份有限公司
PING AN PROPERTY & CASUALTY INSURANCE COMPANY OF CHINA, LTD.

总公司地址:
中国·深圳
八卦岭八卦三路平安大厦
电话(Tel): 0755-82262888
图文传真(Fax): 0755-82414813
邮政编码(Postcode): 518029
Address of Head Office:
Ping An Building, No.3 Ba Gua Road.
Ba Gua Ling, Shenzhen, China

No. 060500087415

货 物 运 输 保 险 单
CARGO TRANSPORTATION INSURANCE POLICY

被保险人
Insured: **SHANGHAI MORNING STAR TRADING CO., LTD.**

中国平安财产保险股份有限公司根据被保险人的要求及所交付约定的保险费, 按照本保险单背面所载条款与下列特款, 承保下述货物水运输保险, 特立本保险单.
This Policy of Insurance witnesses that PING AN PROPERTY & CASUALTY INSURANCE COMPANY OF CHINA, LTD., at the request of the Insurance and in consideration of the agreed premium paid by the Insured, undertakes to insure the undermentioned goods in transportation subject to the conditions of Policy as per the clauses printed overleaf and other special clauses attached hereon.

保单号 Policy No.	2051880130202080915	赔款偿付地点 Claim Payable at	**TORONTO IN US DOLLARS**
发票或提单号 Invoice No. or B/L No.	SMSCINV07210		
运输工具 Per Conveyance S.S.	GLORY OCEAN　　V. 190E	查勘代理人 Survey By:	ROYALTON INSURANCE COMPANY 3470 LAIRD RD. UNIT 6-9 MISSISSAUGA ONTARIO, CANADA
起迄日期 Sig.on or abt	OCT. 26, 2018　自 From　SHANGHAI 至 To　TORONTO		

保险金额 Amount Insured	**US$88,430.54**　SAY U.S. DOLLARS EIGHTY EIGHT THOUSAND FOUR HUNDRED THIRTY AND 54/100 ONLY

保险货物项目、标记、数量及包装:
Description, Marks, Quantity, & Packing of Goods:

承保条件
Conditions:

PORCELAIN DINNERWARES

PARANDA
SMSC-07210
TORONTO
C/NO. 1-564

564CARTONS

COVERING INSTITUTE CARGO CLAUSES (A) AND INSTITUTE CARGO CLAUSES WAR RISKS AS PER ICC DATED 1/1/2009

S/C NO.:　　　　　　SMSC-07210
NUMBER OF CREDIT:　ROYAOBKDLC621501
DATE OF CREDIT:　　AUG. 31, 2018
NAME OF ISSUING BANK:　THE ROYAL BANK OF CANADA

保单正本: 贰份
Number of Originals: TWO

签单日期
Date:　**OCT. 24, 2018**

IMPORTANT
PROCEDURE IN THE EVENT OF LOSS OR DAMAGE FOR WHICH UNDERWRITERS MAY BE LIABLE
LIABILITY OF CARRIERS, BAILEES OR OTHER THIRD PARTIES

DOCUMENTATION OF CLAIMS
To enable claims to be dealt with promptly, the Assured or their Agents are advised to submit all available supporting documents without delay, when applicable:
1. Original policy of insurance
2. Original or certified copy of shipping invoices, together with shipping specification and / or weight notes
3. Original or certified copy of Bill of Lading and / or other contract of carriage
4. Survey report or other documentary evidence to show the extent of the loss or damage
5. Landing account and weight notes at port of discharge and final destination
6. Correspondence exchanged with the Carrier and other Parties regarding their liability for the loss or damage.

For and on behalf of
PING AN PROPERTY & CASUALTY INSURANCE COMPANY OF CHINA, LTD.

地址及电话
Address & Tel.　11/F, 12/F, JING AN PLAZA, 8 CHANG SHU ROAD SHANGHAI, CHINA 52564888×6395

注: 未加盖本公司保单专用章, 保单无效.

保单背书: PAY TO THE ORDER OF THE ROYAL BANK OF CANADA
SHANGHAI MORNING STAR TRADING CO.,LTD.

提交份数:2份

ORIGINAL

1. Goods consigned from (Exporter's business name, address, country) SHANGHAI MORNING STAR TRADING CO., LTD. 375 DONG DA MING ROAD SHANGHAI 200008 P.R. CHINA	Reference No. G183100386150056 GENERALIZED SYSTEM OF PREFERENCES CERTIFICATE OF ORIGIN (Combined declaration and certificate) FORM A Issued in THE PEOPLE'S REPUBLIC OF CHINA (country) See Notes overleaf
2. Goods consigned to (Consignee's name, address, country) PARANDAR INTERNATIONAL INC. 3761 VICTORIA PARK AVE. UNIT#7, TORONTO, ONTARIO CANADA	
3. Means of transport and route (as far as known) FROM SHANGHAI CHINA TO TORONTO CANADA BY SEA	4. For official use

5. Item number	6. Marks and numbers of packages	7. Number and Kind of packages; description of goods	8. Origin criterion (see Notes overleaf)	9. Gross weight or other quantity	10. Number and date of invoices

01	PARANDA
	SMSC-07210
	TORONTO
	C/NO. 1-564
		564 (FIVE HUNDRED AND SIXTY FOUR)
		CARTONS OF PORCELAIN DINNERWARES
		***********************************
		
		NAME OF ISSUING BANK:
		LETTER OF CREDIT NUMBER:
		DATE OF CREDIT:
		S/C NO.:
		
		    THE ROYAL BANK OF CANADA
		    ROYAOBKDLC621501
		    AUG. 31, 2018
		    SMSC-07210
		
		WE STATE THAT THE GOODS ARE OF CHINESE ORIGIN.
			"P"	11154.0KGS	SMSCINV07210
					OCT. 10, 2018

| 11. Certification
It is hereby certified, on the basis of control carried out, that the declaration by the exporter is correct.

SHANGHAI   OCT. 23, 2018
Place and date, signature and stamp of certifying authority | 12. Declaration by the exporter
The undersigned hereby declares that the above details and statements are correct; that all the goods were produced in   CHINA
       (country)
and that they comply with the origin requirements specified for those goods in the Generalized System of Preferences for goods exported to
    CANADA
    (importing country)
SHANGHAI   OCT. 23, 2018
Place and date, signature of authorized signatory |

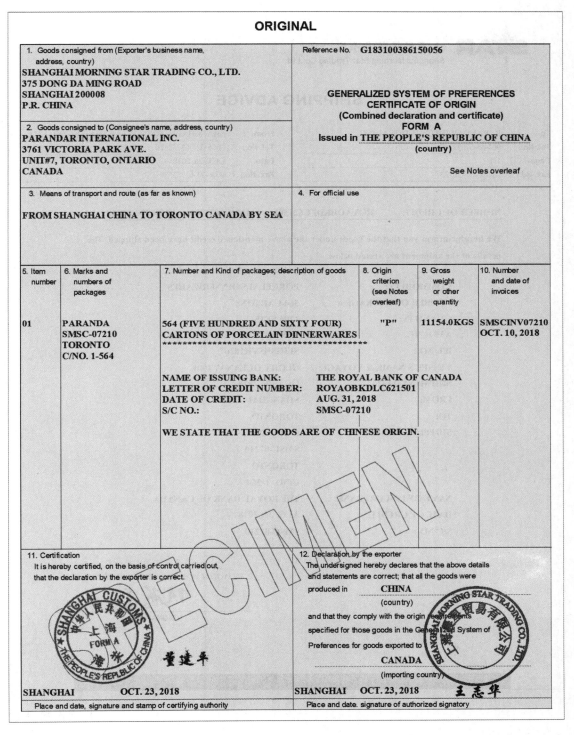

提交份数：2 份

上海晨星贸易有限公司
Shanghai Morning Star Trading Co.,Ltd.

SHIPPING ADVICE

To:	PARANDAR INTERNATIONAL INC.	**From:**	SHANGHAI MORNING STAR TRADING CO., LTD.
Tel. No.:	001-65-67632160	**Tel. No.:**	0086-021-63753526
Page:	1/1	**Date:**	OCT. 26, 2018
Fax. No.:	001-65-67430125	**Fax. No.:**	0086-21-63753529

NUMBER OF CREDIT: ROYAOBKDLC621501   **INVOICE NO.:**   SMSCINV07210

We hereby inform you that the goods under the above mentioned credit have been shipped. The details of the shipment are stated below.

COMMODITY:	PORCELAIN DINNERWARES
NUMBER OF PACKAGES:	564 CARTONS
QUANTITY:	1796 SETS
AMOUNT:	US$80,391.40
B/L NO.:	SITGSHSVK18267
VESSEL'S NAME & VOYAGE:	GLORY OCEAN V. 190E
SHIPMENT DATE:	OCT. 26, 2018
FROM:	SHANGHAI
TO:	TORONTO
SHIPPING MARKS:	PARANDA
	SMSC-07210
	TORONTO
	C/NO. 1-564
NAME OF ISSUING BANK:	THE ROYAL BANK OF CANADA
DATE OF CREDIT:	AUG. 31, 2018
S/C NO.:	SMSC-07210

上海晨星贸易有限公司
SHANGHAI MORNING STAR TRADING CO., LTD.

(SIGNATURE)

上海市东大名路375号(200080) 电话/Tel.86-21-65960332 传真/Fax:86-21-65960328   No.375, Dong Da Ming Rd., Shanghai, P.R.C.

提交份数:1份

2.

出口单据审核记录

汇票：

1）出票日期晚于信用证规定的到期日，应改为：2018 年 12 月 17 日之前出票

2）大写金额有误，应改为：…FIVE HUNDRED AND FIFTY ONLY

3）信用证号码有误，应改为：01DLC077003079

4）货物数量有误，应改为：535 箱货物

5）付款人有误，应改为：COMMERCIAL BANK OF DUBAI P.S.C.

6）出票人未作背书，应改为：由出票人（闵华进出口公司）做背书

商业发票：

1）买方名称有误，应改为：ALABRA…LLC.

2）信用证开证日期有误，应改为：OCT.19，2018

3）合同日期有误，应改为：OCT.3，2018

4）运输标志有误，应改为：SHMHSC-07210

5）货号 2103S 总金额有误，应改为：10304 美元

6）货号 AMZ049 数量有误，应改为：712PCS.

7）援引的客户订单号码有误，应改为：SSTE/363/CN-9

8）货物的总体积有误，应改为：99.743 立方米

9）漏列证实发票真实正确字样，应加上：WE CERTIFY CONTENTS ARE TRUE AND CORRECT.

10）漏列 TERMS OF DELIVERY 字样，应加上：TERMS OF DELIVERY：CFR DUBAI

装箱单：

1）出口商地址有误，应改为：5/F MINHUA BLDG

2）第二个品种的箱号有误，应改为：81-231

3）第三个商品的货号有误，应改为：AMZ049

4）货物的总毛重有误，应改为：9964 公斤

5）未按信用证规定显示开证日期，应加上：L/C DATE：OCT.19，2018

6）开证银行名称有误，应改为：COMMERCIAL BANK OF DUBAI P.S.C.

7）出具人公司名称有误，应改为：SHANGHAI MINHUA IMP. & EXP. COR-PORATION

8）提交份数有误，应改为：三份

海运提单：

1）收货人一栏与信用证规定不符，应改为：TO ORDER OF COMMERCIAL BANK OF DUBAI PSC.

2）被通知人邮政信箱有误，应改为：P.O. BOX 21352

3）运输标志中的件数有误，应改为：C/NO.1-535

4）货物描述有误，应改为：HOUSEHOLD WARES

5）货物件数大写有误，应改为：SAY FIVE HUNDRED AND THIRTY FIVE CARTONS ONLY

6）未按信用证规定显示目的港代理，应加上目的港船代名称、地址和电话

7）未按信用证规定显示总净重，应加上

8）签发日期晚于信用证规定，应不迟于 2018 年 12 月 2 日

9）背书有误，凭开证银行指示抬头，无需发货人背书

原产地证明：

1）运输标志中的目的港拼写有误，应改为：DUBAI

2）货物件数大写有误，应改为：(FIVE HUNDRED AND THIRTY FIVE) CARTONS

3）援引的发票号码有误，应改为：SHMH07210

4）未按信用证规定显示厂商名称和地址，应加上

装运通知：

1）收件人的电传号有误，应改为：46215 BIMEH EM

2）信用证号码有误，应改为：01DLC077003079

3）提单号有误，应改为：COSU85122784

4）未按信用证规定显示预约保单号码，应加上：OPEN POLICY NO.OMP/531/91

5）未按信用证规定显示开证行名，应加上

其他单据：

1）漏交船公司出具的证明，应补上。

第十三章　出口业务善后

1.

发送(S)	收件人(O)...	jmonakin@laseys.com.za
	抄送(C)...	
帐户(A) ▾	主题(U):	Conclusion of 18-G668

Shanghai Feilong Industrial Trading Company

Dear John,

Many thanks for your payment under Contract No. 18-G668.

We are already old friends and this smooth transaction will be a driving force to promote our sound relationship into a new stage. We very much appreciate your great efforts in introducing our products into your market. And we feel sure you have already found the significant improvement in the quality of our products.

We are attaching a pdf of the latest catalogue, in which you may see quite a few new items. If you have any questions, we'll be pleased to hear from you.

We look forward to further business with you.

All the best
Helina

Helina Cai
Shanghai Feilong Industrial Trading Company
222 Siping Road, Shanghai 200080, China
Tel: (86) 21 6357 3210　　Fax: (86) 21 6357 3380
helinacai@shfeilong.com

2.

Shanghai Rainbow Trading Company

906 Xianxia Road, Shanghai, China
Tel: (86) 21 6276 5723   Fax: (86) 21 6277 9800   Zip Code: 200336

Gulfare Commercial Group
P. O. Box453
Dubai
U.A.E

March 16, 2019

Dear Mr. Lamire,

We feel deeply regret when we were informed that the issuing bank rejected payment against L/C No. 18-CS155.

We are extremely sorry that we were unable to ship your order in time. But we would like to explain that it was caused by an unforeseen fire in our warehouse, which damaged a great part of finished products. Although after that we operated production line at its full capacity and gave priority to old customers like you, we could only effect shipment three days later than that was contracted.

However, we are glad the goods will arrive at your end next Tuesday and assume they are just in time for the sales season. We really hope the three-day delay will not bring too much difficulty to you in meeting the requirement of your clients.

So in view of our long-standing relations as well as for our mutual interests, would you please make the payment through your bank?

Thank you very much for your kind understanding.

Yours sincerely,
Shawn Guo
Shanghai Rainbow Trading Company

图书在版编目(CIP)数据

出口贸易模拟操作教程:第四版/祝卫,程洁,谈
英著.—上海:上海人民出版社,2019
ISBN 978－7－208－16000－2

Ⅰ.①出… Ⅱ.①祝…②程…③谈… Ⅲ.①出口贸
易-教材 Ⅳ.①F746.12

中国版本图书馆 CIP 数据核字(2019)第 147774 号

责任编辑　张晓玲
封面设计　甘晓培

出口贸易模拟操作教程(第四版)
祝卫　程洁　谈英 著

出　　版　上海人民出版社
　　　　　(201101　上海市闵行区号景路 159 弄 C 座)
发　　行　上海人民出版社发行中心
印　　刷　启东市人民印刷有限公司
开　　本　787×1092　1/16
印　　张　29.25
字　　数　529,000
版　　次　2019 年 9 月第 1 版
印　　次　2023 年 6 月第 3 次印刷
ISBN 978－7－208－16000－2/F・2598
定　　价　78.00 元